Martin Yan's

FEAST

The Best of Yan Can Cook

Martin Yan
Photography by Geoffrey Nilsen

Bay Books is an imprint of Bay Books & Tapes, Inc., 555 De Haro St., No. 220, San Francisco, CA 94107.

You can reach Yan Can Cook via e-mail at yccook@aol.com

Library of Congress Cataloging-in-Publication Data on file with publisher.

ISBN 0-912333-31-6

Printed in China
10 9 8 7 6 5 4 3 2

Distributed by Publishers Group West

PUBLISHER: James Connolly

EDITORIAL DIRECTOR: Clancy Drake

ART DIRECTOR: Jeffrey O'Rourke

DESIGN AND PRODUCTION: Tania Kac, Jack Meyers, and Tracy Dean of Design Site

COVER DESIGN: Daniel Bowman, Design Site

PROJECT EDITOR: Jan Nix

WRITERS: Stephen Siegelman and Ivan Lai

COPY EDITOR AND GLOSSARY: Margaret McKinnon

FOOD PHOTOGRAPHY: Geoffrey Nilsen

FOOD STYLIST: Susan Massey

PROP STYLIST: Tina Salter

ASSISTANTS: Elizabet der Nederlanden, Mike Procopio, Karen Wang

FOOD PHOTOGRAPHY COORDINATOR: Tina Salter

OTHER PHOTOGRAPHY: Tania Kac, Design Site

Contents

FOREWORD

I love Chinese cooking. Although I never ate Chinese food as a child growing up in France, where Asian restaurants were rare, I did, however, experience Vietnamese cooking. It wasn't until I came to New York nearly forty years ago that I was first exposed to Chinese cooking and found it plentiful, inexpensive, and absolutely delicious.

In the 1960s and '70s, Craig Claiborne, who was then the food editor at the *New York Times*, introduced me to the owner and the head chef of the Shun Lee Palace and Shun Lee Dynasty. It was a time when Chinese cooking really flourished in New York, and some great restaurants opened. Uncle Thai and David K opened on Third Avenue and Sixty-sixth Street, and I became a regular at both restaurants and was introduced to the chef, who was famous in the Chinese community. I had extraordinary meals at these restaurants, and as I became more and more familiar with Chinese cooking, I started to investigate the many different Chinese restaurants on Mott Street in New York's Chinatown. These restaurants became some of my favorite hangouts late at night after a movie or the theater, because we could enjoy great food there at incredibly low prices.

In the 1970s and early '80s, I spent forty weeks each year traveling and teaching. As I began traveling to different parts of the country to conduct cooking classes, I started spending a great deal of time on the West Coast. It was in the mid-1980s that my friend Charlotte Combe, who had recently sold a cooking school she had in the Bay Area and was teaching for Martin Yan, invited me to teach at Martin's cooking school in San Francisco.

This is how I met Martin. We became friends, and I came back several years in a row to teach cooking classes at his school. During one of my visits there, Martin was taping a new series at KQED-TV, the public television station in San Francisco, and he asked me if I wanted to appear with him on one of the shows. I was delighted, and I accepted. It was after my appearance with Martin that one of the executive producers of his series asked me if I would be interested in doing a series. This is really how my television career evolved, even though I had done a series of shows for Florida Public Television in the 1960s.

Always generous when I went to teach on the West Coast, Martin would take me out for dinner at some of the greatest Chinese restaurants in San Francisco and elsewhere in the Bay Area. I came to know him more and more.

I had always thought that Martin's shows were very entertaining, and that he was a colorful, funny, and talented performer; but as I got to know him better, I realized that there is more to Martin than that. When not performing, he is composed, quiet, and a good listener, with a much broader knowledge of the food world than his television persona would lead you to believe. Well-educated and bright, he is a good conversationalist with a great understanding of cooking.

Martin, I learned, had some trying years growing up; and I could identify to a certain extent with this, as I had left home to go into apprenticeship when I was thirteen years old. I think Martin followed much the same road in his learning process. Yet, as he has become more skillful in his trade and more well known in Canada, the United States, and other parts of the world, he has kept wanting to learn and experience more.

This is evident today in this book, which contains the best of *Yan Can Cook*, his national television cooking show. The book is large in scope and gives us some idea of what Chinese cuisine represents. From the basic techniques through appetizers, soups, seafood, and even desserts, with drinks from tea to beer to wine, everything is here.

This is a well-thought-out, well-built cookbook with a lot of depth; in my opinion, it is the most complete and best cookbook that Martin has written. In addition to the recipes, you are treated to his own brand of Chinese philosophy, which is down to earth, straightforward, and works well with his no-fuss, forthright, and user-friendly cuisine.

Being North American as well as Chinese, Martin is well aware of the limitations of markets, and he knows where the tastes of people are today; and in this great book he does succeed in satisfying both the Chinese and the American palate. I know I will cook from it, and I'm sure that once you try some of the recipes, you will do the same.

Happy cooking!

—Jacques Pépin

ACKNOWLEDGMENTS

Over the years, I have had the good fortune of working with many talented individuals. It has been a true privilege and a great learning experience.

First, I want to offer my sincere thanks to Jacques Pépin—master chef extraordinaire, dedicated culinary educator, true gentleman, and good friend for the past two decades. Jacques, along with Julia Child and Graham Kerr, has guided and inspired me and a generation of culinary professionals in the U.S. and around the world. I am honored to be counted among their friends.

Martin Yan's Feast is a labor of love, for me as well as for many others. I want to thank my friends at Bay Books: James Connolly, publisher; Clancy Drake, editorial director; and Jeffrey O'Rourke, art director—all of whom have collectively given this book their utmost professional guidance.

I also thank the creative team, who helped fill the pages of this comprehensive book at record pace. Jan Nix, our project editor, for leading the team; Stephen Siegelman and Ivan Lai for the lively text; Geoffrey Nilsen for the beautiful images of the food; Tina Salter, Susan Massey, Karen Wang, Mike Procopio, and Elizabet der Nederlanden for bringing the food to life in exquisitely stylish photographs; Maura Devlin for her managerial skills and guidance; and Margaret McKinnon, for her tireless efforts to ensure that this volume is as close to perfect as possible. And a special thanks to my friends at Man-U Imports and Takahashi Imports, in San Francisco, for providing the beautiful props for the photographs.

The recipes in *Martin Yan's Feast* are the highlights of many seasons of *Yan Can Cook*. I must therefore take this opportunity to thank Gayle Yamada, my executive producer; Linda Brandt, my senior producer; Katherine Russell, my director; as well as everyone on the production crew. Their talents and hard work have brought the *Yan Can Cook* show numerous honors, including a 1998 Daytime Emmy Award and prestigious James Beard Awards for Best TV Food Journalism (1996) and Best National TV Cooking Show (1994). I am also grateful to all my television sponsors who have supported and believed in *Yan Can Cook* throughout the years.

Finally, I want to thank you, my dedicated readers, who have collected my culinary works since the very beginning when I first wrote the *The Joy of Wokking*. Would you believe that was twenty years ago? You have been my true inspiration. *Martin Yan's Feast* is written as my special gift to all of you.

INTRODUCTION

Making My Way: Reflections on Food, Family, and the Road of Life

To call it a road was a bit of an exaggeration. But it was our road, and that was what we called it. The narrow track that ran past our house along the muddy Pearl River was really more of a path. No one had mapped it out or planned it. It was, like just about everything else in my childhood, a product of necessity. It hugged the curve of the riverbank, widening and narrowing, rising and falling unexpectedly as it headed toward the city. Decades—maybe even centuries—of footsteps, water buffalo hooves, wheelbarrows, and improvised pushcarts had carved it out, pushing back the vines and branches and packing down the dry earth.

The road ran right by the kitchen door of our two-room house on the edge of the southern Chinese city of Guangzhou. Well, strictly speaking, there was no kitchen door, because there was no kitchen wall. It was customary, in those days and in that hot, humid part of the world, for the back of the house to open right onto the garden—in our case, a tiny patch of land that for many years was our main source of food.

From my favorite spot under the kitchen table, I could take in an entire four-year-old's universe: my mom cooking at the wood-burning stove, my little brother crawling around, a chicken or two pecking at the dirt outside in the hot, white sunlight, and, winding off into the distance, the road. Our road. The road to somewhere else.

Believe it or not, I was a quiet kid. Sitting and staring were my two favorite pastimes. I could spend hours under that table, gazing out into the world, taking it all in. And I remember looking down the road, concentrating hard and scrunching up my eyes to see as far as I could. Where did I suppose it led to? Where did I imagine it could take me? Who knows? After all, that was almost half a century ago!

But I do know that I could never have imagined just how long that road really was. How far away it really stretched. How many twists and turns, how many unknown lands and languages, how many hardships, adventures, and beautiful surprises it would reveal. And now, sitting in my home in California and reflecting on my life, it seems somehow fitting that my road began at the back of an open kitchen halfway around the world.

Life in semirural China in the 1950s wasn't easy, especially for a widow with two small children. When I think about how hard my mom, Lam Xi-Mei, worked to keep my little brother and me fed and clothed through years of food rationing and hand-to-mouth poverty, I'm filled with admiration and gratitude. She's a stubborn one, my mom, but she's determined and fearless. I can remember how she used to tell me, "Man-Tat" (that's my Chinese name), "you can't wait for things to happen. You have to make them happen yourself."

My father, Yan Tak-Ming, felt the same way. By the time he married my mother in the late 1940s, he had already done his share of making things happen. He had been to America and back as one of thousands of Chinese emigrants to make the journey to Gum Shan, the "Gold Mountain," in the 1920s.

My father had left China in his teens and settled in Portland, Oregon, where he found work as a barber and ran a small coffee shop. He stuck it out for several years, but in the end, his dreams of making a fortune in the New World never panned out, and he returned home to China.

Eventually, he married my mother, and together they opened a small family-style restaurant in Guangzhou. That was the day care center where I spent a lot of the first years of my life, crawling around unattended on the floor between the tables while my parents worked. I guess you could say that I learned my craft from the ground up!

I never really knew my father. He died when I was just a toddler. But whether he knew it or not, he gave me a wonderful gift that would stay with me all my life. It was the stories of his adventures in America, retold by my mother, embellished here and there over the years, repeated until they became family legends. Those stories awakened in me a longing to see the places he had seen on the other side of the world—the lands at the other end of the road.

To tell the truth, my dad was never a great cook. It was my mom who was the real talent in the kitchen, and my love of food and cooking comes directly from her. To this day, she has the ability of a magician—or maybe I should say a survivor—to transform a few simple ingredients into a truly wonderful meal. If you could see her size up a head of cabbage with the intense concentration of a sculptor examining a block of marble, you'd know what I mean.

It was my mom's cooking that packed their tiny restaurant night after night. When the Communists took over, my parents continued to work as cooks at the local government-run eatery. But after my father died, my mom could no longer put in the long hours and late nights with two little kids to raise, so she became the supervisor of a corner grocery store near our house.

My memories of the next ten years are mostly a blur of unrelieved poverty and day-to-day struggle. We had no real toys, no books, and, of course, no TV. I went to school, helped out around the house, and daydreamed about becoming the world's greatest kung fu master. I had heard about the Shaolin Monastery in the northern province of Henan, where every year a handful of boys were chosen to devote their lives to the study of martial arts, and I spent most of my childhood wishing I could be one of them.

Through all those hard times, my mom never stopped cooking. She used to devote several hours a day to food—walking miles to get it, foraging for it, bargaining for it, and, of course, cooking it. Food was extremely scarce, and she taught us to appreciate every grain of rice and savor every mouthful—lessons that have stayed with me throughout my life and my career.

The kitchen was the one place where my mom could be in complete control of her life, and cooking was her way of connecting with the world. On a good day, she's not quite 5 feet tall. She would stand at the stove in her woven hemp sandals, perched on a block of wood—its edges polished and smoothed by her feet over the years—stirring and sniffing, bobbing up and down like a marionette, all the while talking, singing, and shouting orders to anyone within earshot.

From a single wood burner, she could turn out an impossible array of steamed and fried dumplings, stir-fried vegetables, rice dishes, and wonderful, comforting soups. Her "pantry," a narrow ledge behind the stove, was lined with jars of oils and her own homemade sauces, seasonings, and carefully preserved ingredients—dried tangerine peels, fermented black beans, pickled vegetables, dried shrimp.

I've had the honor of working with a lot of great chefs over the years, but I've never met anyone with as much of a natural instinct for cooking as my mom. She doesn't have recipes or rules. She just knows. And although her food is often simple, it's full of honest, true flavors. To me, it's what food is at its best in Chinese families: a symbol of well-being, harmony, love, and family connection.

So we stuck together, my mom, my brother, and me, until the early '60s. And then, not long after my thirteenth birthday, a letter arrived from an uncle in Hong Kong. And from that day on, my life would never be the same.

My uncle had offered to take me on as an apprentice at his restaurant, the Sun Wong Kee, on Argyle Street. It wasn't the Shaolin Monastery, but it was somewhere new, and I was excited. To be honest, though, I wasn't even thinking about cooking as a career. I just hoped this would be a first step toward better things.

If my mom had mixed feelings about all this, she never showed them. She had meant what she said when she told me, "You have to make things happen yourself."

Even though I would not be leaving for three days, she put down the letter and hauled out our one battered rattan suitcase, left over from my father's years in America. Silently, deliberately, and, I now know, lovingly, she started packing it with clothes and food for my journey. The wait was over. The big, scary, wonderful world was calling my name. The road had opened up for me at last.

My years as a chef's apprentice were what you might call the "school of hard woks." I went to high school all day and spent every evening, night, and weekend in the back of the Sun Wong Kee kitchen. In the summer, when school was out, I worked seven days a week, 14 hours a day. The pay was $20 a month, plus room and board. And I mean that literally. My bed was a board that fit over the top of a booth in the dining room!

I started out scrubbing woks, peeling vegetables, and sweeping the floor. That pretty much sums up the first year's curriculum. Eventually, I was allowed to pick up a cleaver, and once I did, it was "chop till you drop"—thousands of hours of slicing, dicing, mincing, and chopping, and more water chestnuts, bamboo shoots, celery, and bok choy than I care to remember.

But you know, a wonderful thing happens when you repeat a task over and over. Sooner or later, you reach a moment when the technique is coming from inside you and you don't have to think about it any more. The cleaver or the whisk or the paintbrush has become a part of your body, and suddenly you're ready to start really using it. Although I didn't know it at the time, that was what had happened to me. I had begun to master the tools of the culinary trade. The discipline of learning a skill appealed to me in the same way kung fu always had. I looked up to the chefs in that kitchen, and they could tell. For the first time in my life, I started to daydream about becoming one of them.

So while I was still in my last year of high school, I enrolled in the Overseas Institute of Cookery, a school for professional chefs in Hong Kong. I was still working part-time at Sun Wong Kee, and in exchange for my school tuition, I shopped for food for the classes, so I was pretty busy. But I hardly noticed. After a gray, somber childhood, I was beginning to come to life.

One day, a few weeks into school, I got stuck between jobs and showed up late to class. Hoping that no one would notice, I raced to my station and started frantically chopping some carrots to make up for lost time. The instructor, Master Chef Dick Chu, came over and stood beside me, watching.

After some time, he said to the class: "Yan Man-Tat is very fast with the cleaver." Chef Chu was my idol. My years of experience at the restaurant had really paid off, and I felt proud to be singled out for praise.

Until he added: "Perhaps you have heard the saying, Man-Tat: 'It is better to be once perfect than a thousand times adequate.'"

The class was silent as he took the cleaver from my hand. "Like this," he said, and he deftly sliced a pile of carrot circles so thin that you could see the grain of the cutting board right through them.

For weeks, I practiced. Slowly at first, then faster and faster. I would line up stacks of perfect carrot slices in front of me like a gambler hoarding his chips. Chef Chu would nod approvingly. What he didn't know was that out of pride, I was eating all my mistakes. And believe me, there were plenty of mistakes. Let's just say that for a few years after that, I couldn't even look at a carrot. And I'm not even going to tell you what happened when we graduated to turnips!

Chef Chu became my first real mentor, my surrogate father in Hong Kong. He gave me a solid foundation in the culinary arts and encouraged me to pursue a career in cooking. My obsession with cleanliness and order in the kitchen comes from him, along with many of those fancy cleaver moves I do on my show. (Although he didn't smile quite as much while he was demonstrating them!)

Once I had my diploma from the Overseas Institute, I found myself at a crossroads. Should I stay at Sun Wong Kee—or even in Hong Kong? Should I go back to Guangzhou to be with my mom? Or should I set out in search of something entirely new?

One thing was clear: I was finally moving forward, and forward felt like the right direction. So without much of a plan in mind, I made a decision I had always known I would make some day. I would follow the road my father had taken: the road to the West.

That road led me first to Canada, where I stayed briefly with some friends. I started working as a cook in their Chinese restaurant, but somehow, that didn't feel right. Not yet. I wasn't going to let my journey to the West end up the way it had for my father. I wanted to keep learning, to be more than I was. I wanted to get a college degree.

So, I applied to the University of California at Davis. How did I pick that particular school? I confess that the photos in the catalog had a lot to do with my choice. Those leafy paths and bicycles were comforting and familiar—like a dream version of China. And something appealed to me about the school's food science program. Although I wasn't exactly sure what food science was, I knew it would bring my knowledge of food to a higher level and help me rise above the daily grind of restaurant work. In other words, it felt like another step forward. So I put one foot in front of the other, and off I went.

Eventually, I earned both a B.S. and an M.S. in food science at UC Davis, and the years I spent there turned out to be some of the happiest of my life. I practiced my English, studied hard, and met all kinds of wonderful people—including Sue, the woman I have shared my life with ever since.

To help pay for my tuition and living expenses, I signed up to teach Chinese cooking classes in the university's extension program. I was a young man who took himself very seriously, and I had high ambitions for those classes. I made up course titles like "The Art and Science of Chinese Cuisine," and "The Philosophy, History and Heritage of the Chinese Culinary Arts."

But we met in the college coffee shop. And how serious can you be in a coffee shop? Despite my attempts to lecture on history and culture, most of my students just wanted to have a good time, drink a little wine, and enjoy some tasty Chinese food.

That experience taught me a lot. After all my hard work in the kitchen and all those years of training, I had forgotten that cooking isn't just about getting the right answer. As my students and friends reminded me, it's also one of life's greatest pleasures. I lightened up. I started to joke around and have fun. The shy, serious Yan Man-Tat was coming out of his shell. And Martin Yan was coming into his own.

In 1976, with my master's degree in hand, I went back to Hong Kong to be closer to my mother and brother, who, like millions of people in China, had not escaped persecution at the hands of the Red Guards during the Cultural Revolution. I found work as a food technologist for a major Hong Kong food manufacturer and spent two years looking for a way to get my family out of China.

Eventually, I heard that new immigrants to Canada could petition immediately to bring in relatives, so I moved to Calgary, Alberta, hoping to bring my family over from China.

I helped some friends open and run a Chinese restaurant there. But I decided once and for all that the restaurant business just wasn't for me—too much grueling labor and not enough chance to connect with people. So, what next? I kept remembering how much I had enjoyed my cooking classes at Davis, and I began to wonder if I might be able to make a career out of teaching cooking.

Then I heard my mom's voice telling me, "You can't wait for things to happen. You have to make them happen yourself." And she was yelling so loud, I could hear her all the way from Guangzhou! So I made something happen. Actually, I made two things happen: I opened Alberta's first Asian cooking school, and soon afterward, I managed to bring both my mom and my brother over to join me in Canada.

To put it mildly, the cooking school was a concept that was a little ahead of its time. Business was unbelievably slow at first. Sometimes I'd wind up giving private lessons to the building's security guard just for practice. But then one day, I got a phone call that steered my whole life onto a new path.

It was a freezing cold winter morning—the kind of morning when all you have to do is think about going outside and your nostrils immediately freeze shut. The snow had been coming down for days without stopping. I was setting up for a class on soups called "Wok, Stock and Barrel" (I still have the flyer) when the phone rang.

A frantic voice on the other end of the line began babbling at me. I stared at the phone in bewildered amazement. Eventually, I figured out that the caller was the producer and host of a local television show that was broadcast live at a station on the other side of town. It seemed that the famous hotel chef who had been scheduled to do a cooking segment had called in sick. The producer had received a press release about my school. The clock was ticking, and she was desperate.

"Can you be here in an hour?" she asked. I could tell by her tone that "No" was not an acceptable answer. "I'll be there," I said, having absolutely no clue what I was getting myself into, but somehow thinking a TV appearance might help promote the school. I told the security guard not to bother coming to class, then packed a cardboard box full of every ingredient and condiment within easy reach, grabbed a wok, a few tools, and my trusty cleaver, loaded it all into the trunk of my battered old car, and set out through the blizzard. Half an hour later, I skidded into the parking lot of the station, flew out of the car, and jabbed the key into the lock of the trunk.

If you've ever spent any time in -40°F weather, you probably know that trunk locks have an annoying way of freezing shut at the worst times.

I ran into the studio and begged for help. But by the time we got the lock to open, all the food had frozen. There was no time to regroup. I walked onto the set, looked at the few audience members who had braved the snow, and, holding up a head of cabbage covered with ice crystals, blurted out, "I'm Martin Yan. And today...I am cooking with frozen food!"

To my amazement, everybody laughed. I've blanked out most of what happened next. It still feels more like a nightmare than a real experience. I remember smiling a lot and moving around very fast to avoid collapsing from anxiety—banging pots and chopping like a wild man. I wasn't even really trying to be funny. I just kept saying whatever popped into my mind. And they just kept laughing. I chopped. They clapped. I chopped faster. They clapped harder.

The producers told me I was a natural performer, and they asked me back the following week. When I asked them what they'd like me to cover in my segment, they said, "Just be your funny self."

I have a confession to make. I don't think of myself as a funny person. I never have. I think of myself as a cook, a student, and a teacher—a person who loves to share the wonders of Asian food and culture with the world. But as soon as the lights come up and I look out at an audience, this guy called Martin Yan starts to take over, and I hear him joking around and having fun. I've gotten used to sharing the limelight with him over the years, and I'd even say we've become friends. But back then, Martin Yan and I were still kind of getting to know each other.

So no one was more shocked than I was when, two weeks later, that local television station called to offer Martin Yan his own series of half-hour cooking shows. They had already picked out the perfect name: *Yan Can*.

I thought they would want to tape a handful of shows to try out the idea, but they had bigger plans. We would crank out five shows a day—a whopping 130 episodes in just 27 days—and they would pay me $100 for each show, more money than I'd ever imagined earning in my life!

I ended up hosting more than 500 shows in Canada and developed a modest following throughout the country. The whole thing felt like a lark, and I could hardly believe I was getting paid to do it. I loved the fast pace—it was the perfect outlet for all my restless energy—and I didn't even mind the 500-mile train trips to Vancouver to stock up on Chinese ingredients. My career was beginning to take shape. I was finding my way.

Eventually, those long Canadian winters got the better of me, and I found my way back to California. Not wanting to give up the show, I pitched it to the local public television station, KQED, and within six months, *Yan Can Cook* had become a national television series in the U.S. That series has been at the center of my life and my career ever since.

It's hard to believe that was almost 20 years ago. Today, *Yan Can Cook* is seen in more than 70 countries all over the world. In the early days, we had two cameras and two assistants. Today, dozens of talented people work behind the scenes to put it all together and make me look good. We've crisscrossed China and traveled all over Asia, filming on location, and produced more than 1,500 shows.

And in between, I've made nearly two hundred trips to Asia, Europe, and all over the world, teaching, speaking, studying, cooking, tasting, and, of course, occasionally clowning around! It has been a wonderful adventure and a humbling experience. I've learned so much and had the good fortune to meet and work with more wonderful, generous, talented, and remarkable people than I ever imagined the world could contain. And best of all, I've had the opportunity to share my love of Asian cuisines and cultures with all of you.

Which brings me to this collection of my favorite recipes. I put this book together to offer you a compilation of the very best of the *Yan Can Cook* shows, all in one volume. Most of the recipes are based on ones that appear in my nine earlier cookbooks. They're home-style recipes, mostly Chinese, with a few Southeast Asian, Korean, and Japanese dishes tossed into the mix to keep things lively.

I've added new information and tips throughout the book, and the recipes have been revised with an eye toward today's cooking styles: lighter, more healthful ingredients; simpler techniques; quick, easy preparations you can make even on a busy weeknight (I believe that high-quality prepared sauces, seasonings, and ready-to-cook ingredients are great ways to simplify cooking and save time); instructions that don't take a rocket scientist (or even a food scientist) to figure out; and most important, lively, delicious flavors that I hope you and the people you love will enjoy preparing and eating again and again.

The good news is that Asian home cooking is already healthful, fast, sensible, simple, and fabulously flavorful. What I've tried to do is make it accessible to you, keeping in mind the realities of Western kitchens, ingredients, and utensils. It's all food you can make, so have fun, and don't be a stranger—let me know how you like it! (My e-mail address is on page ii.)

These days, I spend more time traveling than I do at home. So, when I am at home, I like to unwind and relax by working in my vegetable garden. Not long ago I found myself with a few free hours, so I decided to do a little spring planting in the backyard. It was a golden California afternoon, and the bushes and oak trees that line the canyon behind our house were still lush and green from the winter rains.

As I crouched down to pat a tomato seedling into place, I happened to glance back over my shoulder and catch a glimpse of the road that winds past our garden and up the side of the canyon. And for one split second, I felt I was looking at that scrappy dirt road where I started out in Guangzhou—looking back down it from the other end, as if the distance from there to here had been just a few short steps.

And then I realized that it had. I have come such a long way, and yet in so many ways, I'm still that quiet kid crouching under the kitchen table, peering out into the light with curiosity and amazement, eager to try new things and explore new worlds.

As I sat there, staring down that road, I thought about the places it had taken me and the people along the way. About my father, dreaming of a life without struggle in a beautiful land of gold and silver. About my mother, still feisty as ever, still doing things her way—the old way. And about the thousands of people all over the world who have shared with me a moment, a meal, a smile, a laugh. Thank you for being one of those people. You have made my life's journey a great adventure and filled my road with joy and wonder.

BASICS AND TECHNIQUES

If Yan Can, You Can!

Repeat after me: *Chi le fan mei you*? That's one of the most common Chinese greetings. And what do you suppose it means? Hello? How are you? Nice to see you? No. It means, "Have you eaten yet?"

That greeting says a lot about the role food plays in Chinese culture. Chinese people spend an average of 40 percent of their disposable income on food. Every region has its own delicacies—from bear paws (not the pastry, the real thing!) to freshwater seaweed to snake meat. Whatever the foods, people are passionate about them, and they'll go to any length and expense to enjoy them on special occasions.

For the Chinese, food is always a surefire conversation starter. They talk all day about where and what they're going to eat. Then when they're finally eating, they talk about what they'll have for their next meal. Food talk was all I heard growing up. Maybe that's why I decided to make a living talking about food myself!

And sharing opinions about food is just the beginning. The food itself must be shared, too. The importance of sharing is instilled in Chinese children from an early age. It would be unthinkable to order a dish all to yourself in a restaurant in China—or to serve a dish to a single person at home. Everything is intended to be experienced and discussed by all the guests. That's why many Chinese tables are round—so you can see and talk to everyone, and everyone has equal access to the food at the center of the table.

It's all about togetherness. In China, family units stay together, with many generations living under one roof. After thousands of years, that's still the way it's done, and I believe that cooking and eating are a huge part of what holds the Chinese social fabric together.

Over the years, I've shared a lot of meals with a lot of people in China. These days, I spend about a quarter of my time there, traveling around, meeting, greeting, and, of course, eating. Between teaching and consulting, I travel so much I've thought about setting up a frequent flyer program for me, and a frequent fryer program for my wok!

And after all those miles and all those meals, the food I still love best is the pure, simple cooking of the Chinese home. The more I learn about the essential principles of Chinese cuisine, the more I understand that they're always the same, whether you're preparing a 36-course banquet or a simple bowl of noodles. What makes any Chinese meal remarkable is a sense of simplicity and a natural balance of flavor, aroma, color, and texture.

Bringing It Home

How about you? When you think of cooking Chinese food at home, do you break into a cold sweat? Do you worry that you'll have to buy some weird root vegetable and you won't know which part to cook and which part to throw away? Do you feel a bit intimidated by all those complicated steps and mysterious techniques—each one an opportunity to incinerate your family's dinner, warp your wok, and wind up ordering take-out? Banish those thoughts from your mind. They couldn't be further from the truth.

In this book, I'm not going to pretend to tell you how to create a grand banquet for a thousand people, or even how to make a meal that rivals what you'd find in an outstanding Chinese restaurant (although you will find versions of some of your favorite restaurant-style dishes here). There are plenty of wonderful cookbooks that handle that job well.

What I'm going to show you here are dishes you can cook for your family for dinner tonight, with minimal equipment, a few simple ingredients, and some very easy techniques. Don't get me wrong: This isn't watered-down Chinese cooking. It's my interpretation of simple, authentic home-style recipes, adapted for Western home cooks like you.

What's Old Is What's New

Why should you be interested in these recipes? Because they represent a whole philosophy of eating that has sustained a quarter of the world's population for thousands of years—and because Americans are discovering that that philosophy is right in line with the way they want to eat today. More fresh vegetables and grains. A healthy balance of proteins and carbohydrates. Less fat. Quick, spontaneous, and convenient preparations. Foods that are exciting and full of flavor. And most importantly, cooking that does more than fill you up—cooking that satisfies the senses and nourishes the soul.

Ten years ago, whenever I taught a class or wrote a recipe, I was constantly suggesting substitutions for Chinese ingredients because people couldn't find them at the grocery store. But all that is changing, and my job is getting easier every day! A wonderful array of authentic Asian products, from prepared sauces to ingredients like noodles, dried mushrooms, and fresh produce, has exploded onto the market during the last decade.

Park your shopping cart in front of the Asian section of your supermarket and open your mind to a new world of adventure and exploration. Buy something you've never tried—a bottle of chili-garlic sauce, a package of dried bean curd skins, some salted black beans. Take them home and start experimenting. Check the glossary of this book if you need a little help or encouragement. Before long, you'll be tasting something you won't believe you made yourself.

Getting Started

Begin by trying a single recipe—a simple soup or a crisp stir-fried vegetable—as part of a regular weeknight dinner. Or practice with one of the one-dish meals (like Stir-Fried Fresh Rice Noodles, page 186, or Chicken in a Clay Pot, page 271). Once you begin to get a feel for the ingredients and techniques, you can start working your way up to a multicourse meal.

Make it easy for yourself. Choose dishes that call for different cooking techniques—a baked dish, a braised dish, a steamed dish, and a stir-fry for example—and eliminate as much last-minute cooking as possible. Spend a little time planning your menu, making a shopping list, and organizing your ingredients, and before long you'll be wokking and rolling like a pro.

That's a lot of words to say a simple message. Chinese cooking is easier than you think. And this book comes with my personal guarantee: If Yan can cook, so can you!

Now, before you get started, let me give you some basic tips and guidelines on equipment, techniques, and cooking methods. Read them first, and you'll find the rest will come naturally.

Equipping Your Kitchen

Like many of my students around the country and around the world, you might be surprised—and I hope you'll be encouraged—to learn that it doesn't take a huge arsenal of equipment to cook Chinese food.

To prepare the recipes in this book, I recommend supplementing your kitchen with a "starter kit" consisting of three basic Chinese cooking tools: a wok or stir-fry pan, some kind of steamer, and a high-quality Chinese chef's knife. These tools have evolved over thousands of years, and, when you treat them right, they

Wok in the Box

If you don't already own a wok, or if you're thinking of upgrading, you might consider buying one of the many complete wok kits on the market. Most contain everything you need to get started, including not only the wok but a lid, wok stand, curved spatula, ladle, brass skimmer, and steaming rack. It's a modest investment that will have you up and wokking as soon as you open the box.

perform perfectly. As your repertoire expands, you'll find that using the right equipment makes cooking easier and a lot more fun.

The Wok

Necessity is the mother of invention. Case in point: the mother of all Chinese cooking utensils, the wok, whose name, meaning "cooking vessel," points to its elemental importance. Many centuries ago, when the wok was born, the necessities in question were limited fuel and food. Cooking had to be done quickly and efficiently.

Originally, the wok was designed to fit into a well in the top of a wood- or coal-burning stove. With the wok's curved, sloping sides, the ingredients cook in a small area of concentrated heat at its center, the part closest to the heat source. Cutting up the ingredients into small, uniform morsels and quickly stir-frying them in batches helped conserve energy and make the cooking process even more efficient. Nutrients, colors, textures, and flavors could be kept at their peak because of the short cooking time. Fats and oils, another precious commodity, could be used sparingly, because once a wok is well seasoned, a light drizzle of oil is all that is needed for stick-resistant cooking. What could be more contemporary than that?

To this day, stir-frying in a wok remains the most frequently used technique in the Chinese kitchen. In rural China, you'll still find heavy, cast-iron woks used just as they were hundreds of years ago, recessed in a well over an open fire. But in most urban home kitchens and restaurants, gas burners have given rise to a more modern kind of wok, the kind you're probably familiar with. Because it sits on the stovetop, the modern wok is lighter in weight for easy handling and comes in a variety of materials, shapes, and sizes.

Wok Options

Once you discover how versatile a wok can be, it might just become the most used piece of cookware you own. You'll discover that stir-frying is just the beginning. A wok is great for steaming, deep-frying, braising, stewing, boiling, poaching, and even smoking.

Finding the best wok for your needs doesn't have to be difficult. Just remember to consider the three S's: shape, size, and substance.

SHAPE: THE BOTTOM LINE. Woks can be grouped into two basic types: round-bottomed and flat-bottomed.

- **Round-bottomed.** Originally designed for wood or charcoal burners, this kind works well when used over gas burners. You can set it directly over the burner or, for greater stability, use a perforated ring-shaped wok stand that sits over the burner and holds the wok in place. If you use a stand with sloping sides, which way is right side up? That depends on your wok and your stove. Position the stand so that the wok sits as close to the heat as possible and has the greatest exposure to the whole flame.

- **Flat-bottomed.** Specifically designed for use with electric burners, these woks can sit right on the heating element without a stand. You'll need to experiment with the heat settings on your range to find the heat intensity that works best.

SIZE: A MATTER OF PORTIONS AND PROPORTIONS. For family cooking like the kind presented in this book, a wok measuring 14 inches in diameter across the top edge is your best bet and will hold enough food to serve four to six people. For a small family or when cooking for one or two people, a 12-inch wok is adequate. Larger ones range from 16 to 36 inches in diameter, but they are heavy and unwieldy for use on the average home stove. Take a good look at the size of your stovetop and plan accordingly.

SUBSTANCE: FROM HEAVY METAL TO LIGHT WOK. Traditional Chinese woks made of unpolished cast iron are rarely sold in North America (though you may find them in Chinatown), but many types of excellent lighter-metal woks are available.

- **Carbon steel.** This time-honored wok is made from a disk of steel that has been shaped on a lathelike contraption. These inexpensive spun or rolled steel woks can be identified by the fine rings in the surface of the metal. They retain heat well, and they're lightweight for easy cooking and handling. Traditional hammered steel woks can also be found in some Asian stores and mail-order companies. Carbon steel woks need to be seasoned when new (see "Seasoning the Wok," page 15) and, when properly cared for, will provide years of use.

- **Anodized aluminum.** Woks and stir-fry pans made of hard anodized aluminum are becoming more and more popular and are readily available in department stores. They need no seasoning, and many offer a nonstick, scratch-resistant cooking surface. Because they require little or no oil, they're great for healthful cooking. These substantial, durable pans—including the popular Circulon and Analon—are also excellent conductors of heat. Stir-fry pans with smooth curved bottoms work well over both gas and electric stoves and are probably the most functional for today's home kitchens.

- **Stainless steel.** These woks, or ones made of aluminum and lined with stainless steel, are shiny and attractive, but food often sticks to their cooking surface, particularly on the plain stainless steel ones. These are not the best for everyday stir-frying.
- **The eclectic electric.** A relative newcomer to the world of wok cookery is the electric wok, with its built-in heating element and thermostat control. Electric woks are designed for all-purpose use, and they're handy because they free up your stovetop. They're particularly suitable for deep-frying, braising, and steaming, since they heat evenly and allow you to set and maintain exact cooking temperatures. And they're pretty good for tabletop cooking or for keeping buffet food warm. But for a stir-crazy guy like me, most electric woks are not hot enough to do a good job.
- **Nonstick coatings.** Some woks, including many electric ones, are coated with a nonstick surface that's easy to clean. Use wooden or plastic utensils for cooking and nonabrasive scrubbers for cleanup. There's a wide range of quality here. My recommendation: It's worth investing in a more expensive nonstick pan with the best nonstick coating you can find.

SEASONING THE WOK. Before using a carbon steel wok, you'll need to remove the protective coating on its surface and reseal the surface with oil. This process, called seasoning, isn't hard to do, and it has its rewards. First, it begins the process of creating a slick, stick-resistant cooking surface that gets better and better with age and repeated use. Second, it seals out moisture so the metal is less prone to rusting. Follow these simple steps for creating a well-seasoned wok:

1. Remove the film of rust-preventive oil that coats most new woks by scrubbing the inside and outside surfaces with warm water, detergent, and steel wool or a scouring pad.

Hey! What's That Amazing Flavor?

There's a mysterious, appetizing flavor that many foods take on when they're cooked in a seasoned wok over high heat—a savory, "wok-charred" taste the Chinese call *wok hey*. That's the mark of a well-seasoned wok—and a seasoned wok chef!

Avoiding "Acid Wok"

Sauces made with acidic ingredients, like vinegar or tomato, can eat away at the seasoning you've been diligently building up, and your sauce may take on a tinny flavor. For very acidic sauces, you're better off cooking the sauce in a separate nonreactive saucepan, then quickly tossing it with the ingredients in the wok at the last minute.

2. Rinse the wok thoroughly and set it over medium heat for several minutes to dry.

3. Moisten a clean rag or paper towel with a little cooking oil. With the wok set over medium heat and holding the towel with an oven mitt, spread the oil evenly over the inside of the wok. Add ½ teaspoon of fine salt and continue to rub the entire inside surface. Soon, the wok will begin to darken and smoke. This would be a good time to turn on the exhaust fan.

4. Using fresh changes of paper towel and a bit more oil and salt if the surface begins to look dry, continue wiping the surface of the wok, rubbing firmly to get the oil into the pores of the metal, until the towel comes away pretty clean. The process can take from 15 to 20 minutes and varies from wok to wok, so consult the manufacturer's directions.

5. Finally, allow the wok to cool, then wash it in warm water with a soft, nylon brush or pad, and dry it on the stove over high heat.

Now you've created the first layer of the seasoned surface. There will be a dark brown area around the center of the wok. As you continue to cook with the wok, that brown area will grow, and eventually, the whole wok will become shiny and dark.

CLEANING THE WOK. After each use, clean the still-hot wok right away with hot water and little or no soap or detergent. To remove persistent burned food, try rubbing the surface of the wok with salt, which acts as a natural abrasive. After cleaning and rinsing, always dry your wok over heat. Towel-drying or air-drying won't remove all the water from the pores of the metal, and rust can form quite quickly.

Handle with Care

Woks generally have either two matching loop-shaped handles or one long one with an optional short one on the opposite side. A long handle makes for easy two-handed stir-frying: you can keep one hand on the spatula and one on the handle, moving the wok around as you work. Advanced cooks love to show off by using the long-handled wok to toss ingredients high in the air. It's fun, but take my advice: Try practicing in the backyard with some dried beans before you perform in front of a live audience.

Wok-cessories

Whether included with your wok or purchased separately, a few traditional accessories can make wok cooking more efficient and enjoyable.

SPATULA. With its shovel-shaped blade that hugs the curves of the wok, the wok spatula is perfect for stir-frying and scooping food out of the traditional steel wok. The long handle keeps you from stir-frying your fingertips. It's fun to toss food around with a clanging Chinese spatula, but if you don't have one, an ordinary wooden or plastic one will do the trick.

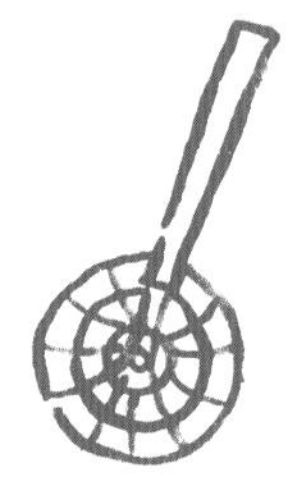

SKIMMER. This is the Chinese version of the Western slotted spoon, but bigger—normally 6 to 8 inches across—and shallower. It's most often used for fishing food out of hot oil or boiling water. The kind most commonly sold in the U.S. is a flat wooden or bamboo slat with a brass wire mesh basket at one end.

LADLE. This one, you know. Chinese ladles are typically a little shallower than Western ones because they're designed to match the curve of the wok. You can use a Chinese ladle as a companion to the spatula for stir-frying or for scooping liquids and cooked foods into and out of the wok.

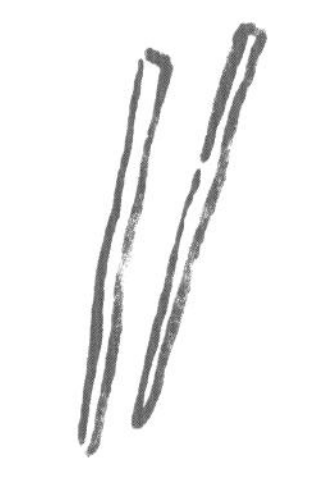

CHOPSTICKS. Extra-long wooden chopsticks are another helpful tool for wok cooking. Use them for frying foods, to separate boiling noodles, and to snatch bits of food from the wok for tasting.

LID. The high, dome-shaped or slope-sided wok lid lets you turn the wok into a braising pot or smoker and creates a natural convection when used for steaming. If your wok didn't come with a lid, look for one that's slightly smaller in diameter than the wok, so it sits solidly just below the wok's rim.

The Steamer

After stir-frying, steaming is probably the most common cooking method in China. Traditional Chinese home kitchens don't have ovens, and the steamer helps fill the void. It's used to cook seafood, meats, poultry, and vegetables, to make silky steamed custards, and to "bake" buns, dumplings, and even cakes over moist heat.

Steaming is simply cooking food on a rack above boiling water in a closed cooking vessel. Your trusty wok makes a fine base. To it, you'll need to add some kind of steaming rack, depending on your recipe, and a lid. The rack can be as simple as four chopsticks, placed tic-tac-toe-style 1 to 2 inches above the boiling water, topped with a plate on which the food is set. You can also use a conventional metal vegetable-steaming rack.

My favorite tool for steaming, though, is the one I grew up with: the old-fashioned but ingenious wok steamer. It's a round, flat basket, handmade of bamboo, that sits right in the wok, an inch or so above the water. These steamers have space between the slats on the bottom to let the steam in, and a lid to keep it there. They can be stacked so you can cook several dishes at once. For a 14-inch wok, look for steamer baskets about 12 inches in diameter; for a 10-inch wok, use 8-inch steamers.

Bamboo steamers have latticed lids of woven bamboo which let just the right amount of steam escape so condensed water doesn't drip onto the food. They're so attractive and unusual-looking that you can serve food right out of them. Some cooks prefer a tiered aluminum steamer set, which has a flat, round pan at its base that's designed to hold water. Fans of the aluminum steamer will tell you that it's more durable than bamboo, and won't mildew or absorb cooking odors as bamboo can if not properly cleaned and dried.

Full Steam Ahead!

I'm happy to see that steaming is coming into fashion in the West, because it's one of my favorite cooking methods. The flavors of steamed foods are outstandingly clean, delicate, and soothing, and their texture moist and tender. Little or no oil is needed for steaming, and most of the vitamins, minerals, and natural juices of foods are retained. Steaming is also convenient; you can place food in a steamer and then move on to other things without needing to keep a constant watch over it. Just remember to add a little bit of water every so often, or you may wind up smoking your food!

This Is Your Knife!

Cutting up food into uniform pieces is one of the most important skills to master in Chinese cooking. And once you learn to use an all-purpose Chinese chef's knife, it's easier than you think. If Yan can cut, so can you!

I like to tell my viewers and students that the Chinese chef's knife is the original Chinese food processor. It can slice, mince, chop, crush, tenderize, and scoop up food—and you can even use the end of the handle to grind spices. Complement it with a smaller paring knife for finer cutting and making garnishes, and you'll be ready for just about anything.

Shop Till You Chop: Buying a Chinese Chef's Knife

Although the lightweight, all-purpose Chinese chef's knife is sometimes called a cleaver and looks like a Western meat cleaver, it's a different tool altogether (and thus should never be used for hacking bones—for that you'll need a heavier one). A good Chinese chef's knife is well balanced, well constructed, and has a fine blade that holds an edge. Always remember that a sharp knife is a safer knife.

Traditional carbon steel Chinese chef's knives are available in Asian hardware stores. They are easy to sharpen, but they rust and will discolor acidic foods like onions and lemons. Ordinary inexpensive stainless steel, on the other hand, can dull quickly and is hard to sharpen. For years, I couldn't find a good, functional all-purpose Chinese kitchen knife. That's why I consulted many professional colleagues and Chinese chefs, and eventually we designed a high-carbon stainless steel blade, Martin Yan's Ultimate Chef's Knife, which I use on the *Yan Can Cook* show. High-carbon stainless steel won't discolor food and keeps a fine, sharp edge.

In some high-quality chef's knives, the end of the blade, called the tang (no relation to the Chinese dynasty of the same name!), extends all the way to the end of the handle and is held in place by three rivets. You can also find traditional knives with cylindrical wooden handles (which tend to loosen and crack over time). Test the balance of the knife and the comfort of the handle as you hold it. It should feel substantial, yet not so heavy that you have to be a bodybuilder to lift it.

Wok On!

Here's my number one tip for keeping your wok happy and perfectly seasoned. Use it! Don't banish it to that extra storage area behind the basement door. Hang it in your kitchen, where you'll reach for it all the time to cook all kinds of food—not just Chinese or Asian dishes.

Getting a Grip

Hold the knife in your writing hand (the Chinese call this the "chopstick hand"). Move your hand all the way up the handle so that your thumb is on one side of the blade and your index finger on the other side. Curling your index finger slightly, grasp the blade firmly between your thumb and index finger. This may feel a bit strange at first, but once you get used to it, you'll find that grasping the blade in this way gives you much more control than simply wrapping all your fingers around the handle.

Use your free hand to hold the food in place, curling your fingertips under. Rest the flat side of the blade alongside the first knuckles of your free hand, and as you slice or chop, slide your free hand along to guide the blade and keep it vertical. To avoid cutting yourself, never uncurl the fingers of your free hand, and never raise the blade higher than the first knuckle. Like I always say, "The idea is to move your fingers, not remove them!" Try not to wiggle the blade while cutting. Use a firm downward and slightly forward motion.

Short Cuts: Knife Technique Made Simple

SLICING: Holding the food and Chinese chef's knife firmly, cut straight down, using the knuckles of your free hand as a guide.

JULIENNE AND SHREDDING: Stack a few slices, and use the slicing technique, cutting straight down through the stack to create sticks. For matchstick julienne, start with ⅛-inch slices, and cut them into ⅛-inch sticks. To shred food into fine slivers, begin by cutting paper-thin slices, then cut across them in the same way to create thin strips.

DICING: Line sticks up perpendicular to the blade, and slice straight down across them, creating cubes.

Here's a Sharp Idea!

An easy way to slice meat thinly is to partially freeze it (or, if it's frozen, partially thaw it) until it's soft enough to cut, but still firm. You'll find it's a simple matter to slice it into paper-thin strips.

MINCING: Start by cutting the ingredient into thin strips, then dice the strips. Hold the knife handle in one hand and, with the other, hold down the tip of the blunt edge of the blade. Using the tip as a pivot, raise and lower the blade in a chopping motion, moving it from side to side to mince everything evenly. Scoop up minced ingredients occasionally, flip them over, and keep chopping to ensure even mincing.

ROLL-CUTTING: This technique is used for long vegetables, like carrots or zucchini. It makes attractive chunks and exposes more of the surface area of the vegetable. Hold the blade perpendicular to the board and cut straight down on the diagonal. Then roll the vegetable a quarter-turn, and cut straight down again at the same diagonal angle. Continue rolling and cutting in this way all along the length of the vegetable.

PARALLEL CUTTING: Used to cut broad, thin slices of meat or vegetables. Lay the food close to the edge of the board with the fingers of your free hand flat on top of it. Angle the Chinese chef's knife so that it's almost parallel to the board, slanting slightly downward. Move it slowly and carefully back and forth to slice the food, paying close attention to avoid cutting your fingers.

CRUSHING: To crush ginger or garlic, place it near the edge of the cutting board, lay the knife blade flat over it with the blade facing away from you, and, with the heel of your free hand, give the side of the blade a good whack, being careful to avoid the edge of the blade.

TENDERIZING: Use the blunt edge of the Chinese chef's knife to tenderize meat by pounding it in a crisscross pattern. It's even more fun to get out your aggressions by turning the blade on its side and slapping the surface of the meat.

Care and Cleaning: Staying on the Cutting Edge

Wash your chef's knife after each use in warm, soapy water and dry it well. To preserve its handle, never soak a chef's knife in water, and never put it in the dishwasher. Store your knife in its own protected place (I use a magnetic knife rack), not in a

A Super Bowl Tip

In a pinch, try my mom's favorite sharpening technique: stroke the blade along the unglazed "foot" of an inverted earthenware bowl, holding the blade flat and angling it slightly downward (this works better with carbon steel knives than with stainless ones).

drawer where its edge might be dulled by knocking against other tools. To maintain a sharp edge, I recommend using a traditional knife sharpening steel.

1. Hold the steel firmly, placing its tip on a cutting board.
2. Position the knife at a 20-degree angle to the steel with the blade facing down and the handle of the knife just below the handle of the steel.
3. Push the blade downward along the steel, pulling it toward you as you go, until you reach the steel's tip.
4. Move the blade back up and place its other side against the steel; repeat the sharpening action, moving the blade from the steel's handle to its tip.
5. Repeat six to eight times on each side of the blade.

If the blade loses its edge and becomes too dull to sharpen with a steel, use a whetstone or have your knife commercially sharpened by your butcher or at a cutlery store.

The Cutting Board

The cutting board is your knife's partner and best friend. Whether you prefer one made of wood or plastic, the key is to use a board that's big enough to hold what you're chopping so things don't go flying all over the place. To keep the board from sliding around, fold a damp kitchen towel in half and lay it under the board. Avoid cutting on hard surfaces such as marble—this is bad for your knife.

We have a built-in butcher block surface at home, but I still like to place a smaller wood or plastic board over it to preserve its surface. These smaller boards are also easier to store and clean. That's especially important when you've been cutting meat, poultry, or fish. Some people like to reserve a separate board just for that purpose to avoid cross-contamination of other foods.

No matter what you're chopping, it's a good idea to scrub your cutting board with soap and hot water after each use and to clean it occasionally with a mild solution of bleach or baking soda and water. Vinegar or lemon juice can also be used to clean and deodorize a cutting board.

The Clay Pot

With a wok, a steamer, and a Chinese chef's knife, you're ready for just about anything. But a traditional Chinese clay pot is one piece of equipment you may want to add to your arsenal just for fun.

Clay pots, also called sand pots because they're made from a mixture of sand and clay, have heavy lids and are often encased in a protective wire cage. They're both functional for cooking and beautiful enough for serving soups and stews right at the table. Clay pots are usually glazed on the inside and unglazed on the outside for better heat absorption, making them ideal for braising, simmering, stewing, and slow-cooking.

You can find inexpensive clay pots in a variety of shapes and sizes in Chinese specialty shops. But what if you can't find a Chinese specialty shop? Just use any flame-resistant casserole with a lid.

Clay Pot Tips

Clay pots are fired at a high temperature so they can withstand intense heat. You can place them directly on a gas burner or in the oven; if you're using an electric burner, place a diffuser under the pot. Clay pots are fragile, so follow these guidelines to avoid breakage:

- Never place an empty clay pot directly over heat. Always add some liquid first.
- Allow the pot to cool completely before immersing it in water or placing it on a damp or cold surface.

The Spice Grinder

Most Asian kitchens, particularly in Southeast Asia, are equipped with a mortar and pestle—a stone bowl and club used for crushing and grinding spices. If you don't have one, you can put spices in a small bowl and use the end of the handle of your chef's knife to pound and crush them. A mini food processor or an electric coffee grinder will also do the trick. Serious spice lovers may want to invest in a second coffee grinder for spice grinding only. They work wonderfully for this purpose, but make sure to label your grinders so you can tell which is which, or you could end up with curried cappuccino!

Techniques and Tips

Here's a quick look at the basic techniques and cooking methods that will help you prepare many of the recipes in this book.

Stir-Fry, Step by Step

Allow me to share with you my ten steps to stir-fry success. Of course, every dish is different, and the recipes in this book will give you exact directions. But these are the basic principles that usually apply.

Getting Ready

1. **CUTTING AND MARINATING.** To ensure even cooking, chop, slice, dice, or shred each ingredient into uniform pieces. Marinate meat, poultry, or seafood if necessary; always marinate under refrigeration.

2. **SEAT THE GUESTS.** No kidding! You don't want your piping hot creation to sit at the table getting cold and soggy while you herd your friends and family to the table. There's an old Chinese saying: "Guests may wait for the food, but the food never waits for the guests." (Once you get the hang of the technique, you can make two stir-fries at a time. Meanwhile, it's always wise to plan a menu with other kinds of dishes, like soups and steamed or roasted foods, so there's less waiting, and you can sit down to enjoy your own cooking.)

3. **SET UP.** Stir-frying is like downhill skiing—once you start, there's no stopping. Read the recipe and make sure you have everything cut up, marinated, measured, and close at hand. Don't forget the serving plate and the garnish.

4. **HEAT FIRST, OIL SECOND.** Place the empty wok or pan over high heat for a minute or two. When you can feel the heat by lowering your hand slightly into the wok, you're ready to add the oil. Drizzle the oil (it doesn't usually take more than a few teaspoons) around the sides of the wok, swirling it to coat the surface. Wait about 5 seconds before adding the other ingredients.

Cooking

5. **KNOW YOUR ORDERS.** Stir-frying is usually done in batches, and the sequence in which ingredients are added is important. The "aromatics"—seasonings like ginger, garlic, or chilies—are usually added first. Stir-fry for a few seconds before adding the meat. Sometimes the meat is removed before vegetables are added; heartier, denser vegetables usually go in before softer or leafier ones. Let the recipe be your guide.

6. **STIR, DON'T STARE.** Use your spatula to flip and toss the food vigorously, breaking up any clumps, so everything cooks evenly without sticking to the wok. I like to give the wok a good shake from time to time to keep everything moving.

7. **AVOID OVERCROWDING.** If you use too big a batch of any ingredient, it becomes hard to stir-fry evenly, and the excess moisture may prevent uniform browning. You end up "steam-frying" or "boil-frying."

8. **SAUCE.** Many recipes call for a final addition of liquid (such as wine or broth) and/or a prepared sauce (such as soy sauce or oyster-flavored sauce). Depending on the type of sauce desired, this liquid is sometimes thickened with a mixture of cornstarch and water. Combine the sauce ingredients ahead, and mix the cornstarch with the water; keep both within easy reach.

9. **TASTE.** Don't forget to taste the dish before you put it on the serving plate. Then quickly adjust the seasonings, if necessary, and serve.

10. **GARNISH.** This is a little touch that makes a big difference. I like to use a bit of an ingredient that's already in the dish (like a slice of lemon with Lemon Chicken). Keep it simple. Even a sprig of cilantro or a sprinkling of toasted sesame seeds adds a special finish to the dish. (For more garnishing ideas, see page 36.)

Steaming

There are two basic methods of steaming, "open" and "closed." In open steaming, food is placed on a heatproof dish or directly on the steamer rack; the steamer is then covered with its lid. In closed steaming, food is placed in a covered earthenware casserole, which is in turn placed in a larger pot. Water is added to the larger pot, which is covered and placed over heat. This technique, also known as "double boiling," usually takes several hours and produces a rich, concentrated broth.

Getting Ready

Place foods that cook in their own juices—like a whole fish—on a heat-resistant plate inside the steamer. An ovenproof glass pie dish makes an ideal liner for steaming fish, custard, and other foods. Choose a dish that's slightly smaller than the steamer basket so the steam can rise around it (it will also be easier to remove if it doesn't fit too snugly). To keep dumplings and buns from sticking, line the steamer with a damp cloth, a piece of parchment paper, or greens, such as napa cabbage or lettuce leaves.

Cooking

- Always bring the water to a boil before adding food to the steamer. As the food cooks, check the water level occasionally. If it's low, add boiling water to avoid lowering the temperature—usually about ½ cup every 8 to 10 minutes.
- To steam larger items, such as a whole chicken, set two cans, emptied, cleaned, and with both ends removed, in the bottom of a large Dutch oven with a lid. Add water to halfway up the cans, and then use them as a support for a plate or dish on which to place the food.
- Don't get steamed! To avoid burns, always open the steamer with care. Wear oven mitts, and lift the lid so that it points away from you.

Deep-Frying

If you suffer from "fear of frying," here's some reassuring news: Your wok makes a wonderful deep-fryer that heats evenly and allows you to use less oil than with a conventional pot. Deep-frying has gotten a bad rap in recent years, and it does require a large amount of oil, but foods that have been properly deep-fried at the right temperature absorb less oil and can be light and crispy without being greasy.

When foods are added to oil that has been heated to between 330° and 375°F (check your recipe for exact temperature), the surface of the food is quickly sealed, forming a coating the oil cannot permeate. If the oil is not hot enough, too much oil soaks in. If it's too hot, the outside of the food can burn before the inside is cooked.

Getting Ready

- Use a flat-bottomed wok (for electric ranges), a round-bottomed wok set securely in a wok stand (for gas ranges), or an electric wok (which has the advantage of a built-in temperature gauge). Make sure the wok is solidly positioned to avoid tipping.

- Pour oil into the wok to a depth of 2 to 3 inches, depending on the size of the pieces of food you're frying. It's best to use enough oil to submerge the food completely so that it cooks quickly and evenly.
- Heat the oil to the temperature called for in the recipe, checking it with a deep-frying or candy thermometer. If you don't have a thermometer, you can test the temperature by carefully dropping a cube of bread into the oil. The bread should start to sizzle immediately; it will soon be coated with bubbles and begin to turn golden brown. Or try my chopstick trick: Place the tip of a clean, dry wooden chopstick into the bottom of the oil; when tiny bubbles emerge from the end of the chopstick, your oil is ready.

Cooking

- Be extra-careful when sliding foods into hot oil to avoid splashing and spattering. Remember: slide, not slam-dunk!
- Bring the ingredients you're going to deep-fry to room temperature before adding them to the oil. This minimizes the lowering of the oil temperature and helps prevent spattering.
- Add the ingredients in small batches so that the oil doesn't overflow. This also helps maintain a constant oil temperature and helps promote even browning.
- Use a Chinese skimmer or a slotted spoon to turn and separate the food as it cooks and to lift it out and transfer it to paper towels for draining.
- Oil used for deep-frying can be reused, although after two to three times, it will begin to break down. To reuse deep-frying oil, allow it to cool, pour it through a fine-mesh strainer to remove particles of food, then store it in an airtight jar in the refrigerator. If, after repeated use, the oil begins to darken or turns cloudy, discard it.

Wok-Smoking

In Chinese cooking, smoking is really more a flavoring method—often used with chicken and duck—than a cooking process. Foods are placed on a rack in the wok over aromatic ingredients like brown sugar, tea, uncooked rice, star anise, or hickory chips. Heat is applied to create smoke, which is sealed in by the lid of the wok.

Typically, food is first marinated and cooked by another method, such as pan-frying, steaming, or roasting, then smoked to add flavor. You can use any deep, heavy pot with a tight-fitting lid for stovetop smoking, but a wok with a high-domed lid works perfectly. Don't use your best wok, though, since smoking is an intense dry-heat process that can harm the pan's seasoning. An old, battered one will work fine. Give wok-smoking a try. The robust aroma and flavor it gives food can be unforgettable.

Getting Ready

- Open some windows, and turn on the exhaust fan.
- Line the wok and the lid with a few layers of aluminum foil, leaving extra foil hanging over the edges.
- Place the aromatic ingredients (tea, brown sugar, etc.) in the bottom of the wok, and set a rack a few inches over them. Choose a rack that will sit stably in the wok. You can use a tic-tac-toe-shaped smoking/steaming rack (one may have been included with your wok), four heavy chopsticks arranged in tic-tac-toe fashion, or a wire rack. I've used everything from a round cake rack to a clean charcoal rack from a round barbecue.

Smoking

- Heat the wok over high heat until smoke begins to form. Place the food to be smoked on the rack, and immediately cover the wok with the lid. Crimp and fold the foil that's sticking out all around the wok and the lid to seal in the smoke. Within a few minutes, the smoke will permeate the meat and impart a robust, smoky flavor.

Braising

Braising is an ideal way to prepare large cuts of meat that need to cook slowly. The food is first browned over high heat, then slowly stewed in liquid in a heavy, covered pot over low heat on the stovetop or in the oven. Braised foods are moist, tender, and richly flavored.

Red Cooking

This is a slow-cooking method in which meats are first browned, then gently simmered over low heat in a liquid consisting mainly of soy sauce and sugar. The food takes on a deep mahogany-colored glaze; a tender, juicy texture; and a rich, full-bodied flavor.

Roasting

In China, roasting happens mostly in restaurants, because home kitchens usually don't have ovens. In restaurants, marinated meat is often roasted in large charcoal- or wood-burning ovens where it can be hung on hooks. This allows air to circulate around the meat, producing a crisp exterior and a moist, tender interior. You can replicate this effect by roasting on a rack over a foil-lined baking pan. Baste the meat with the pan juices and turn it occasionally to ensure even roasting.

Simmering

Simmering means gently cooking food just below the boiling point in enough liquid to cover it. This technique is used to make broths, soups, sauces, and stews.

Marinating

Most of the recipes in this book involve the use of a marinade—one of the cornerstones of Chinese cooking. Marinades vary from one recipe to the next, and serve a variety of purposes. They can add flavor, tenderize, and seal in the flavor of foods.

Common marinade ingredients include soy sauce, wine, and egg white. In Chinese cooking, a marinade isn't always a liquid; it can be a combination of dry ingredients, such as white pepper and cornstarch.

Foods can be marinated for a few minutes or several hours. Marinating should always be done in the refrigerator in a covered nonreactive container (use glass, stainless steel, or ceramic, not aluminum). Marinade left over after marinating meat, poultry, or seafood should be discarded or cooked thoroughly if you're going to use it as a sauce.

Parboiling

Also known as blanching or water-blanching, parboiling refers to immersing foods in boiling water for a few seconds or a few minutes to partially precook it. Once the food is removed from the water (use your Chinese skimmer or a slotted spoon), it is usually placed in cold water to stop the cooking process.

Soaking

This not only refers to what the chef does in a hot tub after cooking all day. It's also a prep technique used to soften certain dried ingredients (including black mushrooms, dried noodles, tangerine peel, and dried shrimp) before cooking them.

- **Dried mushrooms.** To soak dried mushrooms (such as black or shiitake) or black fungus (such as cloud ears or wood ears), place them in a small bowl and cover them with warm water. Let them stand about 20 minutes. Remove them carefully, allowing any grit to settle to the bottom of the soaking water, then rinse them under water to remove residual grit. Trim away and discard tough, fibrous stems with kitchen shears or a paring knife. If you like, you can strain the soaking liquid through a coffee filter and reserve it to enrich broths and sauces.
- **Noodles**. Dried bean thread and rice noodles often need to be softened in water before you add them to a soup or stir-fry dish. Soak them in plenty of warm water (they absorb a surprising amount) for about 10 minutes.

Toasting

Besides being a great way to liven up a meal (bottoms up!), toasting is also a technique used to release the flavor of ingredients such as sesame seeds or Sichuan peppercorns.

To toast, place the ingredient in a small, dry pan, preferably one with a heavy bottom, and place the pan over low heat, shaking it frequently until the ingredient begins to be fragrant and slightly darkened.

You can also toast small amounts of nuts in this way, but for larger amounts, it's best to place them in a single layer in a pie pan and toast them in a 325° to 350°F oven until they're golden brown.

Making a Spice Paste

Spice pastes, pounded together and slowly simmered, are a cornerstone of Southeast Asian cooking. Traditionally, the spice mixture is carefully pounded to a paste in a heavy mortar, but a blender or food processor also works well. For a hotter version, use whole dried red chilies in place of the jalapeños; soak them in water called for in the recipe before proceeding. Spice pastes are equally at home in Western meals. Marinate lamb cubes, chicken thighs, or shrimp in the spice paste for an hour or so, place them on skewers, then grill.

Basic Asian Spice Paste

- 4 *stalks lemongrass*
- 16 *almonds or 8 candlenuts*
- 8 *walnut-sized shallots, peeled and quartered*
- ¾ *cup water*
- 8 *fresh red or green jalapeño chilies, seeded*
- 1 *piece ginger (2 in. long), thinly sliced*
- 8 *cloves garlic*
- 2 *teaspoons dried shrimp paste (blachan)*
- 2 *teaspoons turmeric powder*
- 1½ *teaspoons salt*
- ⅓ *cup cooking oil*

① Trim hard knob at bottom of lemongrass, and cut off and discard dry leaves on top; about 6 inches of tender stalk will remain. Thinly slice this and place in a blender with nuts; process until finely ground. Remove from blender and reserve.

② Purée shallots with water in blender. Add chilies, ginger, and garlic; purée. Add reserved lemongrass and nuts, shrimp paste, turmeric, and salt; process until smooth.

③ Heat oil in a 2-quart pan over medium-low heat until hot. Add spice paste and stir until completely combined with the oil. Cook, stirring frequently, until paste is fragrant, color is richly browned, and oil shows at the edges, about 20 minutes.

④ Let paste cool. Refrigerate in a tightly covered jar for up to a week, or freeze for longer storage.

Makes 1 cup.

Making Perfect Chinese Rice

Here's my foolproof formula for making long-grain rice that's flavorful and fluffy—like the kind you're used to eating in Chinese restaurants—on the stovetop. (If you have an electric rice cooker, follow the manufacturer's directions.)

> To make about 3 cups of cooked rice, start with 1 cup of raw **long-grain rice**. Place it in a medium pan with 1½ cups cold **water**, and bring it to a boil over medium-high heat. Boil, uncovered, until small holes appear in the surface of the rice, about 10 minutes. Reduce heat to low. Cover and simmer until the rice is tender, 18 to 20 minutes. Remove from heat and let stand, covered, 5 minutes longer. Fluff the rice with a fork. It will be perfect every time.

Make-Ahead Sauces and Condiments

Here are some of the essential sauces, condiments, flavored oils, and batters used in Chinese cooking. Most will keep for a week or more in the refrigerator in a tightly sealed container.

All-Purpose Stir-Fry Sauce

This mixture contains the basic seasonings—ginger, garlic, and soy sauce—used to flavor simple stir-fry dishes. Add it to the wok when the dish is nearly done.

In a bowl, combine ⅔ cup **soy sauce**, ½ cup **chicken broth** or water, ⅓ cup **Chinese rice wine** or dry sherry, 3½ tablespoons **sugar**, 1 tablespoon **sesame oil**, and ½ teaspoon **white pepper**. Place a pan over high heat until hot. Add 2 to 3 tablespoons **cooking oil**, swirling to coat sides. Add 1 tablespoon *each* minced **garlic** and minced **ginger**; cook, stirring, until fragrant, 10 to 15 seconds. Add soy mixture, bring to a boil, reduce heat to medium, and cook for 1 minute. Add 3 tablespoons **cornstarch** mixed with 6 tablespoons **water** and cook, stirring, until sauce boils and thickens. Makes about 2 cups. Use as needed; refrigerate remainder.

Hot and Spicy Stir-Fry Sauce

When you want a zestier, chili-spiked dish, stir this in to taste when the dish is nearly done.

In a bowl, combine ⅔ cup **Chinese rice wine** or dry sherry, ⅓ cup *each* **soy sauce** and **chicken broth**, 3 tablespoons **sugar**, ½ teaspoon **white** or black **pepper**, 1½ tablespoons thinly sliced **green onions** (white part only), and 1½ tablespoons **chili garlic sauce** or 1 tablespoon crushed dried red chilies. Place a wok or medium pan over high heat until hot. Add 2 to 3 tablespoons **cooking oil**, swirling to coat sides. Add 1½ tablespoons *each* minced **garlic** and minced **ginger**; cook, stirring, until fragrant, about 20 seconds. Add wine mixture, bring to a boil, reduce heat to medium, and cook for 2 minutes. Add 2 tablespoons **cornstarch** mixed with ¼ cup **water** and cook, stirring, until sauce boils and thickens. Let cool. Makes about 2 cups. Use as needed; refrigerate remainder.

Sweet and Sour Sauce

This makes a good addition to stir-fries, but it's especially good with deep-fried batter-coated cubes of meat or fish.

In a bowl, combine ½ cup *each* **ketchup** and **water**; ⅓ cup *each* packed **brown sugar**, **orange juice**, and **rice vinegar**; 1½ tablespoons **soy sauce**; and ¾ teaspoon **liquid hot pepper sauce** or 1½ teaspoons crushed dried red chilies. Place a medium pan over high heat until hot. Add 3 tablespoons **cooking oil**, swirling to coat sides. Add 2 tablespoons minced **ginger** and cook, stirring, until fragrant, about 20 seconds. Add ketchup mixture, bring to a boil, and cook until sugar dissolves. Add 2 tablespoons **cornstarch** mixed with ¼ cup **water** and cook, stirring, until sauce boils and thickens. Makes about 2½ cups. Use as needed; refrigerate remainder.

Chinese Salad Dressing

Use this whenever you want to give an Asian flavor to salads of raw or cooked vegetables, cold meats, seafood, chicken, or whatever. For creamier texture, whirl in blender to emulsify.

In a small bowl, combine ¾ cup **rice vinegar**, ⅓ cup **sugar** or honey, ⅓ cup **soy sauce**, 1 tablespoon **toasted sesame seeds**, 1 tablespoon minced **garlic**, 2 teaspoons *each* minced **ginger** and minced **cilantro**, and ¼ teaspoon **Chinese five-spice**. Whisk in ⅔ cup **cooking oil** and 3 tablespoons **sesame oil**. Makes about 2 cups. Use as needed; refrigerate remainder.

Sichuan Spicy Salt

Use in place of ordinary salt for seasoning meat and seafood dishes.

Place a wok over medium heat until hot. Add ⅓ cup **salt**, 1½ teaspoons *each* **Chinese five-spice** and **ground toasted Sichuan peppercorns**, ¾ teaspoon **ground red chilies**, and ½ teaspoon **white pepper**. Cook, stirring, until fragrant, 2 to 3 minutes. If desired for extra flavor, add 1 tablespoon **chicken broth powder**. Let cool. Makes about ½ cup. Use as needed; refrigerate remainder.

Chili Oil

Some recipes in this book call for chili oil; it's also popular in dipping sauces for dumplings, or for seasoning a wide variety of foods at the table. Commercial chili oil is available, but it's easy to make your own.

In a small pan over high heat, heat 1 cup **cooking oil** to 375°F. Remove from heat and add 1½ tablespoons **sesame oil**, 1 tablespoon **crushed dried red chilies**, and 2 teaspoons crushed **garlic**. Let stand overnight, strain out seasonings, then transfer to an airtight jar. Makes about 1 cup. Use as a dip, or add a few drops to any dish. Refrigerate remainder.

Five-Flavor Oil

Try this in place of chili oil in dipping sauces; sprinkle a little into a dish at the end of cooking, as you would sesame oil; or use in cold dressings.

In a small pan over medium-low heat, heat 8 slices **ginger**, each the size of a quarter, crushed; 5 cloves **garlic**, crushed; 1 **star anise**; 1 teaspoon **Sichuan peppercorns**; ½ teaspoon **black peppercorns**; and 1 cup **cooking oil** until oil reaches 250°F. Simmer for 15 minutes, stirring occasionally; check oil temperature often to ensure that it does not rise. Remove from heat. Stir in 2 teaspoons sesame oil. Let stand overnight, strain out seasonings, then transfer to an airtight jar. Makes about 1 cup. Use as needed; refrigerate remainder.

Cantonese Crispy Batter Mix

Use this all-purpose batter for deep-frying foods such as shrimp, chicken, fish, or vegetables.

Combine ¾ cup **flour**, 2 tablespoons **cornstarch**, 1¼ teaspoons **baking powder**, and 1 teaspoon **sugar** in a medium bowl. Gradually whisk in ⅔ cup **water**, then 2 to 3 teaspoons **cooking oil** until smooth. Makes about 1 cup.

Chinese Mustard Sauce

Use whenever Chinese or Dijon mustard is called for in a recipe. The sauce gets mellower with time.

In a small bowl, whisk ¾ cup **dry mustard powder**, ⅓ cup **rice vinegar**, ¼ cup **water**, 1 tablespoon **sugar**, 2 tablespoons **sesame oil**, and ¾ teaspoon **cooking oil** to a smooth paste. Makes about 1 cup. Use as needed; refrigerate remainder.

Red-Cooking Sauce

Also known as a master sauce, this can be used again and again for braised or stewed meats or poultry and in casserole dishes. Its flavor deepens with each use. Strain after each use, and refrigerate or freeze.

In a bowl, combine 3 cups **chicken broth**, ½ cup **soy sauce**, ⅓ cup *each* **dark soy sauce** and **Chinese rice wine** or dry sherry, ¼ cup packed **brown sugar** or crushed rock sugar, 2 whole **star anise**, and 2 pieces **dried tangerine peel** or 4 pieces fresh orange peel. Place a medium pan over high heat until hot. Add 2 tablespoons **cooking oil**, swirling to coat sides. Add 8 slices **ginger**, each the size of a quarter, and 6 cloves **garlic**, crushed; cook, stirring, until fragrant, about 20 seconds. Add broth mixture. Bring to a boil, reduce heat, cover, and simmer for 20 minutes, stirring occasionally. Stir in 1 tablespoon **sesame oil**. Strain sauce. Makes about 4 cups. Use as needed; refrigerate remainder.

Lobster Sauce

This sauce contains no lobster; instead, it contains the seasonings typically used in Cantonese lobster dishes. Try it with stir-fried prawns or chicken, or on steamed or poached fish.

Rinse ⅔ cup **salted black beans**; drain and coarsely chop beans. In a bowl, combine ⅔ cup **Chinese rice wine** or dry sherry, ½ cup *each* **chicken broth** and **soy sauce**, ¼ cup packed **brown sugar**, and 2 tablespoons **sesame oil**. Place a wok over medium heat until hot. Add ⅓ cup **cooking oil**, swirling to coat sides. Add ¼ cup minced **garlic** and cook, stirring, until fragrant, about 30 seconds. Add black beans and wine mixture; cook for 2 minutes. Add 2 tablespoons **cornstarch** mixed with ¼ cup **water** and cook, stirring, until sauce boils and thickens. Makes about 2 cups. Use as needed; refrigerate remainder.

All-Purpose Dipping Sauce

Use as a dipping sauce for fried seafood, meats, and vegetables.

In a medium bowl, combine 1 cup **ketchup**, ⅓ cup **soy sauce**, ¼ cup *each* **hoisin sauce** and **chicken broth**, 2½ tablespoons **sugar** or honey, 2 tablespoons *each* **Worcestershire sauce** and **sesame oil**, 1 teaspoon **chili oil**, and ¼ teaspoon **white pepper**; mix well. Makes about 2¼ cups. Use as needed; refrigerate remainder.

Finishing Touches: The Art of Garnishing

A garnish, even a simple one, makes all the difference in presenting food. Believe it or not, I add a garnish even when I'm the only one eating. It just makes a dish feel finished.

- Garnishes don't have to be fancy. They can be made from what you have on hand: a sprig of cilantro; a sprinkling of toasted sesame seeds; a few rings of chopped scallion; a slice or wedge of orange, lemon, or tomato; a chili pepper; or even an edible flower from your garden.
- Call me crazy, but I believe a garnish should be edible (no ceramic pagodas, please) and should relate in some way to the flavors of the dish.
- Set the garnish on the serving plate before you start cooking, so you know right where to find it at serving time.
- Try to avoid repeating a garnish too many times in the same meal.

Here are some simple garnishing ideas for special meals.

Apple Wings

Cut 1 apple in half and place on cutting board. Make 2 diagonal cuts, angling the knife to form a small wedge. Place in lemon juice.

Cut out 4 more wedges, each ¼ inch wider than the previous wedge; place in lemon juice.

Place wedges together and gently move each slice to form layers.

Green Onion Brushes

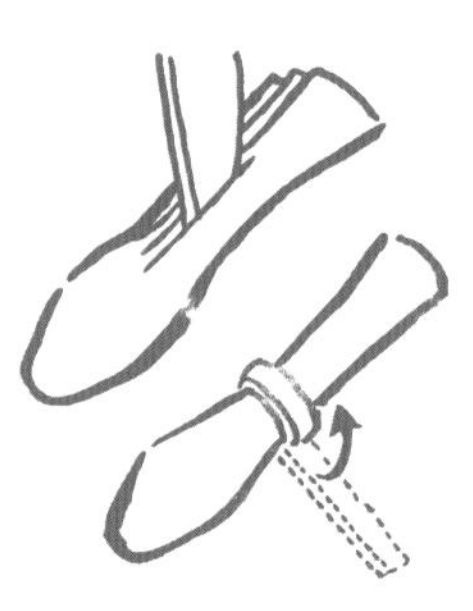

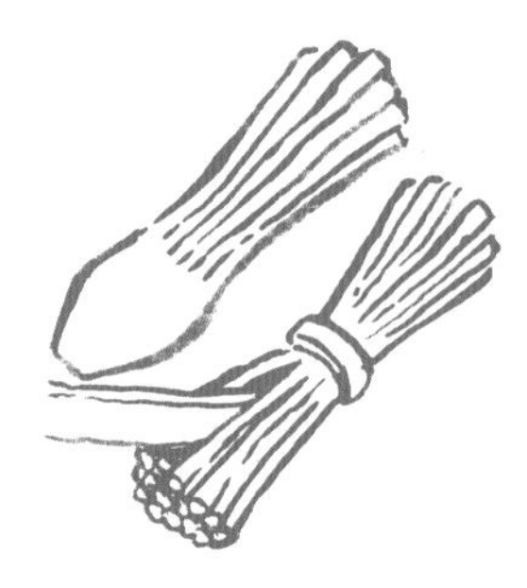

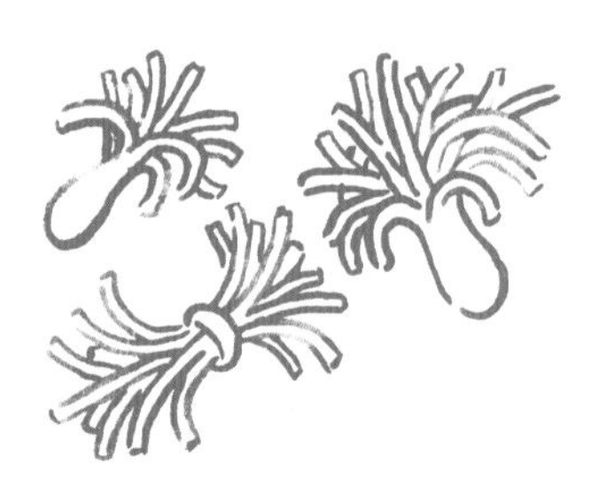

Trim root and green top. For single brush, slash top 2 inches repeatedly. For double brush, slide a ring of red chili peppers onto onion and slash both ends.

Chill in ice water for at least 1 hour.

Carrot and Daikon Knot

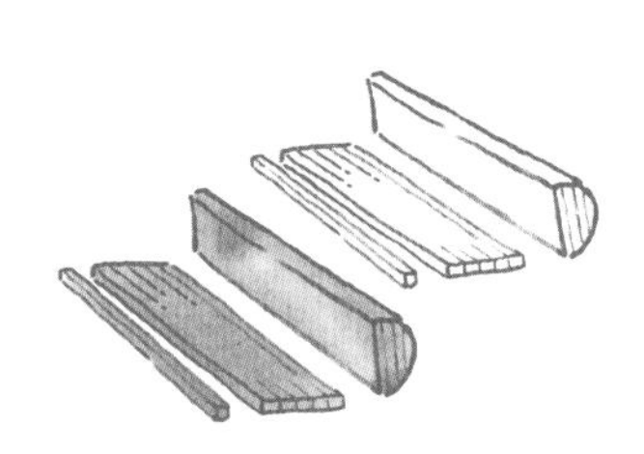

Cut carrot and daikon into ¼- by 6-inch strips. Soak in a solution of 2 cups water and 2 tablespoons salt until pliable.

Make a loop with a carrot strip. Weave daikon loop through carrot loop and pull ends to secure.

Tomato Flower

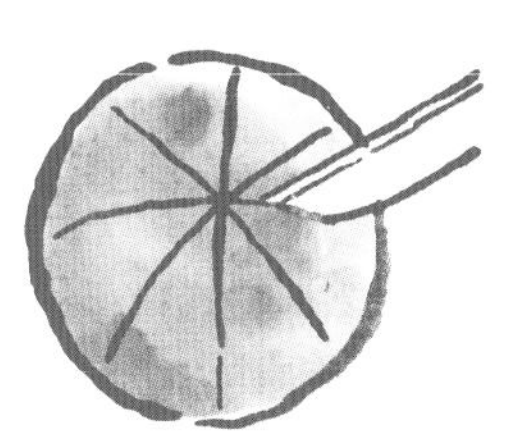

Place tomato stem side down. Cut skin across top and about two-thirds down sides. Repeat three more times to make eight segments.

Carefully lift tips of petals and separate skin from flesh.

Chopsticks 101

In Chinese, chopsticks are called *fai jee*, which means "quick little boys." The name may sound a little odd to you if you're someone who typically uses a single chopstick to spear a few shrimp, then quickly asks the waiter for a fork. But with a little practice, you'll find that chopsticks are surprisingly easy to use, and they're just right for plucking up the perfect mouthful of Chinese food.

Start by placing one chopstick through the crook formed by your thumb and index finger; let the stick rest on the tip of your ring finger. Now insert the second stick above the first one, and hold it the way you would hold a pencil. The idea is to hold the first stick still while you move the second stick up and down, bringing the tips of the two sticks together to pick up food.

Remember, practice makes perfect. If at first you don't succeed, stick with it!

"Don't eat to live, live to eat!"

"Don't eat to live, live to eat!" is my all-time favorite Chinese saying. Cooking is one of the great joys of life. It's the fastest way to get connected to all the things that really matter: goodwill, good friends, good health, good food, and good fun. I hope this book adds a little more of each to your life. Now, as my mom would say, "Enough talking. Let's eat!"

GLOSSARY: THE ASIAN PANTRY

Keeping a well-stocked larder of Chinese dry ingredients and refrigerated and frozen specialty foods will enable you to whip up a Chinese meal on short notice. Stock up on the items below, and all you'll need to buy are a few fresh ingredients like meat, seafood, poultry, bean curd, and vegetables to make most of the recipes in this book. (For definitions and more information, consult the ingredients guide that follows this list.)

Canned Goods

- Bamboo shoots
- Broth (beef, chicken, or vegetable)
- Coconut milk
- Lychees
- Mushrooms, straw
- Water chestnuts

Dry Goods

- Chinese rice wine or Japanese rice wine
- Cloud ear (fungus)
- Cornstarch
- Mushrooms, black
- Nuts (cashews, peanuts, blanched almonds)
- Rice, long-grain, medium-grain, and glutinous
- Sesame seeds

Noodles

- Bean thread noodles (made from mung beans), dried
- Egg noodles, fresh (store in freezer) or dried
- Rice stick noodles, fresh or dried

Oils

- Chili oil
- Cooking oil
- Sesame oil

Sauces and Condiments

- Black bean sauce
- Chili sauce (with or without garlic)
- Hoisin sauce
- Oyster-flavored sauce
- Plum sauce
- Rice vinegar
- Soy sauce (regular, dark, and reduced-sodium)
- Sweet and sour sauce

Spices and Seasonings

- Black beans, salted
- Dried red chilies, whole and crushed
- Five-spice
- Mustard powder
- Sichuan peppercorns, toasted and ground (store in refrigerator)
- Star anise
- Tangerine peel, dried
- White pepper

Wrappers *(store in freezer)*

- Spring roll, egg roll, or gyoza wrappers
- Wonton wrappers

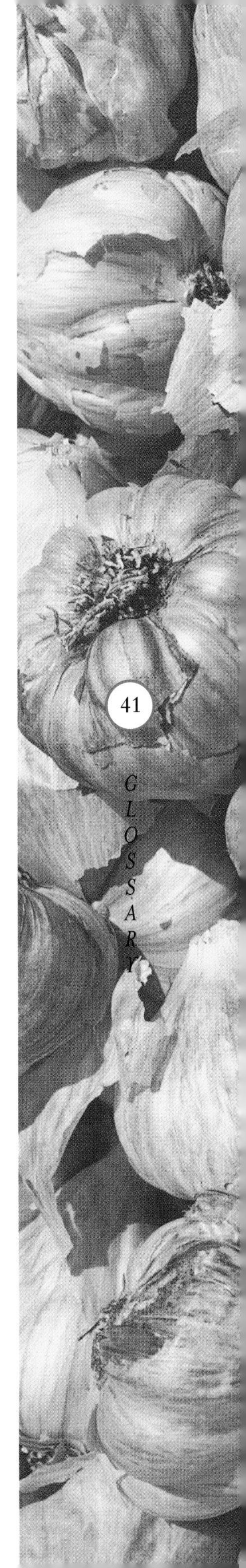

A Guide to Ingredients

While this list isn't all-inclusive, it does include ethnic ingredients used in the recipes in this book. As Asian dishes become more and more a part of home cooking, many of these ingredients can be found in supermarkets. Otherwise, Asian markets (especially ones that cater to a specific country or area) carry good selections including sauces and fresh ingredients.

In many of the recipes, sauces and spice pastes are made from scratch, but if you're a cook in a hurry, don't worry: a lot of them are available ready-made.

Sauces with a greater proportion of whole ingredients are generally thicker and are referred to as pastes. Sauces and pastes of the same name are used interchangeably depending on the desired appearance of the final product. Both are found in various-sized bottles and jars. Once opened, they should be refrigerated. Most will keep for several months to a year.

Store dry seasonings in a tightly sealed container in a cool, dry place. Most will keep for several months. Before using canned vegetables such as bamboo shoots and straw mushrooms, drain and rinse them to remove any trace of the salty canning liquid. If the vegetables have a metallic taste, blanch them in boiling water with a pinch of salt before cooking further.

ASIAN EGGPLANT: see **Eggplant**

Asian Pear

ASIAN PEAR: Also known as apple pears, Asian pears are juicy like pears and crisp like apples; generally they are blander in flavor than European pears.

BAMBOO LEAVES, DRIED: Leaves are used as a wrapper for savory stuffings. Most dishes are grilled, steamed, or boiled, with the leaves imparting an aromatic, smoky flavor to the food. For more details, see page 318.

BAMBOO SHOOTS: These are available as whole tips, young tips, sliced, or diced. All are tender-crisp with a sweet taste, but their texture varies. Young winter bamboo tips are most tender, and sliced shoots are the most fibrous. Asian markets often sell fresh shoots; otherwise use canned ones.

Banana Leaf

BANANA LEAVES: Leaves are used in Southeast Asia as well as in the Americas to wrap foods for steaming or grilling. For more details, see page 324.

BASIL, THAI: Also called holy basil, Thai basil has a pungent, slightly minty flavor. If it is not available, use regular basil.

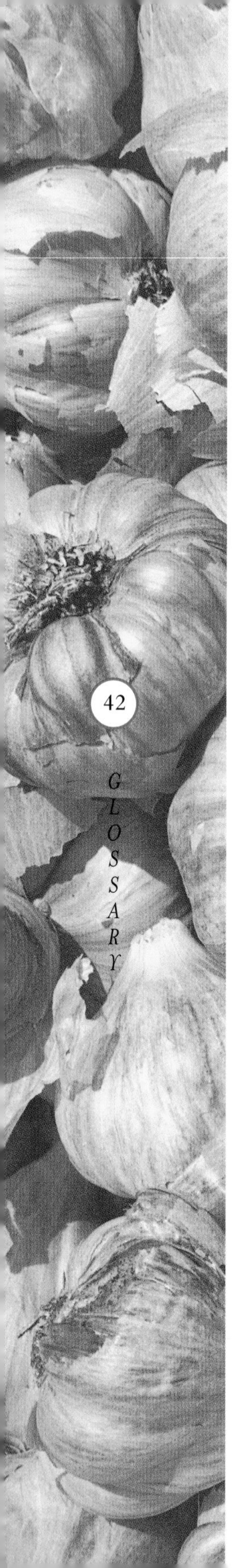

BEAN CURD: see **Tofu**

BEAN PASTE, SWEETENED RED: A paste made from cooked, mashed, and sweetened adzuki beans is used to fill a variety of savory and sweet dishes. The paste is sold canned in Asian markets.

Bean sprouts

BEANS, CHINESE LONG: see **Chinese long beans**

BEAN SAUCE: see **Sauces**

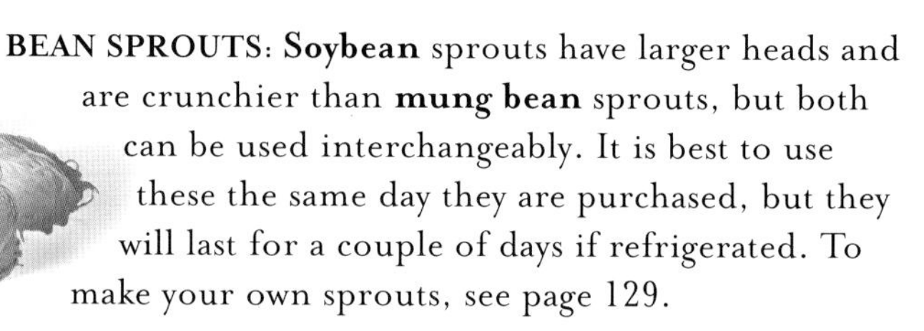

Bean thread noodles

BEAN SPROUTS: **Soybean** sprouts have larger heads and are crunchier than **mung bean** sprouts, but both can be used interchangeably. It is best to use these the same day they are purchased, but they will last for a couple of days if refrigerated. To make your own sprouts, see page 129.

BEAN THREAD NOODLES: see **Noodles**

BLACK BEANS, SALTED: Also called preserved or fermented black beans, these lend a distinctly pungent, smoky flavor to foods. They come in plastic packages and should feel soft and not look dried out.

BLACK BEAN SAUCE: see **Sauces**

BLACK FUNGUS, DRIED: Includes **cloud ears**, **tree ears**, and **wood ears**. Black fungus looks like chips of leather; it is rehydrated in warm water, then used in stir-fries for texture.

BLACK MUSHROOMS: see **Mushrooms**

Bok choy

BOK CHOY: This loose-leaved cabbage has thick white stalks and dark green leaves. Stalks have a mildly tangy taste and a crunchy texture; leaves are peppery and soft. **Baby bok choy** and **Shanghai baby bok choy** are sweeter and less fibrous than regular bok choy. For some other Asian greens, see pages 101 and 128.

BOUILLON, SEAFOOD: As a short-cut to making your own fish broth, use 1 fish bouillon cube and 2 cups water, or dilute as directed in recipe.

CANDLENUTS: This mainstay of Malaysian and Indonesian spice pastes is hard in texture and high in fat. Asian markets sell shelled and roasted candlenuts; almonds, Brazil nuts, or macadamia nuts are substitutes.

Candlenuts

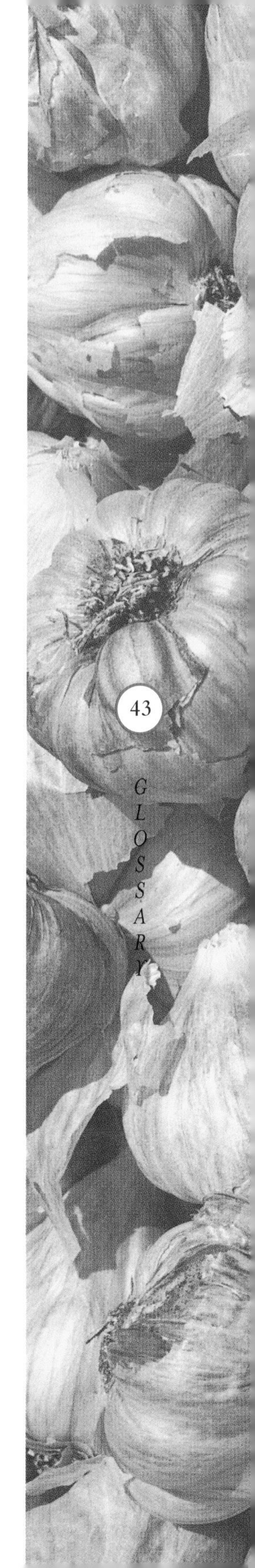

CHAR SIU SAUCE: see **Sauces**

CHILIES, DRIED: Small dried chilies are fiery hot. Use them whole or broken into smaller pieces. Crushed dried red chilies are simply chopped whole ones. Remember to wash your hands after handling because oils in the chilies can burn or irritate your skin and eyes.

CHILIES, FRESH: Most of this book's recipes call for red or green jalapeño chilies, which are hot but not too hot, and are widely available. If you prefer, substitute hotter or milder kinds. Generally, the smaller the chili, the hotter it is. From hottest to mildest, they include the fiery Thai bird, slightly milder serrano, jalapeño, and mild Anaheim.

CHILI GARLIC SAUCE: see **Sauces**

CHILI OIL: This hot, reddish orange oil, used as a flavoring agent and as a condiment, is made by infusing the heat and flavor of dried red chilies in cooking oil. To make your own, see recipe on page 34.

CHINESE BARBECUED PORK (*CHAR SIU*): The honey, soybeans, garlic, and spices in **char siu** sauce give Chinese pork and spareribs their pleasantly sweet, rich taste. To make your own barbecued pork, see page 85.

CHINESE BLACK VINEGAR: see **Vinegar**

Chinese broccoli

CHINESE BROCCOLI: Chinese broccoli (*gai lan*) doesn't look anything like regular broccoli. It has thin, dusty green stems, deep green leaves, and tiny white flowers. When cooked, the tender stems and leaves have a slightly bittersweet taste.

CHINESE FIVE-SPICE: This cocoa-colored powder is made from combinations of cinnamon, **star anise**, cloves, fennel, and **Sichuan peppercorns**. It lends a distinct anise and cinnamon flavor to braised meats, roasts, and barbecues.

CHINESE LONG BEANS: These pencil-thin pale to dark green beans are also called yard-long beans. They are drier, denser, and crunchier than green beans. Their crisp texture and mild flavor make them ideal for stir-frying with bold seasonings.

Chinese long beans

CHINESE PARSLEY: see **Cilantro**

CHINESE RICE WINE: see **Rice wine**

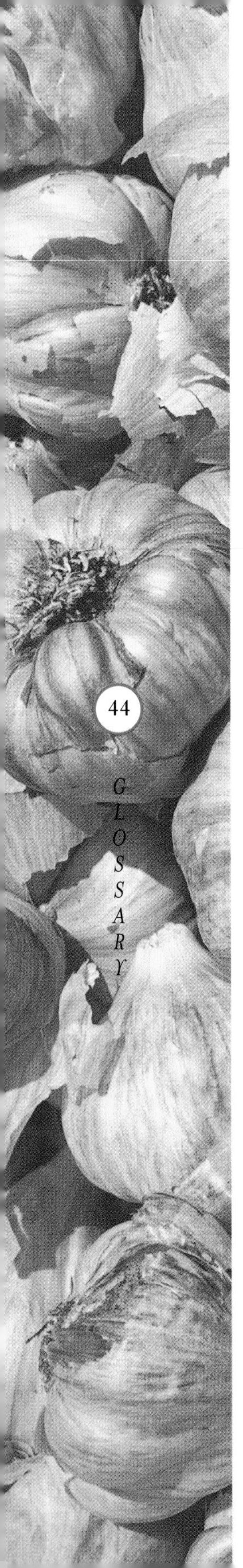

CHINESE SAUSAGE (*LOP CHEONG*): These savory-sweet links, from 4 to 6 inches long, are deep red to brown with a slightly bumpy texture. Most are made from pork, pork fat, duck, or beef simply seasoned with salt, sugar, and rice wine. Look for them in Chinese delis, fresh or in vacuum packages. See also page 88.

CHIVES, CHINESE: see **Garlic chives**

CILANTRO: Cilantro is also known as **Chinese parsley** or fresh coriander. Cilantro has wide, flat leaves and a distinct, refreshing flavor. Don't confuse it with similar-looking Italian parsley.

Coconut

CLOUD EARS: see **Black fungus, dried**

COCONUT: **Coconut water**, **milk**, and **cream** are used throughout Southeast Asia in curries, stews, and desserts. Coconut water, the liquid in the center of a fresh coconut, is not used in cooking but makes a refreshing drink. To "milk" a fresh coconut, see page 333. **Desiccated coconut** is sold shredded or flaked, sweetened or unsweetened, in cans or plastic bags; unless a recipe calls for sweetened coconut, use unsweetened.

COOKING OIL: In Chinese and other Asian cooking, the clear golden oil extracted from **peanuts** is highly prized for cooking. Its fragrant aroma and distinct nutty flavor make it the ideal oil for stir-frying and deep-frying. Other choices include **canola** and **corn oil**.

CORIANDER: The lightly fragrant seeds (more correctly, the dried ripe fruits) of **cilantro** or **Chinese parsley** have a sweet flavor of caraway, lemon, and sage that's not at all like the flavor of the fresh herb.

CRAB: For details on shopping for and cooking both Dungeness and blue crabs, see page 364.

CUCUMBER, ENGLISH: This hothouse-raised cucumber can reach more than a foot long. It is almost seedless, with a thin, bright green skin. Japanese cucumbers are similar to English ones but are only about 1 inch in diameter and 8 inches long.

CUMIN: This tiny aromatic seed, which looks like caraway seed, adds pungent, spicy flavor to Asian foods such as curries and satay, though many diners first encounter it in Latin American dishes such as chili con carne. Cumin is available whole or powdered.

CURRY: The term generally defines a highly seasoned mixture of various ingredients. See page 211.

CURRY LEAF: No relation to **curry** seasoning (see previous page), these lemonlike leaves do have a decided curry fragrance that goes with many Southeast Asian dishes.

Curry leaf

DAIKON: This Japanese radish, 8 to 14 inches long and 2 to 3 inches in diameter, has crisp white flesh and a sweet, peppery taste. Peel and shred or grate to use in Japanese dishes; after cutting, always soak daikon in ice water to make it crisp and eliminate sulfury odors. See also page 109.

Daikon

DASHI: see **Japanese soup stock**

DATES: The jujube, or **Chinese red date**, is small and wrinkled, with a sweet-tart apple flavor. It's sold only in dried form and is no relation to palm dates. When **palm dates** are called for, the large, moist, and sweet Medjool is the best choice.

EGGPLANT, ASIAN: Both Chinese and Japanese eggplants range from short and pudgy 3 inches long to thin and slender 9 inches long. **Chinese** are white to lavender, **Japanese** light purple to purple-black. Because Asian eggplants are sweet and relatively seedless, they do not need to be salted, soaked, or peeled. Use interchangeably in most recipes; one Asian eggplant equals about ¼ pound.

EGG ROLL WRAPPERS: see **Wrappers**

FERMENTED SOYBEAN PASTE: see **Miso**

FISH SAUCE: see **Sauces**

FIVE-SPICE: see **Chinese five-spice**

GALANGAL: This rhizome with translucent pale yellow skin adds a mellow ginger-peppery flavor to stews and Malaysian spice pastes. If you can't find it fresh, look for dried slices or a powder in Southeast Asian markets (it's sometimes sold under its Indonesian name, *laos*). A ½-inch piece of fresh galangal equals about 1 teaspoon of the powder.

GARLIC: Many of the recipes in this book make liberal use of garlic. As a rough equivalent, 1 clove garlic equals 1 teaspoon minced. Fried garlic, often used as a garnish, can be purchased in Asian markets and some supermarkets.

GARLIC CHIVES: Chinese cooking uses several kinds of garlic chives. For details, see page 251.

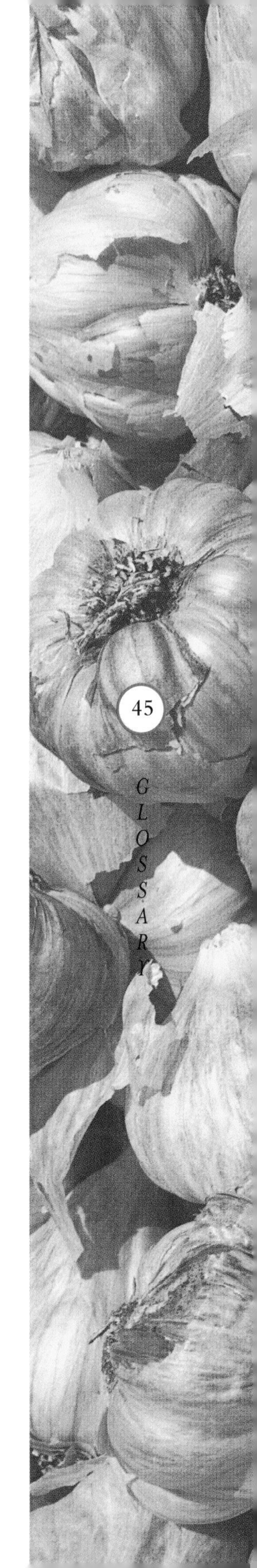

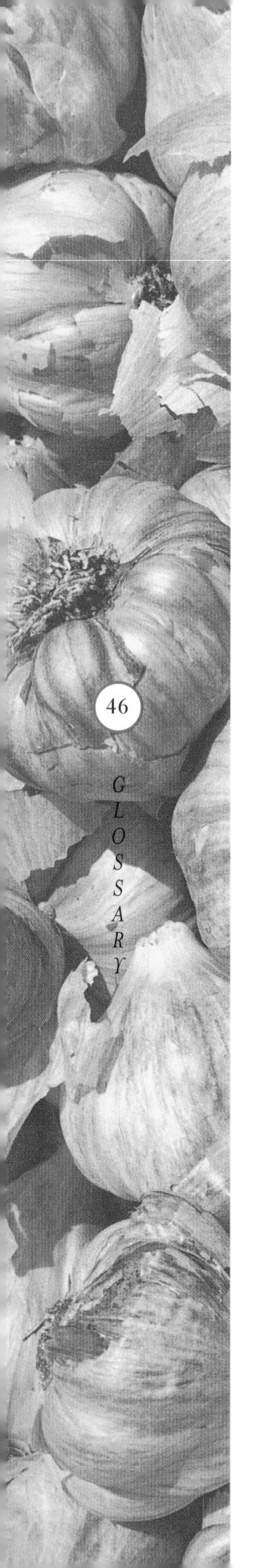

Crystallized ginger

GINGER: **Fresh ginger** has a smooth golden skin, a fibrous yellow-green interior, and a spicy bite and tantalizing aroma. **Young ginger**, available seasonally, has a smoother, more delicate flavor and less fibrous texture. Choose ginger that is hard, heavy, and free of wrinkles and mold. A ginger slice the size of a quarter equals 1 teaspoon minced. **Crystallized ginger** is young ginger cooked in a sugar syrup and coated in sugar. **Pickled ginger**, used in Chinese cooking, is cured in brine, then soaked in a sugar-vinegar solution; red pickled ginger is somewhat sweeter. **Preserved ginger** is packed in a heavy sugar syrup that becomes infused with a mild ginger taste.

GYOZA: see **Wrappers**

HOISIN SAUCE: see **Sauces**

Jackfruit

JACKFRUIT: This spiny and oval or oblong tropical fruit has white or yellowish fruit with a bland, sweet flavor like a combination of banana, pineapple, and mango. Asian markets sell canned jackfruit.

JAPANESE RICE WINE *(SAKE)*: see **Rice wine**

JAPANESE SEAWEED *(NORI)*: see **Seaweed, dried**

JAPANESE SOUP STOCK *(DASHI)*: This basic ingredient for many traditional Japanese soups, marinades, soups, and sauces is easily made from dried giant sea kelp *(konbu)*, flaked dried bonito *(katsuo-bushi)*, and water. Although homemade dashi has the best flavor, many home cooks find it easier to use instant dashi *(dashi-no-moto)* granules, powder, or concentrate.

JAPANESE-STYLE BREAD CRUMBS *(PANKO)*: These dried, toasted flakes, which are larger and coarser than Western-style bread crumbs, give a crunchy coating to deep-fried foods such as Pork Cutlets (recipe on page 254). Use as you would bread crumbs. Unlike some batter- or crumb-coated foods, panko does not taste greasy after frying, and it retains its crisp texture even after standing.

JICAMA: Under its brown, leathery skin is crunchy, slightly fibrous, and sweet white flesh. Although a bit more fibrous and less sweet than fresh water chestnuts, jicama makes a good substitute. Choose small, firm, well-rounded jicama that are free of blemishes and mold.

KUNG PAO SAUCE: see **Sauces**

LEMONGRASS: This herb imparts a delicate lemony flavor and aroma to Southeast Asian foods. To prepare, see page 350. Also see page 104.

Lemongrass

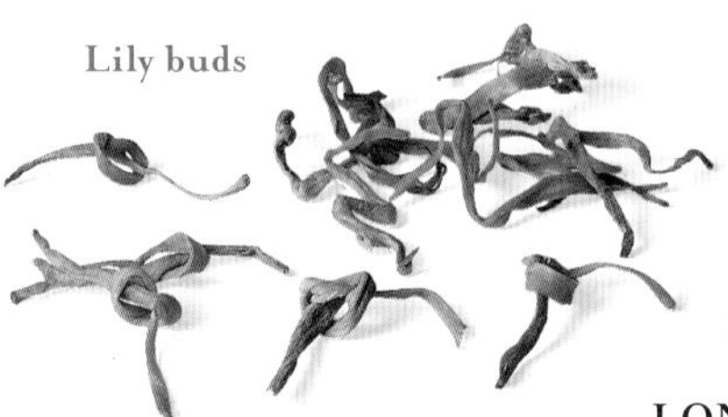
Lily buds

LILY BUDS: These 2- to 3-inch-long brown strands have a delicate musky-sweet flavor. They are usually sold dried, and are used as a vegetable in soups and stir-fried dishes.

LONGAN: Oval fruit, about the size of a small plum, has a smooth brown shell over sweet translucent flesh somewhat similar to that of **lychee**. Longans are available canned or crystallized, and sometimes fresh, in Asian markets.

LONGTONG: see **Rice cakes**

LOP CHEONG: see **Chinese sausage**

LOQUAT: Orange to yellow fruit about the size of an apricot, with sweet, aromatic flesh. They are sometimes available fresh in areas where they grow (such as California) and are also sold canned or dried in Asian markets.

Lotus leaves

LOTUS: **Lotus leaves** are huge, and are used to wrap fillings for steaming. Fresh or dried leaves are available in Asian markets. See also page 318. **Lotus root** looks like a long chain of thick, off-white, hard sausages. Just peel and slice crosswise to reveal an interesting cross-section with air holes that run the length of the root. Lotus root adds a fibrous crunch to soups and braised dishes. **Lotus seeds** have a delicate flavor, are used in desserts, and come in both fresh and dried forms. Asian markets sell them canned or in bulk.

Lotus root

LUMPIA WRAPPERS: see **Wrappers**

Lychee

LYCHEE: Fresh fruit looks like a crimson pink berry 1 to 2 inches across. When the bumpy, leathery peel is slipped off, the semitranslucent, juicy flesh is revealed. See also page 266. Canned lychees are much easier to find.

MALTOSE: A type of malt sugar made mainly from barley and known in ancient China, maltose is used to coat duck skin to make it turn deep brown in roasting. Honey is an acceptable substitute. Chinese markets sell it in 1-pound rocks.

MELON, BITTER: A squash-like vegetable that resembles a bumpy, wrinkled cucumber. It contains quinine, which gives it a cool, bitter taste. The seeds and pulp are scooped out; then it can be parboiled to reduce the bitterness before it is stir-fried or stuffed.

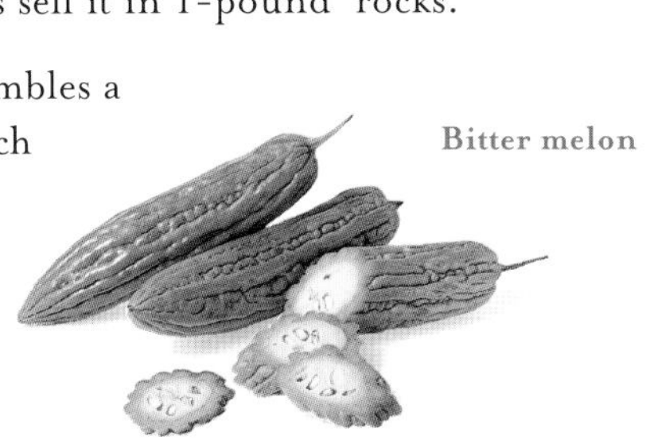
Bitter melon

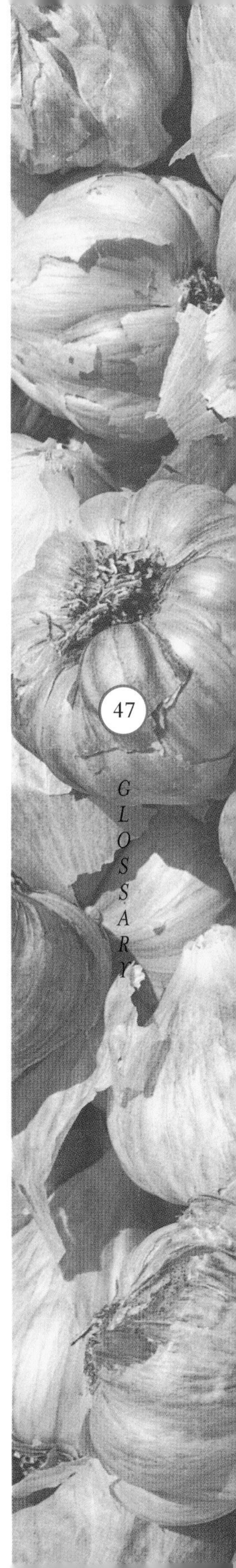

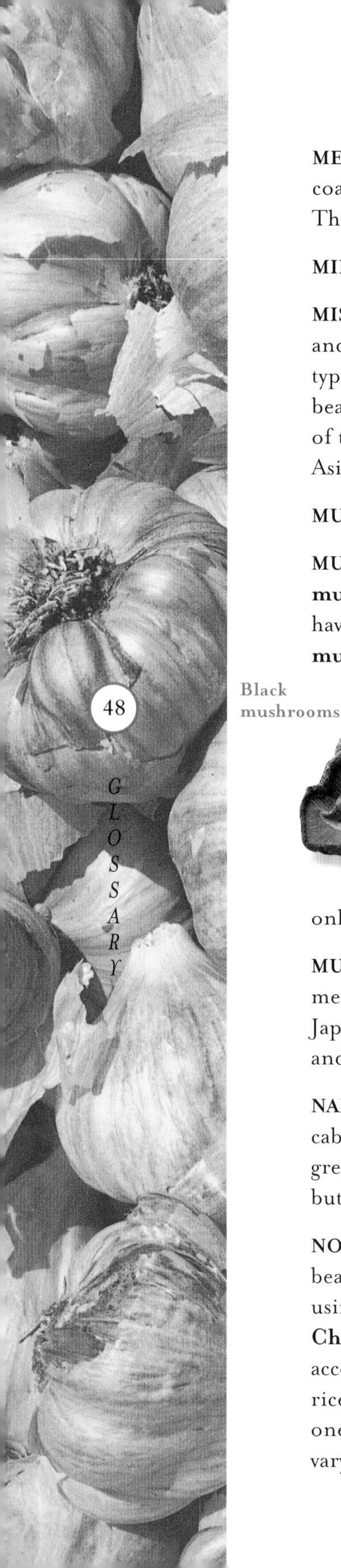

MELON, WINTER: Inside a green skin with a powdery coating is white flesh with a faint sweet-peppery taste. The flesh is used in soups, but never eaten raw.

Winter melon

MIRIN: see **Rice wine**

MISO: Protein-rich and appealing because of its taste and aroma, *miso* is a staple in the Japanese diet. The several types of miso are made by fermenting the same basic ingredients: crushed soybeans and barley, rice, or wheat. Before adding to a dish, dissolve miso with some of the liquid called for in the recipe. Look for it in the refrigerated section of Asian markets.

MUNG BEANS: See **Bean sprouts**

Enoki and oyster mushrooms

MUSHROOMS, FRESH: Long stemmed, tiny-capped **enoki mushrooms** and delicate, shell-shaped **oyster mushrooms** have a delicate, mild flavor. Firm, golden brown **shiitake mushrooms** have a rich, meaty flavor. Both are smooth and velvety in texture.

Black mushrooms

MUSHROOMS, DRIED AND CANNED: Chinese **black mushrooms** and Japanese **shiitake mushrooms** share some characteristics: both kinds have brownish black caps, tan undersides, a rich and meaty texture, and wild mushroom flavor. **Straw mushrooms**, which have a delicate sweetness and a firm, meaty texture, are available peeled or unpeeled, in cans only; drain before using. For details, see page 139.

MUSTARD: Dry mustard powder mixed with liquid is a pungent and fiery condiment, adding a clean-tasting hotness to Chinese appetizers and to sauces for Japanese dishes such as *teppan-yaki*. Chinese, Japanese *(karashi)*, and English-style dry mustards are interchangeable.

NAPA CABBAGE: Both short Chinese and tall Japanese napa cabbages have sweet, cream-colored stalks with ruffled pale green edges. Use either kind as you would regular cabbage, but cooking time is less.

Napa cabbage

NOODLES: **Bean thread noodles** (dried), made from mung bean starch, come in different lengths and thicknesses. Before using, soak in warm water until softened, about 5 minutes. **Chinese egg noodles** (fresh) come in many widths, sizes, and flavors. Cook according to package directions. **Rice flour noodles** (fresh), made from long-grain rice flour, are soft, pliable, and milky white. For details, see page 186. Wide, flat ones are called *kway teow*. Dried rice stick noodles are stiff and brittle, and come in varying widths and lengths; see page 185. Thick ones are called *lai fun*.

NORI: see **Seaweed, dried**

Peas

OYSTER-FLAVORED SAUCE: see **Sauces**

PANKO: see **Japanese-style bread crumbs**

PEARL TAPIOCA: see **Tapioca**

PEAS, EDIBLE-POD: This description applies to both snow peas and sugar snap peas. Snow peas have flat pods with a sweet, sugary flavor and crisp, crunchy texture. Sugar snaps have thicker pods and similar flavor.

PEPPERS, HOT: see **Chilies**

PEPPERS, SWEET: Red and green bell peppers have a mild, sweet flavor and juicy flesh. The red kind are the ripe form of green ones. These bell-shaped peppers also come in yellow, orange, purple, and brown.

PLUM SAUCE: see **Sauces**

Rice

RICE: **Fermented rice** is a byproduct of winemaking. **Glutinous rice**, a kind of short-grain rice, is also known as sweet or sticky rice. Grains resemble rice-shaped pearls. When cooked, grains become soft, sticky, and translucent. **Long-grain rice** is the least starchy of all the kinds of rice; it cooks up dry and fluffy with grains that separate easily. These characteristics make it ideal for fried rice. **Medium-grain rice** is a daily staple in Japan and Korea; it's also the rice used in sushi. For more on cooking perfect rice, see page 31.

RICE CAKES, GLUTINOUS: Compressed glutinous rice cakes, called *longtong* or *ketupat,* are served with satay and other Malaysian dishes. For instructions on how to make them, see page 235.

RICE CRUSTS: Asian markets sell squares of dried rice used in Sizzling Rice Soup and other dishes. For the soup recipe and details on making your own rice crusts, see page 113.

RICE FLOUR: Flour made from ground glutinous rice is used to create sweet doughs for dim sum and for Chinese and Japanese pastries. Boiled dough forms a smooth, chewy casing; deep-frying yields a lightly crisp exterior with a sweet, sticky inside. Flour made from ground long-grain rice is used to make rice paper, rice noodles, steamed cakes, and other dim sum dishes.

RICE PAPER WRAPPERS: see **Wrappers**

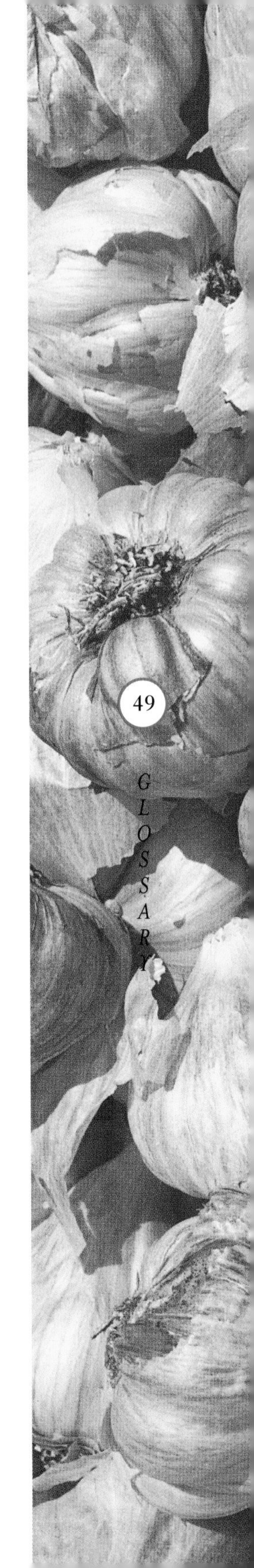

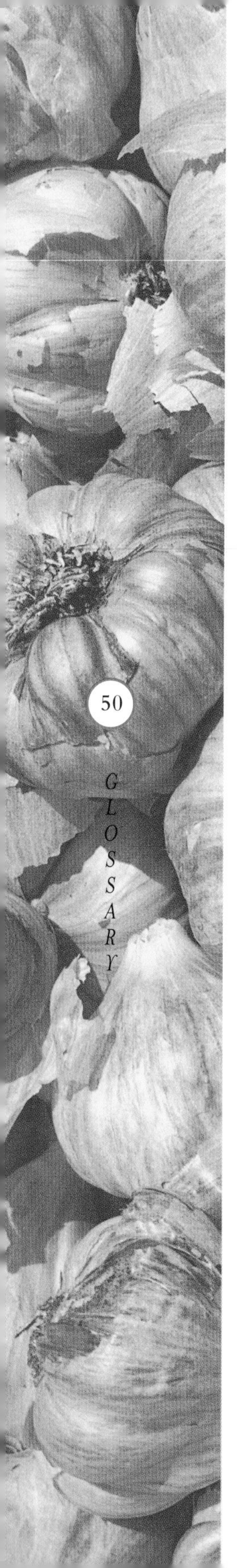

RICE STICK NOODLES, DRIED: see **Noodles**

RICE VINEGAR: see **Vinegar**

RICE WINE: **Chinese rice wine** is a rich amber liquid made from fermented glutinous rice and millet. It is aged 10 to 100 years to achieve its rich, full-bodied flavor. **Shaoxing** (Shao Hsing), in eastern China, produces some of the best-quality rice wines. Japanese sweet cooking rice wine *(mirin)* is also made from glutinous rice; it adds a rich flavor and glossy sheen to cooked dishes. **Japanese rice wine** *(sake)* has a clean, lightly sweet, flowery taste. It is also used in cooking and in marinades to tenderize meats or to remove off-odors and fishy tastes. See also page 286.

ROCK SUGAR: see **Sugar**

SAKE: see **Rice wine**

SAUCES (See also **Soy sauce**): These products are available in Asian markets and some supermarkets. **Black bean sauce** is made from salted black beans and rice wine; it may contain garlic or hot chilies. **Char siu** or **barbecue sauce** is a thick sauce made from fermented soybeans, vinegar, tomato paste, chilies, garlic, honey or sugar, and other spices. **Chili sauce** is made of fresh and dried chilies and vinegar with seasonings such as garlic, ginger, soybeans, and sesame oil. A sweetened version is popular in Malaysia and Singapore. **Curry sauce** contains a mix of spices used in curries. **Fish sauce**, an all-purpose flavoring agent used throughout Southeast Asia and southern China, is a thin, amber-colored fermented fish extract. Its distinct pungent aroma, something like soy sauce and fish, mellows with cooking and adds a delicious, slightly salty taste to foods. **Hoisin sauce** is a robust combination of fermented soybeans, vinegar, garlic, sugar, and spices. Its spicy-sweet flavor complements many dishes, including mu shu variations and Peking duck. **Kung pao sauce** contains red chilies, sesame oil, soybeans, sweet potato, ginger, garlic, and other spices. **Liquid hot pepper sauce** is made from tabasco peppers, vinegar, and salt. **Oyster-flavored sauce** is a thick, dark brown all-purpose seasoning made from oyster extracts, sugar, and seasonings. Its distinct sweet-smoky flavor goes well in any meat or vegetable stir-fry. Hot and vegetarian variations are available. **Peanut-flavored sauce** or satay sauce is best for dipping or barbecuing. **Plum sauce** is a light, amber-colored sauce made from salted plums, apricots, yams, rice vinegar, chilies, and other spices. The sweet-tart chunky sauce is often served with roast duck, barbecued meats, and deep-fried appetizers. **Shrimp sauce**, thick and pungent, is made from salted fermented shrimp; it's a staple in Chinese and Southeast Asian cooking. **Sweet bean sauce** is made from fermented soybeans and sugar. **Sweet and sour sauce** is simply made from vinegar and sugar. Cantonese versions are fruitier. Popular additions

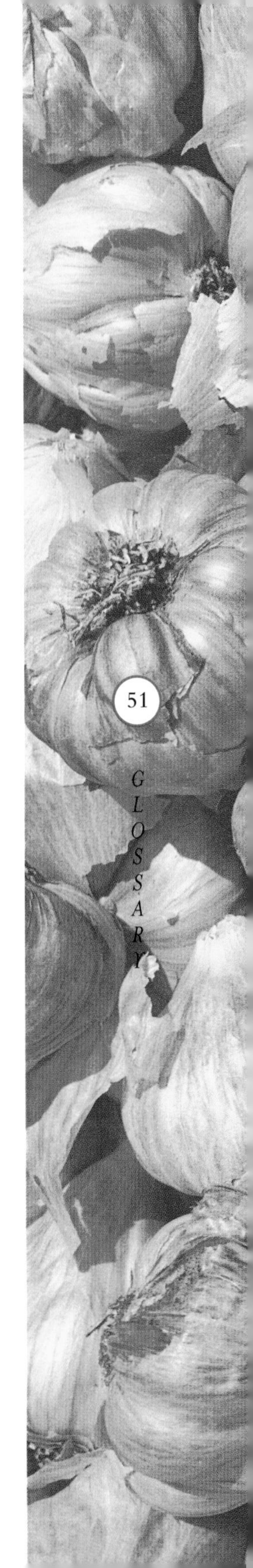

include chili, ketchup, and ginger. **Teriyaki sauce** has a savory, sweet flavor that goes well with any barbecued or grilled meat, poultry, fish, or shellfish. Traditionally, it's made from equal portions of soy sauce and Japanese sweet cooking rice wine; it may include additional ingredients such as pineapple juice, sake, brown sugar, ginger, and garlic.

SEAWEED, DRIED: In Japan, seaweed is harvested, washed, dried, seasoned, and packaged. Deep green sheets of *nori* are used to wrap sushi and are shredded for garnishes, and olive-brown giant sea kelp (*konbu*) is used to make **Japanese soup stock** *(dashi)*.

SESAME OIL: Dark amber Asian sesame oil is pressed from toasted white sesame seeds. The best oils are labeled as 100 percent pure. Use just a small amount to add nutty taste and aroma to marinades, dressings, and stir-fries. Don't confuse Asian sesame oil with the light-colored oil used in salad dressings and for sauté-ing. For more details, see page 131.

SESAME PASTE: Toasted and ground white sesame seeds make a thick paste with a roasted, nutty taste and aroma. It is a common ingredient in Sichuan cooking.

SESAME SEEDS: Both black and white kinds are used to flavor and garnish dishes. White sesame seeds, hulled and unhulled, have a sweet, nutty flavor. Black sesame seeds are slightly bitter. Toasting, particularly of white seeds, intensifies flavor and aroma.

SHALLOTS: They are familiar enough in Western kitchens that they don't need an introduction. But Asian shallots are generally smaller, so when you are shopping look for bulbs each about the size of a walnut. Crisp, deep-fried shallot flakes are a popular Southeast Asian garnish available in some Asian markets. To make your own, peel and very thinly slice shallots; separate each slice into rings. Deep-fry slowly at 325°F until golden brown and crisp, 3 to 5 minutes. Drain on paper towels. Store in an airtight container in the refrigerator.

Shallots

SHAOXING WINE: see **Rice wine**

SHIITAKE MUSHROOMS: see **Mushrooms**

SHRIMP: **Dried shrimp** are tiny shrimp preserved in brine, then dried, creating slightly chewy morsels with a pungent taste. Their flavor will enhance any vegetable dish, soup, or dim sum filling. **Fresh shrimp** come in various sizes; when size is important, it is listed in the recipe. For details on shelling and deveining shrimp, see page 357.

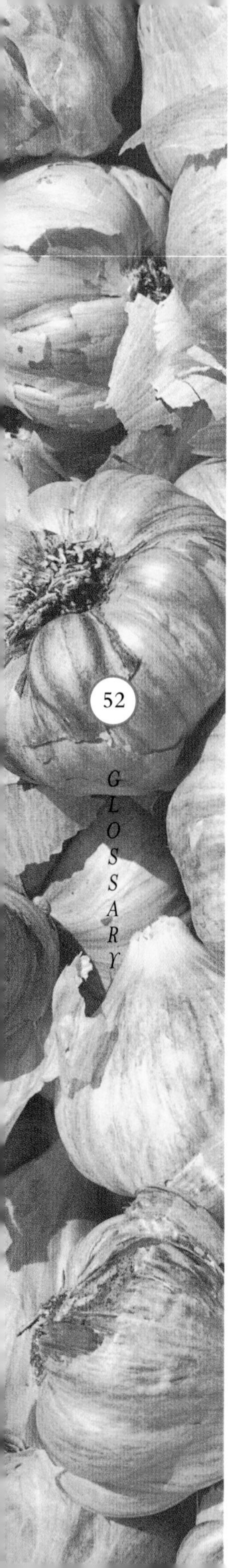

SHRIMP PASTE: Malaysian dried shrimp paste *(blachan)* is the sun-dried version of shrimp sauce, used as a flavoring in many spice pastes (for a spice paste recipe, see page 31). This condiment and flavoring agent is made from salted, cured small fish or shrimp that are then fermented for several weeks. The liquid given off is also used as a sauce or condiment.

SICHUAN PEPPERCORNS: The dried red dish brown berries of the prickly ash tree add a woodsy fragrance to foods and leave a pleasantly numbing feeling in the mouth. To bring out their distinctive aroma and flavor, toast a few handfuls in a frying pan over low heat until fragrant. Use whole, or crush in a spice grinder into a coarse or fine powder. See also page 260.

Sichuan peppercorns

SICHUAN PRESERVED VEGETABLE: Kohlrabi, mustard greens, napa cabbage, or turnips can be the main ingredient in these spicy preserved vegetables. Chili powder and ground Sichuan peppercorns give them a spicy-salty taste. In traditional Chinese cooking, each vegetable is used in a different way, but for American tastes, all can be used interchangeably.

SNOW PEAS: see **Peas, edible-pod**

SOYBEANS, FRESH: Even rice doesn't have as many guises in Asian cooking as soybeans do. These rather bland-tasting legumes with very high nutritive value form the base for products as diverse as **tofu**, soybean oil, **soy sauce** and other flavorings, soybean paste (*miso*), **bean sprouts**, and bean curd sheets.

SOY SAUCE: All the types of soy sauce are made from naturally fermented soybeans and wheat. **Regular soy** sauce gives Chinese dishes their characteristic flavor and rich brown color. **Dark soy** is regular sauce with molasses added. It is thicker, darker, sweeter, and more full-bodied. Use when a richer flavor and deep mahogany color are desired. **Reduced-sodium soy** contains about 40 percent less sodium than regular soy sauce; it tastes less salty but still has all the rich flavor. Sometimes it's called "light" soy sauce. **Thick sweet soy** (*kecap manis*) is very dark brown and thick, sweetened with palm sugar, and seasoned with garlic and star anise.

SPRING ROLL WRAPPERS: see **Wrappers**

STAR ANISE: An inedible 1-inch pod contains eight points, each encasing a shiny, mahogany-colored seed. If you can't find a whole pod, use eight broken points. Star anise adds a distinct spiced licorice flavor to rich braising sauces and stews.

Star Anise

STAR FRUIT: Crosswise slices of this translucent tropical fruit make it obvious why it's called star fruit. Flavor ranges from sweet to tart, with a delicious fragrance. Use in salads and desserts, or eat it by itself, skin and all. Star fruit is also called carambola.

STRAW MUSHROOMS: see **Mushrooms**

Straw mushrooms

SUGAR, ROCK: Also called rock candy, rock sugar looks like large, pale amber-colored crystals. It is made from a combination of refined and raw sugars and honey. It adds a smooth, refreshing sweetness to foods such as braised meat dishes and savory sauces.

SWEET AND SOUR SAUCE: see **Sauces**

TAMARIND: The fibrous, sticky pulp around the seeds of the tamarind tree provide the fruity sour flavor characteristic of Southeast Asian curries, chutneys, soups, and stews. The pulp must be mashed in water, then pressed through a sieve; see instructions on page 106. Tamarind concentrate and powder are also available.

Tamarind

TANGERINE PEEL, DRIED: The gnarled, brittle, rust-colored peel adds a light citrus flavor to sauces, soups, and braised dishes. Before using, soak peel in warm water until softened. Scrape the inside of the peel with a table knife to remove the bitter white layer. To make your own, see page 216.

TAPIOCA: A fine, waxy-textured white powder is made from the root of the cassava plant. Tapioca starch is used as a thickener and with other flours to make dim sum doughs. Pearls come in various sizes; small (1/8-inch) pearls are used in creamy puddings and sweet desserts.

TOFU: Also called bean curd, tofu is made from soybeans and water. Texture varies: **soft tofu** is silky smooth and very light; **regular-firm** and **extra-firm tofu** both have a denser structure and slightly spongy interior. **Fermented bean curd** has a thick custardlike texture with a mildly pungent winelike aroma: **white** and **red** kinds, each with different additives, are available. Tofu is also available as **bean curd sheets**, each about 7 by 21 inches. For handling instructions, see page 102. Diagrams below show how to stuff tofu for Home-Style Tofu with Seafood Mousse (page 145).

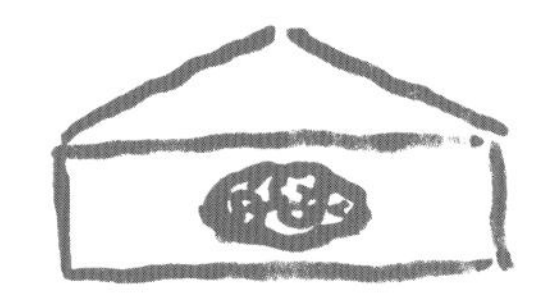

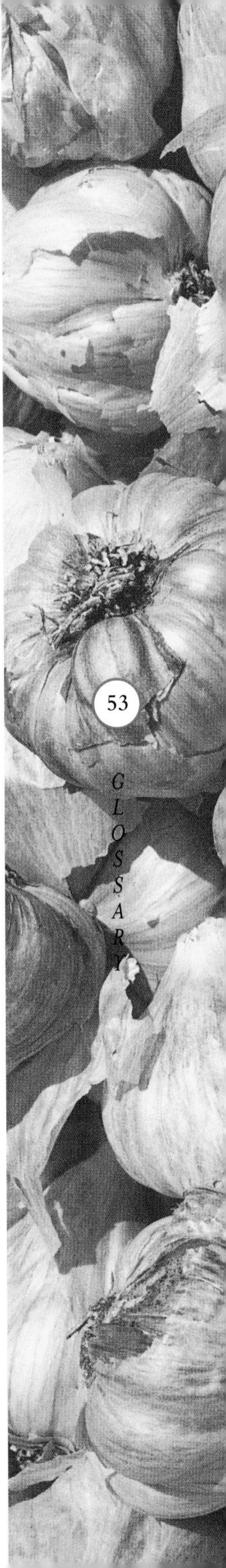

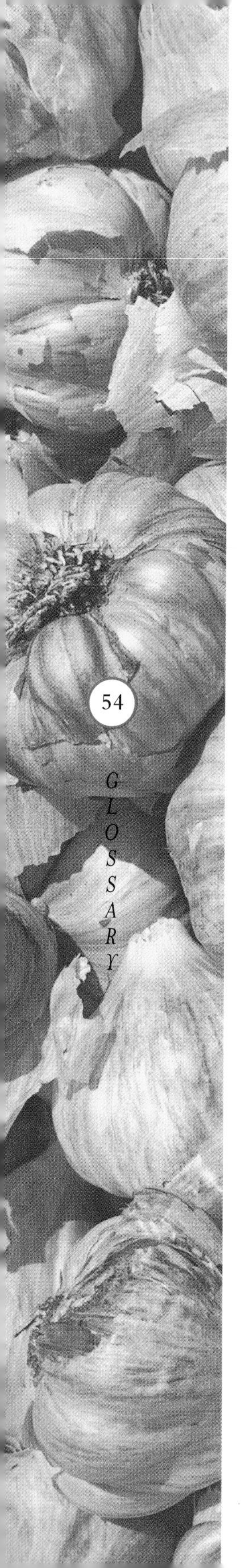

TREE EARS: see **Black fungus, dried**

TURMERIC: This bitter, pungent spice with intense rust color comes from the underground stem of a plant of the ginger family. It is a basic ingredient in many Indian and Southeast Asian spice blends. Look for turmeric powder on supermarket spice shelves.

VINEGAR: **Chinese black vinegar** comes from the fermentation of a mixture of rice, wheat, and millet or sorghum. Compared to distilled white vinegar, it is less tart, smokier, sweeter, and more flavorful. Chinkiang vinegar is a popular type of black vinegar produced in coastal China south of Shanghai. See also page 325. Balsamic vinegar is a substitute for black vinegar; if using it, decrease the amount of sugar the recipe may call for. **Rice vinegar**, made from fermented rice, is milder, less pungent, and sweeter than distilled white vinegar. Popular Chinese and Japanese kinds (such as Chinese black vinegar) range in color from clear or slightly golden to rich amber brown.

WATER CHESTNUTS: **Fresh water chestnuts** are 1½-inch pointy-topped tubers with a shiny, inedible brown skin. Inside is the sweet, slightly starchy flesh. Buy fresh ones that are free of wrinkles and mold. **Canned water chestnuts** have a similar texture but are not as sweet. See also page 146.

WHEAT STARCH: Wheat flour with all the gluten removed is a fine-textured, off-white powder commonly used to make doughs for dim sum dishes. Steamed dough becomes soft, shiny, and opaque white.

WINE, CHINESE RICE: see **Rice wine**

Dried black fungus

WOLFBERRIES: These small, deep red, oval fruits of a medlar tree have a spiced apple flavor. They are used in Chinese dishes; look for them in the dried foods section of Asian markets or at a Chinese herbalist.

WOOD EARS: see **Black fungus, dried**.

WRAPPERS: **Egg roll wrappers** are made from wheat flour, eggs, and water; the dough is rolled into thin, pliable sheets similar to wonton wrappers. They are filled with savory or sweet fillings, then deep-fried until golden brown. **Lumpia wrappers** are the Filipino version of egg roll wrappers; they are a thin skin made of flour or cornstarch, eggs, and water used to wrap around a filling of raw or cooked vegetables, seasonings, and sometimes meat or shrimp. **Potsticker wrappers** are pasta circles made from wheat flour, water, and eggs; they can be used to wrap fillings for gyoza, potstickers, and steamed dumplings *(siu mai)*. Filled wrappers can be deep-fried, pan-fried, or steamed. **Rice paper wrappers** are brittle, semitransparent round or

Wrappers

Folding Made Simple

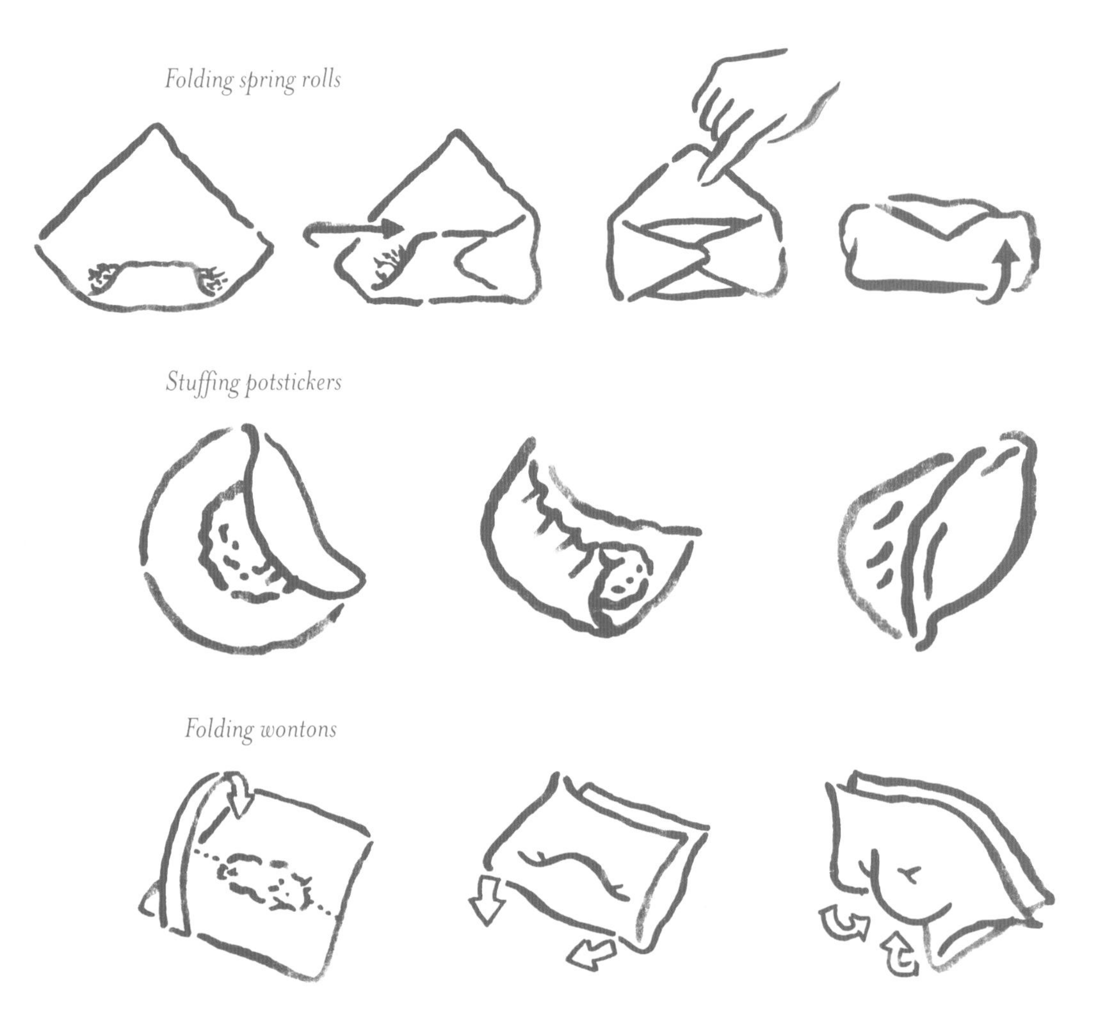

triangular sheets made from rice flour. Before using, soak briefly in water. Use to wrap savory bundles of meats and vegetables and eat as is, or deep-fry until golden brown. **Spring roll wrappers**, made of just wheat flour and water, are thinner than egg roll wrappers. When fried, they become crisp and smooth with a light texture. Square and round wrappers are available. **Wonton wrappers**, made from wheat flour, water, and eggs, are about 3½ inches square and come in two thicknesses. They can hold a variety of fillings, from savory meats to sweet preserves. Thicker ones are used for deep-frying, pan-frying, or steaming; thinner ones in soups.

YARD-LONG BEANS: see **Chinese long beans**

CHAPTER 1

Appetizers and Dim Sum

Golden Shrimp Rolls

Hong Kong chefs are always dreaming up new recipes to make their mark in the world of dim sum. This recipe combines two of my favorites: shrimp and quail eggs. Serve them with Sweet and Sour Dipping Sauce (recipe below) and see if they aren't your favorites, too.

8 *jumbo raw shrimp*

Marinade

1 *tablespoon cornstarch*

½ *teaspoon salt*

¼ *teaspoon white pepper*

8 *hard-cooked quail eggs, shelled*

1 *sheet Japanese seaweed (nori), cut into 8 strips 1 inch wide*

Wooden picks

Cooking oil for deep-frying

Cornstarch

1 *egg, lightly beaten*

1½ *cups Japanese bread crumbs (panko)*

Sweet and Sour Dipping Sauce (recipe below)

Getting Ready

① Shell and devein shrimp, leaving tails intact. Butterfly them along the inside curve, then flatten with the flat side of a cleaver. Combine marinade ingredients in a bowl. Add shrimp and stir to coat; let stand for 10 minutes.

② Place a quail egg at one end of a strip of nori and roll up. Center wrapped egg on inner side of a shrimp. Roll shrimp to enclose egg; secure with a wooden pick. Repeat with remaining eggs, nori strips, and shrimp.

Cooking

① In a wok or 2-quart saucepan, heat oil for deep-frying to 350°F. Dust stuffed shrimp with cornstarch. Dip in egg, drain briefly, then coat with crumbs. Deep-fry, turning once, until golden brown, 2 to 3 minutes. Remove with a slotted spoon; drain on paper towels.

② Cut stuffed shrimp in half horizontally and place on a serving plate. Serve with Sweet and Sour Dipping Sauce.

Makes 16.

Sweet and Sour Dipping Sauce

To make a simple sweet and sour sauce (about 1½ cups), heat 1 tablespoon **cooking oil** in a 1-quart pan over medium-high heat. Add 1 teaspoon minced **fresh ginger** and cook, stirring, until fragrant, about 10 seconds.

Add ¼ cup *each* **orange juice** and **rice vinegar**, 5 tablespoons *each* **brown sugar** and **ketchup**, 2 teaspoons **soy sauce**, and ½ teaspoon **chili oil** or hot pepper sauce.

Cook until sugar dissolves. Mix 1½ tablespoons **cornstarch** with 2 tablespoons **water** and add to sauce; cook, stirring, until sauce boils and thickens.

Shrimp and Scallop Amandine

Almonds are popular in modern Hong Kong cuisine, and this dish creates elegance with casual ease. The wonderful textures of fresh shrimp and scallops are a great contrast to the hot, crunchy almonds and sesame seeds.

- ½ *pound medium raw shrimp*
- ½ *pound sea scallops*

Marinade

- 1 *tablespoon Chinese rice wine or dry sherry*
- 2 *teaspoons cornstarch*
- ½ *teaspoon salt*
- ¼ *teaspoon white pepper*

Dipping Sauce

- 2 *teaspoons dry mustard powder*
- 2 *teaspoons water*
- ¼ *cup sweet and sour sauce* *(see page 33)*

- 1 *cup finely chopped almonds*
- ½ *cup sesame seeds*
- *Cornstarch*
- 1 *egg, lightly beaten*
- ¼ *cup cooking oil*

Getting Ready

① Shell and devein shrimp, leaving tails intact. Butterfly them along the inside curve, then flatten with the side of a cleaver. Combine marinade ingredients in a bowl. Add shrimp and scallops; stir to coat. Let stand for 10 minutes.

② Prepare dipping sauce: In a bowl, blend mustard and water; stir in sweet and sour sauce. Place in a dipping sauce bowl.

③ In a shallow bowl, combine almonds and sesame seeds. Dust each shrimp and scallop with cornstarch. Dip in egg, drain briefly, then coat with almond mixture.

Cooking

① Place a wide frying pan over medium heat until hot. Add oil; when oil is hot, add shrimp and scallops. Pan-fry, turning once, until golden brown, about 1½ minutes on each side.

② Serve hot with dipping sauce.

Makes 6 servings.

Zucchini Siu Mai

Instead of adding zucchini to the filling, I stuff a hollowed-out zucchini with *siu mai* filling, top it with shrimp, and steam it like a dumpling. A new twist to a classic!

Filling

- 1 *dried black mushroom*
- 1/4 *pound ground pork or chicken*
- 1 *tablespoon minced green onion*
- 1 *teaspoon minced ginger*
- 2 *tablespoons water*
- 2 *teaspoons oyster-flavored sauce*
- 1 *teaspoon soy sauce*
- 2 *teaspoons cornstarch*
- 1/4 *teaspoon white pepper*
- 1 *egg white*

- 3 *zucchini, each 8 to 9 inches long and 1 1/2 inches in diameter*
- 18 *small raw shrimp, shelled*
- 1 1/2 *tablespoons cooking oil (optional)*
- 1/3 *cup water (optional)*

Getting Ready

① Soak mushroom in warm water to cover until softened, about 20 minutes; drain. Discard stem and mince cap. Place mushroom in a bowl with remaining filling ingredients; stir briskly until mixture is very smooth, about 30 seconds.

② Trim ends of zucchini; cut each crosswise into 6 pieces. With an apple corer, remove cores from zucchini, leaving a shell 1/4 inch thick.

③ Stuff filling into zucchini cases. Top each case with a shrimp.

Cooking

① Place a wide frying pan over medium heat until hot. Add oil, swirling to coat sides. Stand zucchini in the frying pan and cook until bottoms are lightly browned, about 2 minutes. Add 1/3 cup water; reduce heat to low, cover, and cook until filling is no longer pink, about 5 minutes. Or prepare a wok for steaming (see page 25). Stand zucchini in a heatproof dish. Steam over high heat until filling is no longer pink, about 10 minutes.

② Transfer to a serving plate.

Makes 18.

Steamed Shanghai Buns

At a charming teahouse in a garden in Suzhou, I was served tender pork-filled dumplings like these, lightly steamed and served Shanghai-style with wine vinegar and ginger.

- 2½ *cups flour*
- ½ *cup boiling water*
- ⅔ *cup cold water*

Filling

- ¾ *pound ground pork, beef, or chicken*
- ⅔ *cup chicken broth*
- 3 *tablespoons finely chopped onion*
- 2 *tablespoons oyster-flavored sauce*
- 2 *teaspoons soy sauce*
- 2 *teaspoons sesame oil*

Dipping Sauce

- ¼ *cup red wine vinegar*
- 2 *teaspoons shredded ginger*

Getting Ready

① Place flour in a bowl. Add boiling water, stirring with chopsticks or a fork. Gradually stir in cold water, mixing until dough holds together. On a lightly floured board, knead dough until smooth and satiny, about 5 minutes. Cover and let rest for 30 minutes.

② Combine filling ingredients in a bowl. Combine red wine vinegar and ginger in a dipping sauce bowl.

③ On a lightly floured board, roll dough into a 14-inch cylinder, then cut into 28 portions. Make each bun: Roll a portion of dough into a 4-inch circle about ⅛ inch thick; keep remaining dough covered to prevent drying. Place a rounded tablespoon of filling in center of dough. Gather edges of dough around filling; pinch and pleat to seal. Cover buns and let rest for at least 5 minutes before steaming.

Cooking

① Prepare a wok for steaming (see page 25). One half at a time, place buns, seam side up, in a heatproof dish. Steam buns, covered, over high heat for 10 minutes.

② Transfer to a serving plate. Serve hot with dipping sauce.

Makes 28.

Dumpling Dough

Why are some Chinese doughs made with boiling water? Because it heats and stretches the starch granules in the flour, allowing them to hold more water. This kind of hot-water dough is quite tender and is used to make the kind of chewy wrappers used in dumplings like *siu mai* and potstickers. Of course, you can also buy prepared siu mai or potsticker wrappers, but the hot-water dough is easy to make and has a wonderfully elastic texture.

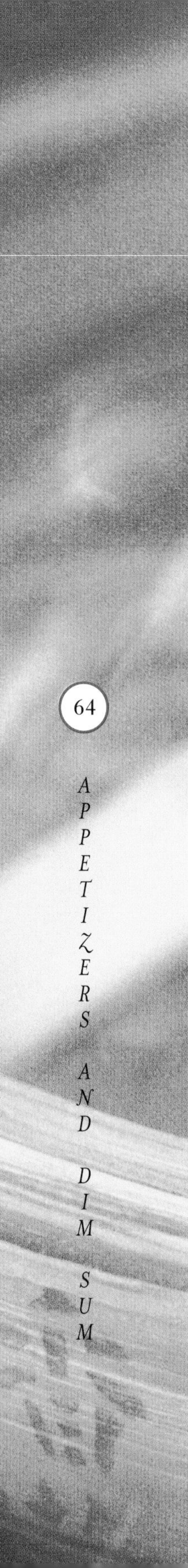

Har Gau

You can't buy wrappers to make *har gau*, but the wrapper dough is easy to make from wheat starch. When these savory dumplings are steamed, the wrappers become shiny and opaque.

Wrappers

- 1 *cup wheat starch*
- ⅓ *cup cornstarch*
- ¼ *teaspoon salt*
- 1 *cup boiling water*

Filling

- ¾ *pound medium raw shrimp*
- ¼ *cup finely chopped bamboo shoots*
- 1 *egg white*
- 1 *tablespoon cornstarch*
- 1 *teaspoon Chinese rice wine or dry sherry*
- 1 *teaspoon sesame oil*
- ¾ *teaspoon salt*
- ⅛ *teaspoon white pepper*

- 1½ *tablespoons cooking oil or solid vegetable shortening*
- *Soy sauce and chili oil*

Getting Ready

① Make wrappers: Combine wheat starch, cornstarch, and salt in a bowl. Add boiling water, stirring with chopsticks or a fork, until dough is evenly moistened. Cover and let rest for 20 minutes.

② Prepare filling: Shell, devein, and coarsely chop shrimp. Place in a bowl with remaining filling ingredients; mix well.

③ On a lightly floured board, knead dough until smooth. A teaspoon at a time, add cooking oil, kneading to blend after each addition, until dough glistens and feels satiny. Divide dough in half. Roll each half into a 15-inch cylinder. Cut each cylinder crosswise into 1-inch pieces; shape each piece into a ball. Cover dough to prevent drying.

④ Shape each dumpling: Roll a portion of dough into a 3- to 3½-inch circle. With your fingers, press edges of dough to make slightly thinner. Place a rounded teaspoon of filling in center of dough; fold dough over filling to form a semicircle. Pinch edges together to seal. Cover with a damp cloth while shaping remaining dumplings.

Cooking

① Prepare a wok for steaming (see page 25). Line the bottom of a steamer with a small damp cloth. Arrange dumplings on cloth without crowding. Cover and steam until dumplings are translucent, 18 to 20 minutes.

② Serve dumplings hot or cold with soy sauce and chili oil for dipping.

Makes 30.

Paper-Wrapped Chicken

In Chinese restaurants, you will find these packages of marinated chicken deep-fried. I think baking is a nice variation, especially for home cooking. Cooking parchment is available in most supermarkets, or you can use aluminum foil.

- ¾ *pound boneless, skinless chicken breasts*

Marinade

- 1 *tablespoon Chinese rice wine or dry sherry*
- 1 *tablespoon oyster-flavored sauce*
- 2 *teaspoons soy sauce*
- 2 *teaspoons sesame oil*
- 1 *teaspoon minced ginger*
- ¼ *teaspoon cornstarch*

- 16 *squares (6 in.) cooking parchment or foil*
- *Sesame oil*
- 1 *ounce Virginia ham, finely julienned*
- 2 *green onions, finely julienned*
- ⅓ *cup sliced water chestnuts*
- ¼ *cup cilantro leaves*

Getting Ready

① Cut chicken into pieces about ¼ inch by ½ inch by 2 inches. Combine marinade ingredients in a bowl. Add chicken; stir to coat. Let stand for 20 minutes.

② Make each packet: Place a square of parchment paper on work surface with one point facing you; brush lightly with sesame oil. Place 2 or 3 pieces of chicken in center of square. Top with a few slivers of ham and green onion, 1 slice of water chestnut, and a few cilantro leaves. Fold bottom over filling; fold right and left corners into center, overlapping and enclosing filling. Fold filled part of packet in half. To seal packet, slide top corner all the way down into space between layers of paper. If making ahead, cover and refrigerate packets for up to 4 hours.

If using foil as a wrapper, fold the filled square in half to make a triangle; double-fold open edges of triangle to seal.

Cooking

① Preheat oven to 375°F. Place packets in a single layer in a shallow baking pan. Bake until chicken is opaque (open a packet to test), about 15 minutes.

② Serve hot. To eat, untuck the flap of paper with your fork or chopsticks and spread out the paper.

Makes 16.

Pearls of Rice

Glutinous rice, sometimes called sweet rice, gives the appearance of translucent pearls on the outside of these steamed balls with centers of seasoned ground pork and mushrooms. They can be made in the morning, then steamed just before serving.

- 1 *cup glutinous rice*
- 2 *dried black mushrooms*
- 1½ *pounds ground pork*
- ¼ *cup chopped water chestnuts*
- 3 *tablespoons minced Sichuan preserved vegetable*
- 2 *tablespoons chopped green onion*
- 1 *tablespoon minced ginger*
- 2 *teaspoons chopped cilantro*
- 1 *tablespoon sesame oil*
- 1 *teaspoon salt*
- ½ *teaspoon white pepper*
- 1 *egg*

Getting Ready

① Soak rice in water to cover for 2 hours.

② Soak mushrooms in warm water to cover until softened, about 20 minutes; drain. Discard stems and mince caps.

③ Place mushrooms in a bowl with remaining ingredients; mix well. With wet hands, roll meat mixture into 24 balls, using 2 tablespoons for each. Drain rice and spread on a plate. Roll each ball in rice to coat completely. Arrange meatballs, without crowding, on two heatproof dishes.

Cooking

① Prepare a wok for steaming (see page 25). Steam meatballs, one dish at a time, over high heat until pork is cooked through, about 25 minutes (cut to test).

Makes 24.

Toast Points

If you go out to eat with friends in Hong Kong, brace yourself for a barrage of toasts. A typical dinner will include several rounds of them, often no more than a quick "*yam seng*" ("down the hatch") or "*gam bui*" ("bottoms up"), and it's polite to drain your glass after each one. Toasting with your water glass or teacup is considered rude, and you should show respect by clinking your glass below your host's. Don't be surprised if some very fine Cognac shows up later in the meal. It's one of Hong Kong's favorite status symbols, and 11 percent of the world's Cognac is consumed here—the highest consumption rate per capita of any place on earth! Many people even have their own personal bottles of Cognac stored at their favorite restaurants.

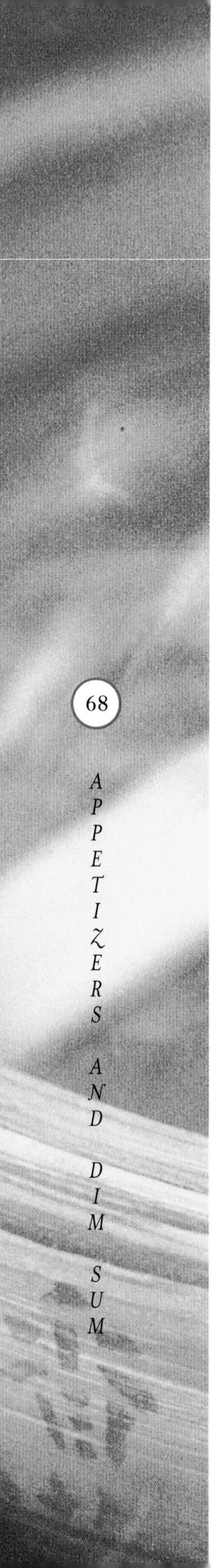

Classic Wontons

There is more to classic wontons than cloudlike dumplings floating in a savory broth. How about light, crispy, and delectable fried wontons that are perfect as a starter or a snack? These are destined to be classics on your dining table. To see how to fold wontons, go to page 55.

Filling

- 1 *bunch spinach (about ¾ lb.)*
- ¾ *pound ground pork*
- ¼ *pound ground beef*
- ¼ *cup finely chopped water chestnuts*
- 2 *tablespoons minced green onion*
- 1 *egg white*
- 1 *tablespoon oyster-flavored sauce*
- 1 *tablespoon chicken broth*
- 2 *teaspoons cornstarch*
- 1 *teaspoon Chinese rice wine or dry sherry*
- 1 *teaspoon sesame oil*
- ¼ *teaspoon salt*

- 1 *package (1 lb.) wonton wrappers*
- 1 *egg, lightly beaten*
- *Cooking oil for deep-frying*
- *Sweet and Sour Sauce* *(see page 33)*

Getting Ready

① Wash spinach and remove coarse stems. Place spinach in a large pot with 1 inch of water. Parboil for 30 seconds; drain, then rinse with cold water. Gently squeeze to remove all water. Coarsely chop spinach.

② Place spinach in a bowl with remaining filling ingredients; mix well.

③ Make each wonton: Place 1 heaping teaspoon filling in center of a wonton wrapper; keep remaining wrappers covered to prevent drying. Brush edges of wrapper with egg; fold wrapper in half to form a triangle. Pinch edges to seal. Pull two opposite corners together, moisten one corner with egg, and overlap with another corner; press to seal. Cover filled wontons with a dry towel to prevent drying.

Cooking

① In a wok or 2-quart saucepan, heat oil for deep-frying to 350°F. Deep-fry wontons, a few at a time, turning occasionally, until golden brown, 3 to 3½ minutes. Remove with a slotted spoon; drain on paper towels. Keep warm in a 200°F oven while cooking remaining wontons.

② Serve hot with sweet and sour sauce.

Makes 6 to 7 dozen.

Potstickers

Potstickers are one of the most famous specialties of Beijing's roadside restaurants. These can be prepared ahead and frozen. If you can't find potsticker wrappers, buy wonton wrappers and cut them into circles with a round biscuit cutter or scissors. To see how to fold potstickers, go to page 55.

Filling

6 *dried black mushrooms*

1 *cup sliced regular cabbage*

¼ *teaspoon salt*

1 *Chinese sausage (2 oz.), chopped*

½ *pound ground chicken, pork, or beef*

2 *cups sliced napa cabbage*

3 *green onions, chopped*

1 *tablespoon minced ginger*

⅓ *cup chicken broth*

1 *tablespoon soy sauce*

1 *tablespoon cornstarch*

½ *teaspoon sugar*

½ *teaspoon white pepper*

24 *potsticker, gyoza, or wonton wrappers*

3 *tablespoons cooking oil*

⅔ *cup chicken broth*

Chili oil and rice vinegar

Getting Ready

① Soak mushrooms in warm water to cover until softened, about 20 minutes; drain. Discard stems and mince caps. Combine regular cabbage and salt in a bowl; let stand for 15 minutes. Squeeze to remove excess liquid. Place a frying pan over high heat until hot. Add Chinese sausage and cook until fat is rendered, about 1 minute. Remove and drain on paper towels.

② Place mushrooms, cabbage, Chinese sausage, and remaining filling ingredients in a bowl; mix well.

③ Make each potsticker: Place a heaping teaspoon filling in center of a potsticker wrapper; keep remaining wrappers covered to prevent drying. Brush edges of wrapper with water; fold wrapper in half, crimping one side, to form a semicircle. Pinch edges together to seal. Set potsticker seam side up in a baking pan. Cover potstickers with a dry towel to prevent drying.

Cooking

① Place a wide frying pan over medium heat until hot. Add 1½ tablespoons cooking oil, swirling to coat sides. Add potstickers, half at a time, seam side up. Cook until bottoms are golden brown, 3 to 4 minutes. Add ⅓ cup broth; reduce heat to low, cover, and cook until liquid is absorbed, 5 to 6 minutes.

② Place potstickers, browned side up, on a serving plate with chili oil and rice vinegar for dipping.

Makes 24.

Flower Petal Dumplings

These delicate meat-filled dumplings are first pan-fried, then steamed in broth or water in the style of potstickers. Or cook them in a steamer.

Filling

- 2 *dried black mushrooms*
- ¼ *pound napa cabbage, finely chopped*
- ½ *pound ground chicken, pork, or beef*
- 1 *tablespoon chopped green onion*
- 2 *teaspoons minced ginger*
- 2 *tablespoons oyster-flavored sauce*
- 1 *teaspoon sesame oil*
- ¼ *teaspoon white pepper*

- 18 *potsticker, gyoza, or wonton wrappers*
- 2 *tablespoons frozen peas, thawed*
- 3 *tablespoons cooking oil*
- ⅔ *cup chicken broth*
- *Soy sauce, chili oil, and rice vinegar*

Getting Ready

① Soak mushrooms in warm water to cover until softened, about 20 minutes; drain. Discard stems and finely chop caps. Place cabbage in a clean towel and squeeze to remove excess water.

② Place mushrooms, cabbage, and remaining filling ingredients in a bowl; mix well. If using wonton wrappers, cut them into circles with a biscuit cutter.

③ Make each dumpling: Place a heaping teaspoon filling in center of a wrapper; keep remaining wrappers covered to prevent drying. Bring sides of wrapper together around filling; line up edges and pinch to seal. Place a pea on top for garnish. Cover dumplings with a dry towel to prevent drying.

Cooking

① Place a wide frying pan over medium heat until hot. Add 1½ tablespoons cooking oil, swirling to coat sides. Add dumplings, half at a time, seam side up. Cook until bottoms are golden brown, 3 to 4 minutes. Add ⅓ cup broth; reduce heat to low, cover, and cook until liquid is absorbed, 5 to 6 minutes.

② Place dumplings on a serving plate with soy sauce, chili oil, and vinegar for dipping.

Makes 18.

Dumpling Tips

Keep wonton or other wrappers covered with a towel as you work so they don't dry out. To keep filled dumplings from sticking to the plate, dust the plate with a little cornstarch. I freeze extra dumplings in a single layer on a baking sheet until firm, then transfer them to a plastic container or freezer bag. Cook frozen dumplings without thawing, adding 3 to 4 minutes to the cooking time.

Shrimp Toast

May I propose a toast? Here's to the inventive Cantonese chefs who created crispy fried shrimp toast. The bread can be cut into any shape you like. I like to cut into rounds with a 2-inch cookie cutter and curl up a half shrimp on top of the shrimp paste.

10 *day-old slices sandwich bread*

Shrimp Paste

¼ *cup water chestnuts*

½ *pound medium raw shrimp, shelled and deveined*

1 *egg white*

2 *teaspoons cornstarch*

2 *teaspoons Chinese rice wine or dry sherry*

½ *teaspoon minced ginger*

½ *teaspoon salt*

⅛ *teaspoon white pepper*

1 *green onion, minced*

10 *medium raw shrimp, shelled and deveined*

Cooking oil for deep-frying

Getting Ready

① With a 2-inch cookie cutter, cut 2 circles from each bread slice.

② Place water chestnuts in a food processor; process until coarsely chopped. Add remaining shrimp paste ingredients except green onion. Process until mixture forms a chunky paste. Transfer to a bowl; stir in green onion.

③ Spread shrimp paste about ¼ inch thick on one side of each bread circle. Cut whole shrimp in half lengthwise. Curl one shrimp half on top of each bread circle, pressing it firmly into shrimp paste.

Cooking

① In a wok, heat oil for deep-frying to 350°F. Deep-fry rounds, a few at a time and shrimp side down, for 1 minute. Turn over and cook until golden brown, about 1 minute longer. Remove with a slotted spoon; drain on paper towels. Serve warm.

Makes 20.

Shrimp Dumplings

Not all shrimp paste ends up on toast. To expand their dim sum repertoire, Chinese chefs roll the paste into balls and steam them. Prepare Shrimp Paste as directed above. With wet hands, shape mixture into 10 balls, each about 1½ inches in diameter. Arrange dumplings on an oiled heatproof dish. Prepare a wok for steaming (see page 25). Steam dumplings over high heat until they become firm and turn pink, about 10 minutes. Serve hot with sweet and sour sauce.

Shrimp with Honey Mustard Sauce

A honey-mustard blend is popular in everything from salad dressings to glazes for meat, but it's especially tasty when spiked with soy sauce and plum sauce, and served with shrimp. Here shrimp are baked, but if you prefer to cook them on the barbecue, thread the shrimp on skewers before putting them on the grill.

Marinade

- 2 *tablespoons soy sauce*
- 2 *tablespoons cooking oil*
- 1 *tablespoon sesame oil*
- 1 *tablespoon Chinese rice wine or dry sherry*
- 2 *teaspoons grated ginger*
- 1 *teaspoon grated orange peel*
- 1 *teaspoon cornstarch*

- 1 *pound medium raw shrimp*

Honey Mustard Sauce

- 3 *tablespoons soy sauce*
- 3 *tablespoons honey*
- 2 *tablespoons lemon or orange juice*
- 1 *tablespoon plum sauce*
- 1½ *teaspoons prepared Chinese mustard*

Getting Ready

① Combine marinade ingredients in a medium bowl.

② Shell and devein shrimp, leaving tails intact. Place shrimp in marinade; cover and refrigerate for 30 minutes.

③ Combine honey mustard sauce ingredients in a small serving bowl.

Cooking

① Preheat oven to 400°F. Place shrimp on a rack in a foil-lined baking pan. Bake until shrimp feel firm and turn pink, about 6 minutes.

② Arrange on a platter. Serve warm or at room temperature with honey mustard sauce.

Makes 8 appetizer servings.

Dim Sum

Savoring the Sum of the Parts

Since the tenth century, southern China has been famous for its teahouses, where family, friends, and business people get together to catch up on the latest news over a pot of tea. And out of this tradition evolved one of China's tastiest contributions to the world: dim sum—Cantonese-style dumplings, pastries, noodles, stuffed breads, and other delectable tidbits, all designed to be eaten with tea as a light breakfast or lunch.

The teahouse roots of dim sum are reflected in the phrase *yum cha* (literally "to drink tea"), the common way to refer to eating a dim sum lunch. I always tell people: "The *cha* part means tea. The *yum* part refers to the food!"

Dim sum is variously translated as "touch the heart" or "point to your heart's delight." Once you've tried it, you'll know why. You've heard of "point and click"? Well, this is "point and eat."

If you live near a Chinatown, you can probably find quite a few Cantonese restaurants serving dim sum. Plan to show up between the hours of 10 A.M. and 2 P.M. Many dim sum houses don't take reservations, and it's best to arrive on the early side to get the best selection and the freshest items.

If the place is any good, there will be a crowd jammed into the front entryway, especially on weekends, when lots of extended families and large groups of friends get together for *yum cha*. Tip number one: Dim sum is a communal affair—the more people in your party, the more variety you can enjoy.

Most dim sum houses offer several types of tea to choose from. As you take your first sip and breathe in the intoxicating aromas of the food, your appetite suddenly becomes voracious and uncontrollable!

Good thing there's no menu to order from, and no waiting necessary. The food comes streaming out of the kitchen in a steady parade of carts loaded with little plates and stacks of small bamboo steamer baskets filled with dumplings and other delicacies—usually three or four pieces to an order. When they say everything is à la carte, they really mean it!

Tip number two: Pace yourself. The individual dishes are small and light, but the "sum" is greater than the parts, and you'll be full sooner than you think. My advice is to take it slow, or instead of "touch the heart," you may experience "touch of heartburn"!

Before long, you'll have a collection of empty little plates and steamers stacked up at the center of the table. At the end of the meal, your bill is calculated by counting the number of plates in the stack (or in some places, the number of stamps on your guest check).

Tip number three: I don't recommend doing what my friends and I once did when we were young and starving. We hid half the plates under the table, somehow imagining that we were the first people ever to have thought of such a clever scheme. But at the end of the meal, the waiter, suspecting foul play, lifted the tablecloth. To our horror, someone else had already left a huge stack of plates, and our bill instantly doubled!

It's been said that there are more than a thousand types of dim sum. But most dim sum chefs draw from a repertoire of 75 to 100 specialties. Generally, dim sum comes two ways—steamed or fried—with a few baked, braised, and stir-fried items thrown in. Allow me to sum up a few of my favorites.

STEAMED

Har gau. Shrimp dumplings.

Siu mai. Cylindrical dumpling, open on top, filled with pork and shrimp.

Fun guor. Crescent of translucent wheat starch dough stuffed with pork, shrimp, and chopped nuts.

Char siu bao. Honey-glazed barbecued pork steamed inside a dome-shaped bun of soft, sweet bread dough.

Churn fun. Steamed soft rice noodle skins rolled around shrimp, minced beef, or barbecued pork.

Noh mai gai. Glutinous rice, marinated chicken, Chinese sausage, mushrooms, and other savory ingredients steamed in a lotus leaf.

FRIED

Chun guen. Crispy deep-fried spring rolls filled with meat, shrimp, and bamboo shoots. (Some Chinese restaurants in North America serve giant egg rolls with a similar filling.)

Har dor see. Golden crisp shrimp toast.

Woo gok. Taro root dumplings filled with shrimp, meat, and mushrooms.

SWEET AND SAVORY

See jup ngau hor. Also known as *chow fun*: stir-fried fresh rice noodles with slices of tender beef or chicken and green and red bell peppers in a fragrant black bean and garlic sauce.

Jin dui jai. Chewy glutinous rice dough wrapped around a sweet bean or lotus seed paste, rolled in sesame seeds, and deep-fried golden brown.

Don tot. One of the most popular dim sum desserts: individual egg custard tarts with a Western-style pastry crust.

If you can't find a dim sum restaurant, don't despair. Even though it would be tricky to create a full dim sum lunch in your own kitchen, it's still a lot of fun to make one or two items. You can get the whole family involved in rolling and stuffing. And don't stop at lunch: Dim sum items make terrific appetizers and party food, too. If you're lucky, you may even find a few frozen dim sum items in Asian supermarkets near you. I always keep three big bags of frozen potstickers in my freezer in case I get "stuck" with unexpected guests.

Crab Puffs

What's in a name? In many parts of North America, these crab puffs are called seafood wontons. Whichever name you use, follow the recipe, and you and your guests are in for a special treat.

Filling

- 4 *ounces cream cheese, softened*
- 2 *tablespoons minced green onion*
- 2 *teaspoons minced ginger*
- 2 *teaspoons oyster-flavored sauce*
- 1 *teaspoon sesame oil*
- ⅛ *teaspoon white pepper*
- ½ *pound cooked crabmeat, flaked*

- 12 *spring roll or lumpia wrappers, or 24 wonton wrappers*
- 1 *egg white, lightly beaten*
- *Cooking oil for deep-frying*

Getting Ready

① Place cream cheese, green onion, ginger, oyster-flavored sauce, sesame oil, and pepper in a medium bowl; mix well. Stir in crabmeat.

② If using spring roll or lumpia wrappers, cut each into 2 strips about 3 inches by 7 inches; keep wrappers covered to prevent drying.

③ Make each puff: Place a rounded teaspoon filling on one short end of a spring roll strip. Fold over one corner to make a triangle. Fold triangle over again on itself. Continue folding, from side to side, as if you were folding a flag. Moisten edges of final fold with egg white and press to seal. Place filled puffs in a baking pan and cover with a dry towel to prevent drying. (If using wonton wrappers, place a rounded teaspoon filling in center of wrapper, brush edges with egg white, fold wrapper in half over filling to form a triangle, and press edges to seal.)

Cooking

① In a wok or 2-quart saucepan, heat oil for deep-frying to 350°F. Deep-fry puffs, a few at a time, turning occasionally, until golden brown, about 1 minute. Remove with a slotted spoon; drain on paper towels.

② Serve warm.

Makes 24.

Here's the Wrap

What's the difference among all those wrappers on the market? Most are made of egg noodle dough (flour, water, and a small amount of egg), and their main difference is their shape and thickness. Wonton wrappers and their larger cousins, egg roll wrappers, are square. Potsticker wrappers, also sold as Japanese gyoza wrappers, are round. Spring roll wrappers, made without the egg, are paper-thin and delicately crisp when fried.

Curried Beef Turnovers

Here's a great treat for high tea, your next cocktail party, or any occasion that calls for a snack wrapped in savory flaky pastry.

Sauce

- 2½ *teaspoons curry powder*
- 2 *teaspoons soy sauce*
- 1 *teaspoon Sichuan chili paste*
- ½ *teaspoon sugar*
- ¼ *teaspoon Chinese five-spice*
- 1 *teaspoon cornstarch dissolved in 2 teaspoons water*

- 1 *tablespoon cooking oil*
- ½ *pound ground beef*
- ¼ *cup finely chopped onion*
- 1 *green onion, minced*

Flaky pastry for a 9-inch double-crust deep-dish pie

- 1 *egg yolk mixed with 1 teaspoon water*

Getting Ready

① Combine sauce ingredients in a small bowl.

Cooking

① Place a wok over high heat until hot. Add oil, swirling to coat sides. Crumble in meat; add onion and green onion. Cook, stirring, until meat is browned, about 3 minutes. Add sauce and cook, stirring, until sauce boils and thickens slightly. Remove from heat and let filling cool.

② Preheat oven to 375°F. Roll out pastry, one half at a time, on floured board to a thickness of ⅛ inch; cut into 3-inch rounds. For each turnover, place 2 teaspoons filling on half of a round, moisten edges of dough with water, then fold other half over to enclose filling. Crimp edges to seal.

③ Place turnovers 1 inch apart on lightly oiled baking sheets; brush with egg yolk mixture. Bake until golden brown, 25 to 30 minutes. Serve warm.

Makes 20.

Nonya Top Hats

My hat's off to the Nonya cooks of Malaysia—descendants of Chinese settlers who came to Malaysia more than 400 years ago and married Malay women. The cooks make these crispy little pastry cups using a top hat–shaped cast-iron mold. The outside of the mold is dipped in hot oil, then in batter, and then again in hot oil. You can find the mold in some Asian markets or, even easier, use my foolproof baked pastry shells made from store-bought potsticker wrappers.

Pastry Shells

- 32 *potsticker, gyoza, or wonton wrappers*

Filling

- 1 *tablespoon cooking oil*
- 2 *teaspoons minced garlic*
- ¼ *pound medium raw shrimp, shelled, deveined, and chopped*
- 2 *cups finely chopped jicama*
- 1 *cup finely chopped carrot*
- 2 *tablespoons chopped cilantro*
- 2 *tablespoons oyster-flavored sauce*
- 1 *teaspoon sugar*

Cilantro leaves

Slivered chilies

Getting Ready

① If using wonton wrappers, trim corners so they become circles. Coat standard-sized muffin pans (2½-in.-diameter cups) with cooking spray. Loosely fit a wrapper into each cup; the edges will be ruffled.

Cooking

① Preheat oven to 375°F. Bake wrapper cases until edges of shells are golden brown, 6 to 7 minutes. Repeat with remaining wrappers. Let shells cool. Store in an airtight container until ready to fill, up to 3 days.

② Make filling: Place a wok over high heat until hot. Add oil, swirling to coat sides. Add garlic and stir-fry for 10 seconds. Add shrimp and stir-fry for 1 minute. Add jicama and carrot; reduce heat to medium and cook for 3 minutes, adding a few drops of water if pan appears dry. Add cilantro, oyster-flavored sauce, and sugar. Cook, stirring frequently, until vegetables are tender-crisp, about 2 minutes. Let mixture cool.

③ To serve, fill each pastry cup with 1 tablespoon of filling and garnish each with a cilantro leaf and a sliver of chili.

Makes 32.

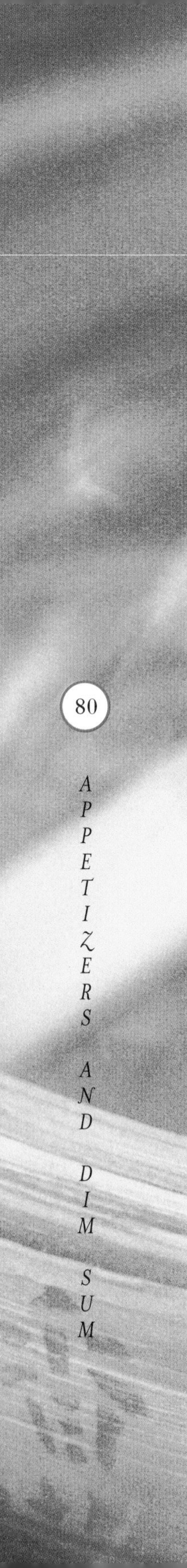

Shrimp-Filled Peppers and Eggplant

Plump stuffed bell peppers are a popular entrée in many countries. In China, we stuff slices of vegetables—bell pepper, eggplant, even bitter melon—to accommodate eating with chopsticks. Dim sum restaurants offer these tasty tidbits with a variety of fillings. My favorite is shrimp.

Shrimp Mousse

- ¾ *pound medium raw shrimp, shelled and deveined*
- 1 *egg white*
- 1 *tablespoon cornstarch*
- 1 *teaspoon minced ginger*
- 2 *teaspoons oyster-flavored sauce*
- 1 *teaspoon sesame oil*
- ¼ *teaspoon white pepper*

Braising Sauce

- ¾ *cup chicken broth*
- 2 *tablespoons oyster-flavored sauce*
- 1 *teaspoon black bean garlic sauce*
- 1 *teaspoon sugar*

- 1 *medium green bell pepper*
- 1 *medium red bell pepper*
- 2 *Asian eggplants*
- *Cornstarch*
- 1 *tablespoon cooking oil*

Getting Ready

① Place shrimp mousse ingredients in a food processor; process to make a smooth paste.

② Combine braising sauce ingredients in a small bowl.

③ Seed bell peppers and cut into about 2-inch squares. Cut eggplants into diagonal slices ½ inch thick. Lightly dust insides of bell pepper squares and tops of eggplant slices with cornstarch. Spread about 2 teaspoons mousse on each piece. Lightly dust filled vegetables with cornstarch; shake off excess.

Cooking

① Place a wide frying pan over medium-high heat until hot. Add oil, swirling to coat sides. Place stuffed vegetables filled side down in pan. Cook, turning once, until lightly browned, 1 to 1½ minutes on each side. Pour braising sauce into pan and bring to a boil. Reduce heat, cover, and simmer until vegetables are tender, 8 to 10 minutes.

② Arrange vegetables filled side up on a platter. Serve hot.

Makes 6 servings.

Five-Spice Fragrant Smoked Fish

One of my most memorable discoveries in Shanghai was delicious smoked fish. It is not actually smoked, but the seasonings give the deep-fried fish its smoky flavor. Serve it at room temperature or, better yet, chilled.

1½ *pounds firm white fish fillets, such as red snapper or cod*

Marinade

3 *tablespoons regular soy sauce*

2 *tablespoons dark soy sauce*

3 *tablespoons Chinese rice wine or dry sherry*

2 *green onions, minced*

2 *teaspoons minced ginger*

Cooking oil for deep-frying

1 *cup chicken broth*

¼ *cup packed brown sugar*

1 *teaspoon Chinese five-spice*

Shredded lettuce

Lemon wedges

Getting Ready

① Cut fish into 3-inch squares. Combine marinade ingredients in a medium bowl. Add fish; stir to coat. Cover and refrigerate for at least 4 hours or up to overnight, turning occasionally. Remove fish and pat dry with paper towels; reserve marinade.

Cooking

① In a wok or 2-quart saucepan, heat oil for deep-frying to 360°F. Deep-fry fish, a few pieces at a time, turning occasionally, until golden brown, 4 to 5 minutes. Remove with a slotted spoon; drain on paper towels.

② In a small pan, combine reserved marinade, broth, brown sugar, and five-spice; heat to boiling, stirring, over medium heat. Remove from heat and place cooked fish in pan; stir to evenly coat with sauce. Lift out fish and drain well on paper towels.

③ Reheat oil in wok to 375°F. Add fish, a few pieces at a time, and deep-fry 3 to 4 minutes longer, turning occasionally. Lift out fish and drain on paper towels.

④ Serve hot or cold. Arrange on a bed of lettuce and garnish with lemon wedges.

Makes 4 servings.

Smile When You Cook That

The best cooks in the world know that cooking is more than recipes. It's about using all six senses: taste, smell, sight, touch, hearing, and my favorite, the sense of humor! There's really no right or wrong in the kitchen, and the more you relax, clown around, and have fun, the more your own style will come through.

Spicy Chicken Wings

Here are some wings that will surely take off. Put out a platter of these spicy delights and watch them disappear in no time. I have the perfect solution to their flight: I make one plate for friends, and save a second one just for me.

- 14 *whole chicken wings*

Marinade

- 2 *tablespoons Chinese rice wine or dry sherry*
- 1 *tablespoon soy sauce*
- *Pinch of white pepper*

Sauce

- ½ *cup chicken broth*
- 2 *tablespoons dark soy sauce*
- 1 *tablespoon Chinese rice wine or dry sherry*
- 1½ *tablespoons packed brown sugar*

- 1 *tablespoon cooking oil*
- 3 *small whole dried red chilies*
- 6 *slices ginger, each the size of a quarter, lightly crushed*
- 2 *green onions, halved*
- 1 *cinnamon stick*
- ½ *teaspoon toasted Sichuan peppercorns*
- 1½ *teaspoons cornstarch dissolved in 1 tablespoon water*

Getting Ready

① Remove tips from chicken wings; save for stock. Cut wings apart at joint. Combine marinade ingredients in a bowl. Add wings and stir to coat; let stand for 15 minutes.

② Combine sauce ingredients in a small bowl.

Cooking

① Place a wok over high heat until hot. Add oil and chilies, swirling to coat sides. Add chicken; cook until chicken is browned on all sides, 3 to 4 minutes. Add ginger, green onions, cinnamon stick, and Sichuan peppercorns; stir-fry for 15 seconds. Add sauce. Bring to a boil; reduce heat, cover, and simmer until wings are tender when pierced, about 12 minutes.

② Remove and discard chilies, ginger, green onions, and cinnamon stick. Add cornstarch solution; cook, stirring, until sauce boils and thickens and wings are glazed. Serve hot.

Makes 28.

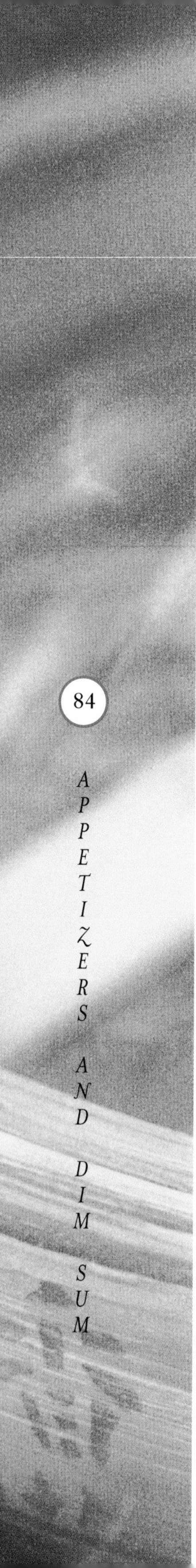

Glazed Sesame Meatballs

I got the idea for this dish at a cocktail party. They were serving plain meatballs, so I thought, why not add a little spice and texture? These meatballs are perfect for any occasion. Make them ahead of time, and keep them chilled or frozen until you are ready to cook them.

2 *tablespoons sesame seeds*

Meatballs

1 *pound ground pork*
⅓ *cup finely chopped jicama*
¼ *cup cornstarch*
2 *tablespoons hoisin sauce*
2 *tablespoons Chinese rice wine or dry sherry*
1 *tablespoon minced ginger*
1 *tablespoon soy sauce*
1 *tablespoon grated lemon peel*
2 *teaspoons sesame oil*

Glaze

3 *tablespoons lemon juice*
2 *tablespoons packed brown sugar*

1 *tablespoon cooking oil*

Getting Ready

① Place sesame seeds in a small frying pan over medium heat; cook, shaking pan frequently, until lightly browned, 3 to 4 minutes. Immediately remove from pan to cool.

② Combine meatball ingredients in a medium bowl; mix well. Shape mixture into 1-inch-diameter balls.

③ Combine glaze ingredients in a small bowl.

Cooking

① Place a wide nonstick frying pan over medium-high heat until hot. Add oil, swirling to coat sides. Add meatballs and cook, turning occasionally, until browned on all sides and meat is no long pink in center, 6 to 8 minutes (cut to test).

② Drain oil from pan. Pour glazing mixture over meatballs; cook over high heat until meatballs are nicely glazed, about 2 minutes.

③ Transfer to a serving platter and sprinkle with sesame seeds.

Makes 36.

Chinese Barbecued Pork

Instead of a grill, Chinese barbecue calls for a roasting oven. I guess you could call it a bar-bake-Q. In Chinese, we call it *char siu*. I always double this recipe. Leftovers are great to have on hand to toss into wonton soup or fried rice.

1 *boneless pork shoulder or butt (about 3 lb.)*

Marinade

¼ *cup soy sauce*

¼ *cup hoisin sauce*

3 *tablespoons Chinese rice wine or dry sherry*

2 *tablespoons ketchup*

2 *tablespoons sugar*

1 *tablespoon grated orange peel*

1 *teaspoon minced garlic*

1 *teaspoon minced ginger*

1 *teaspoon sesame oil*

½ *teaspoon Chinese five-spice*

1 *tablespoon sesame seed paste (optional)*

4–5 *drops red food color (optional)*

Getting Ready

① Trim excess fat from pork. Cut meat into pieces roughly 1 inch thick, 3 inches wide, and 8 inches long.

② Combine marinade ingredients in a large bowl; add pork and stir to coat. Cover and refrigerate at least 4 hours or up to overnight; turn meat occasionally.

Cooking

① Preheat oven to 350°F. Remove meat from marinade; reserve marinade. Place meat on a rack in a foil-lined baking pan. Bake, uncovered, for 30 minutes. Turn slices over and bake for 45 minutes longer, brushing occasionally with reserved marinade.

② Cut into thin slices. Serve hot or cold.

Makes 8 servings.

Golden Meat-Filled Coins

These golden pan-fried dumplings with a meat filling are symbols of good fortune. And they are delicious, too!

- 2¼ *cups flour*
- ½ *cup boiling water*
- ⅓ *cup cold water*

Filling

- ½ *pound ground chicken, beef, or pork*
- 3 *tablespoons chopped green onions*
- 1 *tablespoon minced ginger*
- ¼ *cup chicken broth*
- 1 *tablespoon soy sauce*
- 1 *tablespoon oyster-flavored sauce*
- 2 *teaspoons sesame oil*
- ½ *teaspoon sugar*
- ¼ *teaspoon white pepper*

- 4 *tablespoons cooking oil*

Getting Ready

① Place flour in a bowl. Add boiling water, stirring with chopsticks or a fork. Gradually stir in cold water, mixing until dough holds together. On a lightly floured board, knead dough until smooth and satiny, about 5 minutes. Cover and let rest for 30 minutes.

② Combine filling ingredients in a bowl; mix well.

③ On a lightly floured board, roll dough into a 9-inch cylinder, then cut into 18 portions.

④ Make each coin: Roll a portion of dough into a 3½-inch circle about ½ inch thick; keep remaining dough covered to prevent drying. Place a rounded tablespoon of filling in center of dough. Gather edges of dough around filling; pinch to seal. Roll filled dough into a ball; flatten with the palm of your hand to make a disk ½ inch thick.

Cooking

① Place a wide frying pan over medium heat until hot. Add 2 tablespoons oil, swirling to coat sides. Add half of coins and cook, turning once, until golden brown, 3 to 4 minutes on each side. Repeat with remaining oil and coins.

② Place on a serving platter and serve hot.

Makes 18.

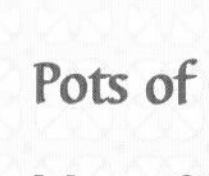

Pots of Gold

Many Chinese dishes are either named after or symbolic of gold coins or money, and eating them is believed to bring prosperity. Nowhere is this symbolism more pronounced than during the New Year celebration, in dishes like red envelope fish (referring to the envelopes in which New Year *lai see* money is given) and spring rolls, designed to evoke tiny bars of gold.

Nori Tofu Rolls

Nori, the thin seaweed wrapper for sushi, is also perfect for wrapping these sesame-coated rolls. Serve them hot with spiced pepper salt.

Pepper Salt

- 2 *teaspoons salt*
- 1 *teaspoon ground toasted Sichuan peppercorns*
- ¼ *teaspoon Chinese five-spice*
- ¼ *teaspoon white pepper*

- ¼ *cup finely diced carrot*
- 1 *sheet Japanese seaweed (nori)*
- 1 *package (14 oz.) extra-firm tofu, drained*
- ¼ *cup finely diced red bell pepper*
- 1 *green onion, finely chopped*
- 1 *tablespoon cornstarch*
- ¾ *teaspoon salt*
- ¼ *teaspoon white pepper*
- 1 *egg white, lightly beaten*
- ½ *cup sesame seeds*
- 3 *tablespoons cooking oil*

Getting Ready

① Make pepper salt: Combine ingredients in a frying pan. Cook, stirring, over low heat, until toasted and fragrant, about 3 minutes. Let cool.

② Parboil carrot in boiling water for 2 minutes; drain. Cut seaweed into 6 strips, each about ¾ inch wide.

③ Mash tofu in a bowl. Place tofu in a clean towel and squeeze to remove excess liquid. Return to bowl and add carrot, bell pepper, green onion, cornstarch, salt, pepper, and ½ of the egg white; mix well.

④ Divide tofu mixture into 6 portions. With oiled hands, roll each portion into a cylinder about 1 inch across by 3 inches long. Roll each cylinder in sesame seeds; press lightly to coat.

⑤ Wrap a strip of seaweed around the middle of each roll; brush edges with remaining egg white and press to seal. Gently flatten roll to make a rectangle about ½ inch thick.

Cooking

① Place a wide frying pan over high heat until hot. Add oil, swirling to coat sides. Add rolls and pan-fry, turning once, until golden brown, about 2 minutes on each side.

② Serve with pepper salt.

Makes 6.

Nori Note

In Shanghai and along China's eastern coast, seaweed is a popular ingredient. In the U.S., it's sold under its Japanese name, *nori*, and mostly used for making sushi. I love to use a ribbon of nori to wrap fried dishes like this one, because it adds an artful stripe of color, a little textural interest, and a savory, oceany flavor.

Lop Cheong Baked Clams

Lop cheong, or Chinese sausage, is a natural with clams.

Filling

- 4 *dried black mushrooms*
- ½ *pound medium raw shrimp, shelled, deveined, and coarsely chopped*
- 1 *Chinese sausage (2 oz.), coarsely chopped*
- 8 *water chestnuts, coarsely chopped*
- 3 *green onions (white parts only), finely chopped*
- 1 *tablespoon chopped cilantro*
- 2 *teaspoons minced ginger*
- 1 *teaspoon minced garlic*
- 1 *egg, lightly beaten*
- 1 *tablespoon Chinese rice wine or dry sherry*
- 2 *teaspoons cornstarch*
- ½ *teaspoon salt*
- ⅛ *teaspoon black pepper*

- 10 *medium hard-shell clams*
- ½ *cup fine dry bread crumbs*
- *Rock salt*

Getting Ready

① Soak mushrooms in warm water to cover until softened, about 20 minutes; drain. Discard stems and coarsely chop caps. Place mushrooms in a bowl with remaining filling ingredients; mix well.

② Scrub clams under cold running water and discard any with open shells that don't close when tapped.

Cooking

① Prepare a wok for steaming (see page 25). Place clams in a heatproof dish. Steam over high heat until shells open, 7 to 8 minutes. Let clams cool, then remove from shells; reserve half of the shells. Coarsely chop clams; stir into filling.

② Mound filling into the shells. Sprinkle with bread crumbs; lightly press onto surface to coat evenly. Arrange clams, filled side up, in an ovenproof serving dish lined with rock salt.

③ Preheat oven to 400°F. Bake clams until golden brown, 10 to 12 minutes.

Makes 10.

Chinese Sausage

In Chinese delis, you often see slim, reddish brown sausage links called *lop cheong* hanging in the window. They're most often made from pork, though some contain duck liver or chicken. Seasoned with salt, sugar, and rice wine, these sausages have a sweet-savory flavor that makes a nice complement to rice and vegetable dishes. They must be cooked before eating.

Classic Spring Rolls

Nothing touches the heart of a dim sum enthusiast like the classic spring roll. Though dim sum chefs everywhere have been inventing new recipes, why tinker with perfection? To see how to fold spring rolls, go to page 55.

Filling

- 5 *dried black mushrooms*
- 2 *tablespoons cooking oil*
- 2 *eggs, lightly beaten*
- ½ *pound boneless pork, finely julienned*
- 2 *green onions, cut into 1-inch slivers*
- 1 *cup shredded cabbage or bok choy*
- 1 *cup bean sprouts*
- ¼ *cup julienned bamboo shoots*
- ¼ *cup chicken broth*
- 2 *tablespoons oyster-flavored sauce*
- 2 *teaspoons soy sauce*
- ⅛ *teaspoon white pepper*
- 1½ *teaspoons cornstarch dissolved in 1 tablespoon water*

- 10 *spring roll or egg roll wrappers*
- 1 *egg white, lightly beaten*
- *Cooking oil for deep-frying*
- *Plum sauce*

Getting Ready

① Soak mushrooms in warm water until softened, about 20 minutes; drain. Discard stems and thinly slice caps.

② Place a wide frying pan over medium heat until hot. Add 1 teaspoon oil, swirling to coat sides. Pour in eggs and cook until lightly browned on bottom and set on top, about 1½ minutes. Remove from pan and let cool; cut into thin strips 1 inch long.

③ Place a wok over high heat. Add remaining oil, swirling to coat sides. Add pork; stir-fry for 2 minutes. Add mushrooms and remaining filling ingredients except cornstarch solution; stir-fry for 2 minutes longer. Add cornstarch solution and cook, stirring, until sauce boils and thickens. Remove from heat; stir in omelet strips. Cool.

④ Make each spring roll: Mound 2 heaping tablespoons filling across wrapper (see illustration on page 55). Fold bottom corner over filling to cover, then fold over right and left corners. Roll over once to enclose filling. Brush sides and top of triangle with egg white. Fold over to seal. Cover filled spring rolls with a dry towel to prevent drying.

Cooking

① In a wok or 2-quart saucepan, heat oil for deep-frying to 360°F. Deep-fry spring rolls, a few at a time, turning occasionally, until golden brown, 2 to 3 minutes. Remove with a slotted spoon; drain on paper towels.

② Serve hot with plum sauce.

Makes 10.

Fresh Spring Rolls

Spring rolls come in all shapes and sizes. This recipe is my interpretation of the Vietnamese interpretation of the Chinese spring roll. Lucky for you, nothing was lost in the translation.

Dipping Sauce

- 3 *tablespoons rice vinegar*
- 2 *tablespoons lime juice*
- 2 *tablespoons honey*
- 1 *tablespoon fish sauce*
- 2 *teaspoons minced garlic*
- 2 *teaspoons chili garlic sauce*

- 2 *ounces dried bean thread noodles*
- 2½ *cups small cooked shrimp*
- 1 *tablespoon fish sauce*
- 1 *tablespoon oyster-flavored sauce*
- 2 *teaspoons sesame oil*
- 2 *teaspoons chopped cilantro*
- ⅛ *teaspoon white pepper*
- 12 *dried rice paper wrappers, each about 8 inches in diameter*
- 1 *small carrot, shredded*
- 2 *green onions, slivered*
- *Mint sprigs*

Getting Ready

① In a bowl, combine dipping sauce ingredients; stir until honey dissolves.

② Soak bean thread noodles in warm water to cover until softened, about 10 minutes; drain. Cut into 4-inch lengths.

③ Place shrimp, fish sauce, oyster-flavored sauce, sesame oil, cilantro, and pepper in a bowl; stir lightly to mix.

Assembly

① Make each spring roll: Brush a rice paper wrapper lightly with warm water. Let stand until it becomes soft and pliable, about 30 seconds. Place about ¼ cup shrimp mixture in center of wrapper and top with a small mound of noodles and carrot and a few slivers of green onion. Fold bottom third of wrapper over filling, then fold in sides.

② Place spring rolls on a serving plate and garnish with mint. Pass dipping sauce at the table.

Makes 12.

Fresh Lumpia

Try this lighter home-style version of the Filipino classic.

Wrappers

- 2 *large eggs*
- 1¼ *cups water*
- ½ *cup cornstarch*
- ½ *cup flour*
- ⅛ *teaspoon salt*

About 3 tablespoons cooking oil

Garlic Dipping Sauce

- ¼ *cup rice vinegar*
- 4 *teaspoons soy sauce*
- 2 *teaspoons minced garlic*
- ¼ *teaspoon sugar*

Filling

- 2 *tablespoons cooking oil*
- ½ *cup julienned onion*
- 1 *teaspoon minced garlic*
- 1 *boneless, skinless chicken breast half, thinly sliced*
- ¼ *pound medium raw shrimp shelled, deveined, and halved*
- 1½ *cups finely julienned jicama*
- ½ *small carrot, finely julienned*
- 2 *green onions, finely julienned*
- 2 *teaspoons oyster-flavored sauce*
- 1 *teaspoon fish sauce*
- ¼ *teaspoon black pepper*
- 5 *tender lettuce leaves*

Getting Ready

① Whisk together eggs, water, cornstarch, flour, and salt until smooth.

② Place a nonstick 8-inch omelet pan over medium heat until hot; brush with ¼ teaspoon oil. Pour ¼ cup batter into pan; tilt pan so batter covers entire surface. Cook until edge of wrapper is lightly browned and surface looks dry, about 45 seconds. Turn wrapper, and cook 10 seconds longer. Remove wrapper from pan. Repeat to use all batter.

③ Combine dipping sauce ingredients in a small bowl.

Cooking

① Prepare filling: Place a wok over high heat until hot. Add 1 tablespoon oil, swirling to coat sides. Add onion and garlic; stir-fry for 30 seconds. Add chicken and shrimp; stir-fry for 2 minutes. Remove from pan. Heat 1 tablespoon oil. Add jicama and carrot; stir-fry for 1 minute. Add green onions; cook until vegetables are tender-crisp, about 2 minutes. Return chicken mixture to pan; add oyster-flavored sauce, fish sauce, and pepper; cook for 1 minute. Cool.

② Cut lettuce leaves in half lengthwise. For each lumpia, place a piece of lettuce on wrapper. Spoon about ⅓ cup filling into center of wrapper. Fold bottom third of wrapper over filling, then fold in sides.

③ Serve with garlic dipping sauce.

Makes 10.

Wonton Chips with Fruit Salsa

A chip off the old block? How about wonton chips? Dip these fried wonton wrappers into a fruit salsa and let the party begin!

Fruit Salsa

1	*mango, peeled and diced*
1	*large tomato, cored and diced*
1	*small red bell pepper, diced*
2	*fresh jalapeño chilies, seeded and minced*
2	*tablespoons finely chopped pickled ginger*
2	*tablespoons chopped cilantro*
2	*teaspoons minced garlic*
2	*tablespoons plum sauce*
2	*teaspoons Chinese chili sauce*

1	*teaspoon salt*
½	*teaspoon Chinese five-spice*
30	*wonton wrappers*
	Cooking oil for deep-frying

Getting Ready

① Combine salsa ingredients in a medium bowl; mix well. Cover and refrigerate for 1 hour for flavors to blend.

② Mix salt and five-spice in a small bowl.

③ Cut wonton wrappers in half diagonally to make triangles.

Cooking

① In a wok, heat oil for deep-frying to 350°F. Deep-fry wonton triangles, a few at a time, until lightly browned, 15 to 20 seconds on each side. Remove with a slotted spoon and drain on paper towels. While triangles are still hot, sprinkle lightly with salt mixture.

② Serve chips in a basket with salsa alongside for dipping.

Makes 6 to 8 servings.

CHAPTER 2

Soups

Cantonese Wor Wonton Soup

Wor in Chinese means a large stockpot. So when we make a large pot of wonton soup and add all kinds of meat and vegetables to the broth, we naturally call it Wor Wonton Soup. This is one soup that is truly a meal in itself.

5 *dried black mushrooms*

Filling

½ *pound ground pork*

¼ *pound medium raw shrimp, shelled, deveined, and coarsely chopped*

3 *tablespoons Chinese rice wine or dry sherry*

1 *tablespoon cornstarch*

2 *teaspoons minced ginger*

2 *teaspoons sesame oil*

½ *teaspoon salt*

⅛ *teaspoon white pepper*

24 *wonton wrappers*

6 *cups chicken broth*

1 *cup bok choy, cut into 1-inch pieces*

2 *ounces snow peas, trimmed*

1 *teaspoon sesame oil*

⅛ *teaspoon white pepper*

½ *pound Chinese Barbecued Pork (page 85) or Virginia ham, thinly sliced*

1 *green onion, thinly sliced*

Getting Ready

① Soak mushrooms in warm water to cover until softened, about 20 minutes; drain. Discard stems and thinly slice caps.

② Combine filling ingredients in a bowl; mix well.

③ Make each wonton: Place 1 heaping teaspoon filling in center of a wonton wrapper; keep remaining wrappers covered to prevent drying. Brush edges of wrapper with water and fold wrapper in half to form a triangle. Pinch edges to seal. Pull two opposite corners together, moisten one corner with water, and overlap with another corner; press to seal. Cover filled wontons with a dry towel to prevent drying.

Cooking

① Place broth in a large pot; bring to a boil. Add mushrooms and bok choy and cook for 2 minutes. Add wontons and cook for 3 minutes. Add snow peas and cook for 1 minute. Stir in sesame oil and pepper.

② Ladle wontons, vegetables, and broth into 6 deep soup bowls. Garnish each serving with slices of barbecued pork and green onion.

Makes 6 servings.

Tomato Egg Flower Soup

Egg flower is not something you grow in your garden. It opens up as you drizzle beaten egg into soup before you serve it. Drizzle slowly and let your soup be your canvas.

- 4 *dried black mushrooms*
- 1¼ *cups warm water*
- 1 *medium tomato*
- 6 *cups chicken broth*
- 1 *tablespoon Chinese rice wine or dry sherry*
- 2 *tablespoons cornstarch dissolved in ¼ cup water*
- 1 *egg, lightly beaten*
- 1 *teaspoon sesame oil*
- ¼ *teaspoon white pepper*
- *Salt*
- 1 *green onion, thinly sliced*

Getting Ready

① Soak mushrooms in warm water to cover until softened, about 20 minutes. Remove mushrooms and reserve 1 cup liquid. Discard mushroom stems and dice caps.

② Peel, seed, and dice tomato.

Cooking

① Place broth, wine, reserved mushroom soaking liquid, and mushrooms in a 2-quart pan; bring to a boil. Reduce heat and simmer for 5 minutes. Add tomato and cook for 1 minute.

② Add cornstarch solution and cook, stirring, until soup boils and thickens. Turn off heat. Add egg, stirring, until it forms long threads. Stir in sesame oil, pepper, salt to taste, and green onion.

Makes 6 servings.

Stock Options

Many recipes in this book call for chicken broth. Chinese soup stocks are simpler than Western ones, so it's easy to make your own: In a large pot, heat 8 cups **water** and 2½ pounds **chicken bones** to boiling. Skim off any foam that forms. Reduce heat, cover, and simmer for 1½ hours. Add 4 halved **green onions**, 8 thin slices **ginger**, each the size of a quarter, and ⅛ teaspoon *each* **salt** and **white pepper**. Simmer for 30 minutes. Strain broth, discarding bones and seasonings. If using canned broth, look for brands labeled "Oriental broth" or "reduced-sodium broth."

Velvet Corn Soup

Traditional Chinese cuisine rarely uses cream or dairy products, but you can hardly tell their absence in this smooth, velvety corn soup. It has all the creamy taste and rich texture without the fat and calories. Who says you can't have soup and eat it, too? Minced chicken or crabmeat is also traditional in place of shrimp.

- ¼ *pound medium raw shrimp*
- 6 *cups chicken broth*
- ½ *cup diced cooked ham*
- ¼ *cup coarsely chopped water chestnuts*
- 1 *can (16 oz.) cream-style corn*
- 3 *tablespoons cornstarch dissolved in ⅓ cup water*
- 2 *egg whites, lightly beaten*
- 1 *green onion, thinly sliced*
- 2 *teaspoons sesame oil*
- ⅛ *teaspoon white pepper*
- *Salt*

Getting Ready

① Shell, devein, and coarsely chop shrimp.

Cooking

① Place broth in a large pot; bring to a boil. Add shrimp, ham, water chestnuts, and corn. Reduce heat to medium; heat to simmering, stirring frequently. Add cornstarch solution and cook, stirring, until soup boils and thickens slightly. Turn off heat. Add egg whites, stirring until they form long threads.

② Stir in green onion, sesame oil, pepper, and salt to taste.

Makes 6 to 8 servings.

Vegetable Broth

Heat a large pot over medium-high heat. Add 1 tablespoon **cooking oil**, swirling to coat sides. Add 8 slices **ginger**, each the size of a quarter, lightly crushed; 3 cloves **garlic**, crushed; 1 large **onion**, cut into 1½-inch squares; and 4 **green onions**, cut into 2-inch pieces. Cook, stirring, for 2 minutes. Add 9 cups **water**, 4 **carrots**, cut into ½-inch slices; 2 stalks **celery**, cut into 2-inch pieces; 2 sprigs **cilantro** (optional); 2 tablespoons **soy sauce**; 2 teaspoons **salt**; ½ **star anise**; ½ teaspoon toasted **Sichuan peppercorns**; and ½ teaspoon **white pepper**. Bring to a boil; reduce heat, cover, and simmer for 1½ hours. Strain broth, discarding vegetables and seasonings.

Watercress Soup with Crab

This is a popular Cantonese treat, yet ironically watercress is not of Chinese origin. It was brought to China by Western traders, and over the centuries it has found a perfect home in Chinese cuisine, as in this savory seafood broth.

Marinade

- 2 *teaspoons cornstarch*
- ½ *teaspoon salt*

- ¼ *pound cooked crabmeat, flaked*
- 2 *teaspoons cooking oil*
- 3 *slices ginger, each the size of a quarter, lightly crushed*
- 4 *cups chicken broth*
- 1 *cup water*
- 1 *bunch watercress (about ¾ lb.), coarse stems trimmed*
- ½ *cup sliced carrot*
- ½ *teaspoon sesame oil*
- ¼ *teaspoon white pepper*

Getting Ready

① Combine marinade ingredients in a small bowl. Add crabmeat and stir to coat. Let stand for 10 minutes.

Cooking

① Place a 2-quart pan over high heat until hot. Add cooking oil, swirling to coat sides. Add ginger and cook, stirring, until fragrant, about 10 seconds. Add crabmeat and stir-fry for 1 minute.

② Add broth and water; bring to a boil. Add watercress and carrot. Reduce heat to low and simmer until vegetables are tender-crisp, about 5 minutes.

③ Stir in sesame oil and pepper.

Makes 4 servings.

Color Me Green

Asian greens are showing up in more and more American grocery stores. Let me tell you about three of my favorites: Chinese broccoli (*gai lan*) looks nothing like regular broccoli. It has dusty green stems, deep green leaves, and tiny white flowers. With its slightly bitter taste, it's great stir-fried or steamed with oyster-flavored sauce. Bok choy, baby bok choy, and the beautiful jade green Shanghai bok choy are delicately crunchy and slightly tangy. Chinese mustard greens (*gai choy*) have a slightly peppery flavor. Stir-fry them with a little garlic, or add them to soups.

Tofu Seafood Soup

This is typical family fare, tofu and spinach in a broth. It is tasty and nutritious. I chose seafood because I could never get enough of it as a child. A bowl of this and I am nine years old again. Who needs the Fountain of Youth?

6	*dried black mushrooms*
½	*pound firm white fish fillets, such as sea bass or red snapper*
½	*pound sea scallops*
⅛	*teaspoon white pepper*
½	*bunch (about 6 oz.) spinach or watercress*
1	*package (16 oz.) soft tofu*
6	*cups chicken broth*
2	*tablespoons fish sauce*
1	*teaspoon sesame oil*
	Salt

Getting Ready

① Soak mushrooms in warm water to cover until softened, about 20 minutes; drain. Discard stems and thinly slice caps.

② Cut fish into ½-inch cubes; cut scallops in half horizontally. Place fish and scallops in a bowl and sprinkle with pepper.

③ Wash spinach and trim coarse stems.

④ Drain tofu and cut into ½-inch cubes.

Cooking

① Place broth and fish sauce in a large pot; bring to a boil. Add fish, scallops, spinach, and tofu. Reduce heat and simmer until seafood is opaque and spinach is slightly wilted, 2 to 3 minutes.

② Stir in sesame oil and salt to taste.

Makes 6 servings.

Bean Curd Basics

Bean curd (tofu) is fragile stuff, especially the soft or silken kind. To transfer cubes of it from the cutting surface to the pan without breaking them, don't pick them up with your hands. Instead, slide the flat blade of a chef's knife or cleaver under the tofu and gently lift it, holding it in place on the blade with your hand. If you're pan-frying tofu, a nonstick pan is indispensable for keeping the soft cubes intact. Try to resist the temptation to push and prod the cubes, letting them brown nicely on each side before you turn them. To prolong the life of tofu sold in plastic tubs, pour out the liquid in the tub, refill the tub with tap water, and cover it with plastic wrap. Store it in the refrigerator for several days, changing the water daily. If tofu develops a strong odor, throw it away.

Hot and Sour Seafood Chowder

Mention seafood chowder, and most people would bring up images of rustic New England. I, on the other hand, think of exotic Southeast Asia and this exciting seafood chowder. The combination of red chili, fish sauce, mint, basil, and cilantro gives this soup quite a punch.

- ½ *pound medium raw shrimp*
- ¼ *pound firm white fish fillet, such as red snapper*
- 1 *stalk lemongrass*
- 1 *tablespoon cooking oil*
- 6 *cups chicken broth*
- 2 *slices ginger, each the size of a quarter, lightly crushed*
- 1 *small whole dried red chili*
- ½ *cup canned straw mushrooms, drained*
- 3 *tablespoons lime juice or lemon juice*
- 1½ *tablespoons fish sauce*
- 1 *green onion, thinly sliced*
- 2 *tablespoons chopped cilantro*
- 1 *tablespoon shredded fresh mint leaves*
- 1 *tablespoon shredded fresh basil leaves*

Getting Ready

① Shell and devein shrimp; reserve shells. Cut shrimp in half horizontally. Cut fish into ½-inch cubes.

② Lightly crush bottom 6 inches of lemongrass; discard remainder.

Cooking

① Prepare spicy broth: Place a large pot over high heat until hot. Add oil, swirling to coat sides. Add shrimp shells; cook until they turn pink, about 30 seconds. Add broth, lemongrass, ginger, and chili; bring to a boil. Reduce heat, cover, and simmer for 20 minutes. Strain broth and discard seasonings.

② Return broth to pot and heat to simmering. Add shrimp, fish, and straw mushrooms; simmer until shrimp turn pink, about 2 minutes. Stir in lime juice, fish sauce, and green onion.

③ Combine cilantro, mint, and basil. Ladle soup into bowls and sprinkle with fresh herbs.

Makes 4 to 6 servings.

Coconut-Flavored Chicken Soup

On hot summer nights, nothing perks up my appetite like a spicy soup. The coconut milk in this recipe serves as a balance between the fragrant lemongrass, pungent fish sauce, and hot chili. The amounts listed are for a milder soup. If you can take the heat, add more lemongrass and chili. Just don't cry over spilled coconut milk!

- ¾ *pound boneless, skinless chicken breasts*
- 1 *stalk lemongrass*
- 2 *slices ginger, each the size of a quarter, lightly crushed*
- 3 *cups chicken broth*
- 1 *can (13½ oz.) unsweetened coconut milk*
- 3 *tablespoons fish sauce*
- ½ *cup canned straw mushrooms, drained*
- 3 *tablespoons lime juice or lemon juice*
- 1 *fresh jalapeño chili, seeded and thinly sliced*
- 2 *tablespoons chopped cilantro*

Getting Ready

① Thinly slice chicken. Lightly crush bottom 6 inches of lemongrass; discard remainder.

Cooking

① Place lemongrass, ginger, and broth in a 2-quart pan; bring to a boil. Reduce heat to simmer and add coconut milk and fish sauce; cover and simmer for 8 minutes.

② Add chicken, straw mushrooms, lime juice, and chili; stir once to separate slices of chicken. Simmer until chicken turns opaque, 4 to 5 minutes.

③ Just before serving, stir in cilantro.

Makes 4 servings.

Lemongrass

Lemongrass is commonly used in Thai and Vietnamese cooking, but I love to throw it into a few Chinese dishes every now and then. A slender, pale green stalk that looks a bit like a green onion, lemongrass gives foods a delicately fragrant citrus flavor. If you've ever bitten into a piece of lemongrass in a dish and thought you were chewing on a matchstick, you know that even after it's cooked it remains tough and woody. That's why it's often simmered in broths and sauces, then discarded before serving.

Seafood Medley in Chili Broth

The chefs in Sichuan know all about chili, but there is more to this soup than hot spice. Double cooking is the key. The squid, shrimp, and fish are first stir-fried, then a quick simmer releases their deep, rich flavors.

- 2 *small squid, cleaned*
- ¼ *pound medium raw shrimp, shelled and deveined*
- ¼ *pound firm white fish fillet, such as sea bass or red snapper*

Marinade

- 2 *teaspoons cornstarch*
- 1 *teaspoon salt*

- 4 *cups chicken broth*
- ½ *cup sliced carrot*
- 2 *tablespoons julienned ginger*
- 2 *tablespoons cooking oil*
- 6 *small whole dried red chilies*
- ¼ *cup Chinese rice wine or dry sherry*
- 1 *tablespoon soy sauce*
- 1 *teaspoon sesame oil*
- 2 *tablespoons cornstarch dissolved in 3 tablespoons water*
- 1 *egg white, lightly beaten*

Getting Ready

① Cut squid, shrimp, and fish into ¾-inch pieces. Combine marinade ingredients in a medium bowl. Add seafood and stir to coat. Let stand for 10 minutes.

Cooking

① Place broth, carrot, and ginger in a 2-quart pan; bring to a boil. Reduce heat to low and simmer for 2 minutes.

② Place a wok over high heat until hot. Add oil, swirling to coat sides. Add chilies and cook, stirring, until fragrant, about 10 seconds. Add seafood and stir-fry for 1 minute.

③ Pour seafood into broth and simmer for 1 minute. Add wine, soy sauce, and sesame oil. Add cornstarch solution and cook, stirring, until soup boils and thickens. Turn off heat. Add egg white, stirring until it forms long threads.

Makes 4 servings.

Tangy Seafood Soup

Any visitor to the Philippines will remember the famous *sinigang*: a rich, tangy soup made with tamarind. Drop in egg noodles and you will have a fabulous one-dish meal.

- 2 *teaspoons cooking oil*
- ½ *small onion, thinly sliced*
- 1 *teaspoon minced garlic*
- 2½ *cups seafood bouillon (from bouillon cube and water)*
- 1 *cup green beans, cut into 1-inch lengths*
- 1 *medium tomato, peeled and diced*
- 1½ *tablespoons tamarind powder*
- 2 *tablespoons soy sauce or oyster-flavored sauce*
- 1 *tablespoon fish sauce*
- ¼ *teaspoon black pepper*
- ¼ *pound firm white fish fillet, such as sea bass, diced, or bay scallops*
- ¼ *pound medium raw shrimp, shelled and deveined*
- 1 *cup packed spinach leaves, coarse stems trimmed*
- 4 *ounces fresh Chinese egg noodles (optional)*

Cooking

① Heat a 3-quart pan over high heat. Add oil, swirling to coat sides. Add onion and garlic; cook, stirring, until fragrant, about 1 minute. Add bouillon, beans, tomato, tamarind powder, soy sauce, fish sauce, and pepper. Bring to a boil; simmer for 2 minutes.

② Add fish and shrimp; simmer for 3 minutes. Add spinach and cook for 1 minute.

③ If using noodles, cook in a large pot of boiling water according to package directions. Drain, rinse, and drain again; divide among 4 soup bowls. Ladle soup over noodles.

Makes 4 servings.

Tamarind Tips

Tamarind pulp gives many Southeast Asian dishes their fruity, sour flavor, and it's one of the "secret ingredients" in Worcestershire sauce. You can buy tamarind pods or tamarind paste (sold in brick form or in jars) in Southeast Asian markets. To make tamarind water, combine ½ cup **hot water** with 2½ tablespoons **tamarind pulp** (scraped from the pod) or prepared paste. Soak 10 to 15 minutes, then squeeze the pulp to extract all the juices, and strain through a sieve to remove the seeds. You can also buy tamarind in concentrated or powdered form.

West Lake Beef Soup

Over the centuries, the beautiful West Lake has inspired works by many famous Chinese poets. Why let the poets have all the fun? I am sure that West Lake is equally inspiring to Chinese chefs. Would a broth by any other name taste as sweet?

Marinade

- 3 *tablespoons water*
- 2 *tablespoons Chinese rice wine or dry sherry*
- 1 *tablespoon cornstarch*

- ½ *pound ground beef*
- 5 *cups beef broth*
- 2 *tablespoons regular soy sauce*
- 1 *tablespoon dark soy sauce*
- ½ *teaspoon white pepper*
- ½ *leek (white part only), julienned*
- ⅓ *cup frozen peas, thawed*
- ¼ *cup diced carrot*
- 1 *tablespoon chopped cilantro*
- 3 *tablespoons cornstarch dissolved in ¼ cup water*
- 2 *egg whites, lightly beaten*
- 1 *teaspoon sesame oil*

Getting Ready

① Combine marinade ingredients in a medium bowl. Add beef and mix well. Let stand for 10 minutes.

Cooking

① Place broth, soy sauces, and pepper in a 2-quart pan; bring to a boil. Add beef and stir to separate. Add leek, peas, carrot, and cilantro. Reduce heat and simmer for 5 minutes.

② Add cornstarch solution and cook, stirring, until soup boils and thickens. Turn off heat. Add egg whites, stirring, until they form long threads. Stir in sesame oil.

Makes 4 to 6 servings.

Fragrant Beef Soup

Slow simmering brings out the full, rich flavor of this hearty soup. Take your time and enjoy the enticing aroma of ginger and star anise. Goodness requires patience: this is as true in life as it is in the kitchen.

- ¾ *pound boneless beef shank*

Marinade

- 2 *tablespoons dark soy sauce*
- 2 *teaspoons cornstarch*

- 2 *stalks celery*
- 1 *carrot*
- ½ *pound daikon*
- 2 *tablespoons cooking oil*
- 4 *cups beef broth*
- 1 *cup water*
- 4 *slices ginger, each the size of a quarter, lightly crushed*
- 2 *whole star anise*
- 1 *tablespoon regular soy sauce*
- 2 *teaspoons sugar*
- ¼ *teaspoon white pepper*

Getting Ready

① Cut beef into ½-inch pieces. Combine marinade ingredients in a medium bowl. Add beef and stir to coat. Let stand for 10 minutes.

② Thinly slice celery. Roll-cut carrot and daikon.

Cooking

① Place a wide frying pan over high heat until hot. Add oil, swirling to coat sides. Add beef and cook until browned on all sides, 2 to 3 minutes.

② Lift beef from pan and place in a 2-quart pan. Add broth, water, ginger, and star anise; bring to a boil. Reduce heat, cover, and simmer until meat is tender, 45 to 50 minutes.

③ Add celery, carrot, and daikon. Cover and simmer until vegetables are tender, 15 to 20 minutes. Add soy sauce, sugar, and pepper; simmer for 5 minutes.

Makes 4 to 6 servings.

On Daikon

Daikon is the Japanese name for a long white radish that looks like an oversize carrot. It's also known as the Chinese turnip or Chinese radish. Raw daikon has a delicious, sweet, mildly peppery flavor. It's used in Japanese cooking in a variety of ways: in salads, shaved into thin threads as an accompaniment to sashimi, and made into pickles. In China, it's most often used in slow-cooked stews, soups, and braised dishes, much like the Western turnip or potato.

A Sense of Balance

The Wisdom of Yin and Yang

For as long as I've lived in the West, I've marveled at the way food trends come and go here. I've seen the pendulum swing back and forth from the indulgent '80s to the fat-free '90s and now back to a resurgence of indulgence. I am getting seasick just from watching!

What's next? I believe that people are getting tired of all that swinging. I think that the swings will grow smaller as we move toward the still point in the center. I think what's next is *balance*. Nothing forbidden and everything in moderation. The sensible voices of the food world—people like my good friends Julia Child and Jacques Pépin, and my number-one culinary advisor, my mom—have been talking about balance and moderation for years. And people are finally listening.

So, it's no coincidence that, right now, Chinese food is more popular in the West than ever. After all, like much of Asian food, Chinese food is all about balance. As long ago as the fourth century B.C., the Chinese had identified five essential tastes: salty, sweet, sour, bitter, and spicy-hot. Over the centuries, the balancing of these tastes created a cuisine of infinite variety, subtlety, and sophistication—a cuisine that loves to play with contrasting textures and colors, with light and heavy, rich and simple, mild and fiery hot. Now that's what I call a balanced diet!

This is the ancient Chinese symbol of yin and yang. I'm sure you've seen it before. But did you know that in Chinese culture and cuisine, yin and yang are alive and well today?

To put it simply, yin and yang are two cosmic forces, opposite yet equal, balanced in perfect harmony. Yin represents the feminine, yielding, cooler, more mysterious forces, while yang stands for the masculine, harder, richer, and hotter ones.

The Chinese believe that a healthy person is a person in whom yin and yang forces are in equilibrium. When the lips crack or the nose bleeds, the body is too dry, and the system has too much yang force. When the weather is humid, the body retains too much moisture and feels weak and tired—too much yin. How do you maintain the right balance? You start by eating foods with the right yin and yang qualities.

Yin foods might be cooler, moister, softer ones, like fish and shellfish, tofu, winter melon, or asparagus. Steaming and simmering are yin cooking methods. Yang might take the form of red meat, chilies, ginger, garlic, or fried foods. Yin and yang are important in combining colors and textures, too: bright colors balancing pale ones, toothsome textures setting off softer ones.

If all this sounds mystical and difficult, don't panic! There's no right or wrong attached to yin and yang. What matters is creating a lively harmony of complementary ingredients within a single dish and within a meal. It's as simple as pairing a mild steamed fish (yin) with a sprinkling of minced ginger and sizzling oil (yang), or serving a cool, refreshing Shrimp Salad with Tropical Fruit Salsa (page 122) to balance a hot and spicy Hunan Beef with Dry-Fried Beans (page 227).

Keep this ancient principle in mind the next time you walk into the kitchen. Whether you're cooking a classic Chinese dish or just making a midnight meat loaf sandwich, a sense of balance makes for better eating and better health. Remember, if Yan can use yin and yang, so can you!

Sizzling Rice Soup

Here's a soup that sings for its supper. It's always a treat to watch the "oohs" and "aahs" when this soup is brought to the table in a Chinese restaurant. Now you can put on your own show.

- ½ *pound boneless, skinless chicken*

Marinade

- 1 *tablespoon Chinese rice wine or dry sherry*
- 1 *teaspoon cornstarch*

- 4 *dried black mushrooms*
- 6 *cups chicken broth*
- ¼ *cup canned straw mushrooms, drained*
- ½ *cup sliced bamboo shoots*
- ½ *cup sliced carrot*
- ½ *cup sliced zucchini*
- ½ *cup frozen peas, thawed*
- 3 *tablespoons Chinese rice wine or dry sherry*
- ½ *teaspoon salt*
- ¼ *teaspoon white pepper*
- *Cooking oil for deep-frying*
- 8 *pieces dried rice crusts, each about 2 inches square*

Getting Ready

① Cut chicken into thin slices, then cut slices into thin strips. Combine marinade ingredients in a medium bowl. Add chicken and stir to coat. Let stand for 10 minutes.

② Soak black mushrooms in warm water to cover until softened, about 20 minutes; drain. Discard stems and thinly slice caps.

Cooking

① Place broth in a large pot; bring to a boil. Add chicken, black mushrooms, and straw mushrooms. Reduce heat to low, cover, and simmer for 2 minutes. Add bamboo shoots, carrot, zucchini, peas, wine, salt, and pepper; simmer for about 2 minutes.

② In a wok or 2-quart saucepan, heat oil for deep-frying to 375°F. Deep-fry rice crusts, 4 pieces at a time, turning continuously, until puffed and golden, 15 to 20 seconds. Remove with a slotted spoon/spatula; drain on paper towels.

③ Bring soup to the table in a tureen. Slide hot rice crusts into the soup. Break rice crusts with ladle and serve.

Makes 6 to 8 servings.

Rice Crusts

Asian markets sell dried rice cakes, or you can make your own. In a medium pan, bring 1 cup medium-grain rice and 1 cup water to a boil; reduce heat and simmer for 25 minutes. Let stand off the heat for 20 minutes. Spread rice in a ¼-inch-thick layer on an oiled baking sheet. Cut rice into 2-inch squares with a wet knife. Bake in a 325°F oven until firm and dry, about 50 minutes.

Chicken and Bean Thread Soup

Long, transparent bean thread noodles are called *fun see* in Chinese. They are not only fun to see, but they are also great-tasting. Bean threads in soup can be quite slippery, so the real fun may be in trying to pick them up with chopsticks. More than a soup and a meal, this dish is a chopstick exercise.

- 2 *tablespoons dried shrimp*
- 4 *ounces dried bean thread noodles*
- 6 *cups chicken broth*
- 2 *tablespoons soy sauce*
- ⅛ *teaspoon white pepper*
- ½ *pound boneless, skinless chicken or boneless pork, thinly sliced*
- 1 *small carrot, julienned*
- 2 *cups packed spinach leaves, coarse stems removed*
- 2 *teaspoons sesame oil*

Getting Ready

① Soak dried shrimp in warm water to cover until softened, about 20 minutes; drain.

② Soak bean thread noodles in warm water to cover until softened, about 5 minutes; drain. If desired, cut noodles into shorter lengths.

Cooking

① Place broth, soy sauce, and pepper in a large pot; bring to a boil. Add shrimp, noodles, chicken, and carrot. Reduce heat and simmer for 3 minutes. Add spinach and cook 2 minutes longer.

② Stir in sesame oil.

Makes 6 servings.

Soup's On

In Chinese restaurants everywhere, the menu begins with appetizers and soups. Everywhere but in China, that is. Whether served at home or as part of a restaurant banquet, soup is seldom a course of its own in China. It's intended more as a beverage, to accompany the meal and wash down the mouthfuls of rice, meat, and vegetables. At a banquet, a richer soup might be served with a light vegetable dish, and a vegetable soup with a meat dish. Hot, sweet soups might be served toward the end of the meal.

Chicken and Vegetable Soup

If two heads are better than one, then two soups must be better than one. To serve these two green and white soups together, you need two pairs of steady hands and one very large bowl. I can't think of a better way to enjoy a dish than to prepare it with my friends.

¼ *teaspoon* each *white and black sesame seeds*

Vegetable Soup

- 2 *bunches (¾ lb. each) spinach, coarse stems trimmed*
- ¾ *teaspoon salt*
- 2 *cups chicken broth*
- ¼ *teaspoon white pepper*
- 2 *tablespoons cornstarch dissolved in 3 tablespoons water*
- 1 *teaspoon sesame oil*

Chicken Soup

- 3 *tablespoons Chinese rice wine or dry sherry*
- 1½ *tablespoons cornstarch*
- 1 *teaspoon sugar*
- ¼ *teaspoon white pepper*
- 1¾ *cups chicken broth*
- ½ *pound boneless, skinless chicken, minced*
- ½ *cup mashed potato*
- 1 *egg white, lightly beaten*

Getting Ready

① Place white sesame seeds in a small frying pan over medium heat; cook, shaking pan frequently, until lightly browned, 3 to 4 minutes. Immediately remove from pan to cool. Repeat with black sesame seeds; cook until seeds smell toasted, 3 to 4 minutes.

Cooking

① Prepare vegetable soup: Place spinach and salt in a large pot with 1 inch of water. Parboil for 2 minutes; drain, then rinse with cold water. Gently squeeze to remove all water. Coarsely chop spinach.

② Place spinach, broth, and pepper in the same pot; bring to a boil. Add cornstarch solution and cook, stirring, until soup boils and thickens. Add sesame oil. Keep soup warm.

③ Prepare chicken soup: Combine wine, cornstarch, sugar, pepper, and broth in a 2-quart nonstick pan. Add chicken and mashed potato; mix well. Let stand for 15 minutes. Stirring constantly, bring to a boil over medium heat. Continue to stir and cook until thickened and creamy, about 3 minutes. Turn off heat. Add egg white, stirring, until it forms long threads.

④ Pour vegetable and chicken soups into two separate large heatproof glass measuring cups. Slowly pour the soups simultaneously into the opposite sides of a large bowl. Sprinkle white sesame seeds in center of vegetable soup and black sesame seeds in center of chicken soup.

Makes 6 servings.

Eight Treasure Winter Melon Soup

Winter melon is wonderful any season of the year. My favorite way of enjoying it is to put it in a rich savory broth together with eight different treasured ingredients. Imagine, a treasure hunt right at your dining table!

- 6 *dried black mushrooms*
- ½ *pound boneless, skinless chicken breasts*
- ¼ *pound boneless pork*

Marinade

- 1 *tablespoon soy sauce*
- 2 *teaspoons Chinese rice wine or dry sherry*
- ½ *teaspoon cornstarch*
- ½ *teaspoon salt*

- ½ *pound winter melon*
- 6 *cups chicken broth*
- ⅓ *pound medium raw shrimp, shelled, deveined, and coarsely chopped*
- 2 *ounces cooked crabmeat, flaked*
- 1 *ounce Virginia ham, diced*
- ¼ *cup canned straw mushrooms*
- ¼ *cup frozen peas, thawed*
- 1 *egg white, lightly beaten (optional)*
- ½ *teaspoon sesame oil*
- ⅛ *teaspoon white pepper*

Getting Ready

① Soak mushrooms in warm water until softened, about 20 minutes; drain. Discard stems and coarsely chop caps.

② Cut chicken and pork into ½-inch cubes. Combine marinade ingredients in a medium bowl. Add meats and stir to coat. Let stand for 10 minutes.

③ Trim hard skin off melon; cut flesh into ½-inch cubes.

Cooking

① Place broth, mushrooms, and melon in a large pot; bring to a boil. Reduce heat, cover, and simmer until melon begins to turn transparent, 12 to 15 minutes.

② Add chicken and pork, stirring once to separate cubes. Cook for 3 minutes. Add shrimp, crabmeat, ham, straw mushrooms, and peas. Cook, stirring once or twice, for 2 minutes.

③ Turn off heat. Add egg white, stirring, until it forms long threads. Stir in sesame oil and pepper.

Makes 6 to 8 servings.

CHAPTER 3

Salads

Chinese Chicken Salad

In recent years, chicken salad has become a popular starter item in Chinese restaurants all over North America. Here's my do-it-yourself version. When you want to entertain at home, just supply your own fortune cookies (see recipe on page 382).

Cooking oil for deep-frying

8 *wonton wrappers, cut into ¼-inch-wide strips*

Dressing

¼ *cup Chinese black vinegar or balsamic vinegar*

2 *tablespoons cooking oil*

2 *tablespoons sesame paste or peanut butter*

2 *tablespoons oyster-flavored sauce*

2 *tablespoons honey*

1 *tablespoon sesame oil*

2 *teaspoons sweet chili sauce*

1½ *teaspoons hot pepper sauce*

2 *cups shredded iceberg lettuce*

2 *cups mixed salad greens*

1½ *cups shredded cooked chicken*

¼ *cup chopped cilantro*

Fresh basil sprigs

Getting Ready

① In a wok or 2-quart saucepan, heat oil for deep-frying to 350°F. Deep-fry wonton strips, a few at a time, until lightly browned, 15 to 20 seconds. Remove with a slotted spoon; drain on paper towels. Let cool, then place in a tightly covered container until ready to use (up to 4 days).

② Combine dressing ingredients in a small bowl.

Assembly

① Place lettuce, salad greens, chicken, and cilantro in a wide, shallow bowl.

② Pour dressing over salad and toss. Surround salad with wonton strips; garnish with basil.

Makes 4 to 6 servings.

Chopstick Taboos

Chinese food is somehow more satisfying when you master the art of eating with chopsticks—maybe because they help you slow down and really enjoy the food. Here's what not to do with them: Pointing or playing with your chopsticks between mouthfuls is considered rude in polite company. Setting them down in a crossed position is said to bring bad luck. And sticking your sticks straight down into your rice bowl evokes ancient funeral rites—a downer at dinner!

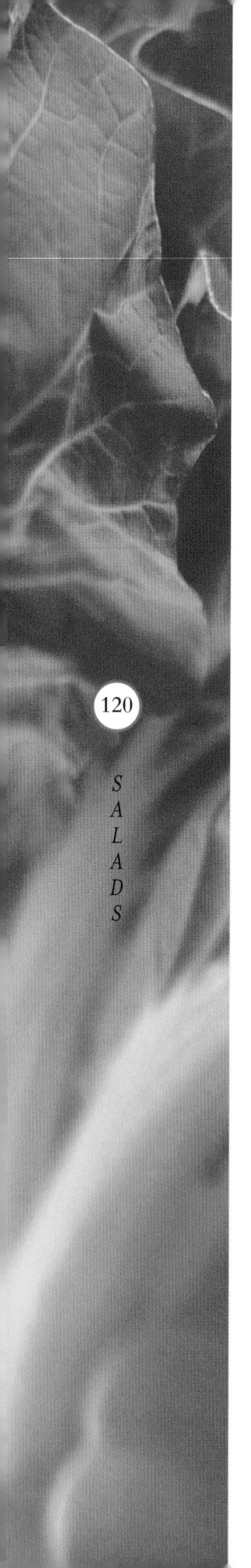

Warm Chicken Salad

This memorable banquet dish is from the famous Chengdu Restaurant in Chengdu, Sichuan. Instead of being served chilled, the shredded chicken and vegetables were tossed in a warm sauce, which in turn heats them enough to take away the raw edge. Try this salad tonight using leftover poached or roasted chicken, and turn your dining room into a royal banquet hall.

- 1½ *cups shredded cooked chicken breast*
- ½ *cup julienned English cucumber*
- 1 *small carrot, julienned*
- 1 *red bell pepper, julienned*
- 1 *green onion, julienned*

Sauce

- ⅓ *cup rice vinegar*
- 2 *tablespoons soy sauce*
- 1 *tablespoon sesame oil*
- 2 *teaspoons chili garlic sauce*
- 1 *teaspoon chili oil*
- 4 *teaspoons sugar*

- 1 *teaspoon sesame seeds*
- 2 *teaspoons cooking oil*
- 1 *tablespoon minced garlic*
- 1 *teaspoon cornstarch dissolved in 2 teaspoons water*
- *Toasted walnut halves*

Getting Ready

① In a large bowl, combine chicken, cucumber, carrot, bell pepper, and green onion.

② Combine sauce ingredients in a small bowl.

③ Place sesame seeds in a small frying pan over medium heat; cook, shaking pan frequently, until lightly browned, 3 to 4 minutes. Immediately remove from pan to cool.

Cooking

① Place a wok over high heat until hot. Add oil, swirling to coat sides. Add garlic and cook, stirring, until fragrant, about 10 seconds. Add sauce and bring to a boil. Add cornstarch solution and cook, stirring, until sauce boils and thickens. Let cool slightly.

② Pour warm sauce over chicken mixture and toss to coat. Arrange on a serving plate; garnish with sesame seeds and walnuts.

Makes 4 to 6 servings.

Grilled Beef Salad

I came across this dish in Thailand, and I've added a touch of white pepper and oyster-flavored sauce for my personal taste. This salad is fun to prepare outdoors during barbecue season. And for true beef lovers who appreciate a good salad, this dish can be a complete meal.

Marinade

3 *tablespoons Chinese rice wine*
2 *tablespoons oyster-flavored sauce*
2 *tablespoons fish sauce*
1 *tablespoon minced garlic*
¼ *teaspoon white pepper*

¾ *pound flank steak*

Dressing

¼ *cup rice vinegar*
2 *tablespoons cooking oil*
1 *tablespoon sesame oil*
2 *teaspoons chili garlic sauce*
¼ *teaspoon freshly ground black pepper*

4 *cups mixed salad greens*
½ *small red onion, thinly sliced*
1 *small carrot, cut in half lengthwise and thinly sliced*
¼ *cup cilantro leaves*
Fresh basil sprigs

Getting Ready

① Combine marinade ingredients in a shallow pan. Add meat and turn to coat. Cover and refrigerate for at least 30 minutes.

② Combine dressing ingredients in a small bowl; whisk until blended.

③ Place salad greens, onion, carrot, and cilantro in a wide, shallow serving bowl.

Cooking

① Lift meat from marinade; drain briefly. Place meat on an oiled grill 3 to 4 inches above a solid bed of hot glowing coals. Cook until meat is browned on the outside but still pink within, 4 to 5 minutes on each side.

② Cut meat across the grain into thin, slanting slices. Arrange warm meat over the salad. Pour dressing over the salad and toss. Garnish with basil sprigs.

Makes 4 to 6 servings.

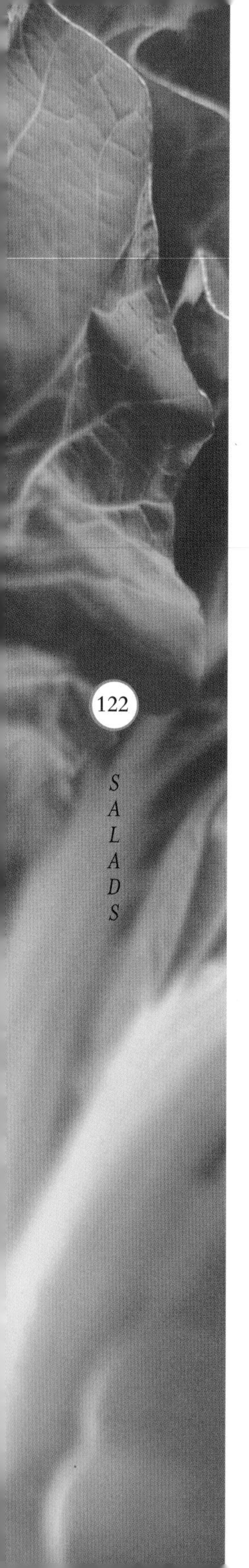

Shrimp Salad with Tropical Fruit Salsa

Fruit-based sauces and dressings are relatively new innovations by creative young Chinese chefs, and this shrimp salad is a delicious example. Instead of grilling the shrimp, you can also broil, poach, steam, or pan-fry them.

Marinade

1 *tablespoon Chinese rice wine or dry sherry*
1 *teaspoon sesame oil*
¼ *teaspoon salt*
¼ *teaspoon white pepper*

¾ *pound medium raw shrimp, shelled and deveined*

Dressing

3 *tablespoons lime juice or rice vinegar*
2 *tablespoons plum sauce*
2 *tablespoons cooking oil*
1½ *tablespoons honey*
1 *tablespoon sesame oil*
¼ *teaspoon white pepper*

Salsa

1 *mango or small papaya*
¼ *cup golden raisins*
¼ *cup diced red bell pepper*
1 *tablespoon chopped cilantro*
1 *tablespoon chopped crystallized ginger*
3 *tablespoons rice vinegar*
1 *teaspoon chili garlic sauce*

4 *cups mixed salad greens*

Getting Ready

① Combine marinade ingredients in a bowl. Add shrimp and stir to coat. Let stand for 10 minutes. Place shrimp on an oiled grill 3 to 4 inches above a solid bed of glowing coals. Cook until shrimp turn pink, 1½ to 2 minutes on each side. Let cool.

② Combine dressing ingredients in a bowl.

③ Prepare salsa: Peel mango. Cut half of flesh into 4 slices; reserve for garnish. Cut the remaining fruit into ¼-inch cubes; place in a bowl with remaining salsa ingredients.

Assembly

① Place salad greens in a large bowl; toss with dressing. Divide greens among 4 salad plates. Arrange shrimp on one side of greens; spoon salsa on greens opposite shrimp. Garnish with mango.

Makes 4 servings.

Warm Shrimp Salad with Ginger Vinaigrette

A touch of ginger can do much to enhance a vinaigrette dressing, especially when you pour it over sizzling hot stir-fried shrimp on a bed of cool salad greens. Red bell pepper adds just the right amount of sweetness and provides great color contrast.

Ginger Vinaigrette

- ¼ *cup rice vinegar*
- 2 *tablespoons cooking oil*
- 2 *tablespoons soy sauce*
- 1 *tablespoon sesame oil*
- 2 *tablespoons honey*
- 2 *tablespoons grated ginger*
- 1 *teaspoon finely minced garlic*
- ⅛ *teaspoon white pepper*

- ¾ *pound medium raw shrimp, shelled and deveined*
- 2 *teaspoons cornstarch*
- ¼ *teaspoon salt*
- 4 *cups mixed salad greens*
- ½ *red bell pepper, julienned*
- 4 *fresh shiitake mushrooms, stems discarded, thinly sliced*
- 1 *tablespoon cooking oil*

Getting Ready

① Combine vinaigrette ingredients in a small bowl; whisk until blended.

② In a bowl, toss shrimp with cornstarch and salt; let stand for 10 minutes.

③ Place salad greens, bell pepper, and mushrooms in a wide, shallow bowl.

Cooking

① Heat a wok over high heat until hot. Add oil, swirling to coat sides. Add shrimp and stir-fry until they turn pink, 2 to 3 minutes.

② Arrange warm shrimp over the salad. Pour dressing over the salad and toss.

Makes 4 to 6 servings.

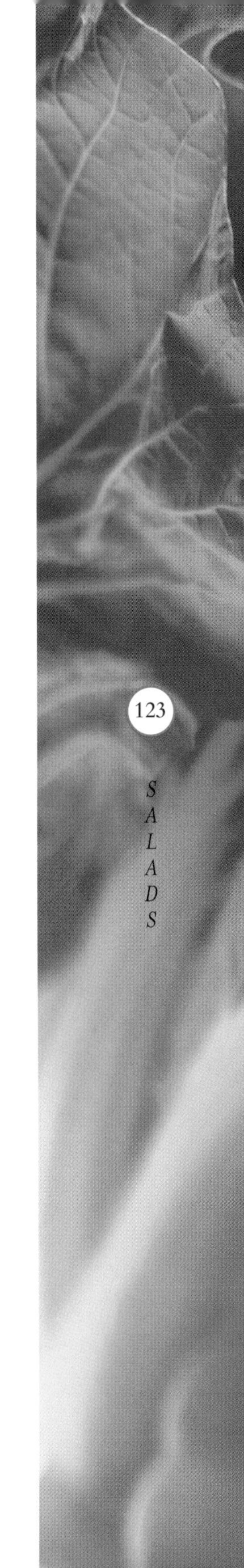

Spicy Fun See Noodle Salad

This cold salad, made with slippery, translucent bean thread noodles (*fun see*) and julienned vegetables in a sesame vinaigrette dressing, makes a perfect dish for a picnic or a light meal at home. See how much fun noodles can be?

8 *ounces dried bean thread noodles*

Dressing

2 *tablespoons soy sauce*

2 *tablespoons rice vinegar*

1 *tablespoon oyster-flavored sauce*

2 *teaspoons chili garlic sauce*

2 *teaspoons sesame oil*

1 *teaspoon sugar*

1 *teaspoon sesame oil*

2 *green onions, julienned*

1 *carrot, julienned*

½ *English cucumber, julienned*

Getting Ready

① Soak bean thread noodles in warm water to cover until softened, about 5 minutes; drain. Cut into 4-inch lengths.

② Combine dressing ingredients in a small bowl.

Cooking

① In a large pot of boiling water, cook noodles for 1 minute; drain, rinse with cold water, and drain again. Pat dry with paper towels.

② Place noodles in a salad bowl and toss with sesame oil. Add dressing, onions, carrot, and cucumber; toss to coat.

Makes 4 to 6 servings.

Fun

Fun is the Chinese word for noodles. But it's also the English word for having a good time! I think having fun in the kitchen and "playing with your food" are among the most rewarding parts of cooking. When you try new ingredients and recipes with a sense of adventure, you're doing more than just putting food on the table. You're sharing the excitement of creating something new. Serve your creation with a smile, and you add a little happiness to the world. And that, after all, is what fun is all about.

Hawaiian Fish Salad

Cultural ties between Japan and Hawaii date back to the last century. Today, many of these cross-cultural influences are prominent in everyday Islands life, and of course, in the kitchen. Thanks to talented local chefs, the traditional sashimi recipe has become Hawaiian *aku poke*, with pineapple and papaya adding a special sweet flavor to the fish.

Dressing

- 2 *tablespoons oyster-flavored sauce*
- 1 *tablespoon plum sauce*
- 1 *teaspoon soy sauce*
- 1½ *teaspoons sesame oil*
- 1 *fresh red or green jalapeño chili, seeded and minced*

- ½ *pound tuna or salmon fillet*
- 1 *medium tomato, diced*
- ½ *medium onion, diced*
- ½ *cup diced pineapple*
- ½ *cup diced papaya*
- 1 *green onion, thinly sliced*
- 1 *teaspoon sesame seeds*
- ½ *sheet Japanese seaweed (nori)*

Getting Ready

① Combine dressing ingredients in a large bowl.

② Remove skin and any bones from fish, then cut fish into ½-inch cubes. Place in the bowl with dressing. Add tomato, onion, pineapple, papaya, and green onion; toss to coat.

③ Place sesame seeds in a small frying pan over medium heat; cook, shaking pan frequently, until lightly browned, 3 to 4 minutes. Immediately remove from pan to cool.

Assembly

① Place fish mixture in a serving bowl.

② Fold nori into layers, such as quarters, then cut with scissors into fine strips. Sprinkle nori and sesame seeds on top for garnish.

Makes 4 servings.

A Winning Toss

Besides being full of flavors and textures, New Year Fish Salad (opposite page) is loaded with symbolic meaning. The raw ingredients signify the renewal of life, and the word for fish in Cantonese sounds like the word for prosperity. The most important part of eating this salad is the mixing together of the ingredients. To ensure good luck for the coming year, diners all call out, "*Lo hei!*" which means "to mix it up" but also sounds like "to prosper more and more," while they use their chopsticks to toss the ingredients as high in the air as they can.

New Year Fish Salad

During the lunar New Year celebration, many Chinese restaurants in Singapore serve *yu sheng*, a colorful salad of raw fish and crunchy vegetables. In recent years, the ingredients have become more elaborate and exotic: jellyfish, preserved papaya, pickled shallots, etc. My version is light, flavorful, and simpler to make—no need to spend the entire year preparing for next New Year's banquet.

Salad Mixture

- ½ *cantaloupe or ¼ honeydew melon*
- 1 *grapefruit*
- ¼ *cup thinly sliced sweet pickled ginger*
- 1 *medium carrot, shredded*
- ¼ *pound (3-inch wedge) jicama, shredded*

Dressing

- 3–4 *tablespoons cooking oil*
- 1 *teaspoon sesame oil*
- 3 *tablespoons plum sauce*

- 1 *tablespoon sesame seeds*
- 6 *ounces salmon fillet*
- 6 *ounces firm white fish fillet, such as sea bass*
- 1 *tablespoon lime juice*
- 1 *tablespoon cooking oil*
- ½ *teaspoon white pepper*
- ¼ *cup chopped roasted peanuts*
- 1 *green onion, slivered*

Getting Ready

① Peel melon and cut into crescents. Segment grapefruit by cutting away the peel and white pith; cut and lift out segments. In a bowl, combine melon, grapefruit, pickled ginger, carrot, and jicama.

② Combine dressing ingredients in a small bowl.

③ Place sesame seeds in a small frying pan over medium heat; cook, shaking pan frequently, until lightly browned, 3 to 4 minutes. Immediately remove from pan to cool.

④ Remove skin and any bones from fish. Thinly slice fish across the grain to make pieces about 1 by 2 inches. Fan slices on a serving platter, alternating pink and white fish. In a small bowl, combine lime juice, oil, and pepper.

Assembly

① Drizzle lime juice mixture over fish. Mound salad mixture in center of fish. Spoon dressing over the salad. Garnish with peanuts, sesame seeds, and green onion.

Makes 4 to 6 servings.

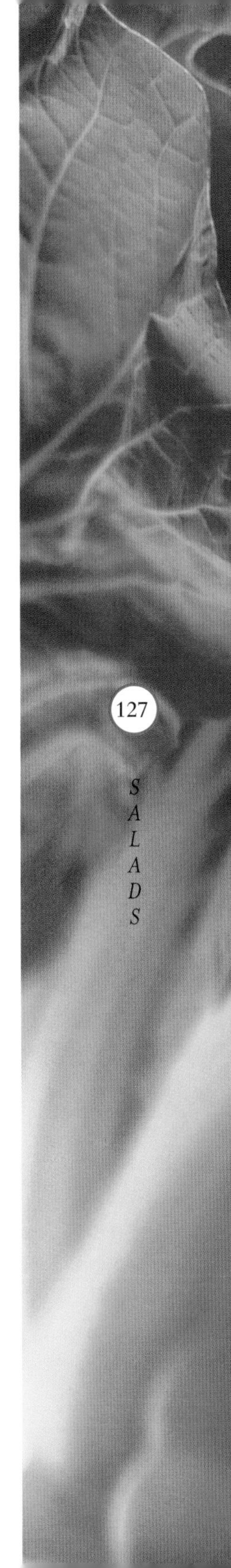

Ready, Set, Grow!

Planting Your Own Asian Vegetable Garden

I've been a devoted gardener all my life. When I was growing up, every inch of the small patch of earth behind our house was planted and cultivated to yield fresh vegetables all year long, and my brother, my mother, and I would spend hours planting, weeding, and watering.

Today, my garden is my sanctuary. Our whole house is built around it, and from every room, you can look out and see what's growing. To me, an afternoon spent working in the garden is the best form of meditation and relaxation there is. When I get back from a long trip, I head straight for the garden to check on things—even if it's the middle of the night.

Originally, my garden was mostly ornamental—shrubs and flowers neatly landscaped around a little koi pond. But during the last few years, I've been returning to my roots and trying out all kinds of Asian vegetables like the ones I grew up raising and eating. And now I really have the best kind of hobby of all—the kind you can eat!

Asian vegetables are becoming easier to find in supermarkets these days, but growing your own is fun, and there's nothing better than the flavor of a vegetable plucked right from the soil. Even if you don't live in California, as I do, there are all kinds of Asian vegetables you can grow throughout the year. You can buy seeds at a nursery or from a mail-order catalog.

Generally speaking, these vegetables can be divided into cool-weather and warm-weather varieties.

The leafy green vegetables, like bok choy, mustard (*gai choy*), and cilantro (also known as Chinese parsley, or *yim*

sike), as well as vegetables that mature underground, like Chinese turnips (*law bok*), grow well during the cooler months of early spring. Chinese broccoli (*gai lan*) and snow peas also do well during these months.

Later in the spring, you can plant warm-season squashes and gourds, like winter melon (*doan gwa*), yard-long beans (*dou gog*), and Chinese okra (*see gwa*), which mature in the summer and fall.

If your garden is 3 square feet on a fire escape, don't despair. Cilantro, garlic chives, and even snow peas can all be grown in pots. Just don't get carried away, or you'll block the fire escape!

What? You don't even have a fire escape? Okay, try this: grow your own fresh bean sprouts. You can harvest a whole crop right in your kitchen in just three to four days! (This is a great project for kids, too.)

Start by washing ½ cup of dried green mung beans, discarding any broken ones. Place the beans in a 1-quart jar with 2 cups of cold water. Cover the jar with a piece of cheesecloth held in place with a rubber band. After one day, drain the beans, rinse them, drain them again, and let them stand overnight. Repeat this process one or two more times. When the white stems reach 2½ to 3 inches in length, pluck them from the jar and rinse them in a bowl of cold water to remove the green husks. Drain well and use immediately, or store in a plastic bag in the refrigerator for up to three days.

You can even grow ginger in a pot indoors. All you need is a fresh ginger root from the grocery store. Cut the root into 2-inch lengths, and let the cut surfaces dry. Then plant the sections just below the surface of the soil. Soon, green leafy shoots will appear. Once the roots begin to grow, you can harvest them to use in cooking at any time.

So what are you waiting for? Isn't it time you turned your garden into a growing concern?

Orange Papaya Salad with Raspberry Vinaigrette

In my early childhood memories, there is nothing quite like burying my face in a slice of freshly cut papaya at a road-side fruit stand. Since then, my taste for papaya has expanded, and this salad with raspberry vinaigrette is a good example. Sweet papaya, tangy citrus, and crisp salad greens tossed with toasted nuts are a classic in the making.

Dressing

- ¼ *cup raspberry vinegar*
- 2 *tablespoons cooking oil*
- 1½ *tablespoons honey*
- 2 *tablespoons finely chopped crystallized ginger*

- 2 *oranges*
- 1 *small papaya*
- 3 *cups mixed salad greens*
- 1 *pear*
- ¼ *cup chopped toasted nuts*

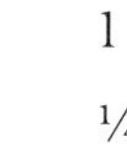

Getting Ready

① Combine vinegar, oil, and honey in a small bowl; whisk until blended. Stir in ginger.

② Segment oranges by cutting away the peel and white pith; cut and lift out segments. Peel papaya, remove seeds, and cut into crescents.

Assembly

① Divide salad greens among 4 salad plates. Peel, core, and slice pear. Arrange pear slices, orange segments, and papaya crescents on top of the greens. Sprinkle with nuts. Drizzle dressing over greens and fruit.

Makes 4 servings.

Feng Shui

Feng shui (pronounced "fung shway"), the Chinese art of balancing the flow of energy (*ch'i*), is a part of everyday life in Hong Kong. It would be unthinkable to choose a site or design a new building, home, or business without consulting a feng shui master. The placement of doors, mirrors, windows, and water (often in the form of fish tanks) helps channel good energy to bring in prosperity, happiness, and health. Whether or not you believe in the underlying principles, it can produce dramatic results. A friend of mine in San Francisco who owned a failing restaurant was told by a feng shui master to rebuild the front door 8 inches to the left. He did, and within three weeks his business was booming.

Spicy Cucumber Salad

Cool as cucumbers may be, you can fire them up in this spicy salad. A dash of fish sauce and a couple of teaspoons of chili garlic sauce should do the trick. By the way, cucumbers really are cool. A cucumber's pulp can be 20°F cooler than the outside air temperature.

Dressing

- ¼ *cup lemon juice or lime juice*
- 2 *tablespoons fish sauce*
- 1½ *tablespoons sesame oil*
- 1 *tablespoon honey*
- 1 *tablespoon finely minced garlic*
- 2 *teaspoons grated ginger*
- 2 *teaspoons chili garlic sauce*

- 2 *teaspoons sesame seeds*
- 1 *English cucumber*
- 1 *small red onion*
- ½ *red bell pepper*
- 1 *cup small cooked shrimp*

Getting Ready

① Combine dressing ingredients in a small bowl; whisk until blended.

② Place sesame seeds in a small frying pan over medium heat; cook, shaking pan frequently, until lightly browned, 3 to 4 minutes. Immediately remove from pan to cool.

③ Peel cucumber, leaving a few strips of green for color. Cut cucumber in half lengthwise, then thinly slice; place in a large bowl. Thinly slice onion and julienne bell pepper; place in bowl with cucumber. Cover and refrigerate until ready to serve.

Assembly

① Add shrimp to cucumber mixture. Pour dressing over salad and toss. Sprinkle with sesame seeds.

Makes 4 servings.

Sesame Oil

Asian-style sesame oil has a deep amber color because it's extracted from toasted sesame seeds. Don't confuse it with the clear type sold in some natural foods stores, which has a completely different flavor. Because sesame oil burns easily and has a strong flavor and aroma, it is used sparingly, as a condiment and seasoning, and in marinades, sauces, and dressings, rather than as a cooking oil. It's often sprinkled on foods at the end of the cooking process as a final flavor booster.

Southeast Asian Sweet Potato Salad

How do you spell potato? In my book it's spelled S-W-E-E-T. Sweet and delicious in fact, as in this colorful fruit and vegetable salad. Southeast Asian chefs like to add fruits to their salads for taste and texture contrast. This kind of salad is called *rojak*, which in Malay means a "mixture of all kinds."

- ¾ *pound sweet potatoes or yams*
- 2 *cups bean sprouts*
- 1 *mango, cut into ½-inch cubes*
- ½ *fresh pineapple, peeled and cut into ½-inch cubes*
- ½ *English cucumber, halved lengthwise and thinly sliced*
- ¼ *small jicama, peeled and cut into ½-inch cubes*

Dressing

- 2 *fresh red jalapeño chilies, seeded*
- ¼ *cup lemon juice*
- 2 *tablespoons packed brown sugar*
- 2 *tablespoons peanut butter*
- 2 *tablespoons soy sauce*

Lettuce leaves

Getting Ready

① In a medium pan, boil sweet potatoes in water to cover until tender when pierced, 20 to 30 minutes; drain and let cool. Peel, cut into ½-inch cubes, and place in a large bowl; add bean sprouts.

② To sweet potatoes and bean sprouts, add mango, pineapple, cucumber, and jicama. Cover and chill until ready to serve.

③ In a blender, process dressing ingredients until smooth.

Assembly

① Pour dressing over salad and toss. Arrange on a lettuce-lined serving plate.

Makes 6 servings.

Asian Cabbage Salad

Asian pears are making quick inroads into the North American market. Juicy like pears but crisp like apples, they are perfect for salads. Asian pear lovers take heart, these are not exotic imports but homegrown in California. Maybe we should rename them Asian American pears.

Dressing

- ¼ *cup raspberry vinegar*
- 2 *tablespoons cooking oil*
- 2 *tablespoons honey*
- 1 *tablespoon oyster-flavored sauce*
- 2 *teaspoons prepared Chinese mustard*
- 1 *teaspoon grated ginger*

- 2 *teaspoons sesame seeds*
- 3 *cups packed shredded napa cabbage*
- ½ *red bell pepper, finely julienned*
- 1 *Asian pear or sweet-tart apple*

Getting Ready

① Combine dressing ingredients in a small bowl.

② Place sesame seeds in a small frying pan over medium heat; cook, shaking pan frequently, until lightly browned, 3 to 4 minutes. Immediately remove from pan to cool.

③ In a salad bowl, combine cabbage and bell pepper. Cover and chill until ready to serve.

Assembly

① Peel, core, and julienne pear. Add to cabbage mixture. Pour dressing over salad and toss. Sprinkle with sesame seeds.

Makes 4 servings.

Napa Cabbage

Psst. There's something you need to know about napa cabbage: It has nothing to do with the Napa Valley, which, after all, is famous as California's wine country, not California's cabbage patch! Its name probably comes from the Japanese word *nappa*, meaning "greens." Now that we've cleared that up, what is napa cabbage? It's a pale green and yellow oblong cabbage also sold as Chinese or Tientsin cabbage. I love it in simple salads and stir-fries, and the broad outer leaves are great for stuffing and for lining a steamer basket.

CHAPTER 4

Tofu and Eggs

Braised Spicy Tofu

So you think of tofu as bland, eh? This fiery and flavorful Hunanese dish—tofu braised with garlic, chilies, black beans, and ham—will make you think again!

1	*package (16 oz.) soft tofu or 1 package (14 oz.) regular-firm or extra-firm tofu, drained*
2	*ounces cooked ham, sliced ⅛ inch thick*

Sauce

½	*cup chicken broth*
1	*tablespoon soy sauce*
2	*teaspoons sugar*
1	*teaspoon sesame oil*

1	*tablespoon cooking oil*
½	*cup sliced onion*
4	*cloves garlic, thinly sliced*
1	*fresh jalapeño chili, thinly sliced*
2	*teaspoons salted black beans, rinsed and drained*
3	*green onions, cut into 2-inch lengths*
2	*teaspoons cornstarch dissolved in 1 tablespoon water*

Getting Ready

① Cut tofu into pieces about ¼ inch thick and 1½ inches square. Cut ham slices into 1½-inch squares.

② Combine sauce ingredients in a bowl.

Cooking

① Place a nonstick frying pan over high heat until hot. Add oil, swirling to coat sides. Add onion, garlic, chili, and black beans; cook, stirring, until fragrant, about 10 seconds. Add tofu and cook, turning once, until golden brown, about 2 minutes. Add ham and green onions; cook for 1 minute.

② Add sauce and bring to a boil. Add cornstarch solution and cook until sauce boils and thickens.

Makes 4 servings.

Chilled Tofu with Bean Sprouts

Fresh mung bean sprouts (usually just sold as "bean sprouts") can be eaten raw, but they taste even better when you quickly parboil them, then chill them for use in salads like this one. Here, they're paired with soft tofu and drizzled with a sweet and spicy dressing.

- ½ *pound bean sprouts*
- 1 *teaspoon sesame seeds*

Dressing

- 3 *tablespoons rice vinegar*
- 2 *tablespoons soy sauce*
- 2 *tablespoons sesame oil*
- 2 *teaspoons chili garlic sauce*
- 2 *teaspoons sugar*

- 1 *package (16 oz.) soft tofu, drained*
- ¼ *cup chopped roasted almonds*

Getting Ready

① Bring a pot of water to a boil. Add bean sprouts and parboil for 1 minute. Drain, rinse with cold water, and drain again. Place on a serving plate, cover, and refrigerate until chilled.

② Place sesame seeds in a small frying pan over medium heat; cook, shaking pan frequently, until lightly browned, 3 to 4 minutes. Immediately remove from pan to cool.

③ Combine dressing ingredients in a bowl.

Assembly

① Cut tofu into ½-inch cubes. Place over chilled bean sprouts. Drizzle dressing over tofu; garnish with sesame seeds and nuts.

Makes 4 servings.

Meatless Miracles

Vegetarian cooking was introduced to China in the kitchens of Buddhist and Taoist monasteries more than 2,000 years ago. The practice of abstaining from eating meat was originally tied to a belief in reincarnation. Over the centuries, Chinese vegetarian cooking has developed into a sophisticated cuisine in its own right. Cooks use a variety of protein-rich foods to simulate the flavors and textures of meat. Bean curd skin, for example, becomes mock poultry, and wheat gluten stands in for meat. I often like the understudy better than the real thing!

Vegetarian's Delight

You'll find vegetable and tofu dishes like this one, sometimes called "Buddhist's Delight," all over southern China, where fresh produce is plentiful. Served over rice, it will delight you even if you're not a vegetarian!

- 8 *dried black mushrooms*
- ½ *of a 14-ounce package regular-firm tofu, drained*

Sauce

- ¾ *cup vegetable broth*
- 2 *tablespoons soy sauce*
- 2 *teaspoons sesame oil*
- 2 *teaspoons sugar*

- 1 *tablespoon cooking oil*
- 1 *teaspoon minced ginger*
- 1 *small carrot, sliced*
- ½ *cup sliced bamboo shoots*
- 1 *can (15 oz.) straw mushrooms, drained*
- ½ *pound napa cabbage, cut into 1- by 2-inch pieces*
- 2 *teaspoons cornstarch dissolved in 1 tablespoon water*

Getting Ready

① Soak dried mushrooms in warm water to cover until softened, about 20 minutes; drain. Discard stems and quarter caps.

② Cut tofu into ½-inch cubes.

③ Combine sauce ingredients in a bowl.

Cooking

① Place a wok over high heat until hot. Add oil, swirling to coat sides. Add ginger and cook, stirring, until fragrant, about 10 seconds. Add black mushrooms, carrot, bamboo shoots, straw mushrooms, and cabbage; stir-fry for 1 minute.

② Add tofu and sauce; bring to a boil. Reduce heat to low, cover, and simmer until vegetables are tender, 4 to 5 minutes. Add cornstarch solution and cook, stirring, until sauce boils and thickens.

Makes 4 to 6 servings.

Straw Mushrooms

Canned straw mushrooms are widely available in the Asian sections of supermarkets. If you think canned mushrooms are boring, give straw mushrooms a try. True, their flavor is somewhat mild, but they have a wonderful meaty texture and a delightfully velvety feeling on the tongue. They're also cute to look at. With their tall, oblong caps and short bodies, they look like little cartoon characters that are just about to start dancing around and singing: "Hi ho, hi ho, it's off to wok we go!"

Braised Tofu and Mushrooms

When tofu is pan-fried until golden, its surface becomes slightly spongy, and it absorbs sauces well. Here, it's first stir-fried, then braised in a rich brown sauce and paired with three kinds of mushrooms.

- 1 *package (14 oz.) extra-firm tofu, drained*

Sauce

- ⅔ *cup vegetable broth*
- 2 *teaspoons black bean garlic sauce*
- 2 *teaspoons oyster-flavored sauce*
- 1 *teaspoon sugar*
- ½ *teaspoon sesame oil*

- 2 *tablespoons cooking oil*
- 1 *leek (1-in. diameter), white part only, cut into ¼-inch-thick rounds*
- ½ *pound small white button mushrooms*
- ¼ *pound oyster mushrooms*
- 6 *medium fresh shiitake mushrooms, stems discarded*
- 1½ *teaspoons cornstarch dissolved in 1 tablespoon water*

Getting Ready

① Cut tofu in half horizontally to make 2 pieces, each about ¾ inch thick. With a 2-inch biscuit cutter, cut 6 rounds from each half to make a total of 12 rounds.

② Combine sauce ingredients in a bowl.

Cooking

① Place a nonstick frying pan over medium-high heat until hot. Add 1 tablespoon oil, swirling to coat sides. Add tofu and cook, turning once, until golden brown, 1½ to 2 minutes on each side. Remove pan from heat.

② Place a wok over high heat until hot. Add remaining 1 tablespoon oil, swirling to coat sides. Add leek and all mushrooms; stir-fry for 1 minute. Add sauce, reduce heat to low, cover, and simmer until mushrooms are tender, about 5 minutes. Add cornstarch solution and cook, stirring, until sauce boils and thickens.

③ To serve, arrange tofu in a circle around edge of serving plate. Place mushroom mixture in the center.

Makes 4 to 6 servings.

Tougher Tofu

Soft or "silky" tofu has a custardy texture that's best for soups or dressings. Firm tofu, in more solid blocks, is best for stir-frying and deep-frying. If tofu is a bit too soft, you can easily make it firmer. Cut the block of tofu in half horizontally and lay the two halves on a flat surface lined with paper towels. Top with a flat weight, such as a platter, and let sit for half an hour. Some liquid will be extracted, and the tofu will become more solid. Parboiling briefly in water will also help firm it up before using.

Tofu Scallop Butterflies

This is a great dish for tableside showmanship. You emerge from the kitchen and announce: "Butterflied scallops!" Then you present this fanciful dish that actually looks like little butterflies. Applause guaranteed.

8 *dried black mushrooms*

1 *package (16 oz.) soft tofu, drained*

8 *sea scallops or 8 medium raw shrimp*

Marinade

1 *tablespoon cornstarch*

¾ *teaspoon salt*

¼ *teaspoon white pepper*

2 *ounces Virginia ham, sliced ⅛ inch thick*

Getting Ready

① Soak mushrooms in warm water to cover until softened, about 20 minutes; drain. Discard stems and leave caps whole.

② Cut tofu in half horizontally to make 2 pieces, each about ¾ inch thick. Cut each half into quarters to make a total of 8 rectangles.

③ Butterfly scallops. (If using shrimp, shell, devein, and butterfly them.) Combine marinade ingredients in a bowl. Add scallops and stir to coat; let stand for 10 minutes. Cut ham to make 8 strips, each about ¾ inch wide and 2 inches long.

④ Place tofu in a heatproof glass pie dish. Top each piece with a scallop. Center a mushroom on each scallop, then place a strip of ham across the middle of each mushroom so topping resembles a butterfly.

Cooking

① Prepare a wok for steaming (see page 25). Steam over high heat until scallops turn opaque, 5 to 6 minutes.

② With a slotted spatula, transfer tofu to a serving plate; discard steaming liquid.

Makes 4 servings.

What Service!

The Chinese love to invent beautiful and whimsical ways to serve food. Here are some easy tips: Prepare a simple garnish in advance—something edible that relates to the food and adds a little color to the plate. Choose serving dishes that complement the colors and shapes of the food. Vary the serving style: some dishes on individual plates or bowls, some on platters, some in unusual vessels, like a bamboo steamer. Name your creation, and present it with a flourish and, of course, a smile.

Spicy Ma Po Tofu

Legend says that an old freckle-faced woman from Sichuan created this dish to feed her poor family. She cut creamy tofu into cubes and stir-fried them with slivers of meat and hot chilies. Minced pork is the traditional meat, but this dish is just as delicious if you prefer to use ground beef or ground chicken.

1 *tablespoon oyster-flavored sauce*
2 *teaspoons cornstarch*
½ *pound ground pork*

Spicy Sauce

⅓ *cup chicken broth*
2 *tablespoons soy sauce*
2 *teaspoons sugar*
2 *teaspoons chili garlic sauce*
2 *teaspoons sesame oil*

1 *package (16 oz.) soft tofu or 1 package (14 oz.) regular-firm tofu, drained*
1 *tablespoon cooking oil*
2 *teaspoons minced garlic*
2 *teaspoons minced ginger*
4 *small whole dried red chilies*
1½ *teaspoons cornstarch dissolved in 1 tablespoon water*

Getting Ready

① Combine oyster-flavored sauce and cornstarch in a bowl. Add pork and mix well; let stand for 10 minutes.

② Combine spicy sauce ingredients in a bowl.

③ Cut tofu into ½-inch cubes.

Cooking

① Place a wok over high heat until hot. Add oil, swirling to coat sides. Add pork and stir-fry until lightly browned and crumbly, about 1 minute. Add garlic, ginger, and chilies; cook for 2 minutes.

② Add tofu and spicy sauce; bring to a boil. Cook for 1 minute. Add cornstarch solution and cook, stirring, until sauce boils and thickens.

Makes 4 to 6 servings.

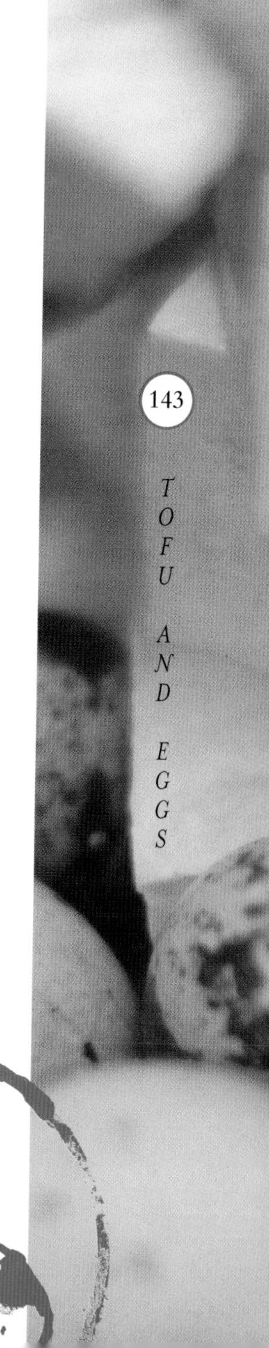

Home-Style Tofu with Seafood Mousse

This is my version of the famous southern specialty, Hakka bean curd. Triangles of tofu are stuffed with minced seafood, browned in a wok, and braised with vegetables in a seasoned broth.

6 *ounces firm white fish fillets or medium raw shrimp, shelled and deveined*

Marinade

1 *teaspoon chopped cilantro*

1 *tablespoon Chinese rice wine or dry sherry*

1 *tablespoon soy sauce*

1 *tablespoon egg white, lightly beaten*

2 *teaspoons cornstarch*

¼ *teaspoon salt*

1 *package (14 oz.) regular-firm tofu, drained*

2 *tablespoons cooking oil*

Seasoned Broth

2½ *cups chicken broth*

2 *tablespoons oyster-flavored sauce*

2 *tablespoons soy sauce*

1 *teaspoon sesame oil*

⅛ *teaspoon white pepper*

½ *cup sliced bamboo shoots*

½ *cup sliced carrot*

½ *cup sliced zucchini*

Getting Ready

① Finely mince seafood. Combine marinade ingredients in a bowl. Add seafood and mix well; let stand for 10 minutes.

② Cut tofu in half horizontally to make 2 pieces, each about ¾ inch thick. Cut each piece diagonally to make a total of 4 triangles (see illustration on page 53).Using a melon baller or teaspoon, remove about 1 tablespoon tofu from the longest side of each triangle.

③ Stuff each triangle with a heaping tablespoon of seafood mixture; smooth the mounded filling with the back of a wet spoon.

Cooking

① Place a wok over medium heat until hot. Add oil, swirling to coat sides. Add tofu triangles, filling side down, and cook until golden brown, 1 to 2 minutes. Place triangles in a clay pot or a 2-quart pot.

② Add seasoned broth ingredients and bring to a boil over medium heat. Reduce heat to low; cover and simmer for 8 minutes. Add bamboo shoots, carrot, and zucchini. Cover and simmer until vegetables are tender-crisp, 3 to 4 minutes.

Makes 4 to 6 servings.

Braised Tofu with Nuts

The creamy texture of tofu and the crunch of cashews, water chestnuts, and carrots make a delightfully yin-and-yang combination in this vegetarian stir-fry—all brought together in a sweet and spicy sauce.

1 *package (14 oz.) regular-firm or extra-firm tofu*

Sauce

½ *cup vegetable broth*

2 *tablespoons hoisin sauce*

1 *tablespoon regular soy sauce*

1 *tablespoon dark soy sauce*

1 *teaspoon chili garlic sauce*

1 *teaspoon sesame oil*

1½ *tablespoons cooking oil*

4 *small dried red chilies*

4 *medium white button mushrooms, sliced*

½ *cup canned straw mushrooms, drained*

1 *can (5 oz.) sliced water chestnuts, drained*

¼ *cup diced carrot*

1½ *teaspoons cornstarch dissolved in 1 tablespoon water*

¾ *cup roasted cashews or peanuts*

Getting Ready

① Cut tofu into ½-inch cubes.

② Combine sauce ingredients in a bowl.

Cooking

① Place a wok over high heat until hot. Add oil, swirling to coat sides. Add chilies and cook, stirring, until fragrant, about 10 seconds. Add tofu, button and straw mushrooms, water chestnuts, and carrot; stir-fry until carrot is tender-crisp, about 1½ minutes.

② Add sauce and bring to a boil. Add cornstarch solution and cook, stirring, until sauce boils and thickens. Add nuts and toss to coat.

Makes 4 to 6 servings.

Water Chestnuts

Canned water chestnuts are widely available. Fresh ones are a little harder to find, but worth searching for (look in Asian groceries). Their meat is sweeter and their texture crisper than their canned counterparts. Don't be put off by fresh water chestnuts' muddy exterior. Rinse them well, then peel the brown skin with a paring knife, placing the peeled ones in water as you work to prevent discoloration. Fresh jicama can be used as a substitute for water chestnuts.

Vegetarian Tofu Casserole

Not all bean curds are alike. Some are silky soft, some are firm, and some are extra-firm from being pressed with a weight. For vegetarian cooking, pressed bean curd is a logical choice. Its chewy texture makes it a good stand-in for meat.

2 *ounces dried bean thread noodles*

6 *dried black mushrooms*

4 *dried cloud ears*

Sauce

2 *cups vegetable broth*

2 *tablespoons Chinese rice wine or dry sherry*

2 *tablespoons soy sauce*

1 *tablespoon oyster-flavored sauce*

1 *teaspoon sesame oil*

2 *tablespoons cooking oil*

2 *teaspoons minced garlic*

2 *tablespoons fermented bean curd, mashed*

8 *ounces pressed bean curd, cut into thin slices*

1 *large carrot, julienned*

1 *can (8 oz.) sliced bamboo shoots, drained*

Getting Ready

① In separate bowls, soak noodles, mushrooms, and cloud ears in warm water to cover until softened, about 5 minutes for noodles, 20 minutes for mushrooms and cloud ears; drain. Leave noodles long. Discard mushroom stems and slice caps. Slice cloud ears.

② Combine sauce ingredients in a bowl.

Cooking

① Place a wok over high heat until hot. Add oil, swirling to coat sides. Add garlic and cook, stirring, until fragrant, about 10 seconds. Add noodles, mushrooms, cloud ears, fermented bean curd, pressed bean curd, carrot, and bamboo shoots; cook and toss for 1 minute.

② Stir in sauce and bring to a boil. Reduce heat, cover, and cook, stirring occasionally, until vegetables are tender-crisp and noodles absorb most of the liquid, about 10 minutes.

Makes 4 servings.

Vegging Out in the Kitchen

Some Thoughts about Vegetarianism in Chinese Cooking

Okay, first of all, let me say that I have never been too fond of "isms." Maybe it's because I have seen firsthand what the vast, sweeping power of "isms" can do to individual people and centuries-old traditions.

Most "isms" are too simple, too limiting, too black and white—especially when it comes to the marvelously complex world of food. That's why I am a self-avowed omnivore. I always say, "Better a little of all things than too much of one!"

But don't get me wrong. I'm not entirely opposed to food "isms." I'm just in favor of keeping them in perspective. While I'm not a vegetarian, for example, I do have a healthy respect for the ancient Chinese principles of vegetarianism, and my mom often prepares delicious meatless meals at our house.

Those principles go all the way back to the rise of Buddhism, which came to China from India almost 2,000 years ago. The vegetarian part originally had less to do with diet, and more to do with the act of killing animals: Buddhist doctrine is based on principles of nonviolence and respect for the sanctity of all living things.

Understandably, killing the thing you might yourself become in another life was not considered the best way to reach nirvana, the ultimate state of enlightenment.

Over the centuries, as Chinese Buddhism spread and became interwoven with Taoism and Confucianism, Buddhist temples were built in most cities and towns. We have those temples to thank for most of the wonderful vegetarian dishes that are so much a part of Chinese cooking today.

The temples were bound by monastic law to feed visitors during festivals, and eventually, as a means of financial survival, many temples opened restaurants to attract secular visitors, too. Motivated by the need to attract customers (some things never change!), the monks were compelled to invent all kinds of ingenious and delicious vegetarian dishes.

They turned to the protein-rich soybean for help, elevating bean curd (tofu), and its various by-products (like soy milk, fermented bean curd, and bean curd skin) to new culinary heights. The Mahayana Buddhist monks, in particular, became famous for creating a vast array of mock meat delicacies—beef, ham, pork, chicken, goose, abalone, and more—made from bean curd and wheat gluten. These are still prepared in many parts of China today.

When I was growing up, most of our meals were vegetarian by necessity, because meat, poultry, and seafood were in short supply, and we were able to grow our own vegetables. But my mom's mostly meatless cooking was neither about religion nor about fooling the palate with foods that masquerade as meat. It was unapologetic—a celebration of the foods of the earth, prepared with great respect for their integrity, flavor, and nutritional value.

The words "not till you eat your veggies" were never spoken at our table. Looking back, I'm glad I grew up appreciating the infinite possibilities of fresh vegetables without any of the stigmas that kids attach to them in other parts of the world. I've tasted some great cooking over the years, but to this day, a simple plate of steamed *gai lan* (Chinese broccoli) with a drizzle of oyster sauce is still one of the ultimate culinary pleasures to me.

Whether you're a vegetarian or just want to make the occasional meatless meal a part of your diet, here are five simple tips I've learned from my mom—and a few other great cooks—over the years. (P.S.: They're by no means limited to Chinese cooking.)

① **Shop first, plan second.** Go to the best produce market you can find, and buy what's fresh and in season (it's often the best deal, too). Then bring home your bounty and design your menu around it.

② **Discover flavor boosters.** Ingredients like soy sauce, oyster-flavored sauce (strict vegetarians can buy vegetarian oyster-flavored sauce made with shiitake mushrooms), fermented black beans, mushrooms, onions, garlic, ginger, and tomatoes help enhance flavor and add intensity and "meatiness" to a dish.

③ **Check out the magic of tofu.** It's truly the most versatile ingredient in the world. Braised Spicy Tofu (page 137), and Buddhist's Bean Curd Rolls, (page 150) are great places to start.

④ **Keep it simple.** Take a cue from those Buddhist monks: Less is more. Treat your vegetables with respect and the rewards will be great. Avoid overcooking them; keep seasonings clean and simple; and go for bright colors and contrasting textures.

⑤ **Don't mention it.** Finally, if you're cooking for guests who are used to having meat as the centerpiece of the meal, for Pete's sake, don't use the words "vegetarian" or "meatless." Take it from me, if you don't call people's attention to the absence of meat, half the time they don't even notice!

Buddhist's Bean Curd Rolls

These crispy rolls look like egg rolls, but there's a difference. The savory rice and mushroom filling is wrapped in bean curd sheets for extra protein.

Filling

1 *cup glutinous rice*

1 *cup plus 2 tablespoons water*

6 *dried black mushrooms*

1 *tablespoon cooking oil*

1 *teaspoon minced garlic*

1 *small carrot, cut into 1-inch slivers*

6 *asparagus spears, cut into ½-inch pieces*

2 *green onions, sliced*

2 *tablespoons oyster-flavored sauce*

1 *tablespoon hoisin sauce*

2 *teaspoons sesame oil*

2 *dried bean curd sheets, each about 7 by 21 inches*

2 *tablespoons flour mixed with 1 tablespoon water*

About 2 tablespoons cooking oil

Getting Ready

① Soak rice in warm water to cover for 1 hour.

② Soak mushrooms in warm water to cover until softened, about 20 minutes; drain. Discard stems and thinly slice caps.

Cooking

① Drain rice. Place in a medium pan with the water. Bring to a boil; cover, reduce heat, and simmer until small craterlike holes appear on the surface and rice is tender, 20 to 25 minutes.

② Make filling: Place a wok over high heat until hot. Add oil, swirling to coat sides. Add garlic and cook, stirring, until fragrant, about 10 seconds. Add carrot and asparagus; stir-fry for 2 minutes. Add mushrooms, green onions, oyster-flavored sauce, hoisin sauce, and sesame oil; stir-fry for 2 minutes. Off heat, stir in rice. Cool.

③ Soak bean curd sheets in warm water to cover until softened, about 15 minutes; drain and cut each sheet into three 7-inch squares.

④ Make each roll: Place a bean curd square on work surface with 1 corner facing you. Place 2 rounded tablespoons of filling across wrapper slightly above the corner. Fold corner over filling, then roll over once. Fold in left and right sides. Brush sides and top of triangle with flour paste, then roll up completely to enclose filling. Flatten roll slightly with your hand.

⑤ Place a nonstick frying pan over medium heat until hot. Add 2 tablespoons oil, swirling to coat sides. Place rolls in pan and cook until golden, about 3 minutes on each side; add more oil if needed.

⑥ Cut rolls into thirds; serve hot.

Makes 6 rolls.

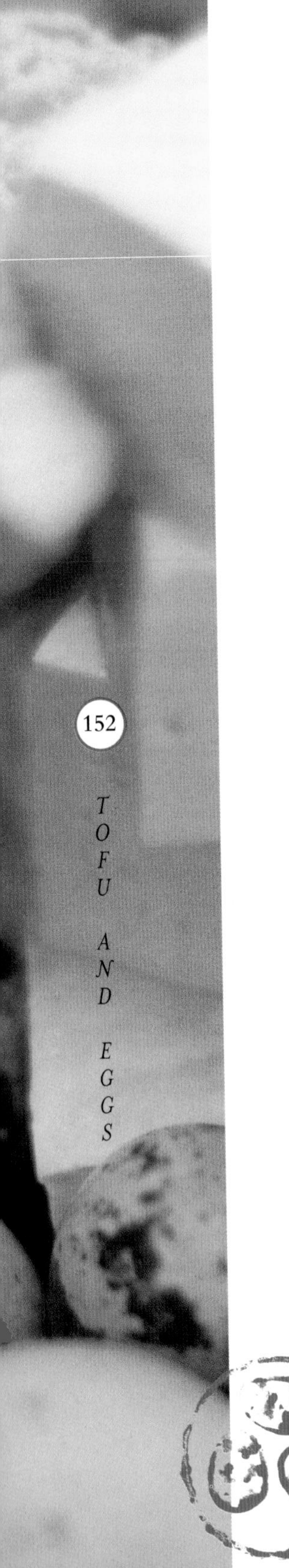

Crispy Tofu

In my old neighborhood, there was a man who sold fried tofu slices from his portable wok stand. He cooked it right in front of us, and it was quite a sensation to sink your teeth into those piping hot crispy tofu slices dripping with a sweet and spicy sauce.

1 *package (16 oz.) soft tofu or 1 package (14 oz.) regular-firm tofu, drained*
¼ *teaspoon cayenne*
¼ *teaspoon salt*
¼ *teaspoon white pepper*
2 *eggs*
1 *cup flour*
½ *cup Japanese bread crumbs (panko)*

Sauce

⅓ *cup vegetable broth*
1 *tablespoon soy sauce*
1 *tablespoon Chinese rice wine or dry sherry*
1½ *teaspoons sugar*
1 *teaspoon sesame oil*
¾ *teaspoon cornstarch*

2 *tablespoons cooking oil*

Getting Ready

① Cut tofu in half horizontally to make 2 pieces, each about ¾ inch thick. Cut each half into quarters to make a total of 8 rectangles.

② In a small bowl, combine cayenne, salt, and pepper. In a wide bowl, beat eggs until well blended. On a plate, combine flour and bread crumbs.

③ Combine sauce ingredients in a pan.

Cooking

① Bring a pot of water to simmering. Add tofu and parboil for 2 minutes. Lift out with a slotted spoon; pat dry with paper towels. Sprinkle with cayenne mixture.

② Place a wide nonstick frying pan over medium heat until hot. Add oil, swirling to coat sides. Dip tofu pieces in egg, drain briefly, then dip in flour-crumb mixture. Cook, turning once, until golden brown, 2 to 3 minutes on each side. Remove pan from heat.

③ Heat sauce over medium heat, stirring, until it boils and thickens.

④ Pour sauce onto a serving plate. Arrange tofu pieces on sauce.

Makes 4 to 6 servings.

Steamed Egg Custard

If you're looking for authentic Chinese comfort food, look no further. The time-honored method of steaming eggs produces a custard of delicate texture, so light you can eat it any time of day. To keep the eggs smooth and soft, steam them slowly over medium heat. The custard is ready to eat the moment a knife inserted in the center comes out clean.

- ¼ *pound medium raw shrimp, shelled, deveined, and diced*
- 2 *tablespoons chopped Virginia ham*
- ½ *teaspoon salt*
- ¼ *teaspoon white pepper*
- 4 *eggs, lightly beaten*
- 1¼ *cups water*

Dressing

- 1 *tablespoon chopped green onion*
- 2 *teaspoons soy sauce*
- 1 *teaspoon sesame oil*
- ½ *teaspoon hot pepper sauce*

Getting Ready

① In a bowl, combine shrimp, ham, salt, and white pepper; mix well. Combine eggs and water in another bowl.

② Combine dressing ingredients in a small bowl.

③ Pour shrimp mixture and egg mixture into a heatproof glass pie dish; cover with another heatproof glass pie dish.

Cooking

① Prepare a wok for steaming (see page 25). Place pie dish in wok, cover, and steam over medium heat for 15 minutes.

② Spoon dressing on top and serve.

Makes 4 servings.

Full Steam Ahead

I'm happy to see that steaming is coming into fashion in the West, because it's one of my favorite cooking methods. The flavors of steamed foods are outstandingly clean, delicate, and soothing, and their texture is moist and tender. Little or no oil is needed for steaming, and most of the vitamins, minerals, and natural juices of foods are retained. Steaming is also convenient; you can place food in a steamer and then move on to other things without needing to keep a constant watch over it.

Scrambled Eggs with Shrimp

From start to finish, scrambled eggs take less than 5 minutes, but you don't want to rush the cooking process. Cook the eggs slowly, and remove the pan from the heat when eggs are still creamy; they will finish cooking in their own heat.

Marinade

1 *teaspoon cornstarch*
½ *teaspoon salt*
Dash of white pepper

¾ *pound medium raw shrimp, shelled, deveined, and diced*
4 *eggs*
1 *teaspoon sesame oil*
Salt
2 *tablespoons cooking oil*
1 *teaspoon minced garlic*
1 *teaspoon minced ginger*
2 *tablespoons finely chopped onion*
¼ *cup frozen peas, thawed*
Cilantro leaves

Getting Ready

① Combine marinade ingredients in a bowl. Add shrimp and stir to coat; let stand for 10 minutes.

② In a bowl, lightly beat eggs with sesame oil, and salt to taste.

Cooking

① Place a wok or nonstick frying pan over high heat until hot. Add 1 tablespoon oil, swirling to coat sides. Add garlic, ginger, and onion; cook, stirring, until fragrant, about 20 seconds. Add shrimp; stir-fry until pink, about 2 minutes. Add peas and cook for 30 seconds. Remove mixture from pan.

② Heat the remaining 1 tablespoon oil in nonstick frying pan over medium-high heat. Add eggs. Cook, without stirring, until eggs are cooked around the edges. Return shrimp mixture to pan, stir toward center, and cook until eggs form large, soft, moist curds.

③ Place on a serving plate and garnish with cilantro leaves.

Makes 4 servings.

Light Reading

Here are a few of my favorite ways to lighten up the foods you love:

- Substitute egg whites with a little milk for whole eggs.
- Try soy milk as a substitute for dairy products.
- Ask your butcher to help you choose leaner cuts of meat.
- Check out reduced-sodium soy sauce.
- Eat slowly, savor the moment, and have a little extra rice.

Crab Egg Foo Yung

Egg foo yung is one of the best-known dishes in Chinese restaurants, but do you know that *foo yung* actually refers to the beauty of a peony? In ancient China, a beautiful woman was often described as someone with the face of a peony, and this omelet is as colorful as the flower in bloom.

3 *dried black mushrooms*
3 *eggs*
¼ *cup cooked crabmeat, flaked*
2 *tablespoons chopped cilantro*
1 *teaspoon minced ginger*
1 *teaspoon sesame oil*
Salt and white pepper

Sauce

⅓ *cup chicken broth*
2 *tablespoons oyster-flavored sauce*
2 *teaspoons Chinese rice wine or dry sherry*
¾ *teaspoon cornstarch*

1½ *tablespoons cooking oil*

Getting Ready

① Soak mushrooms in warm water to cover until softened, about 20 minutes; drain. Discard stems and thinly slice caps.

② In a bowl, lightly beat eggs. Stir in mushrooms, crabmeat, cilantro, ginger, sesame oil, and salt and pepper to taste.

③ Combine sauce ingredients in a small pan.

Cooking

① Place an 8-inch nonstick frying pan over medium heat until hot. Add oil, swirling to coat sides. Pour egg mixture into pan and cook without stirring. As edges begin to set, lift with a spatula and shake or tilt pan to let eggs flow underneath. When eggs no longer flow freely, turn omelet over and brown lightly on the other side.

② Bring sauce to a boil over medium-high heat; cook, stirring, until sauce thickens.

③ Slide omelet onto a warm serving plate and pour sauce over.

Makes 2 servings.

Ham or Shrimp Egg Foo Yung

Substitute ¼ cup diced cooked ham or small cooked shrimp for the crab.

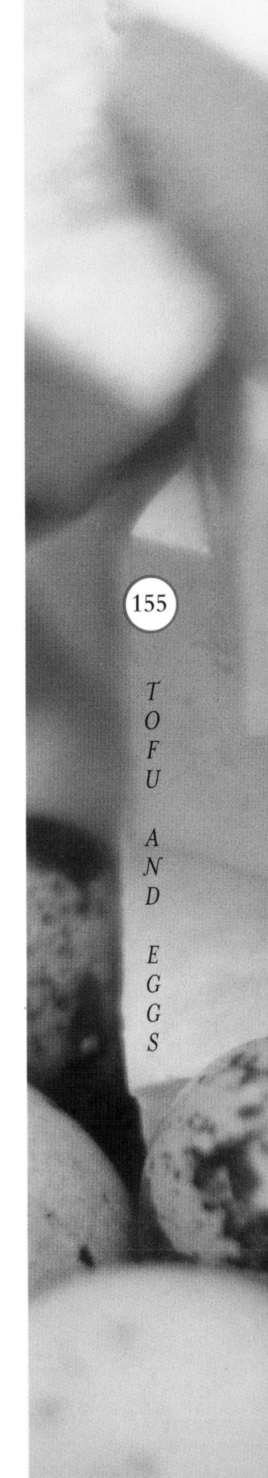

川味小吃
四川人民出版社
入廚三十年
食品衛生學
文京圖書有限公司

Open-Faced Omelet with Savory Garlic Sauce

When I was growing up, we often made a light meal of an omelet topped with a tangy vegetable sauce.

- 4 *eggs, lightly beaten*
- ¼ *teaspoon salt*
- ⅛ *teaspoon white pepper*
- 2 *teaspoons chopped green onion*

Sauce

- ⅓ *cup vegetable broth*
- 2 *tablespoons soy sauce*
- 1 *tablespoon black vinegar or balsamic vinegar*
- 2 *teaspoons chili garlic sauce*
- 1 *teaspoon sesame oil*
- 2 *teaspoons sugar*

- 1½ *tablespoons cooking oil*
- 1 *teaspoon minced garlic*
- 1 *teaspoon minced ginger*
- ½ *cup diced tomatoes*
- ½ *cup chopped water chestnuts*
- ¼ *cup frozen peas, thawed*
- 1 *teaspoon cornstarch dissolved in 2 teaspoons water*

Getting Ready

① Combine eggs, salt, pepper, and green onion in a bowl.

② Combine sauce ingredients in another bowl.

Cooking

① Place an 8- to 9-inch nonstick frying pan over medium heat until hot. Add 1 tablespoon oil, swirling to coat sides. Add eggs and cook without stirring. As edges begin to set, lift with a spatula and shake or tilt pan to let egg flow underneath. When egg no longer flows freely, turn omelet over and brown lightly on the other side. Slide omelet onto a warm serving plate. Cut into 6 to 8 wedges.

② Place a pan over high heat until hot. Add remaining ½ tablespoon oil, swirling to coat sides. Add garlic and ginger; cook, stirring, until fragrant, about 10 seconds. Add tomatoes, water chestnuts, peas, and sauce; bring to a boil. Add cornstarch solution and cook, stirring, until sauce boils and thickens. Pour over omelet and serve.

Makes 4 servings.

Yin, Yang, and Yolk

To the Chinese, the egg is an important symbol, not only of the beginning of life but also of yin (the white) and yang (the yolk) held in a circle (the shell, representing creation). Yin and yang create a balance of wisdom, truth, purity, propriety, and kindness, making the egg the "food of five virtues."

Marble Eggs

Usually these eggs are quartered and served as part of a cold appetizer selection, but they make great picnic fare, too. First, the eggs are hard-cooked. Then the shells are lightly cracked, so, when the eggs simmer again in a tea-soy mixture, they are marbled with fine dark lines.

8–10 *eggs*

Seasonings

- 2 *green onions, crushed*
- 4 *slices ginger, each the size of a quarter, lightly crushed*
- ¼ *cup regular soy sauce*
- ¼ *cup dark soy sauce*
- 3 *tablespoons oolong or lychee tea leaves*
- 2½ *tablespoons packed dark brown sugar*
- 1 *teaspoon Sichuan peppercorns*
- ¼ *teaspoon Chinese five-spice*
- 2 *whole star anise*
- 1 *cinnamon stick*

About 4 cups water

Shredded lettuce

Cooking

① Place eggs in a large pan, cover with cold water, and bring to a simmer. Simmer for 15 minutes. Drain; rinse eggs with cold water until cool enough to handle.

② Gently crack shells of eggs with the back of a spoon to make a network of hairline cracks all over the shells; do not remove shells.

③ Return eggs to pan. Add seasonings and enough water to cover eggs. Heat to simmering; simmer, covered, over low heat for 1 hour. Let cool, then refrigerate eggs in the liquid for at least 8 hours or up to 2 days.

④ To serve, shell eggs; leave whole or cut into quarters. Serve on a bed of lettuce.

Makes 8 to 10 servings.

Eggs Any Style

In China, eggs go way beyond hard-boiled. "Thousand-year-old eggs" (really only about 100 days old) are coated with a mixture of clay, lime, salt, tea, and bits of straw, which cures and "cooks" the egg, turning it into a dark green gelatinous delicacy that's an acquired taste for most Westerners. Marble eggs, sold by street vendors and eaten as between-act snacks at the Chinese opera, are first boiled, then steeped in a spicy tea mixture, giving them a beautiful marbled appearance. Scarlet eggs are dyed bright red and used as birth announcements—a basket of 8 or 10 eggs means it's a girl; 9 or 11 means it's a boy.

CHAPTER 5

Rice, Noodles, and Breads

Fragrant Lentil Rice

Rice is the basic staple of Asian diets, but in Malaysia how it is cooked is anything but basic. The infinitely varied *nasi* (the word for cooked rice) dishes are perfumed with spices, simmered with coconut milk and nuts, or combined with legumes and vegetables, as in this tasty dish. Serve it as the centerpiece of a meatless meal (lentils and rice make a complete protein).

- 1/3 *cup lentils*
- 1 *cup long-grain rice*
- 2 *tablespoons cooking oil*
- 2 *teaspoons minced ginger*
- 1 *walnut-sized shallot, chopped*
- 1 *green onion, sliced*
- 2 1/4 *cups water*
- 1/2 *carrot, cut into 1/4-inch cubes*
- 8 *green beans, cut into 1/4-inch pieces*
- 1/2 *teaspoon salt*

Getting Ready

① Soak lentils in warm water to cover for 30 minutes; drain. Wash and drain rice.

Cooking

① Place a 2-quart pan over medium heat until hot. Add oil, swirling to coat sides. Add ginger, shallot, and green onion. Cook, stirring, for 2 minutes.

② Add lentils and rice; mix well. Add water and bring to a boil. Cook, uncovered, until craterlike holes appear on the rice, 8 to 10 minutes.

③ Reduce heat to low. Add carrot and green beans; cover and continue cooking until liquid is absorbed and rice is tender, about 15 minutes.

④ Add salt and mix well.

Makes 4 to 6 servings.

Rice for the Rushed

If you don't own an electric rice cooker, it's a modest investment that will be quickly repaid in convenience. It frees up space on the stove and frees up your brain to worry about more important things. A 3- to 5-cup rice cooker is a good size for 1 to 4 people. Most rice cookers now have a "warmer" setting that keeps the rice hot once it's cooked. Microwave tip: Make extra rice and freeze it in heavy freezer bags. On busy nights, just zap and eat! (Before reheating, vent the bag by opening it slightly.)

Mushroom Tea Rice

The flavors of tea and rice are often combined in Chinese cooking, especially in Shanghai. This recipe is based on the Shanghainese method of cooking rice and vegetables in the same pot. For a fancier presentation, spoon cooked rice into custard cups, unmold onto serving plates, and top with chopped toasted walnuts.

- 3 *dried black mushrooms*
- 1 *cup boiling water*
- 3 *tablespoons oolong or Japanese green tea leaves*

Sauce

- 2 *tablespoons oyster-flavored sauce*
- 2 *teaspoons soy sauce*

- 1 *tablespoon cooking oil*
- 2 *teaspoons minced ginger*
- 2 *green onions, cut into 1-inch pieces*
- ⅓ *cup diced carrot*
- 1 *stalk celery, julienned*
- 1 *cup long-grain rice*
- 1½ *cups vegetable broth*
- ¼ *cup frozen peas, thawed*
- ½ *cup coarsely chopped toasted walnuts*

Getting Ready

① Soak mushrooms in warm water to cover until softened, about 20 minutes; drain. Discard stems and thinly slice caps.

② Combine boiling water and tea leaves in a bowl; let steep for 15 minutes. Strain liquid; discard tea leaves.

③ Combine sauce ingredients in a bowl.

Cooking

① Place a 2-quart pan over high heat until hot. Add oil, swirling to coat sides. Add ginger and cook, stirring, until fragrant, about 10 seconds. Add mushrooms, green onions, carrot, and celery; stir-fry for 3 minutes. Add rice and mix well. Add tea and broth; bring to a boil. Reduce heat to medium-high and cook, uncovered, until craterlike holes appear on rice. Reduce heat to low, cover, and continue cooking until liquid is absorbed and rice is tender, 18 to 20 minutes.

② Add peas and sauce; mix well. Place in a serving bowl and garnish with walnuts.

Makes 4 to 6 servings.

Chicken Rice

Ironically, you won't find Hainanese Chicken Rice (recipe on opposite page) on the island of Hainan in the South China Sea. But you'll find plenty of it in Singapore, where everyone calls it "chicken rice." Singaporeans will drive from one end of the island to the other in pursuit of their favorite version.

Hainanese Chicken Rice

This dish is one of the most popular lunch items throughout Singapore and Malaysia.

- 1 *pound chicken thighs*
- 4 *cups water*
- 1 *teaspoon salt*

Seasoned Rice

- 2 *tablespoons cooking oil*
- 1 *walnut-sized shallot, finely chopped*
- 1 *teaspoon minced ginger*
- ½ *teaspoon minced garlic*
- 1½ *cups long-grain rice*
- 2 *cups chicken broth*
- ½ *teaspoon sesame oil*

Ginger Sauce

- ⅓ *cup chopped ginger*
- ¼ *cup chicken broth*
- 1 *teaspoon salt*
- ½ *teaspoon sugar*
- 1 *teaspoon sesame oil*
- 2 *tablespoons cooking oil*

Chili Sauce

- 2 *fresh red jalapeño chilies, seeded*
- ¼ *cup chicken broth*
- 1 *tablespoon minced garlic*
- 2 *tablespoons lime juice*
- ½ *teaspoon sugar*
- ½ *teaspoon salt*
- 2 *tablespoons cooking oil*

Thick sweet soy sauce (kecap manis)

Oyster-flavored sauce

Cooking

① Place chicken, water, and salt in a 2-quart pan and bring to a boil. Reduce heat; cover and simmer until chicken is no longer pink when cut near bone, 30 to 40 minutes. Lift out chicken and let cool; reserve broth.

② Make seasoned rice: Place a 2-quart pan over high heat until hot. Add cooking oil, swirling to coat sides. Add shallot, ginger, and garlic; stir-fry until fragrant, about 20 seconds. Add rice and cook, stirring, for 2 minutes. Add broth and sesame oil. Bring to a boil; cover, reduce heat, and simmer until rice is tender and liquid is absorbed, about 20 minutes.

③ Make ginger sauce: Place all ingredients except cooking oil in a blender and process until smooth. Heat oil in a small pan over medium heat. Add oil, swirling to coat sides. Add purée and cook until slightly thickened, about 2 minutes.

④ Make chili sauce: Place all ingredients except cooking oil in a blender and process until smooth. Heat oil in a small pan over medium heat. Add purée and cook until slightly thickened, about 2 minutes.

⑤ Place rice in a wide, shallow bowl. Top with chicken. Serve with sauces.

Makes 4 servings.

Rice with Chicken and Egg

Every cuisine has its unique one-dish meal, and in Japan it's *donburi:* a healthy helping of steamed white rice with a variety of toppings. This original Japanese fast food is served in small mom-and-pop restaurants all over the country. Donburi may be topped with pork cutlet and egg (*katsudon*), tempura (*tendon*), or my favorite, chicken and egg, whose name, *oyako donburi*, literally means "parent and child."

- 1 *dried shiitake mushroom*
- ¾ *cup Donburi Sauce (recipe follows)*
- 1 *green onion, cut diagonally into ½-inch lengths*
- 3 *ounces boneless, skinless chicken breast, thinly sliced*
- 1 *egg, lightly beaten*
- ½ *cup coarsely chopped spinach or thinly sliced napa cabbage*
- 1½ *cups hot cooked medium-grain rice*
- *Japanese seaweed (nori), cut into thin strips*

Getting Ready

① Soak mushroom in warm water to cover until softened, about 20 minutes; drain. Discard stem and slice cap.

Cooking

① Heat Donburi Sauce in a small frying pan or 1-quart pan over medium heat. Add mushroom, green onion, and chicken. Simmer until chicken is no longer pink, 3 to 4 minutes.

② Pour egg over chicken; sprinkle spinach over egg. Reduce heat to low, cover, and cook until egg is softly set, 2 to 3 minutes.

③ Place rice in a donburi bowl or deep soup bowl. Spoon topping and broth over rice. Garnish with nori.

Makes 1 serving.

Donburi Sauce

- 1 *cup Japanese soup stock (dashi)*
- ¼ *cup sweet cooking rice wine (mirin)*
- ¼ *cup soy sauce*
- 2 *tablespoons sugar*

Cooking

① In a saucepan, combine stock, wine, soy sauce, and sugar. Cook, stirring, over medium heat until sugar dissolves. Use, or refrigerate up to 1 week.

Makes 1½ cups.

Curried Coconut Rice

There are infinite ways to make fried rice—you can use whatever you have handy, and it comes out different every time. This combination of curry and coconut is inspired by Southeast Asian flavors.

- ½ *cup unsweetened shredded coconut*

Sauce

- ⅓ *cup chicken broth*
- 2 *tablespoons soy sauce*
- 1 *tablespoon fish sauce*
- 2½ *teaspoons curry powder*
- 2 *teaspoons sesame oil*
- *Dash of white pepper*

- 2 *tablespoons cooking oil*
- 2 *teaspoons minced ginger*
- 1 *teaspoon minced garlic*
- 1 *fresh red jalapeño chili, seeded and sliced*
- ½ *small onion, diced*
- 4 *cups cold cooked long-grain rice*
- ½ *cup small cooked shrimp*
- ½ *cup frozen peas and carrots, thawed*
- ½ *cup chopped roasted cashews*

Getting Ready

① Spread coconut in a pie pan; toast in a 350°F oven, stirring frequently, until lightly browned, 4 to 5 minutes.

② Combine sauce ingredients in a bowl.

Cooking

① Place a wok over high heat until hot. Add oil, swirling to coat sides. Add ginger, garlic, chili, and onion; cook, stirring, until onion is softened, about 1½ minutes. Reduce heat to medium and stir in rice, separating grains with the back of a spoon.

② Add sauce, shrimp, and peas and carrots. Cook, stirring, until well blended and heated through.

③ Place in a serving bowl and sprinkle with coconut and cashews.

Makes 4 servings.

Rituals of Rice

Have you ever wondered why people throw rice at weddings? That tradition must have started in Southeast Asia, where rice is used to mark nearly all the major milestones and ceremonies. It is scattered on the wedding couple, and used to purify and bless everything from a new house to a new baby. Cooked rice, raw rice, and rice wine or brandy are offered to friends, relatives, and deities to cement relationships and bring good fortune. In Malaysia and elsewhere, superstitions surrounding rice are common, for example, putting too much sauce on your rice can bring on a flood.

Rice Congee

In China, we can eat congee for breakfast, lunch, dinner, and often as a midnight snack. We eat it at home and on the road. It is versatile, filling, and economical. At times, it is also nourishment for the infirm, when their system can't digest solid food. Rice congee is the ultimate comfort food.

1½ *cups uncooked long-grain rice*

4 *slices ginger, each the size of a quarter, lightly crushed*

12 *cups chicken broth*

6 *squid (about 4 oz.), cleaned*

¼ *pound medium raw shrimp*

¼ *pound sea scallops*

Marinade

1 *tablespoon Chinese rice wine or dry sherry*

2 *teaspoons cornstarch*

¼ *teaspoon salt*

⅛ *teaspoon white pepper*

1 *teaspoon sesame oil*

Toppings

Chopped cilantro

Thinly sliced green onion

Deep-fried wonton strips

Deep-fried dried bean thread noodles

Roasted peanuts

Cooking

① In a large pot, combine rice, ginger, and broth; bring to a boil. Reduce heat, cover, and simmer, stirring occasionally, until rice becomes very soft and creamy, about 1½ hours.

② While rice is cooking, prepare seafood. Cut squid tentacles and bodies into 1-inch pieces. Shell and devein shrimp. Cut sea scallops in half horizontally. Combine marinade ingredients in a bowl; add seafood and stir to coat. Let stand for 10 minutes.

③ Remove ginger slices from cooked rice. Add seafood and simmer, stirring occasionally, for 10 minutes. Stir in sesame oil.

④ To serve, ladle congee into individual soup bowls and offer with a variety of toppings.

Makes 6 to 8 servings.

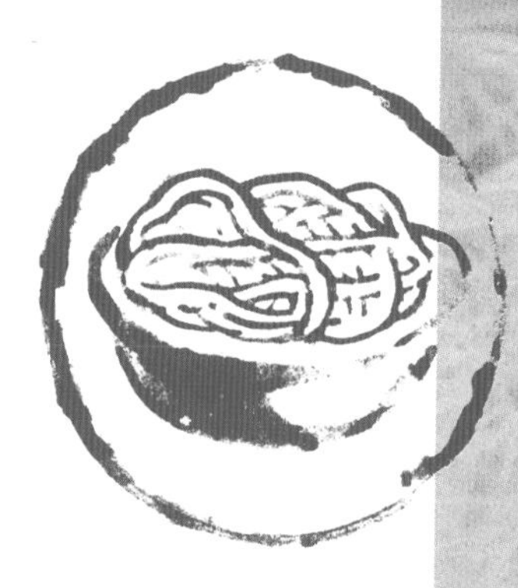

Rice in Lotus Leaves

The Cantonese name for this dish means "glutinous rice chicken." It's a very popular choice on the dim sum menu. I love unwrapping the lotus leaves and catching the first whiff of freshly steamed rice. It is truly a magical moment.

- 4 *dried black mushrooms*
- ¼ *cup dried shrimp*
- 2 *large dried lotus leaves*
- 1 *tablespoon cooking oil*
- 2 *walnut-size shallots*
- 1 *Chinese sausage (2 oz.), cut diagonally into ⅛-inch-thick slices*
- ½ *cup diced Virginia ham*
- ¼ *cup diced celery*
- 1 *teaspoon chopped cilantro*
- 2 *tablespoons soy sauce*
- 1 *tablespoon sesame oil*
- 3 *cups cold cooked medium-grain rice*

Getting Ready

① In separate bowls, soak mushrooms and dried shrimp in warm water until softened, about 20 minutes; drain. Discard mushroom stems and thinly slice caps.

② Heat a large pot of water to simmering. Submerge lotus leaves in water until softened, about 15 minutes; drain.

③ Place a wok over high heat until hot. Add oil, swirling to coat sides. Add shallots, sausage, and dried shrimp; stir-fry for 1 minute. Add mushrooms, ham, celery, and cilantro; stir-fry for 1 minute longer. Stir in soy sauce and sesame oil. Stir in rice, separating grains with the back of a spoon. Remove from heat and let cool.

④ Spread 1 lotus leaf on work surface; cover with second leaf. Place rice mixture in center of leaves; fold edges of leaves over so rice is completely covered.

Cooking

① Prepare a wok for steaming (see page 25). Place lotus leaf packet on a heatproof dish. Steam over high heat for 30 minutes. If cooked ahead of time, reheat in a microwave oven or in a bamboo steamer before serving.

Makes 4 to 6 servings.

Ham It Up

Chinese cooks love to "ham it up" in the kitchen, and I'm no exception (in case you hadn't noticed!). The most famous Chinese ham comes from the south-western province of Yunnan. It's cured and smoked, and can be eaten as is, though it's mostly used in cooked dishes. Yunnan ham is not exported to the West, where Chinese cooks often use Smithfield ham, a deep red, highly flavored salted ham from Virginia, as a substitute. Italian prosciutto will also do the trick.

Tomato Beef Fried Rice

Fried rice provides an easy way to convert bits of leftovers into a quick snack or one-dish meal. There are no strict guidelines for the embellishments, but you must start with cold cooked rice so the grains remain separate when stir-fried. A wok is traditional for cooking fried rice, but I find a nonstick frying pan works even better and is much easier to clean.

Sauce

3 *tablespoons ketchup*
2 *tablespoons soy sauce*
2 *teaspoons sesame oil*
¼ *teaspoon salt*

2 *tablespoons cooking oil*
½ *pound ground beef*
1 *small onion, chopped*
2 *green onions, thinly sliced*
4 *cups cold cooked long-grain rice*
1 *medium tomato, peeled, seeded, and chopped*
½ *cup frozen peas, thawed*
2 *eggs, lightly beaten*

Getting Ready

① Combine sauce ingredients in a small bowl.

Cooking

① Place a wide nonstick frying pan over high heat until hot. Add oil, swirling to coat sides. Add beef and stir-fry for 1 minute. Add onion and green onions; stir-fry for 2 minutes.

② Reduce heat to medium; stir in rice, separating grains with the back of a spoon. Add tomato, peas, and eggs. Cook, stirring constantly, for 1 minute. Add sauce and cook, stirring, until heated through.

Makes 4 to 6 servings.

Rice Ideas

When I was growing up in Guangzhou, rice was served at every meal as a porridge (called *congee* or *jook*) for breakfast, and boiled, steamed, or fried for lunch and dinner. Rice symbolizes nourishment and well-being in China. Spilling a bowl of rice is thought to bring bad luck, and serving poorly cooked rice to a guest is a great offense. When I was a kid, my mom used to tell me that for every grain of rice left behind in my bowl a freckle would appear on the face of my future wife. It worked! My wife doesn't have freckles, and I still never waste a grain of rice.

Eight Precious Noodle Soup

This simple Sichuan-style dish makes a colorful first course or a light meal-in-a-bowl. Humble vegetables become treasures when you julienne them and serve them with egg noodles in a savory broth.

- 2 *teaspoons sesame seeds*
- 12 *ounces fresh Chinese egg noodles*
- 8 *asparagus spears, thinly sliced diagonally*
- ½ *cup julienned bamboo shoots*
- ½ *cup julienned carrot*
- ½ *cup julienned celery*
- ½ *cup julienned green onions*
- ½ *cup omelet strips (recipe below)*
- ¼ *cup julienned Sichuan preserved vegetable*
- 3½ *cups chicken broth*
- 2 *tablespoons oyster-flavored sauce*
- 2 *tablespoons soy sauce*
- 1 *teaspoon chili garlic sauce*

Getting Ready

① Place sesame seeds in a small frying pan over medium heat; cook, shaking pan frequently, until lightly browned, 3 to 4 minutes. Immediately remove from pan to cool.

Cooking

① In a large pot of boiling water, cook noodles according to package directions. Drain, rinse with cold water, and drain again. Place noodles in 4 soup bowls or 1 large serving bowl.

② Parboil asparagus, bamboo shoots, and carrot separately for 2 minutes in a pot of boiling water. Drain each, rinse with cold water, and drain again. Arrange asparagus, bamboo shoots, carrot, celery, green onions, omelet strips, and preserved vegetable decoratively over noodles.

③ In the same pot, combine broth, oyster-flavored sauce, soy sauce, and chili garlic sauce; bring to a boil. Pour over noodles. Garnish with sesame seeds.

Makes 4 servings.

Omelet Strips

Chinese cooks often use lacy ribbons of cooked egg as a garnish. To make them, beat 2 **eggs** with a pinch of **salt**. Heat an 8-inch nonstick frying pan over medium heat. Add ¼ teaspoon **cooking oil**. Pour in ⅓ of eggs and swirl pan to cover entire bottom. Cook until eggs are lightly browned on bottom and set on top, about 1 minute. Turn sheet over and cook 5 seconds; slide out of pan. Repeat to make 2 more egg sheets. When sheets are cool, cut into strips.

Beef and Rice Noodle Soup

Vietnamese cuisine is very popular in North America, and this delicious soup is one of the reasons why. The beef must be sliced paper-thin to cook up quickly in the hot broth. If you can't find very thin slices in the market, slice the meat yourself; just partially freeze it first.

Marinade

- 2 *tablespoons Chinese rice wine or dry sherry*
- 1 *tablespoon soy sauce*
- 2 *teaspoons cornstarch*

- ½ *pound boneless tender beef, sliced paper-thin*
- ½ *pound dried or fresh flat rice noodles, about ¼ inch wide*
- 1 *cup bean sprouts*
- 2 *green onions, julienned*
- 6 *cilantro sprigs*
- 6 *fresh mint leaves*
- 4 *cups chicken broth*
- 3 *thin slices of lime*
- ½ *fresh jalapeño chili, thinly sliced*
- 2 *tablespoons minced lemongrass*
- 1 *tablespoon fish sauce*
- 2 *teaspoons sesame oil*
- 2 *teaspoons lime juice*

Getting Ready

① Combine marinade ingredients in a bowl. Add beef and stir to coat; let stand for 10 minutes.

② If using dried rice noodles, soak in warm water to cover until softened, about 30 minutes; drain. Divide rehydrated or fresh noodles among 3 large soup bowls. Place ⅓ of beef slices, bean sprouts, green onions, cilantro, and mint in each bowl.

Cooking

① Combine broth, lime slices, chili, and lemongrass in a pan and bring to a boil. Reduce heat and simmer for 10 minutes.

② Ladle hot broth over noodles and meat in bowls. Season each serving with fish sauce, sesame oil, and lime juice.

Makes 3 servings.

Cold Mixed Noodles, Sichuan-Style

Sichuan is famous for its cold noodle dishes, which are often tossed in a spicy sesame or peanut dressing like this one. You can use any kind of cooked chicken breast meat in this salad—roasted, poached, pan-fried, or grilled—but it's particularly delicious with Poached Chicken with Pepper Salt (page 293).

- 12 *ounces fresh Chinese egg noodles*
- 2 *teaspoons sesame oil*
- ½ *English cucumber, julienned*
- ½ *red bell pepper, julienned*
- ¼ *pound bean sprouts*
- 2 *cups shredded cooked chicken breast*

Dressing

- ⅓ *cup chicken broth*
- ⅓ *cup sesame seed paste or chunky peanut butter*
- 2 *tablespoons soy sauce*
- 2 *tablespoons rice vinegar*
- 2 *teaspoons sesame oil*
- 2 *teaspoons chili sauce*
- ½ *teaspoon sugar*
- ½ *teaspoon ground toasted Sichuan peppercorns*

Cooking

① In a large pot of boiling water, cook noodles according to package directions; drain, rinse, and drain again. Add sesame oil and toss to coat.

② Add cucumber, bell pepper, and bean sprouts; toss to mix. Place on a serving plate and arrange chicken on top. Cover and refrigerate until ready to serve.

③ Prepare dressing: Combine broth and sesame seed paste in a bowl; whisk until blended. Add remaining dressing ingredients and mix well.

④ Just before serving, pour dressing over noodles and toss.

Makes 4 to 6 servings.

Peanut Gallery

When is a nut not a nut? When it's a peanut! It's actually a legume, like the soybean, the lentil, or the pea (which explains how it got its name in the first place). By Chinese standards, peanuts are a relatively new ingredient, having arrived from the New World a mere 400 years ago. But in that time, they've become China's most important source of cooking oil and, being rich in protein, a dietary staple. They're eaten as a snack, added to stir-fries and sweets, and ground for use in dressings, sauces, and soups.

Glass Noodles with Peanut Sauce

Western traders introduced peanuts to China a few hundred years ago, long before they imported the beer. But seriously, peanuts have been leading an active life in the Chinese kitchen: peanut oil, peanuts in stir-fry dishes, and two of my favorites—peanuts in rice congee or sprinkled over noodles.

Marinade

1 *tablespoon soy sauce*

2 *teaspoons Chinese rice wine or dry sherry*

2 *boneless, skinless chicken breast halves, thinly sliced*

8 *ounces dried bean thread noodles*

Peanut Sauce

¼ *cup peanut butter*

3 *tablespoons soy sauce*

2 *tablespoons rice vinegar*

1 *tablespoon chicken broth or water*

1 *tablespoon sesame oil*

2 *teaspoons sugar*

2 *teaspoons chili oil*

2 *tablespoons cooking oil*

2 *teaspoons minced ginger*

1 *teaspoon minced garlic*

½ *red onion, thinly sliced*

½ *English cucumber, peeled, seeded, and julienned*

1 *medium carrot, shredded*

½ *cup roasted peanuts, coarsely chopped*

Getting Ready

① Combine marinade ingredients in a bowl. Add chicken and stir to coat. Let stand for 10 minutes.

② Soak bean thread noodles in warm water to cover until softened, about 10 minutes. Drain noodles and cut in half.

③ Combine peanut sauce ingredients in a bowl.

Cooking

① Place a wok over high heat until hot. Add oil, swirling to coat sides. Add ginger and garlic; cook, stirring, until fragrant, about 10 seconds. Add chicken and stir-fry for 2 minutes. Add onion and stir-fry for 1 minute. Add cucumber, carrot, and peanut sauce. Cook, stirring, until sauce thickens slightly.

② Remove pan from heat. Add bean thread noodles and toss to coat evenly. Place on a serving platter and sprinkle with peanuts.

Makes 4 servings.

Spicy Chicken Noodle Soup

Older Singaporeans will tell you about the good old days when the man selling spicy chicken noodle soup—locals call it *soto ayam*—used to come around with his portable stall and wooden clappers. The sound of the clappers was enough to bring people running from their homes.

Spice Paste

- 2 *stalks lemongrass*
- 6 *cloves garlic*
- 5 *walnut-sized shallots*
- 2 *slices ginger, each the size of a quarter, lightly crushed*
- 16 *almonds*
- ¼ *cup water*

- 2 *chicken legs and thighs*
- 6 *cups water*
- 2 *tablespoons cooking oil*
- 2 *teaspoons ground coriander*
- 1 *teaspoon galangal powder (optional)*
- 1 *teaspoon turmeric powder*
- 1 *teaspoon chili garlic sauce*
- 3 *tablespoons soy sauce*
- 12 *ounces fresh Chinese egg noodles*
- ½ *pound bean sprouts*
- 4 *hard-cooked eggs, shelled and halved*
- *Deep-fried shallots (see page 51)*
- *Cilantro sprigs*
- *Sliced fresh red or green jalapeño chili*

Getting Ready

① Thinly slice bottom 6 inches of lemongrass. Place in a blender with remaining spice paste ingredients and process until smooth.

Cooking

① Place chicken and water in a large pan; bring to a boil. Reduce heat, cover, and simmer for 30 minutes.

② Place a wok over medium-low heat until hot. Add oil, swirling to coat sides. Add spice paste and cook, stirring, until fragrant, 6 to 8 minutes. Add coriander, galangal, turmeric, and chili garlic sauce; cook for 1 minute.

③ Add spice paste to chicken; simmer until chicken is no longer pink near the bone, about 20 minutes longer. Lift out chicken. When it is cool enough to handle, remove and discard skin and bones; shred meat.

④ Pour broth through a strainer; discard solids and return broth to the pan. Skim fat from broth and add soy sauce; heat to simmering.

⑤ In a large pot of boiling water, cook noodles according to package directions; drain, rinse, and drain again. Divide noodles, chicken, and bean sprouts among 4 individual bowls. Pour broth over noodles. Garnish with eggs, shallots, cilantro, and chili.

Makes 4 servings.

Seafood and Garlic Chive Lo Mein

This is my homage to the noodle shops of Hong Kong. You can also serve the stir-fried seafood over a crispy noodle pancake (recipe below).

16 *ounces fresh Chinese egg noodles*
2 *teaspoons sesame oil*
6 *squid (about 4 oz.), cleaned*
¾ *pound medium raw shrimp, shelled and deveined*
1 *tablespoon cornstarch*
½ *teaspoon salt*

Sauce

⅔ *cup chicken broth*
1 *tablespoon soy sauce*
1 *tablespoon oyster-flavored sauce*
1 *teaspoon sesame oil*

4 *dried black mushrooms*
1 *tablespoon cooking oil*
1 *tablespoon minced ginger*
¼ *pound yellow garlic chives, cut into 2-inch lengths*
4 *green onions, cut into 2-inch lengths*

Getting Ready

① In a large pot of boiling water, cook noodles according to package directions; drain, rinse, and drain again. Add sesame oil and toss to coat.

② Cut off squid tentacles. Cut squid bodies in half lengthwise; with a knife score the inside diagonally several times in a crosshatch pattern. Combine squid tentacles and bodies, shrimp, cornstarch, and salt in a bowl. Stir to coat; let stand for 10 minutes. Combine sauce ingredients in bowl.

③ Soak dried mushrooms in warm water to cover until softened, about 20 minutes; drain. Discard stems and thinly slice caps.

Cooking

① Place a wok over medium-high heat until hot. Add oil, swirling to coat sides. Add mushrooms, ginger, garlic chives, and green onions; stir-fry for 2 minutes. Add shrimp and squid; stir-fry for 2 minutes.

② Add sauce, stirring, until it boils and thickens. Toss in noodles and mix well.

Makes 4 to 6 servings.

Baked Noodle Pancake

Here's a simple way to make noodle pancake in the oven. Cook 16 ounces fresh Chinese egg noodles according to package directions; drain, rinse with cold water, and drain again. Place two 12-inch pizza pans in a 500°F oven. When pans are very hot, brush 1 tablespoon cooking oil evenly onto each pan. Spread noodles evenly in pans and brush top of each noodle pancake with 1 teaspoon cooking oil. Bake until golden brown on top and bottom, 20 to 25 minutes.

Dan Dan Noodles

This is perhaps the most famous of Sichuan's street foods, and there are many variations on the basic formula of egg noodles with a spicy, creamy sesame sauce. My version includes minced meat and a last-minute sprinkling of chopped Sichuan preserved vegetable.

Marinade

- 2 *tablespoons Chinese rice wine or dry sherry*
- 2 *tablespoons soy sauce*
- 2 *teaspoons cornstarch*

- ½ *pound minced chicken, pork, or beef*

Sauce

- ½ *cup sesame seed paste*
- 3 *tablespoons chicken broth*
- 2 *tablespoons oyster-flavored sauce*
- 1 *tablespoon soy sauce*
- 1 *tablespoon rice vinegar*
- 2 *teaspoons chili garlic sauce*

- 12 *ounces fresh Chinese egg noodles*
- 1 *tablespoon cooking oil*
- *Chopped Sichuan preserved vegetable*

Getting Ready

① Combine marinade ingredients in a bowl. Add meat and mix well. Let stand for 10 minutes.

② Combine sauce ingredients in a bowl.

Cooking

① In a large pot of boiling water, cook noodles according to package directions; drain, rinse with cold water, and drain again. Place noodles in a large serving bowl.

② Place a wok over high heat until hot. Add oil, swirling to coat sides. Add meat and stir-fry until browned and crumbly, about 2 minutes. Add sauce and cook until it is heated through.

③ Pour sauce over noodles and garnish with preserved vegetable.

Makes 4 servings.

Dan Dan Derivations

The origin of *dan dan* noodles has passed into legend. Some say it all began with a street vendor in Sichuan who carried his entire kitchen on his back, using a contraption called a *dan*. Others claim that the name *dan dan* imitates the sound of the noodle vendors, who announce their arrival by walking up and down the street clapping their hands. As for me, I'm content to simply say that *dan dan* means delicious, and leave it at that!

Command Performances

Making the Most of Leftovers

Poor leftovers. They have always gotten a bad rap. As in"It's nothing special, we're just having leftovers." Let's give them a new name. How about "extended meal opportunities"? Okay, maybe not. But you get what I mean. Whatever you call them, with a little extra attention, leftovers can be more than just the stuff that piles up in your refrigerator.

In China, wasting food is unheard of, and leftovers are a treasured part of the larder. That's how it was in our house. My mom doesn't just use up leftovers, she loves them and even creates them on purpose! Example: when she roasts chicken, she roasts two. It's the same amount of work, and we wind up with cold chicken to use for days in soup, noodle dishes, stir-fries, sandwiches, and more.

The same goes for other foods. When you buy meat in larger quantities, the price goes down. So whether you cook just for yourself or a whole bunch of people, buy more than a meal's worth, and use what's left to give you a head start on the next meal.

Store leftovers in glass or plastic containers, plastic wrap, or resealable plastic bags. Add a piece of tape on which you have written the date you stored the food. That way, you won't have to resort to carbon-dating mysterious "fridge fossils."

Soups, noodle dishes, stir-fries, salads, omelets, fried rice, sandwiches, tortilla wraps, and casseroles are all great ways to use up leftover food.

Let's imagine we've just opened your refrigerator. Here are some creative uses for some of the gems that might be waiting inside.

Leftover Chinese food. Reheat stir-fried and steamed food in a wok, steamer, saucepan, or microwave oven (transfer food from cardboard cartons into microwave-safe dishes and cover loosely with plastic wrap). Reheat crispy fried foods in a 300°F oven. If you have small amounts of food, use them to make fried rice. Or make a flat Chinese omelet: Chop the leftover food and combine it with beaten eggs, green onions, bean sprouts, and a sprinkling of salt, pepper, and sesame oil. Heat cooking oil in a nonstick skillet and add egg mixture. When bottom browns, invert omelet onto plate, then slide back into pan to brown second side; drizzle with a few drops of soy sauce and top with cilantro.

Cooked rice. Use to make fried rice (page 170), or divide into single servings and freeze in airtight plastic bags that can be reheated in the microwave as the base for a quick one-dish meal.

Fresh vegetables. Toss into hot broth along with noodles to make a speedy soup.

Steak. I usually buy more than I need and freeze the unused portion. Steak that is partially frozen is much easier to slice thinly across the grain for use in stir-fries and other dishes.

Cooked noodles. Rinse unused cooked noodles in cold water to keep them from sticking, then drain and sprinkle with a few drops of sesame oil. To make a noodle pancake, add beaten egg, green onion, and a little salt. Brown in a small amount of oil in a nonstick frying pan, inverting pancake halfway through cooking to brown both sides. Now you have a sensational, golden brown noodle pancake, crisp on the outside, moist and tender inside.

Wonton wrappers, egg roll skins, potsticker rounds, or fresh noodles. These can be turned into crispy low-fat snacks. Slice them into strips or wedges; spray a baking sheet with nonstick spray and arrange strips in a single layer on sheet. Spray strips with nonstick spray and sprinkle with sesame seeds or Parmesan cheese. Bake in a 350°F oven until golden, 5 to 6 minutes. Another option: Deep-fry the strips until they're golden brown and serve like croutons with salad.

Tofu. Dice and add to soup or chili. Crumble and add to meat loaf, hamburgers, or burrito fillings. Purée in a blender or food processor and add to creamy dips. Dice and season with soy sauce, chili oil, chopped green onion, and dried shrimp for a refreshing warm-weather salad. You can even purée tofu to make a smoothie or low-fat "ice cream."

Cilantro. Wash and dry in a lettuce spinner, then store in a plastic bag with as little air as possible (this is not one of those herbs you should store stems-down in a glass of water). Use to make pesto with pine nuts or walnuts, chili oil, garlic, and a dash of white vinegar.

Tortillas or leftover mu shu pancakes. Make an Asian quesadilla: Spread tortilla with a small amount of hoisin sauce, then sprinkle with green onions, mozzarella cheese, and bits of cooked chicken, duck, shrimp, or pork. Top with second tortilla, and brown both sides of the quesadilla in a skillet in a small amount of oil.

Chinese sauces and condiments. Most of these will keep for a long time in the refrigerator. Just be sure to transfer canned sauces to glass jars and label them with the contents and date.

So don't look at that crowded fridge as another cleaning chore. Think of it as a culinary treasure chest. I wish you happy eating and lots of fun with your leftovers . . . I mean "extended meal opportunities"!

Noodle Cake with Spicy Meat Sauce

This elegant appetizer or great party dish will impress all your guests. It's crispy and crunchy on the outside, moist and delicious inside, and to top it all, has a sauce that can kick-start any party. Who says noodles have to be served in a bowl?

Marinade

- 2 *tablespoons oyster-flavored sauce*
- 1 *tablespoon Chinese rice wine or dry sherry*
- 1 *teaspoon cornstarch*

- ½ *pound ground pork or ground beef*

Spicy Sauce

- ⅓ *cup chicken broth*
- 2 *tablespoons oyster-flavored sauce*
- 1 *tablespoon soy sauce*
- 2 *teaspoons chili garlic sauce*
- 2 *teaspoons sesame oil*

- 8 *ounces fresh Chinese egg noodles*
- 3 *tablespoons cooking oil*
- 2 *teaspoons minced garlic*
- 1 *Chinese sausage (2 oz.), chopped*
- ½ *cup chopped celery*
- ¼ *cup chopped onion*
- 2 *green onions, chopped*
- 2 *teaspoons cornstarch dissolved in 1 tablespoon water*

Getting Ready

① Combine marinade ingredients in a bowl. Add ground meat and mix well. Let stand for 10 minutes.

② Combine spicy sauce ingredients in another bowl.

Cooking

① In a large pot of boiling water, cook noodles according to package directions; drain, rinse with cold water, and drain again.

② Place a 10- to 12-inch nonstick frying pan over medium-high heat until hot. Add 1 tablespoon oil, swirling to coat sides. Spread noodles in pan and press lightly to make a firm cake. Cook until bottom is golden brown, about 5 minutes. Turn pancake over, add 1 more tablespoon oil around edges of pan, and cook until the other side is golden brown, 3 to 4 minutes longer.

③ Place a wok over high heat until hot. Add remaining 1 tablespoon oil, swirling to coat sides. Add garlic and Chinese sausage; stir-fry for 1 minute. Add ground meat and stir-fry until browned and crumbly, about 2 minutes. Add celery, onion, and green onions; cook for 1 minute. Add sauce and cornstarch solution and cook, stirring, until sauce boils and thickens.

④ Place noodle cake on a serving dish. Cut into wedges or serve whole, topped with spicy meat sauce.

Makes 4 to 6 servings.

Shanghai Chow Mein

There are noodles and there are noodles. The Shanghai kind are slightly thicker than regular Chinese egg noodles. Their fuller, more robust texture definitely comes through in *chow mein*, or pan-fried noodles.

Marinade

1 *tablespoon soy sauce*

2 *teaspoons cornstarch*

2 *boneless, skinless chicken breast halves, thinly sliced*

Sauce

3 *tablespoons soy sauce*

1 *tablespoon Chinese rice wine or dry sherry*

2 *tablespoons sweet bean sauce*

2 *tablespoons black vinegar or balsamic vinegar*

4 *teaspoons sesame oil*

16 *ounces fresh Shanghai-style noodles or Chinese egg noodles*

2 *tablespoons cooking oil*

1 *teaspoon minced garlic*

1 *leek (1-in. diameter), white part only, julienned*

1 *red bell pepper, julienned*

Getting Ready

① Combine marinade ingredients in a bowl. Add chicken and stir to coat. Let stand for 10 minutes.

② Combine sauce ingredients in a bowl.

Cooking

① In a large pot of boiling water, cook noodles according to package directions; drain, rinse with cold water, and drain again.

② Place a wok over high heat until hot. Add oil, swirling to coat sides. Add garlic and cook, stirring, until fragrant, about 10 seconds. Add chicken and stir-fry for 2 minutes. Add leek and bell pepper and stir-fry for 2 minutes. Add sauce and noodles. Gently toss until heated through.

Makes 6 servings.

Noodles at the Ready

Noodles are among the best emergency resources to have on hand in your kitchen. When you're out of ideas, out of time, or just plain out of food, it doesn't take much to turn fresh or dried noodles into a satisfying, nutritious meal. You can stir-fry them with a little meat or cut-up vegetables and a prepared sauce. Or add them to broth, along with a bit of something green, like spinach, bok choy, or peas. Throw in a few flavor accents—a drizzle of oyster sauce, soy sauce, or sesame oil; a dash of white pepper; or a splash of white vinegar—and you've made something from nothing. Now that's using your noodle!

Thai-Style Rice Noodles

Whenever I think of Thai cuisine, my mouth begins to water. Maybe it is the symphony of spices even in a simple stir-fry. The Thai name for this dish is *pad Thai*; I call it noodle nirvana.

8 *ounces dried or fresh flat rice noodles, about ¼ inch wide*

Sauce

⅓ *cup chicken broth*

2 *tablespoons fish sauce*

2 *tablespoons sweet chili sauce*

1 *tablespoon sugar*

2 *tablespoons cooking oil*

2 *teaspoons minced garlic*

1 *fresh red jalapeño chili, seeded and sliced*

¼ *pound ground pork or beef*

¼ *pound medium raw shrimp, shelled and deveined*

2 *eggs, lightly beaten*

1½ *cups bean sprouts*

1 *lime, cut into wedges*

2 *green onions, thinly sliced*

2 *tablespoons chopped cilantro*

Getting Ready

① If using dried rice noodles, soak in warm water to cover until softened, about 15 minutes; drain.

② Combine sauce ingredients in a bowl.

Cooking

① Place a wok over high heat until hot. Add oil, swirling to coat sides. Add garlic and chili. Cook, stirring, until fragrant, about 10 seconds. Crumble in pork and cook for 2 minutes. Add shrimp and stir-fry until barely pink, about 1 minute. Add sauce and cook for 1 minute. Add noodles; toss to coat evenly with sauce. Add eggs. Stir-fry until eggs are cooked, about 1 minute.

② Place on a serving plate. Garnish with bean sprouts and lime wedges, and sprinkle with onions and cilantro.

Makes 4 servings.

Rice Noodle News

Dried rice noodles come in two widths, thin (sold as "rice vermicelli") and wide (like fettuccine and sometimes called "rice sticks"). To use them in a soup or a stir-fry, soak them in warm water to soften (about 15 minutes). Thin dried rice noodles are deep-fried (without soaking) to create those fluffy nests and garnishes you see in Asian restaurants. Separate the noodles inside a bag (so they don't fly all over), and deep-fry them a handful at a time in hot oil. They will puff up immediately on contact with the oil; it's a dramatic trick, so make sure you have an audience!

Stir-Fried Fresh Rice Noodles

This Singaporean dish is all about contrasts: soft fresh rice noodles, tender seafood and poultry, and crunchy bok choy and bean sprouts.

Sauce

- 1/4 *cup chicken broth*
- 2 *tablespoons regular soy sauce*
- 1 *tablespoon dark soy sauce*
- 1 *teaspoon chili garlic sauce*
- 1 *teaspoon sesame oil*
- 1/4 *teaspoon white pepper*

- 1/3 *pound medium raw shrimp; or thinly sliced boneless, skinless chicken*
- 1/3 *pound squid, cleaned*
- 3 *baby bok choy*
- 2 *tablespoons cooking oil*
- 2 *teaspoons minced garlic*
- 1 *pound fresh rice noodles, about 1/4 inch wide*
- 1 *cup bean sprouts*
- 1 *egg, lightly beaten*
- 1/2 *lime, cut into wedges*

Getting Ready

① Combine sauce ingredients in a small bowl.

② Shell and devein shrimp; cut in half lengthwise. Cut squid crosswise into 1/4-inch slices to make rings; leave tentacles whole. Quarter bok choy lengthwise, then slice crosswise into 1-inch pieces.

Cooking

① Heat a wok over high heat until hot. Add oil, swirling to coat sides. Add garlic and cook, stirring, until fragrant, about 10 seconds. Add shrimp and squid; cook, stirring, for 1 minute. Add bok choy and cook, stirring, for 30 seconds.

② Add sauce; cook for 30 seconds. Add noodles and bean sprouts; stir-fry for 1 minute. Stir in egg and cook until set, about 1 minute.

③ Place on a serving plate and garnish with lime wedges.

Make 4 servings.

Fresh Rice Noodles

These noodles, made of water and rice flour, fry up crispy around the edges and soak up sauces like no other pasta. You can find them in the refrigerated section of Asian markets, where they're sold as folded sheets (left whole so you can roll a filling around them or cut them into whatever width noodles you need) or as precut ribbons or spaghetti-thin strands. It's best to use fresh rice noodles the day you buy them. With prolonged refrigeration, they become stiff; rinse them gently in warm water to soften them up.

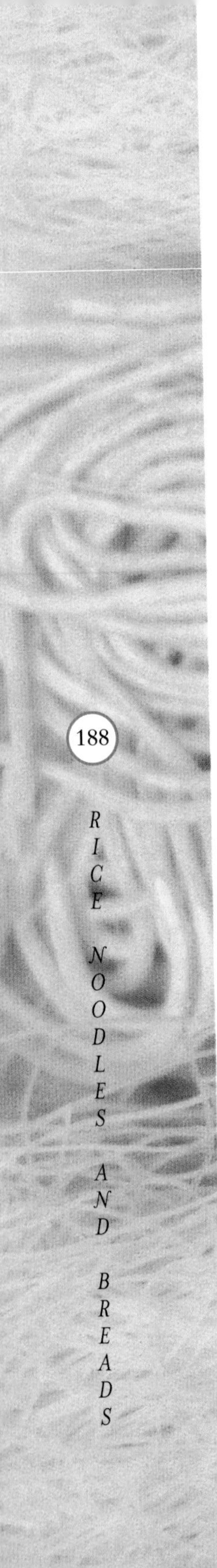

Baked Pork Buns

These could be cousins to Steamed Pork Buns (facing page).

Dough

- 4 *tablespoons sugar*
- ½ *cup warm milk (110°F)*
- ⅓ *cup warm water (110°F)*
- 2 *teaspoons active dry yeast*
- *About 2½ cups flour*
- ½ *teaspoon salt*

Filling

- 8 *dried black mushrooms*
- 2 *tablespoons cooking oil*
- ½ *cup minced green onions*
- 2 *teaspoons minced garlic*
- ½ *cup water*
- 4 *teaspoons hoisin sauce*
- 4 *teaspoons oyster-flavored sauce*
- 1 *tablespoon sugar*
- 2 *teaspoons cornstarch dissolved in 2 tablespoons water*
- 1½ *cups chopped Chinese Barbecued Pork (see page 85)*

- 1 *egg yolk, lightly beaten*

Getting Ready

① Dissolve 2 tablespoons of the sugar in milk and water. Sprinkle in yeast; let stand in a warm place until bubbly, about 10 minutes. Gradually mix in remaining 2 tablespoons sugar, 2 cups flour, and salt. Add more flour as needed until dough is no longer sticky.

② Place dough on a lightly floured board and knead until smooth and elastic, 6 to 8 minutes. Place in an oiled bowl, cover, and let rise in a warm place until doubled in bulk, about 1 hour.

③ Meanwhile prepare filling: Soak mushrooms in warm water to cover until softened, about 20 minutes; drain. Discard stems and coarsely chop caps.

④ Heat a wok over high heat. Add oil, swirling to coat sides. Add green onions, garlic, and mushrooms; stir-fry for 1 minute. Stir in water, hoisin sauce, oyster sauce, and sugar. Add cornstarch solution and stir until sauce boils and thickens. Stir in pork. Cool.

Cooking

① Punch down dough, then roll into a cylinder. Cut cylinder into 12 equal pieces. Roll each into a ball; cover.

② Flatten each ball and roll into a circle 4 to 6 inches in diameter. Place 1 heaping tablespoon filling in center. Gather edges of circle over filling; twist and pinch edges together to seal. Place buns, seam side down, 2 inches apart on an oiled baking sheet. Cover and let rise in a warm place until puffy and light. Brush tops with egg yolk.

③ Preheat oven to 350°F. Bake buns until golden brown, 18 to 20 minutes.

Makes 12.

Mandarin Pancakes

My early exposure to Mandarin cuisine was through a few "northern" restaurants in southern China. I was fascinated by their bread and pancakes, and the variety of noodle dishes. Since then, I've visited northern China many times, but strangely enough, the aroma of Mandarin pancakes still reminds me of my hometown.

- 2 *cups flour*
- ¾ *cup boiling water*
- 2 *tablespoons sesame oil*

Getting Ready

① Place flour in a bowl. Add boiling water, stirring with chopsticks or a fork until dough is evenly moistened. On a lightly floured board, knead dough until smooth and satiny, about 5 minutes. Cover and let rest for 30 minutes.

② On a lightly floured board, roll dough into a cylinder; cut into 16 equal pieces. Roll each piece into a ball, then flatten slightly into a pancake. Brush top of each pancake with a light coating of sesame oil.

③ Place 1 pancake on top of a second pancake, oiled sides together. With a rolling pin, roll to make a circle 6 inches in diameter. Stack and roll remaining pairs of pancakes the same way. Cover with a damp cloth to prevent drying.

Cooking

① Place a nonstick frying pan over low heat until hot. Add 1 pair of pancakes and cook, turning once, until lightly browned and bubbles appear on the surface, about 2 minutes on each side. Remove from pan and separate into 2 pancakes while still hot. Stack cooked pancakes on a plate while cooking remaining pairs of pancakes.

② Serve pancakes hot. If making ahead, reheat pancakes in a microwave oven or wrap in a clean dish towel and steam in a bamboo steamer for 5 minutes.

Makes 16.

Steamed Pork Buns

A bamboo steamer is ideal for steaming: Its woven top allows steam to escape so no moisture condenses under the lid to drip down on the buns. For steaming instructions, see page 25. Follow directions for baked buns (opposite) but place a 3-inch square of waxed paper under each bun before it rises, and don't brush the tops with egg yolk. When buns have risen, steam them over high heat until tops are glazed and smooth, 12 to 15 minutes. Both baked and steamed buns can be made ahead and frozen. Thaw baked buns and serve at room temperature, or heat in a 350°F oven for 10 minutes. Reheat frozen steamed buns by steaming for about 10 minutes or zap them in the microwave until hot, 2 to 3 minutes.

Green Onion Cakes

These unleavened fried breads are thin and flat, crisp outside, moist and chewy inside, and bursting with onion flavor. I like to serve them the traditional way, as street vendors in Beijing do: sliced into wedges and eaten out of hand, plain or with a spicy chili-garlic dipping sauce.

3⅓ *cups flour*
1¼ *cups boiling water*

Dipping Sauce

½ *cup chicken broth*
2 *tablespoons soy sauce*
2 *teaspoons chopped green onion*
1 *teaspoon minced garlic*
1 *teaspoon chili sauce*

¼ *cup solid vegetable shortening or cooking oil*
2 *teaspoons sesame oil*
1 *cup chopped green onions*
2 *teaspoons salt*
½ *teaspoon white pepper*
Cooking oil

Getting Ready

① Place flour in a bowl. Add boiling water, stirring with chopsticks or a fork until dough is evenly moistened. On a lightly floured board, knead dough until smooth and satiny, about 5 minutes. Cover and let rest for 30 minutes.

② Combine dipping sauce ingredients in a bowl.

③ On a lightly floured board, roll dough into a cylinder; cut into 12 equal portions.

④ Make each cake: Roll a portion of dough into an 8-inch circle about ⅛ inch thick; keep remaining dough covered to prevent drying. Brush with a thin film of shortening. Sprinkle with a small portion of sesame oil, green onions, salt, and pepper. Roll dough into a cylinder and coil dough into a round patty; tuck end of dough underneath. Roll again to make an 8-inch circle about ⅛ inch thick.

Cooking

① Place a wide frying pan over medium heat until hot. Add 2 tablespoons cooking oil, swirling to coat sides. Add 1 cake and cook, turning once, until golden brown, 2 to 3 minutes on each side. Remove and drain on paper towels. Repeat with remaining cakes, adding more cooking oil as needed.

② Cut cakes into wedges. Serve hot with dipping sauce.

Makes 12.

Curried Rice Stick Noodles

Dried rice stick noodles, made from long-grain rice flour, need to be softened with a good soaking before cooking. In addition to stir-frying, rice stick noodles are also ideal for soups and clay pot dishes.

6	*dried black mushrooms*
8	*ounces thin dried rice stick noodles*

Sauce

3	*tablespoons chicken broth*
3	*tablespoons soy sauce*
4	*teaspoons curry powder*
2	*teaspoons sesame oil*
¼	*teaspoon turmeric powder*
¼	*teaspoon salt*
⅛	*teaspoon Chinese five-spice*

2½	*tablespoons cooking oil*
2	*eggs, lightly beaten*
1	*walnut-sized shallot, thinly sliced*
½	*small onion, thinly sliced*
2	*green onions, cut into 2-inch pieces*
½	*cup julienned Chinese Barbecued Pork (see page 85)*
½	*cup small cooked shrimp*
1	*cup bean sprouts*

Getting Ready

① In separate bowls, soak mushrooms and noodles in warm water to cover until softened, about 20 minutes for the mushrooms and 15 minutes for the noodles. Drain. Discard mushroom stems and thinly slice caps.

② Combine sauce ingredients in a small bowl.

③ Place a nonstick 8- to 9-inch frying pan over medium heat until hot. Brush with ½ teaspoon cooking oil. Add half of eggs and cook until lightly browned on bottom and set on top, about 1 minute. Turn over and cook for 5 seconds longer; remove from pan. Repeat with ½ teaspoon oil and remaining egg. Cut omelets into ¼-inch-wide strips.

Cooking

① Place a wok over high heat until hot. Add remaining oil, swirling to coat sides. Add shallot, onion, and green onions; stir-fry until onions are limp, about 1 minute. Add mushrooms, pork, shrimp, and bean sprouts. Stir-fry for 1 minute.

② Reduce heat to medium. Stir in noodles and sauce; toss to coat noodles evenly with sauce. Cook until noodles are moist but not wet, about 1 minute.

③ Remove to a serving plate and garnish with omelet strips.

Makes 4 servings.

Sesame Seed Pillows

These flaky breads, a classic street food of northern China, are traditionally stuffed with slices of roasted lamb. Instead of layering butter into the dough as the French do, Chinese bakers use a roux made from oil and flour.

Roux

- ¼ *cup cooking oil*
- ½ *cup flour*

- 2½ *cups flour*
- ¾ *cup boiling water*
- ¼ *cup cold water*
- ¾ *teaspoon salt*
- ¼ *cup sesame seeds*

Getting Ready

① Prepare roux: Place a small, heavy saucepan over medium-high heat until hot. Add oil, swirling to coat sides. Add flour and cook, stirring, until mixture turns golden brown. Let cool.

② Place 2½ cups flour in a bowl. Add boiling water, stirring with chopsticks or a fork. Gradually add cold water, stirring until dough is evenly moistened. On a lightly floured board, knead dough until smooth and satiny, about 5 minutes. Cover and let rest for 30 minutes.

③ On a lightly floured board, roll dough into a 10- by 16-inch rectangle. Spread cooled roux over dough; sprinkle with salt. Fold dough into thirds; pinch edges to seal. Roll dough again into a 10- by 16-inch rectangle; fold and pinch again. Turn dough 90° and repeat rolling, folding, and pinching. Again turn dough 90° and repeat rolling, folding, and pinching. Roll dough into a 10- by 16-inch rectangle one last time. Roll dough into a cylinder, then cut into 16 equal portions.

④ Place sesame seeds on a plate. Make each pillow: Roll each portion of dough into a 2- by 3½-inch rectangle; keep remaining dough covered to prevent drying. Lightly press one side of dough onto sesame seeds. Place, seed side up, on a baking sheet; let rest for at least 5 minutes before baking.

Cooking

① Preheat oven to 375°F. Bake pillows until golden brown, 25 to 35 minutes. Serve hot.

Makes 16.

Seeds of Success

What's black and white and used all over China? Sesame seeds! The white kind are sweet and nutty, while black seeds (which come from a different kind of sesame plant) have a slightly bitter taste. Both are much cheaper when bought in bulk at Asian markets. To bring out their flavor, toast them in a small frying pan over medium heat for a few minutes, then keep them on hand for a quick garnish.

Chinese Pizza

OK. I admit it. I don't eat Chinese food every night. Sometimes I take a break and order a good old-fashioned pizza. But what if pizza were Chinese? Chances are it would taste a lot like this.

Dough

- ¼ *cup warm water (110°F)*
- 1 *package (¼ oz.) active dry yeast*
- ¾ *cup cold water*
- 2 *tablespoons cooking oil*
- 1 *tablespoon honey*
- 3 *cups flour*
- 1 *teaspoon salt*

Sauce

- ⅔ *cup tomato sauce*
- 2 *tablespoons chili garlic sauce*
- 1½ *tablespoons char siu sauce*
- 1½ *tablespoons hoisin sauce*

Toppings

- 2 *Chinese sausages (2 oz. each), thinly sliced diagonally*
- ½ *cup shredded roast duck meat*
- 1 *red bell pepper, julienned*
- 4 *green onions, sliced*
- 8 *white button mushrooms, sliced*
- 1½ *cups shredded mozzarella cheese*

Getting Ready

① In a small bowl, combine warm water and yeast; let stand in a warm place until bubbly, about 10 minutes. Combine cold water, oil, and honey in a measuring cup.

② Place flour and salt in a food processor fitted with a metal blade; process for 10 seconds. With motor running, pour water-honey mixture, then dissolved yeast, down feed tube. Process until dough forms a ball.

③ Place dough on a lightly floured board and knead until smooth and elastic, about 5 minutes. Place in an oiled bowl, cover, and let rise in a warm place until doubled in bulk, about 1 hour.

④ Combine sauce ingredients in a bowl.

Cooking

① Punch down dough, then divide in half. Roll each half to form a 12-inch circle. Transfer each circle to a greased 12-inch pizza pan; pat dough firmly into pan edge.

② To assemble each pizza, spread half of sauce over dough. Arrange half of toppings, except cheese, over sauce; sprinkle cheese on top.

③ Preheat oven to 450°F. Bake pizzas, one at a time, in lower third of oven until cheese melts and bottom of crust is browned, about 15 minutes.

Makes two 12-inch pizzas.

CHAPTER 6

Vegetables

Asparagus with Sweet and Pungent Dressing

When the weather warms up and asparagus is in season, I like to prepare it Sichuan-style: quickly blanched in boiling water until tender-crisp, then chilled and tossed in a sweet mustardy dressing. This dish is easy to prepare ahead of time, but wait until the last minute to add the dressing so the asparagus retains its bright green color.

- 1 *pound asparagus*
- 1 *teaspoon cooking oil*
- ½ *teaspoon salt*
- ⅓ *cup walnuts*

Dressing

- 2 *tablespoons plum sauce*
- 2 *tablespoons rice vinegar*
- 2 *tablespoons soy sauce*
- 1 *tablespoon sesame oil*
- 2 *teaspoons sugar or honey*
- 1 *teaspoon chili oil*
- ½ *teaspoon mustard powder*

Getting Ready

① Trim asparagus; cut spears diagonally into 1½-inch pieces. In a pan, heat 2 inches of water to boiling. Add oil, salt, and asparagus; cook until tender-crisp, 1 to 2 minutes. Drain, rinse with cold water, and drain again. Pat dry with paper towels. Chill until ready to serve.

② Spread walnuts in a pie pan; toast in a 350°F oven, stirring once or twice, until lightly browned, about 10 minutes. Let nuts cool, then coarsely chop.

③ Combine dressing ingredients in a bowl.

Assembly

① Just before serving, pour dressing over asparagus and toss lightly to mix. Place on a serving plate and sprinkle with walnuts.

Makes 4 servings.

Mustard's a Must

Dried mustard gives foods a mysterious, pleasantly hot flavor, especially when you use it in moderation, adding just a pinch to sauces and dressings. In China, prepared mustard is often served as a condiment with appetizers and cold platters. To make your own, pour some powdered Chinese or English mustard into a bowl and whisk in drops of water until you get the consistency you want. If you let it stand for an hour or more, you'll find that the flavor develops and the bitterness disappears.

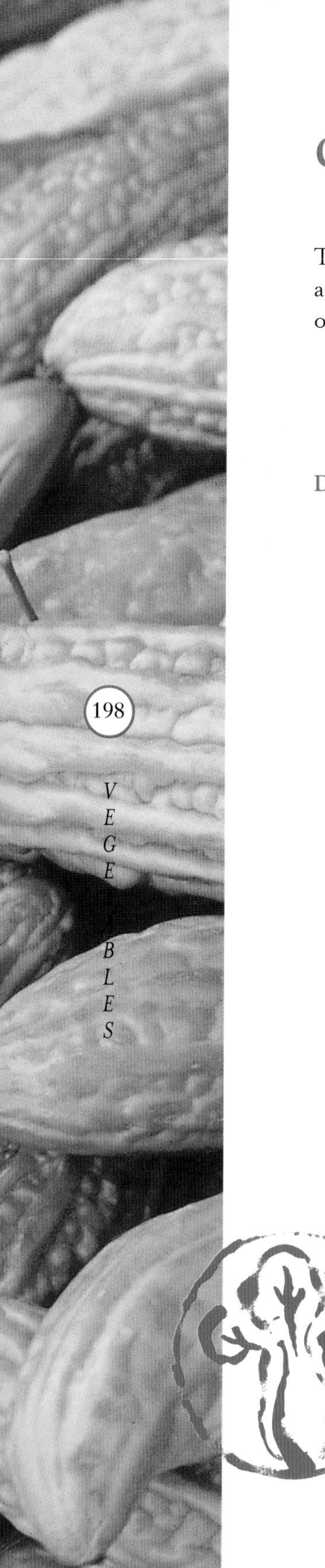

Green Beans with Sesame Dressing

Toasted black and white sesame seeds add a nutty flavor to this simple salad of tender-crisp green beans.

1 *teaspoon black sesame seeds*

¼ *cup white sesame seeds*

Dressing

2 *tablespoons oyster-flavored sauce*

2 *tablespoons sweet rice cooking wine (mirin)*

2 *teaspoons rice vinegar*

1 *tablespoon sugar*

1 *teaspoon cooking oil*

½ *teaspoon salt*

¾ *pound green beans, cut in half*

Getting Ready

① Place black sesame seeds in a small frying pan over medium heat; cook, shaking pan frequently, until seeds smell toasted, 3 to 4 minutes. Immediately remove from pan to cool. Repeat with white sesame seeds but cook until lightly browned, 3 to 4 minutes. Leave black seeds whole; grind white seeds in a spice grinder.

② In a small pan, heat dressing ingredients over medium heat just until sugar dissolves. Remove from heat and whisk in ground seeds until dressing is smoothly blended. Let cool.

Cooking

① In a saucepan, bring 2 inches of water to a boil. Add oil, salt, and beans; cook until tender-crisp, 4 to 5 minutes. Drain, rinse with cold water until cold, and drain again.

② Place beans in a bowl, add dressing, and toss lightly to mix.

③ Place on a serving plate and sprinkle with black sesame seeds.

Makes 4 servings.

Spicy Snap Peas

Fresh snap peas are sweet and crunchy, and since they cook in a hurry, they make a snappy stir-fry. A snazzy one too, cooked in this spicy chili-garlic sauce.

8	*dried black mushrooms*

Sauce

¼	*cup chicken broth*
2	*tablespoons soy sauce*
1	*tablespoon oyster-flavored sauce*
2	*teaspoons sesame oil*
1½	*teaspoons sugar*
1	*teaspoon chili garlic sauce*

1	*tablespoon cooking oil*
6	*small dried red chilies*
2	*slices ginger, each the size of a quarter, finely julienned*
1	*small onion, thinly sliced*
¼	*pound white button mushrooms, thinly sliced*
¼	*cup chicken broth*
½	*pound sugar snap peas, ends removed*
1	*teaspoon cornstarch dissolved in 2 teaspoons water*

Getting Ready

① Soak dried mushrooms in warm water to cover until softened, about 20 minutes; drain. Discard stems and thinly slice caps.

② Combine sauce ingredients in a bowl.

Cooking

① Place a wok over high heat until hot. Add oil, swirling to coat sides. Add chilies and ginger; cook, stirring, until fragrant, about 30 seconds. Add dried mushrooms and onion; stir-fry for 1 minute. Add button mushrooms and broth; cover and cook for 2 minutes. Add peas, cover, and cook until peas are tender-crisp, about 1 minute.

② Add sauce and bring to a boil. Add cornstarch solution and cook, stirring, until sauce boils and thickens.

Makes 4 servings.

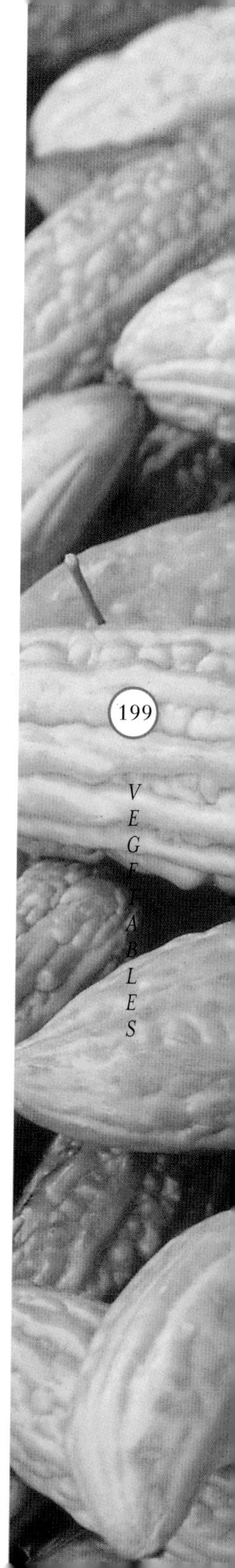

Grandma's Cabbage Rolls

If your grandma were anything like mine, she would be reminding you all the time to eat your vegetables. Thank goodness for her cabbage rolls. These lovely vegetable-stuffed rolls make obeying your elders a true pleasure.

8	*dried black mushrooms*

Sauce

2	*tablespoons rice vinegar*
2	*tablespoons oyster-flavored sauce*
2	*teaspoons sesame oil*
1/8	*teaspoon Chinese five-spice*
1/8	*teaspoon white pepper*

1	*tablespoon cooking oil*
2	*teaspoons minced garlic*
1	*small carrot, julienned*
3	*tablespoons julienned Sichuan preserved vegetable*
1/4	*pound bean sprouts*
1	*teaspoon cornstarch dissolved in 2 teaspoons water*
2	*tablespoons chopped cilantro*
8	*large napa cabbage leaves*

Getting Ready

① Soak mushrooms in warm water to cover until softened, about 20 minutes; drain. Discard stems and thinly slice caps.

② Combine sauce ingredients in a bowl.

Cooking

① Place a wok over high heat until hot. Add oil, swirling to coat sides. Add garlic; cook, stirring, until fragrant, about 10 seconds. Add mushrooms, carrot, and preserved vegetable. Stir-fry for 2 minutes, adding a few drops water if wok appears dry. Add bean sprouts; stir-fry for 1 minute. Add sauce and bring to a boil. Add cornstarch solution and cook, stirring, until sauce boils and thickens. Remove from heat and stir in cilantro. Let filling cool.

② In a large pot of simmering water, parboil cabbage leaves just until limp, 2 to 3 minutes. Drain, rinse with cold water, and drain again. Pat leaves dry with paper towels.

③ Trim leaves to make rectangles about 4 by 8 inches; discard heavy stem ends. If necessary, use a knife to shave any remaining thick white ribs to make leaves easier to roll. Make each roll: Place a leaf on work surface with stem end facing you. Spread 3 tablespoons filling in a band across bottom of leaf. Roll leaf tightly to enclose filling. If making ahead, cover and chill until ready to serve.

④ To serve, trim ends of each roll; cut rolls in half. Stand rolls on a serving plate so filling shows.

Makes 16.

Steamed Garden Vegetables

As a Southerner, I grew up eating and loving simple foods like steamed vegetables and savory egg custards, drizzled with a little oyster-flavored sauce. Here's a typical Cantonese-style recipe that's light and healthful, and works well with almost any kind of steamed seasonal vegetables.

Sauce

- ½ *cup chicken broth*
- 2 *tablespoons oyster-flavored sauce*
- 1 *tablespoon Chinese rice wine or dry sherry*
- ⅛ *teaspoon white pepper*

- 3 *Shanghai baby bok choy, cut in half lengthwise*
- 1 *cup broccoli florets*
- 1 *cup cauliflower florets*

- 2 *teaspoons cornstarch dissolved in 1 tablespoon water*

Getting Ready

① Combine sauce ingredients in a small pan.

② Place bok choy, broccoli, and cauliflower in a heatproof dish.

Cooking

① Prepare a wok for steaming (see page 25). Cover and steam vegetables over high heat until tender-crisp, 5 to 6 minutes.

② Heat sauce to boiling. Add cornstarch solution and cook, stirring, until sauce boils and thickens.

③ Place vegetables on a serving plate and pour sauce on top.

Makes 4 servings.

I ♥ Broccoli

I am on a cruciferous crusade: Save the endangered broccoli stem! So many people cook the florets and toss the stems in the trash. At our house, it's just the opposite. We think of the stems as the vegetable, and the florets as a cute little garnish. Here's the thing: Peeling broccoli stems transforms them from something chewy and fibrous into a tender, tasty delicacy. The easiest way to do this is to make a small cut with a paring knife at the bottom of the stem, about 1/16 inch under the surface of the peel; grab a bit of peel between the knife and your thumb, and pull toward you. A ribbon of peel about ¼ inch wide will pull right off the stem. Repeat until you've removed all the peel. Now you have hearts of broccoli julienned for steaming and stir-frying. Eat your hearts out, floret fans!

Mu Shu Vegetables

Mu shu pork is a popular restaurant dish, but other foods can be cooked and served mu shu–style as well. This version I found in Beijing's Wong Fu Jin Market. If you use spring roll wrappers or Mandarin pancakes, wrap them in a towel and steam them for 5 minutes. Heat flour tortillas in the microwave.

- 4 *dried black mushrooms*
- 6 *dried cloud ears*
- 2 *ounces dried bean thread noodles*
- 1½ *tablespoons cooking oil*
- 2 *eggs, lightly beaten*
- 1 *teaspoon minced garlic*
- 1 *cup thinly sliced cabbage*
- ¼ *cup julienned carrot*
- ½ *cup chicken broth*
- 1 *cup bean sprouts*
- 2 *tablespoons oyster-flavored sauce*
- 2 *teaspoons sugar*
- 2 *teaspoons sesame oil*
- *About 12 spring roll wrappers, Mandarin Pancakes (see page 189), or flour tortillas*
- *Hoisin sauce*
- *Cilantro sprigs*

Getting Ready

① In separate bowls, soak mushrooms and cloud ears in warm water to cover until softened, about 20 minutes; drain. Discard mushroom stems. Thinly slice mushroom caps and cloud ears.

② Soak noodles in warm water to cover until softened, about 5 minutes; drain. Cut noodles into 4-inch lengths.

③ Place a nonstick 8- to 9-inch frying pan over medium heat until hot. Brush with ½ teaspoon oil. Add half of eggs and cook until lightly browned on bottom and set on top, about 1 minute. Turn over and cook for 5 seconds; remove from pan. Repeat with ½ teaspoon oil and remaining egg. Roll omelets into cylinders and cut into ¼-inch-wide strips.

Cooking

① Place a wok over high heat until hot. Add remaining oil, swirling to coat sides. Add garlic and cook, stirring, until fragrant, about 10 seconds. Add mushrooms, cloud ears, cabbage, and carrot; stir-fry for 30 seconds. Add bean thread noodles and broth; cook for 2 minutes.

② Add bean sprouts, omelet strips, oyster-flavored sauce, sugar, and sesame oil; cook until heated through.

③ Place mu shu mixture on a serving plate. Place wrappers and a small bowl of hoisin sauce alongside. To eat, spread a small amount of hoisin sauce on a wrapper. Place about 3 tablespoons of vegetable mixture in center of wrapper and top with a cilantro sprig. Wrap like a burrito and eat out of hand.

Makes 6 servings.

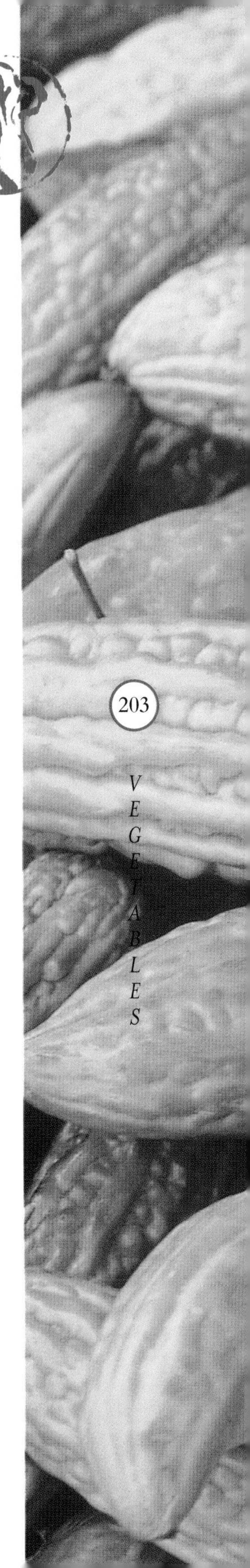

Hakka-Style Eggplant with Mint

Here eggplants are double-cooked using a technique called oil-blanching. First, they're quickly deep-fried so they're crisp on the outside and moist inside. Then they're stir-fried with bell pepper and seasonings and finished with a spicy chili garlic sauce. If you can't find Thai basil, use regular basil.

Sauce

- ¼ *cup chicken broth*
- 2 *tablespoons oyster-flavored sauce*
- ½ *teaspoon chili garlic sauce*
- ½ *teaspoon sesame oil*

- ½ *cup lightly packed mint leaves*
- ¾ *pound Asian eggplants*
- *Cooking oil for deep-frying*
- 6 *cloves garlic, peeled*
- 2 *teaspoons cooking oil*
- 1 *fresh red jalapeño chili, seeded and thinly sliced*
- ½ *small onion, cut into ½-inch cubes*
- 1 *small green bell pepper, cut into 1-inch diamond-shaped pieces*
- ½ *cup lightly packed Thai basil leaves*

Getting Ready

① Combine sauce ingredients in a bowl. Wash mint leaves and dry thoroughly. Roll-cut eggplants.

Cooking

① In a wok or 2-quart pan, heat oil for deep-frying to 375°F. Deep-fry eggplants and garlic until golden brown, about 2 minutes. Lift out with a slotted spoon and drain well on paper towels.

② Deep-fry mint leaves until crisp, about 30 seconds. Remove with a slotted spoon; drain well on paper towels.

③ Place a wok over high heat until hot. Add 2 teaspoons oil, swirling to coat sides. Add chili, onion, and bell pepper; cook, stirring, until fragrant, about 30 seconds. Add eggplants, garlic, basil, and sauce. Reduce heat to medium and cook until eggplants are tender, 5 to 6 minutes.

Makes 4 servings.

A Hakka Feast

Centuries ago, the Hakka people fled the river plains of central China to avoid persecution. In the 17th century, many settled in what is now the New Territories of Hong Kong. On special occasions, they put on a traditional "farmer's bucket" banquet, and recently I got to help. Twenty chefs worked for days preparing chicken, pork, squid, tofu, eel, and vegetable dishes, and over 1,000 people ate and laughed under the stars all night long.

Shop Till You Drop!

The Fresh New World of Asian Ingredients

The other day, my wife called me on the car phone and said, "On your way home, can you pick up a lotus root?" She wasn't joking. Admittedly it was for a recipe we were testing—we don't use that much fresh lotus root in our everyday cooking at home. But the fact remains, there are at least three stores within easy driving distance of our house in Northern California where we can buy it.

My wife's phone call made me think about how much the world of Asian ingredients has changed in North America. When I began writing Chinese cookbooks twenty years ago, the challenge was always finding ways to approximate Asian flavors using Western ingredients: cabbage stood in for bok choy, sherry for Shaoxing rice wine.

I still like to suggest those kinds of substitutions, but nowadays it's getting easier all the time to find great Asian produce and dry goods all over America and all around the world. As more and more Asians pour into North America, Europe, Australia, and New Zealand, and as the Pacific Rim emerges as a major force in the new global economy, Asian foods have entered the mainstream in most of the world's major metropolises.

If you live in an area that has a Chinatown, you're in luck. My advice is to set aside a few hours and prepare yourself for a culinary adventure. You may find that the people working in the stores speak very little English, but don't let that frustrate you. Just dive into the experience and take it all in stride.

For years, I've led walking tours of San Francisco's Chinatown. And I always tell people that it is more than just an exotic neighborhood. It's a cook's paradise—and not just for Asian ingredients. In my opinion, most Chinatown markets offer the freshest produce, fish, meat, and poultry in the whole city—not to mention the best prices—because Chinese shoppers are obsessed with freshness and value.

"Fresh" often means "still alive" (like the seafood swimming in tanks in many Chinese fish markets). And in an era of mass production, transcontinental refrigerator trucks, and week-old fruits and vegetables, much of the produce in these small markets is locally grown, restocked every morning, and sold within hours of being harvested. What's in season is what you get. There's very little produce flown in from elsewhere.

You can also find some great bargains in Chinatown, though I go there more for the quality than for the price. And best of all, if you get hungry while you're shopping, every Chinatown in the world is a snacking opportunity waiting to happen. There's everything from hot delis selling roast pork, chicken, and duck to restaurants, dim sum houses, and bakeries.

Equally remarkable in their own way are a new breed of Pan-Asian supermarkets (99 Ranch in Northern and Southern California is a good example) that are showing up in more and more U.S. cities.

For a first timer, these places can be a little disorienting. Or maybe I should say "dis-Orienting"! You walk into what looks at first glance like an enormous conventional Western supermarket. But then you notice that the music on the P.A. system is alternating between Dixieland band and classic Chinese string orchestra. And on closer inspection, you realize that the shelves are stocked with equal proportions of familiar Western brand names and exotic Asian imports. Canned chicken soup sits comfortably alongside coconut milk. Cartons of farm-fresh eggs are stacked next to boxes of preserved duck eggs. The deli case features specials on both lunch meat and neatly labeled plastic take-out boxes filled with stewed pork ears. Live eels swim in tanks in the fish section, right above the 2-foot-long squid stacked on ice.

These markets make me happy. I love to stand and watch as people of every race poke, prod, and sniff at foods they've never seen before. It feels like the edge of a new frontier. It's fun. It's exciting. It's exactly what I try to achieve in my books and on my show: a sense of curiosity and a lively culinary and cultural exchange. If you're looking for an afternoon of free entertainment and education, this is the best new food show around!

Finally, a word about another heartwarming development in food shopping: the local farmers' market. Of course, these markets are not exactly new. But they're experiencing a wonderful revival, fueled by consumer demand for high-quality, flavorful fresh fruits and vegetables—and, in some states, by government support as well. Like Chinatowns, they're often the places that offer the best and freshest local produce. They can also be great sources for all kinds of exotic and traditional Asian vegetables and herbs.

One piece of advice: Unlike supermarket produce, much of which must be harvested before it is ripe so that it can survive the journey to the store, the produce at local farmers' markets is usually sold at the peak of ripeness. If you let it sit around on the counter, it may not last long. It's best to enjoy it within a day of buying it.

Mixed Vegetable Stir-Fry

I've always been a lover of lotus root—its flavor, texture, and beautiful appearance. Here, I've used it in a bright, fresh vegetable stir-fry with typically Shanghainese flavor accents: wine, soy sauce, and sugar. For a special presentation, try cutting vegetables into fancy shapes.

Sauce

- ½ *cup vegetable broth (see page 99)*
- 1 *tablespoon Chinese rice wine or dry sherry*
- 1 *tablespoon soy sauce*
- 2 *teaspoons sugar*
- 1 *teaspoon sesame oil*

- 1 *tablespoon cooking oil*
- ½ *teaspoon minced garlic*
- ½ *teaspoon minced ginger*
- ½ *cup sliced carrots*
- ½ *cup sliced lotus root*
- ½ *cup sliced jicama*
- ½ *cup sliced zucchini*
- 8 *white button mushrooms*
- 2 *tablespoons water*
- ½ *cup red bell pepper, cut into 1-inch squares*
- 4 *asparagus spears, trimmed and cut diagonally into 1½-inch lengths*
- 2 *teaspoons cornstarch dissolved in 1 tablespoon water*

Getting Ready

① Combine sauce ingredients in a bowl.

Cooking

① Place a wok over high heat until hot. Add oil, swirling to coat sides. Add garlic and ginger; cook, stirring, until fragrant, about 10 seconds. Add carrots, lotus root, jicama, zucchini, and mushrooms; stir-fry for 1 minute.

② Add water, cover, and cook for 3 minutes. Add bell pepper and asparagus; stir-fry for 1 minute.

③ Add sauce and bring to a boil. Add cornstarch solution and cook, stirring, until sauce boils and thickens.

Makes 4 servings.

Land of the Lotus Eaters

The beautiful lotus flowers that grace the surface of many lakes and ponds in China are more than just decorative. The entire lotus plant is also a versatile cooking ingredient. The root, with its lacy pattern of Swiss cheese–like holes, is used in vegetable and meat dishes, or is candied and eaten as a sweet. The seeds are eaten fresh or dried as a snack and are also ground into a paste that's used in desserts and pastry fillings. And the leaves are used to wrap foods for steaming.

Braised Stuffed Shiitake Mushrooms

If you like stuffed mushrooms, wait till you taste them cooked Japanese-style. Shiitakes filled with shrimp and chicken and braised in a sweet *dashi* sauce make a great accompaniment to Grilled Sesame Beef (page 232) or Chicken Teriyaki (page 286).

- 5 *large raw shrimp*
- 2 *ounces ground chicken*
- 2 *teaspoons Japanese rice wine (sake)*
- 2 *teaspoons soy sauce*
- ½ *teaspoon grated ginger*
- ½ *teaspoon sesame oil*
- 6 *large fresh or dried shiitake mushrooms or white button mushrooms, each 2½ inches in diameter*

Braising Sauce

- ⅔ *cup Japanese soup stock (dashi)*
- 3 *tablespoons soy sauce*
- 3 *tablespoons sweet cooking rice wine (mirin)*
- 1 *tablespoon sugar*

Getting Ready

① Shell, devein, and finely chop shrimp.

② Place shrimp in a bowl with chicken, sake, soy sauce, ginger, and sesame oil; mix well.

③ If using fresh shiitake mushrooms, discard stems. If using dried mushrooms, soak in warm water to cover until softened, about 20 minutes; drain. Discard stems.

④ Spread 1 tablespoon of filling inside each mushroom cap.

Cooking

① Combine braising sauce ingredients in an 8-inch frying pan. Place mushrooms, filled side up, in sauce.

② Bring to a boil; reduce heat, cover, and simmer until mushrooms are tender and filling is cooked, about 25 minutes. Remove cover and simmer until sauce is slightly syrupy, about 5 minutes.

③ Lift mushrooms from sauce and place on a serving plate; drizzle remaining sauce over mushrooms.

Makes 6.

Mushrooms, Cut & Dried

When you are served black mushrooms at a Chinese restaurant, you're actually eating reconstituted dried mushrooms, not fresh ones. Like sun-dried tomatoes or raisins, dried black mushrooms have a much more intense, concentrated flavor than their fresh counterparts—a flavor the Chinese prefer. Dried black mushrooms, also known by their Japanese name, shiitake, are one of my favorite "chef's secrets." They keep almost indefinitely, they're easy to rehydrate (see page 30) and they give foods a rich, meaty flavor—the essence of mushroominess!

Four-Color Vegetable Fan

I'm a big fan of vegetables. And this dish is a slightly smaller one. Its charming banquet-style presentation demonstrates a classic Chinese approach: start with a handful of simple vegetables, add a dash of flavor—in this case, curry—and a little imagination, and you end up with a healthful, tasty work of art.

7	*dried black mushrooms*
9	*large asparagus spears*

Sauce

½	*cup vegetable broth (see page 99)*
3	*tablespoons prepared curry sauce, or 1½ tablespoons curry powder*
2	*tablespoons Chinese rice wine or dry sherry*
2	*teaspoons sesame oil*

1	*teaspoon salt*
1	*teaspoon cooking oil*
6	*large white button mushrooms*
8	*ears baby corn*
1	*green onion (bottom 5 in. only)*
2	*teaspoons cornstarch dissolved in 1 tablespoon water*

Getting Ready

① Soak dried mushrooms in warm water to cover until softened, about 20 minutes; drain. Discard stems; leave caps whole. Trim asparagus so spears are the same length as baby corn.

② Combine sauce ingredients.

Cooking

① Bring a pot of water to a boil. Add salt, oil, black and button mushrooms, corn, and asparagus. Cook until asparagus is tender-crisp, 1 to 2 minutes. Add green onion and cook for 10 seconds. Drain, rinse with cold water, and drain again.

② Arrange vegetables so they resemble a fan: Alternate asparagus and baby corn across top half of serving plate. Place black mushrooms at base of fan. Arrange button mushrooms below black mushrooms. Place green onion below mushrooms to form a handle.

③ Heat sauce to boiling. Add cornstarch solution and cook, stirring, until sauce boils and thickens. Pour sauce over vegetables.

Makes 4 servings.

Currying Flavor

Curry came to China by way of India more than a thousand years ago and was gradually adapted to fit Chinese cooking styles and tastes. Today it is used all over southern China as a flavor accent in vegetable and meat dishes as well as noodles and dumplings. Curry is a blend of spices like cumin, cardamom, coriander, chilies, cinnamon, cloves, turmeric (which makes it yellow), and tamarind.

Grilled Vegetables with Miso Glaze

Japanese cooks grill vegetables on an iron griddle called a *teppan*, then finish them with a miso glaze. But you don't need special equipment to make these tasty vegetables. Cook them in a frying pan or grill them on your barbecue, moving them to a cooler spot on the grill when you apply the glaze.

Miso Glaze

- ¼ *cup Japanese soup stock (dashi)*
- 3 *tablespoons sweet cooking rice wine (mirin)*
- 2 *tablespoons sugar*
- 1 *tablespoon soy sauce*
- 2 *tablespoons fermented soybean paste (red miso)*

- 1 *tablespoon cooking oil*
- 1 *tablespoon sesame oil*
- 2 *Asian eggplants, each about 5 inches long*
- 1 *small acorn squash*
- 4 *ears baby corn*
- 4 *baby carrots*
- 2 *fresh shiitake mushrooms*
- 1 *teaspoon sesame seeds*

Getting Ready

① In a small pan, heat dashi, mirin, sugar, and soy sauce over medium heat just until sugar dissolves. Remove from heat and whisk in miso until glaze is smoothly blended.

② Combine cooking oil and sesame oil in a small bowl.

③ Cut eggplants diagonally to make ovals about ¼ inch thick and 3 inches long. Cut squash crosswise into ½-inch-thick slices. Discard mushroom stems, and cut caps in half.

④ Place sesame seeds in a small frying pan over medium heat; cook, shaking pan frequently, until lightly browned, 3 to 4 minutes. Immediately remove from pan to cool.

Cooking

① Heat a griddle or wide frying pan over medium heat. Brush griddle with some of the oil mixture. Place vegetables on griddle and brush with oil. Cook, turning once and brushing again with oil, until vegetables are tender, about 3 minutes on each side.

② Reduce heat to low. Brush half of miso glaze on vegetables and cook for 30 seconds. Turn vegetables, brush with remaining glaze, and cook 30 seconds longer. Place on a serving plate and sprinkle with sesame seeds.

Makes 4 servings.

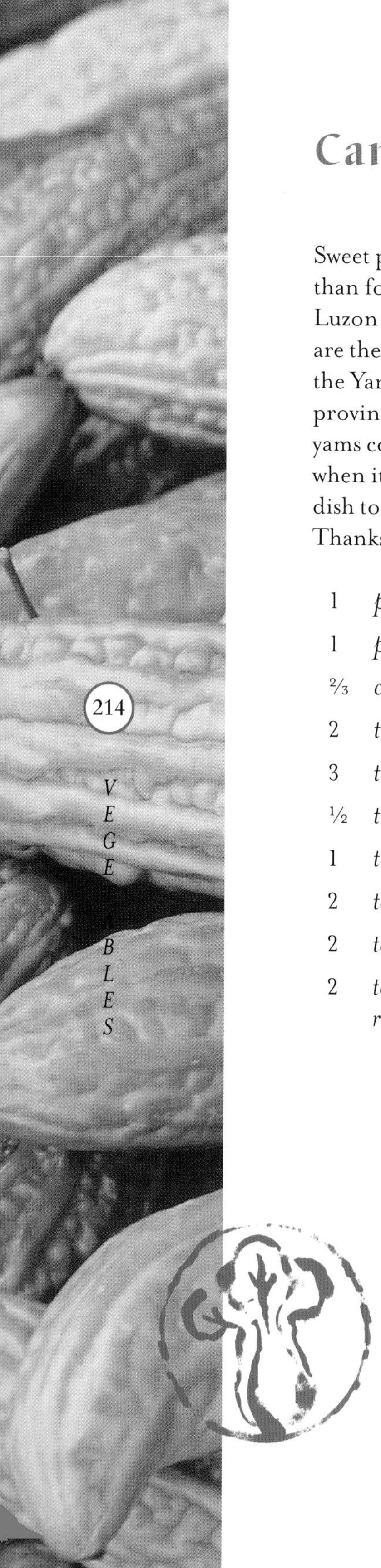

Candied Yams and Sweet Potatoes

Sweet potatoes came to China more than four centuries ago by way of Luzon in the Philippines. Today they are the most important root crop in the Yangtze Valley and Yunnan province. I like sweet potatoes and yams cooked with sugar, especially when it's caramelized. Make this dish to go with turkey for your next Thanksgiving dinner.

1	*pound yams*
1	*pound sweet potatoes*
⅔	*cup sugar*
2	*tablespoons water*
3	*tablespoons butter*
½	*teaspoon salt*
1	*teaspoon grated lemon peel*
2	*tablespoons lemon juice*
2	*tablespoons unsweetened coconut*
2	*tablespoons finely chopped roasted peanuts*

Getting Ready

① In a 3-quart pan, boil yams and sweet potatoes in water, covered, until tender when pierced, 20 to 30 minutes; drain and let cool. Peel and slice crosswise ¼ inch thick.

② Alternating yam and sweet potato, overlap slices slightly in a buttered 1½-quart baking dish. Start from the outer edge and work toward the center.

③ In a small heavy pan, heat sugar and water over medium heat. Shake pan frequently until sugar melts and turns a light caramel color. Remove from heat and stir in butter, salt, lemon peel, and lemon juice. Pour syrup over the slices.

Cooking

① Preheat oven to 425°F. Bake, uncovered, until hot and bubbly, 10 to 15 minutes. Sprinkle coconut and peanuts over the top, and serve.

Makes 8 servings.

CHAPTER 7

Meat

Tangerine Peel Beef

This is a lighter, stir-fry version of the Sichuan restaurant favorite, in which the beef is usually deep-fried.

- 2 *pieces (each about 1½ in. square) dried tangerine peel*

Marinade

- 2 *tablespoons soy sauce*
- 1 *tablespoon cornstarch*

- ¾ *pound flank steak, thinly sliced across the grain*

Sauce

- ⅓ *cup orange juice*
- 2 *tablespoons Chinese rice wine or dry sherry*
- 1 *tablespoon soy sauce*
- ½ *teaspoon chili garlic sauce*
- 2 *teaspoons sugar*

- 2½ *tablespoons cooking oil*
- 6 *small dried red chilies*
- 1 *small onion, cut into 1-inch pieces*
- 1 *stalk celery, cut into ½-inch pieces*
- 1½ *teaspoons cornstarch dissolved in 1 tablespoon water*
- ½ *orange, sliced*

Getting Ready

① Soak tangerine peel in warm water to cover until softened, about 20 minutes; drain. Thinly slice peel.

② Combine marinade ingredients in a bowl. Add beef and stir to coat. Let stand for 10 minutes.

③ Combine sauce ingredients in a bowl.

Cooking

① Place a wok over high heat until hot. Add 2 tablespoons oil, swirling to coat sides. Add chilies and cook, stirring, until fragrant, about 10 seconds. Add beef and stir-fry until no longer pink, 1½ to 2 minutes. Remove meat and chilies from pan.

② Add remaining ½ tablespoon oil, swirling to coat sides. Add tangerine peel, onion, and celery; stir-fry for 1 minute. Return meat and chilies to wok and add sauce; bring to a boil. Add cornstarch solution and cook, stirring, until sauce boils and thickens.

③ Place on a serving plate and garnish with orange slices.

Makes 4 servings.

Homemade Appeal

The dried peels of tangerines and oranges are a flavoring staple in many Chinese dishes. It's easy to make your own at home. Peel the fruit, cut the peel into pieces, and cut or scrape away the white pith from the inside of the peel. Let the pieces sun- or air-dry until they're firm but still flexible, then store them in an airtight jar.

Spicy Hunan Beef

Chefs from Hunan province, in southwestern China, are experts in cooking with chilies. They stir-fry them whole over high heat, thus releasing just enough of their spiciness to make this beef stir-fry a mouth-tingling treat.

Marinade

- 2 *tablespoons soy sauce*
- 1 *tablespoon Chinese rice wine or dry sherry*
- 2 *teaspoons cornstarch*

- ¾ *pound flank steak, thinly sliced across the grain*

Sauce

- 3 *tablespoons Chinese black vinegar or balsamic vinegar*
- 1 *tablespoon soy sauce*
- 1 *tablespoon Chinese rice wine or dry sherry*
- 2 *teaspoons sugar*
- 2 *teaspoons chili garlic sauce*
- 1 *teaspoon sesame oil*

- 2 *cups broccoli florets*
- 2 *tablespoons cooking oil*
- 2 *teaspoons minced garlic*
- 4 *small dried red chilies*
- 1 *teaspoon cornstarch dissolved in 2 teaspoons water*

Getting Ready

① Combine marinade ingredients in a bowl. Add beef and stir to coat. Let stand for 10 minutes.

② Combine sauce ingredients in a bowl.

Cooking

① Place broccoli in a large pot with 1 inch of boiling water. Boil until tender-crisp, 2 to 3 minutes; drain.

② Place a wok over high heat until hot. Add oil, swirling to coat sides. Add garlic and chilies and cook, stirring, until fragrant, about 10 seconds. Add beef and stir-fry until no longer pink, 1½ to 2 minutes.

③ Add broccoli and sauce to wok; bring to a boil. Add cornstarch solution and cook, stirring, until sauce boils and thickens.

Makes 4 servings.

A Cut Above

I've always loved to use flavorful flank steak in beef stir-fries. Cut across the grain in thin slices and quickly cooked, it can be deliciously tender. It used to be one of the most economical cuts, but nowadays the demand for flank steak has increased, and so has the price. Some other beef cuts that work well for stir-fries include top sirloin, strip loin, rib eye, tri-tip, and tenderloin.

Three Ginger Beef

The combination of young ginger, candied ginger, and pickled ginger makes every bite a tasty surprise! If you can't find young ginger, substitute regular fresh ginger, though you may want to reduce the quantity slightly, to taste.

Marinade

- 2 *tablespoons oyster-flavored sauce*
- 2 *teaspoons cornstarch*

- ¾ *pound flank steak, thinly sliced across the grain*

Sauce

- 2 *tablespoons chopped red pickled ginger*
- 1 *tablespoon chopped crystallized ginger*
- ¼ *cup water*
- 1½ *tablespoons plum sauce*
- 1 *tablespoon dark soy sauce*
- 2 *teaspoons sesame oil*
- ½ *teaspoon sugar*

- 2 *tablespoons cooking oil*
- 2 *tablespoons julienned young ginger*
- ½ *cup pineapple chunks*
- 1 *teaspoon cornstarch dissolved in 2 teaspoons water*

Getting Ready

① Combine marinade ingredients in a bowl. Add beef and stir to coat. Let stand for 10 minutes.

② Combine sauce ingredients in a bowl.

Cooking

① Place a wok over high heat until hot. Add oil, swirling to coat sides. Add beef and stir-fry until no longer pink, 1½ to 2 minutes. Add young ginger and stir-fry for 30 seconds.

② Add pineapple and sauce; bring to a boil. Add cornstarch solution and cook, stirring, until sauce boils and thickens.

Makes 4 servings.

Gingerly Yours

Ginger is one of the oldest and most used ingredients in Chinese and Japanese cooking. The Chinese believe it can stimulate the appetite, suppress a cough, improve your memory, and other things that I can't quite remember! It makes foods like meat and fish taste fresher, even when they're a little over the hill. Young ginger has a delicate flavor and a thin, pinkish skin. Crystallized ginger has a strong, sweet-spicy bite. Red pickled ginger is tangy and sweet.

Triple Pepper Steak

Beef lovers, this one's for you: wok-seared slices of steak in a robust brown sauce with colorful bell peppers.

Marinade

- 2 *tablespoons oyster-flavored sauce*
- 2 *teaspoons cornstarch*
- ¼ *teaspoon black pepper*

- ¾ *pound flank steak, thinly sliced across the grain*

Sauce

- ⅓ *cup beef broth*
- 2 *tablespoons Chinese rice wine*
- 2 *tablespoons dark soy sauce*
- 1 *teaspoon sugar*
- ¼ *teaspoon black pepper*

- 2 *tablespoons cooking oil*
- 1 *teaspoon minced garlic*
- ½ *teaspoon minced ginger*
- ½ each *green, red, and yellow bell peppers, julienned*
- 2 *tablespoons water*
- 1 *teaspoon cornstarch dissolved in 2 teaspoons water*
- ½ *fresh jalapeño chili, sliced*

Getting Ready

① Combine marinade ingredients in a bowl. Add beef and stir to coat. Let stand for 10 minutes.

② Combine sauce ingredients in a bowl.

Cooking

① Place a wok over high heat until hot. Add 1½ tablespoons oil, swirling to coat sides. Add garlic and ginger and cook, stirring, until fragrant, about 10 seconds. Add beef and stir-fry until no longer pink, 1½ to 2 minutes. Remove meat from pan.

② Add remaining ½ tablespoon oil to wok, swirling to coat sides. Add bell peppers and stir-fry for 1 minute. Add water and stir-fry until peppers are tender-crisp, 2 to 3 minutes. Return meat to wok and add sauce; bring to a boil. Add cornstarch solution and cook, stirring, until sauce boils and thickens.

③ To serve, garnish with chili slices.

Makes 4 servings.

Pepper Prep

Cut off the top and bottom of the pepper. Next, make a single cut along the side, to open the pepper. Pull out and discard the central core of membranes and seeds. Now lay the pepper, skin side down, on a cutting board, spreading it out flat. Holding a sharp knife or cleaver flat against the pepper, trim away any remaining membrane. You now have a long flat rectangle that's easy to slice crosswise.

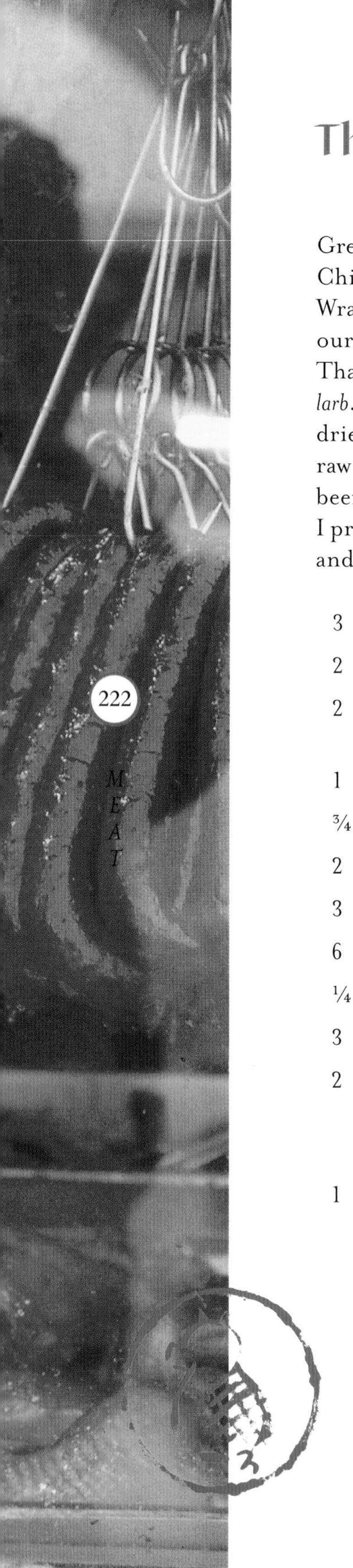

Thai-Style Lettuce Cups

Great chefs often think alike. In China, we have the famous Crystal Wrap, a special dish we serve during our New Year celebration. Northern Thailand has a similar dish, called *larb*. Instead of diced shrimp and dried vegetables, Thai cooks spoon raw or sometimes water-blanched beef into lettuce cups. For my taste I prefer to stir-fry the ground beef and use the Thai seasonings.

- 3 *tablespoons uncooked rice*
- 2 *tablespoons cooking oil*
- 2 *walnut-sized shallots, finely chopped*
- 1 *teaspoon crushed dried red chilies*
- ¾ *pound ground beef*
- 2 *green onions, thinly sliced*
- 3 *tablespoons chopped cilantro*
- 6 *fresh mint leaves, chopped*
- ¼ *cup lime juice*
- 3 *tablespoons fish sauce*
- 2 *teaspoons sugar*
- *Iceberg lettuce cups, washed and crisped*
- 1 *lime, cut into wedges*

Getting Ready

① Place rice in a small frying pan over medium heat; cook, shaking pan frequently, until lightly browned, 3 to 4 minutes. Immediately remove from pan to cool. When rice is cool, grind to a fine powder in a spice grinder.

Cooking

① Place a wok over high heat until hot. Add oil, swirling to coat sides. Add shallots and chilies; cook, stirring, until fragrant, about 20 seconds. Add beef and cook until browned and crumbly, 3 to 4 minutes.

② Discard excess liquid from pan. Add green onions, cilantro, mint, lime juice, fish sauce, and sugar; mix well. Add ground rice and stir until liquid is absorbed, about 30 seconds.

③ Place meat mixture on a platter; surround with lettuce cups and lime wedges. Serve warm or at room temperature. To eat, place a spoonful of meat in a lettuce cup, wrap it up, and eat out of hand.

Makes 4 servings.

Mongolian Beef

With its rich, savory sauce, fragrant with garlic and chilies, Mongolian Beef is a favorite dish in northern China and a favorite dish in Chinese restaurants throughout the world. For an authentic and dramatic presentation, serve it over deep-fried snowy bean thread noodles (see instructions below).

Marinade

- 2 *tablespoons dark soy sauce*
- 2 *tablespoons Chinese rice wine or dry sherry*
- 1 *teaspoon cornstarch*

- ¾ *pound flank steak, thinly sliced across the grain*
- 2½ *tablespoons cooking oil*
- 2 *tablespoons minced garlic*
- 10 *small dried red chilies*
- 10 *green onions, cut into 3-inch pieces*
- 2 *tablespoons hoisin sauce*
- 1 *tablespoon soy sauce*

Getting Ready

① Combine marinade ingredients in a bowl. Add beef and stir to coat. Let stand for 10 minutes.

Cooking

① Place a wok over high heat until hot. Add 2 tablespoons oil, swirling to coat sides. Add beef and stir-fry until no longer pink, 1½ to 2 minutes. Remove meat from pan.

② Add remaining ½ tablespoon oil to wok, swirling to coat sides. Add garlic and chilies; cook, stirring, until fragrant, about 10 seconds. Add green onions and stir-fry for 1 minute.

③ Return meat to wok and add hoisin sauce and soy sauce; cook until heated through.

Makes 4 servings.

Crispy Bean Threads

If you've never made crispy fried bean thread noodles, you're in for a surprise. On contact with the hot oil, the dried noodles puff up instantly, creating a snowy white nest. Pull apart a small bundle of dried bean thread noodles. In a wok, heat cooking oil for deep-frying to 375°F. Deep-fry bean threads in small batches until they puff and expand, about 5 seconds. Turn them over to cook the other side, then drain on paper towels.

Beef Tomato

Many casual eateries in Hong Kong feature rice plates—meat and vegetables with steamed rice. These inexpensive dishes are popular choices for a quick lunch, and beef stir-fried with tomato is a favorite.

Marinade

- 2 *tablespoons soy sauce*
- 2 *tablespoons Chinese rice wine or dry sherry*
- 2 *teaspoons cornstarch*

- ¾ *pound flank steak, thinly sliced across the grain*

Sauce

- ¼ *cup chicken broth*
- ¼ *cup ketchup*
- 2 *tablespoons hoisin sauce*
- 1 *tablespoon soy sauce*
- 1 *tablespoon Worcestershire sauce*
- 2 *teaspoons sesame oil*
- 1 *teaspoon chili garlic sauce*

- 2 *tablespoons cooking oil*
- 1 *teaspoon minced garlic*
- 1 *small onion, cut into ½-inch squares*
- 2 *green onions, cut into 1-inch pieces*
- 3 *small tomatoes, peeled and cut into 1-inch cubes*
- 2½ *teaspoons cornstarch dissolved in 2 tablespoons water*

Getting Ready

① Combine marinade ingredients in a bowl. Add beef and stir to coat. Let stand for 10 minutes.

② Combine sauce ingredients in a bowl.

Cooking

① Place a wok over high heat until hot. Add 1½ tablespoons oil, swirling to coat sides. Add beef and stir-fry until no longer pink, 1½ to 2 minutes. Remove meat from pan.

② Add remaining ½ tablespoon oil to wok, swirling to coat sides. Add garlic, onion, and green onions; stir-fry for 1 minute. Add tomatoes and sauce; bring to a boil. Return meat to wok. Add cornstarch solution and cook, stirring, until sauce boils and thickens.

Makes 4 servings.

Ready, Set, Cook!

Chinese cooking is easier when you do what experienced chefs do: take the time to set up in advance so there are no last-minute surprises. Cut up everything. Soak dried ingredients. Marinate meats. Measure ingredients and place them in small bowls. Group everything you'll need for each recipe, and set utensils and pans within easy reach. When the prep is well done, the cooking's more fun!

Venison with Leeks

Venison stir-fried with leeks or onions is the kind of dish you might find in the province of Yunnan, to the south of Sichuan. This remote region, separated from central and coastal China by tall mountains, has developed its own unique cuisine. The most famous local specialty is Yunnan ham, but many dishes also feature a variety of exotic ingredients, such as snails, sparrows, and bear's paws, along with the meat of game animals, such as venison and rabbit.

Marinade

- 2 *tablespoons oyster-flavored sauce*
- 2 *teaspoons cornstarch*

- ¾ *pound venison steaks, cut ½ inch thick*

Sauce

- 2 *tablespoons hoisin sauce*
- 1 *tablespoon Chinese rice wine or dry sherry*
- 1 *teaspoon dark soy sauce*
- 1 *teaspoon chili garlic sauce*

- 1 *leek (1-in. diameter), white part only*
- 2 *tablespoons cooking oil*
- 2 *teaspoons minced garlic*

Getting Ready

① Combine marinade ingredients in a bowl. Cut venison across the grain into ⅛-inch-thick slices. Add to marinade and stir to coat. Let stand for 10 minutes.

② Combine sauce ingredients in a bowl.

③ Julienne leek. Parboil for 1 minute in a small pan with 1 inch of boiling water; drain.

Cooking

① Place a wok over high heat until hot. Add oil, swirling to coat sides. Add garlic and cook, stirring, until fragrant, about 10 seconds. Add venison and stir-fry until no longer pink, 1½ to 2 minutes. Add leek and sauce. Cook until heated through.

Makes 4 servings.

Leek Tips

When buying leeks, look for bright green leaves and a clean, firm white portion. Grit and mud often get trapped between the layers of leeks, so it's important to clean them thoroughly before using them in cooking. Start by cutting off and discarding the dark green tops and the root end, then cut an X in the root end about 2 inches deep. Rinse the leeks thoroughly under cold water, spreading out the layers at the root end and forcing water between them until the leek is completely clean.

Hunan Beef with Dry-Fried Beans

Dry-frying is a typical western Chinese cooking method in which vegetables are first deep-fried, then stir-fried. Here's an easier method—the beans are quickly parboiled before stir-frying.

Marinade

- 1 *tablespoon soy sauce*
- 1 *tablespoon cornstarch*

- ¾ *pound flank steak, cut into ½-inch cubes*

Sauce

- ¼ *cup chicken broth*
- ¼ *cup Chinese rice wine or dry sherry*
- 2 *tablespoons soy sauce*
- 1 *tablespoon black bean sauce*
- 2 *teaspoons chili garlic sauce*
- 2 *teaspoons sesame oil*
- ½ *fresh jalapeño chili, seeded and minced*
- 1 *tablespoon sugar*

- ¾ *pound green beans, trimmed and cut into 2-inch pieces*
- 3 *tablespoons cooking oil*
- 6 *small dried red chilies*
- 1 *tablespoon minced garlic*
- 1½ *teaspoons cornstarch dissolved in 1 tablespoon water*

Getting Ready

① Combine marinade ingredients in a bowl. Add beef and stir to coat. Let stand for 10 minutes.

② Combine sauce ingredients in a bowl.

③ Parboil green beans in a pot of boiling water for 3 minutes; drain.

Cooking

① Place a wok over high heat until hot. Add oil, swirling to coat sides. Add green beans; stir-fry until wilted, 3 to 4 minutes. Remove beans from pan with a slotted spoon.

② Remove all but 1½ tablespoons oil from wok. Add chilies and garlic; cook, stirring, until fragrant, about 10 seconds. Add beef and stir-fry until no longer pink, 1½ to 2 minutes.

③ Return beans to wok and add sauce; bring to a boil. Add cornstarch solution and cook, stirring, until sauce boils and thickens.

Makes 4 servings.

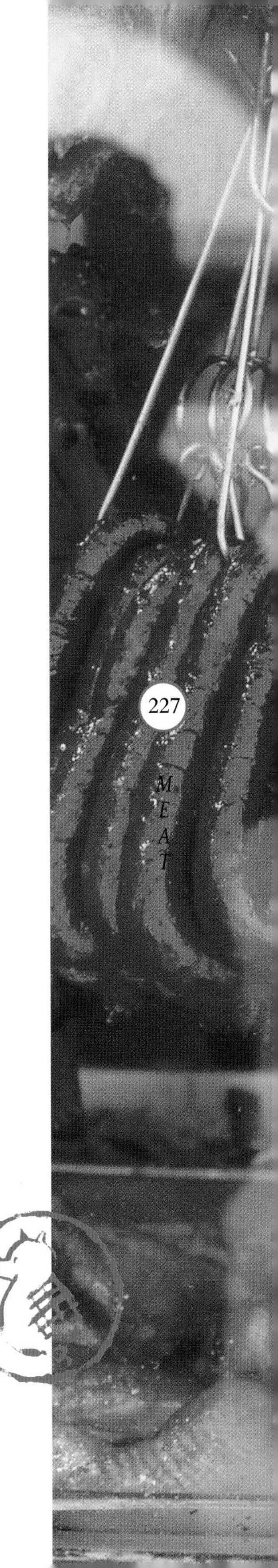

Mango Beef

Like many Hong Kong–trained chefs, I love to combine the flavors of meat and fresh fruit. Here, it's a case of meat meets mango in a sizzling sweet-and-savory stir-fry. If you can't find mangoes, you can substitute pears or peaches.

Marinade

1 *tablespoon oyster-flavored sauce*
1 *teaspoon cornstarch*

¾ *pound beef sirloin, cut into ½-inch cubes*

1 *ripe mango (about 1 lb.) or pear*
1 *large Granny Smith or other tart apple*
2 *tablespoons cooking oil*
1 *teaspoon minced ginger*
¼ *cup diced red bell pepper*
2 *tablespoons plum sauce*
1 *tablespoon Chinese rice wine or dry sherry*
2 *teaspoons soy sauce*
¼ *cup whole macadamia nuts or blanched almonds*
½ *fresh jalapeño chili, sliced*

Getting Ready

① Combine marinade ingredients in a bowl. Add beef and stir to coat. Let stand for 10 minutes.

② Peel mango and cut flesh from the pit; cut flesh into ¾-inch cubes. Peel and core apple; cut into ½-inch cubes.

Cooking

① Place a wok over high heat until hot. Add 1½ tablespoons oil, swirling to coat sides. Add ginger and cook, stirring, until fragrant, about 10 seconds. Add beef and stir-fry until no longer pink, 1½ to 2 minutes. Remove meat from pan.

② Add remaining ½ tablespoon oil to wok, swirling to coat sides. Add mango, apple, and bell pepper; stir-fry for 2 minutes. Return meat to wok and add plum sauce, wine, and soy sauce; cook until heated through. Add nuts and mix well.

③ Place on a serving plate and garnish with chili slices.

Makes 4 servings.

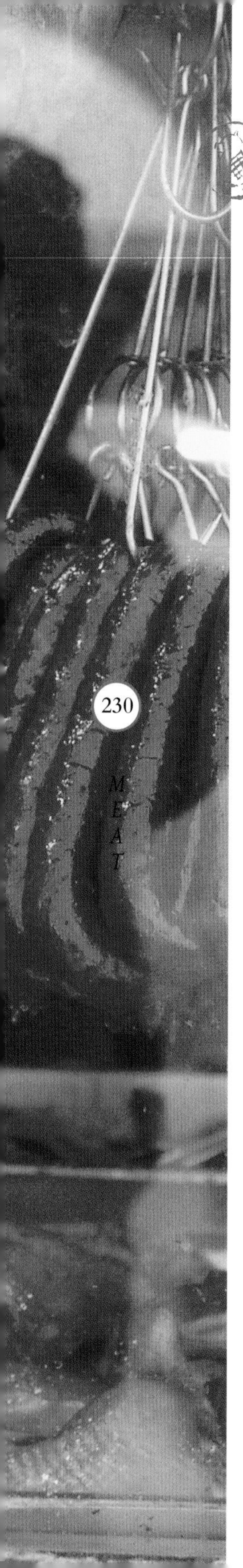

Grilled Beef and Vegetables

Dinner and a show? You can enjoy both in a Japanese *teppan-yaki* restaurant. With great panache, chefs grill beef and vegetables on a griddle right in front of their dinner guests. For you budding teppan-yaki chefs at home, grill half of the meat and vegetables, serve them, and then grill the rest. For variety, you can also grill Asian eggplant, sweet potato rounds, green onions, snow peas, and napa cabbage.

- 4 *small boneless beef steaks, such as New York, each about ½ inch thick*
- *Salt and pepper*
- 1 *medium onion*
- 1 each *red and yellow bell peppers*
- 1 each *zucchini and crookneck squash*
- ¼ *pound bean sprouts, rinsed and drained*
- 8 *fresh shiitake mushrooms, stems discarded*

Mustard Sauce

- 1½ *tablespoons dry mustard powder*
- ¼ *cup soy sauce*
- 2 *tablespoons Japanese sweet cooking rice wine (mirin)*
- ½ *teaspoon sesame oil*

- 1 *tablespoon cooking oil*
- 2 *tablespoons butter, cut into small cubes*

Getting Ready

① Trim fat from steaks; sprinkle meat lightly with salt and pepper. Cut onion in half lengthwise, then crosswise into half-moons about ¼ inch thick; run a wooden pick through all layers of onion to hold rings together. Cut peppers into ¼-inch-thick slices; remove seeds and veins. Cut squash into ¼-inch-thick slices. Cover and chill meat and vegetables until ready to cook.

② In a bowl, combine mustard sauce ingredients until evenly blended; pour into 4 dipping sauce bowls.

Cooking

① Heat a Japanese iron griddle (teppan) or electric frying pan to medium-high. Brush griddle with half the oil. Place half of meat and vegetables on griddle. Place half of the butter on top of the vegetables. Cook, turning once, until meat is done to your liking, about 2 minutes per side for rare, and vegetables are tender-crisp. Repeat with remaining meat, vegetables, and butter.

② Before serving, cut meat into thin strips. Serve with mustard sauce for dipping.

Makes 4 servings.

Korean-Style Short Ribs

The aroma of beef ribs slowly sizzling on a grill is what makes me a frequent diner at my favorite Korean restaurant. For this specialty, chefs use Korean-style or flanken ribs: short ribs that have been sawed across the bone to make ¼-inch-thick strips about 2 inches wide and 6 inches long.

Marinade

- 2 *tablespoons sesame seeds*
- ½ *cup chicken broth*
- ⅓ *cup soy sauce*
- ¼ *cup Chinese rice wine or dry sherry*
- 2½ *tablespoons sugar*
- 2 *tablespoons minced garlic*
- 1 *tablespoon minced ginger*
- 2 *green onions, finely chopped*
- 2 *teaspoons chili garlic sauce*

- 2 *pounds Korean-style beef short ribs*
- 1 *teaspoon cornstarch dissolved in 2 teaspoons water*

Getting Ready

① Prepare marinade: Place sesame seeds in a small frying pan over medium heat; cook, shaking pan frequently, until lightly browned, 3 to 4 minutes. Immediately remove from pan to cool. When seeds are cool, grind in a spice grinder. Place seeds in a large bowl with remaining marinade ingredients. Add ribs; turn to coat. Cover and refrigerate for 4 hours or overnight.

Cooking

① Lift meat from marinade and drain briefly; reserve marinade in a small pan. Place ribs on an oiled grill 3 to 4 inches above a solid bed of low-glowing coals. Cook, turning once, until done to your liking, about 3 minutes per side for medium-rare.

② While meat is cooking, simmer marinade for 3 minutes. Add cornstarch solution and cook, stirring, until sauce bubbles and thickens slightly. Pour sauce into a small bowl.

③ Serve ribs with sauce on the side.

Makes 4 servings.

Beef Tips

Here are a few simple tips for buying and preparing beef. In the store, pick it up last so it stays cool, and place it in a plastic bag to keep it from dripping onto other foods. Thaw frozen beef in the refrigerator or the microwave, never at room temperature. Marinate in the refrigerator. Discard the leftover marinade that was in contact with the raw meat, or bring it to a rolling boil for 1 minute before using it on cooked meat. To test doneness, use a quick-read meat thermometer. For burgers, the internal temperature should 160°F. For steaks, medium-rare is 145°F, medium is 160°F, and well done is 170°F.

Grilled Sesame Beef

Beef is a real treat in Japanese cuisine, and chefs certainly take extra care in its preparation as well as its presentation. The garnishes suggested here are of classical Japanese design, and make this dish as pleasing to the eye as it is to the palate.

Marinade

- 2 *tablespoons sesame seeds*
- ¼ *cup soy sauce*
- ¼ *cup Japanese rice wine (sake)*
- 1 *tablespoon lemon juice*
- 1 *tablespoon sesame oil*
- 1 *tablespoon sugar*
- 2 *green onions, minced*
- 2 *teaspoons minced garlic*
- 2 *teaspoons minced ginger*

- 1 *pound boneless tender beef steaks, such as rib eye or New York, cut into 2- to 3-inch squares*
- 1 *teaspoon cornstarch dissolved in 2 teaspoons water*
- *Thinly sliced green onion*

Getting Ready

① Place sesame seeds in a small frying pan over medium heat; cook, shaking pan frequently, until lightly browned, 3 to 4 minutes. Immediately remove from pan to cool. Reserve ½ teaspoon whole seeds for garnish; crush remaining seeds in a spice grinder.

② Place crushed sesame seeds in a bowl with remaining marinade ingredients. Add beef to marinade; turn to coat. Cover and refrigerate for 4 hours or up to overnight.

Cooking

① Place a cast-iron frying pan or griddle over medium-high heat until hot. Lift meat from marinade and drain; reserve marinade in a small pan. Place meat in frying pan and cook, turning once, until done to your liking, about 2 minutes per side for rare.

② While meat is cooking, simmer marinade for 3 minutes. Add cornstarch solution and cook, stirring, until sauce bubbles and thickens slightly.

③ To serve, pour sauce onto a serving plate. Cut meat into crosswise slices, then reassemble in its original shape on sauce. Garnish with sesame seeds and green onion.

Makes 4 servings.

Satay

Satay is one of Malaysia's best-loved snacks. Serve it with Satay Peanut Sauce, along with pieces of Pressed Rice Cake (recipes on opposite page) and wedges of cucumber and red onion.

Spice Paste

2 *stalks lemongrass*
4 *walnut-sized shallots*
3 *cloves garlic*
1 *teaspoon fennel seeds*
¼ *cup water*
2 *tablespoons packed brown sugar*
1 *teaspoon ground cumin*
1 *teaspoon ground coriander*
1 *teaspoon turmeric powder*
1 *teaspoon galangal powder*
1 *tablespoon soy sauce*

1 *pound boneless beef sirloin or top round or boneless, skinless chicken*
20 *bamboo skewers*
Satay Peanut Sauce (opposite)
Pressed Rice Cakes (opposite)
Sliced cucumber, onion, and red chili

Getting Ready

① Thinly slice bottom 6 inches of lemongrass; discard remainder. Place in a blender with shallots, garlic, fennel seeds, and water; process until smooth. Pour into a medium bowl. Add brown sugar, cumin, coriander, turmeric, galangal, and soy sauce; mix well.

② Cut meat across the grain into thin diagonal slices, then cut crosswise into 2-inch pieces. Add meat to spice paste and stir to coat. Cover and refrigerate for 2 hours or up to overnight.

③ Soak skewers in water for 15 minutes or until ready to use.

Cooking

① Thread 2 pieces of meat on each skewer. Place skewers on a preheated oiled grill. Cook, turning skewers frequently, until meat is seared, 2 to 3 minutes.

② Serve with satay peanut sauce for dipping, and garnish with rice cakes, cucumber, onion, and chili.

Makes 4 servings.

Satay Secrets

Here are some tricks that will turn you into a seasoned satay pro. To keep the skewers from burning, weave the skewer in and out of the meat, exposing the skewer as little as possible. For a glossy finish, brush satay just before cooking with 1 tablespoon sugar dissolved in ¼ cup water. Baste several times during cooking with a mixture of 2 tablespoons oil and ⅓ cup water. To add flavor, make a basting brush from a crushed stalk of lemongrass.

Satay Peanut Sauce

This peanut dipping sauce is the classic accompaniment to satay. You can substitute ¾ cup chunky peanut butter for the peanuts, but make sure it's made only from peanuts with no additives. Before adding the peanut butter to the wok, blend it with half of the water.

Spice Paste

- 1 *stalk lemongrass*
- 1 *walnut-sized shallot*
- 2 *cloves garlic*
- ½ *teaspoon ground cumin*
- ½ *teaspoon ground coriander*
- ½ *teaspoon galangal powder*
- ¼ *cup water*

- 1 *cup roasted peanuts*
- 3 *tablespoons cooking oil*
- 1 *cup water*
- ¼ *cup packed brown sugar*
- 3 *tablespoons chili garlic sauce*
- 2 *tablespoons soy sauce*

Getting Ready

① Thinly slice bottom 6 inches of lemongrass; discard remainder. Place in a blender with remaining spice paste ingredients and process until smooth.

② In a food processor, chop peanuts very fine.

Cooking

① Place a wok over medium-low heat until hot. Add oil, swirling to coat sides. Add spice paste and cook, stirring, until fragrant, 6 to 8 minutes.

② Add water, peanuts, brown sugar, chili garlic sauce, and soy sauce; stir until evenly blended. Bring to a boil. Reduce heat and simmer, stirring frequently, until sauce is slightly thickened, 4 to 5 minutes.

③ Serve with satay for dipping.

Makes about 2 cups.

Pressed Rice Cakes

Compressed rice cakes are eaten with Satay (recipe opposite), and a slice or two will often be used to garnish a bowl of Spicy Chicken Noodle Soup (page 176). Here's my technique for making rice cakes at home: Wash and drain 2 cups **glutinous rice**. Place in a medium pan with 3 cups **water**; bring to a boil, reduce heat, and simmer until all liquid is absorbed, 35 to 40 minutes. Spoon hot rice into a 9-inch-square pan lined with lightly oiled foil or banana leaves. Cover with more oiled foil or leaves and a second square pan; weight with large cans or other heavy objects. Let stand 8 hours or overnight. Invert onto a cutting board, remove foil or leaves, and slice into 1½-inch squares with a wet knife. Serve at room temperature.

Asian Burgers

Western fast food has made inroads all over the world, but to Asian chefs, burgers are a lot more than beef patties in buns. Bite into this version, and you will find the crunchiness of water chestnuts and onion. Yes, you can put onion in the beef instead of on top of it. And since the beef is already marinated, you may not even need that splatter of ketchup.

2	*dried black mushrooms*
1	*pound ground beef*
½	*medium onion, finely chopped*
¼	*cup chopped water chestnuts*
2	*green onions, chopped*
2	*tablespoons minced garlic*
2	*tablespoons soy sauce*
1	*tablespoon oyster-flavored sauce*
1	*teaspoon sesame oil*
1	*tablespoon cornstarch*
4	*hamburger buns*

Getting Ready

① Soak mushrooms in warm water to cover until softened, about 20 minutes; drain. Discard stems and finely chop caps.

② Crumble meat into a large bowl. Add mushrooms, onion, water chestnuts, green onions, garlic, soy sauce, oyster-flavored sauce, and sesame oil; mix well. Sprinkle cornstarch over meat mixture; mix well. Divide mixture into 4 equal portions; lightly shape each portion into a patty about 1 inch thick.

Cooking

① Place patties on an oiled grill 3 to 4 inches above a solid bed of low-glowing coals. Cook, turning once, until done to your liking, 3 to 4 minutes per side for medium-rare.

② Serve in buns with your favorite condiments.

Makes 4 servings.

Doing the Twist

Whenever people ask me how I come up with recipes and ideas for new dishes, I always answer that my favorite Chinese cooking technique is one you can't find in any book: imagination. There's nothing more fun than taking a familiar idea and giving it a new twist. Take something you love to eat, and try changing a few ingredients. Say it's meat loaf. Why not add a little soy sauce instead of salt? How about cilantro instead of parsley? Throw in some water chestnuts for texture. Add oyster-flavored sauce to the glaze. You get the idea: Have fun and follow your nose!

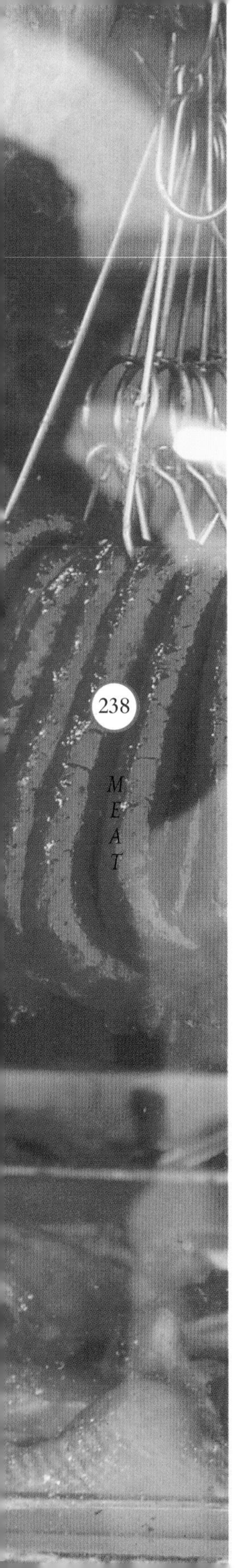

Grilled Steak with Shiitake Mushrooms

Here's an Asian version of a French classic, steak with mushroom sauce. The velvety texture of shiitake mushrooms and the exciting seasonings make this dish a classic in its own right. Of course, in Asia the steak is sliced thin, a perfect pickup for your chopsticks!

Marinade

- 3 *tablespoons soy sauce*
- 2 *tablespoons Chinese rice wine or dry sherry*
- 1 *tablespoon grated ginger*
- ¼ *teaspoon white pepper*

- 1¼ *pounds boneless tender beef steaks, such as rib eye or New York*
- 6 *fresh shiitake mushrooms or dried black mushrooms*

Sauce

- ½ *cup beef broth*
- 2 *tablespoons Chinese rice wine or dry sherry*
- 2 *tablespoons hoisin sauce*
- 1 *tablespoon Worcestershire sauce*
- 1 *teaspoon hot pepper sauce*
- 2 *teaspoons sesame oil*

- 1 *tablespoon cooking oil*
- 2 *teaspoons minced garlic*
- 2 *teaspoons minced ginger*
- 1½ *teaspoons cornstarch dissolved in 1 tablespoon water*

Getting Ready

① Combine marinade ingredients in a bowl. Score beef lightly on each side with shallow crosshatch marks. Add beef to marinade; turn to coat. Cover and refrigerate for 4 hours or overnight.

② Discard mushroom stems and thinly slice caps. (If using dried mushrooms, soak in warm water to cover until softened, about 20 minutes; drain. Discard stems and thinly slice caps.)

③ Combine sauce ingredients in a bowl.

Cooking

① Lift meat from marinade and drain briefly. Place steaks on an oiled grill 3 to 4 inches above a solid bed of low-glowing coals. Cook, turning once, until done to your liking, about 3 minutes per side for medium-rare.

② While meat is cooking, place a wok or small frying pan over medium heat until hot. Add oil, swirling to coat sides. Add garlic and ginger and cook, stirring, until fragrant, about 10 seconds. Add mushrooms and cook until tender, about 2 minutes. Add sauce and bring to a boil. Add cornstarch solution and cook, stirring, until sauce boils and thickens.

③ Cut steaks into ½-inch-thick slices and place on a serving plate. Top with sauce.

Makes 4 servings.

Braised Beef Shanks with Vegetables

Braising is a wonderful way of cooking beef; it allows plenty of time for the seasonings to sink in and complement the flavor of the meat. Of course all the attention makes the meat extra-tender.

4 *dried black mushrooms*

Braising Sauce

3 *cups chicken broth*

½ *cup Chinese rice wine or dry sherry*

3 *tablespoons hoisin sauce*

3 *tablespoons regular soy sauce*

1 *tablespoon dark soy sauce*

2 *teaspoons sesame oil*

1 *whole star anise*

2 *tablespoons cooking oil*

2 *pounds beef shanks, sliced about 1 inch thick*

5 *cloves garlic, peeled and lightly crushed*

4 *slices ginger, each the size of a quarter, lightly crushed*

1 *large carrot, cut into ½-inch slices*

1 *pound daikon, cut into 1-inch chunks*

1 *medium onion, cut into 1-inch pieces*

3 *tablespoons cornstarch dissolved in ¼ cup water*

Getting Ready

① Soak mushrooms in warm water to cover until softened, about 20 minutes; drain. Discard stems and leave caps whole.

② Combine braising sauce ingredients in a bowl.

Cooking

① Heat oil in a 5-quart pan over medium-high heat. Add shanks and brown lightly on all sides, 5 to 6 minutes. Add garlic and ginger; cook, stirring, until fragrant, about 10 seconds. Add braising sauce. Bring to a boil; reduce heat, cover, and simmer until meat is tender, about 1½ hours.

② Add mushrooms, carrot, daikon, and onion to pan. Cover and simmer for 30 minutes or until all vegetables are tender when pierced. Add cornstarch solution and cook, stirring, until sauce boils and thickens.

Makes 6 servings.

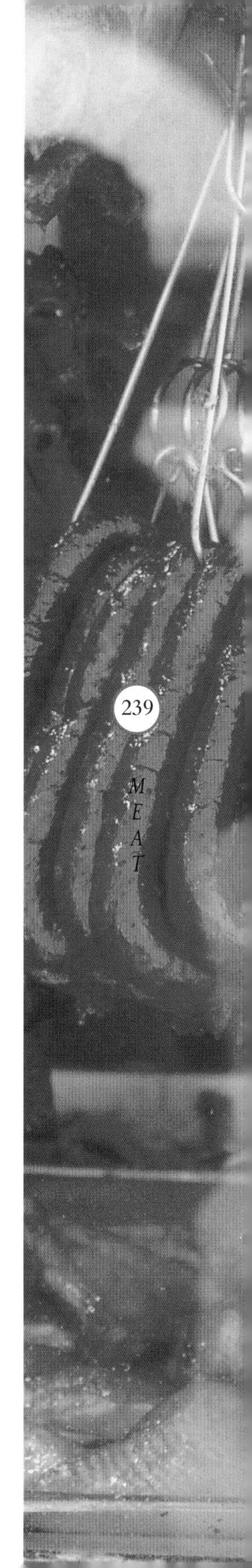

Entertaining Asian-Style

Five Tips for Overcoming Dinner-Partyphobia

There are all kinds of books that will tell you how to have a novel kind of dinner party by creating a classic Chinese banquet-style meal. They'll give you tips on how to plan one dish per person plus rice. How to balance meat, poultry, vegetables, and seafood. How to balance hot and cold, sweet and savory. Even how to make your own fortune cookies. Now, as a Chinese chef, I love these books. I've even written some of them! But that's not what we're talking about here.

Reality check: When was the last time you planned a formal banquet—Chinese or otherwise—at your house? If your answer is "last Saturday," congratulations. You are a devoted culinary artist and a master entertainer. But if you're like most people I know, even the thought of planning a potluck with one other family makes your heart start beating irregularly.

There's the shopping, the cleaning, the cooking. And what if the food turns out badly? Or people just sit there staring at their plates, with only the occasional clink of a knife and fork to break the awkward silence?

Well, as far as the cleaning part is concerned, you're going to need to get over that one yourself. But I can offer a few suggestions about how to make entertaining a little easier and a lot more fun—especially if you're planning an Asian meal.

- **Remember, you are not a restaurant.** In Asia, kitchens are usually tiny. They're really only set up to feed a single family. People often use restaurants to entertain guests, and when they do entertain at home, they have no choice but to keep things fairly simple. Good idea. Restaurant meals are wonderful, but that doesn't mean you need to apply those standards to your cooking! Take it from someone who has cooked in restaurants: What your friends want when they come over to your place is a relaxed, home-style meal.

- **Plan ahead to avoid traffic jams.** Planning a meal is all about figuring out what foods will taste good together and make up a satisfying whole. But if you want to have any fun at your own party, it's equally important to think about traffic flow in the kitchen. Can the soup and the clay-pot dish be made ahead? Can you make the rice in the rice cooker to free up a burner? Can you really make two stir-fries in quick succession? What about an "interactive" dish, like Mongolian Hot Pot (page 262) that gives you a breather while the guests cook their own food?

- **Put the guests to work.** There's no better icebreaker, and besides, your load is instantly lightened. In our house, we almost always leave a few things for the guests to do. The adventurous ones get to roll out flatbread, chop veggies, or fill dumplings. The more timid ones stir the soup. One beer later, they've usually switched places!

- **Set yourself up for success.** I've gotten spoiled by my show. Those hardworking people in the back kitchen set out all the ingredients for each dish on a separate tray, all nicely measured and ready to go. I recommend this technique for home entertaining, too, particularly if you're preparing an Asian menu. With a kitchen full of guests, you've got enough on your mind without having to search for that box of cornstarch you could swear you bought last year.

- **Cheat.** Yes, cheat. You are a busy person. It really is okay to round out a meal with some delicious frozen potstickers or to use a high-quality store-bought sauce here and there. You have my permission. One tip, though: It's best to confess up front before anyone finds out!

Entertaining can be a lot of work, it's true. But it's also an act of true generosity that makes you and the people you care about feel good. Just remember: Stay loose, keep things casual, and do what all great entertainers do—keep smiling.

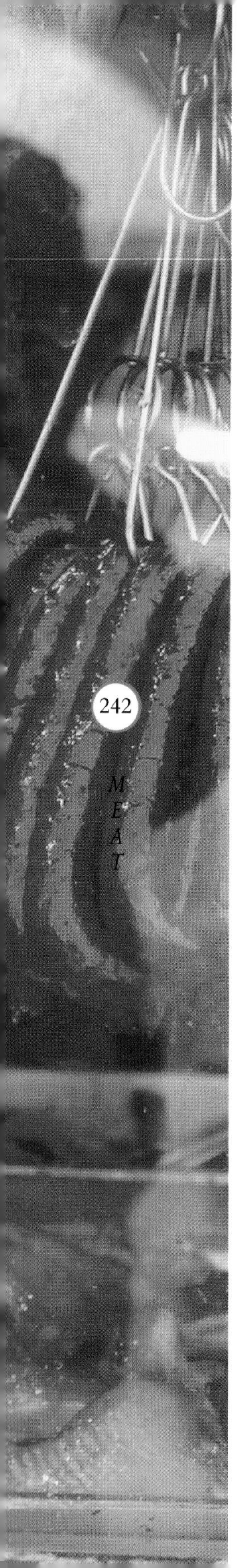

Sweet and Sour Pork

Sweet and sour pork needs no introduction—it's probably on the menu of every Chinese restaurant in the Western world. But you may be surprised at how delicious a homemade version can be, especially if the sauce is not too sweet.

Marinade

- 2 *tablespoons soy sauce*
- 1 *tablespoon Chinese rice wine or dry sherry*

- ¾ *pound boneless pork, cut into ¾-inch cubes*

Sweet and Sour Sauce

- ⅓ *cup distilled white vinegar*
- ⅓ *cup packed brown sugar*
- ¼ *cup ketchup*
- ¼ *cup water*
- 1 *tablespoon cornstarch*
- 2 *teaspoons soy sauce*
- 1 *teaspoon chili garlic sauce*

- 1 *egg, lightly beaten*
- *Cornstarch*
- *Cooking oil for deep-frying*
- ½ *cup lychees*
- ¾ *cup pineapple chunks*
- 1 *small red bell pepper, cut into 1-inch chunks*

Getting Ready

① Combine marinade ingredients in a bowl. Add pork and stir to coat. Let stand for 10 minutes.

② Combine sauce ingredients in a small pan and set aside.

③ Place egg and cornstarch in separate bowls. Dip pork in egg, drain briefly, then dredge in cornstarch; shake off excess.

Cooking

① In a wok, heat oil for deep-frying to 360°F. Deep-fry pork, a few pieces at a time, turning occasionally, until golden brown, about 3 minutes. Remove with a slotted spoon/spatula; drain on paper towels.

② Cook sauce over medium-high heat, stirring, until sauce boils and thickens. Stir in lychees, pineapple chunks, and bell pepper. Reduce heat and simmer for 1 minute.

③ Place pork on a serving plate. Pour sauce on top.

Makes 4 servings.

Spareribs with Black Bean Sauce

Black bean sauce is classic in southern Chinese cooking. The fermented black beans are versatile and work well in enriching the flavor of the braising sauce of this popular dish. It is perfectly acceptable to eat spareribs with your fingers, and you will have a great time licking them afterwards.

2 *pounds pork spareribs, cut Chinese-style into 1-inch pieces*

Braising Sauce

1 *cup chicken broth*

1 *tablespoon soy sauce*

1 *tablespoon Chinese rice wine or dry sherry*

1 *teaspoon sugar*

1 *tablespoon cooking oil*

1 *tablespoon minced garlic*

1 *teaspoon minced ginger*

1 *fresh jalapeño chili, seeded and minced*

2½ *tablespoons salted black beans, rinsed, drained, and coarsely chopped; or 2 tablespoons black bean sauce*

2 *teaspoons cornstarch dissolved in 1 tablespoon water*

Getting Ready

① Cut spareribs between bones into individual pieces. In a large pan, parboil ribs in water to cover for 3 minutes; pour into a colander and drain.

② Combine braising sauce ingredients in a bowl.

Cooking

① Place a wok over high heat until hot. Add oil, swirling to coat sides. Add garlic, ginger, and chili; cook, stirring, until fragrant, about 10 seconds. Add ribs and black beans; stir-fry until ribs are browned on all sides, 3 to 4 minutes.

② Add braising sauce. Bring to a boil; reduce heat, cover, and simmer, stirring occasionally, until meat is tender when pierced, 25 to 30 minutes. Add cornstarch solution and cook, stirring, until sauce boils and thickens.

Makes 4 servings.

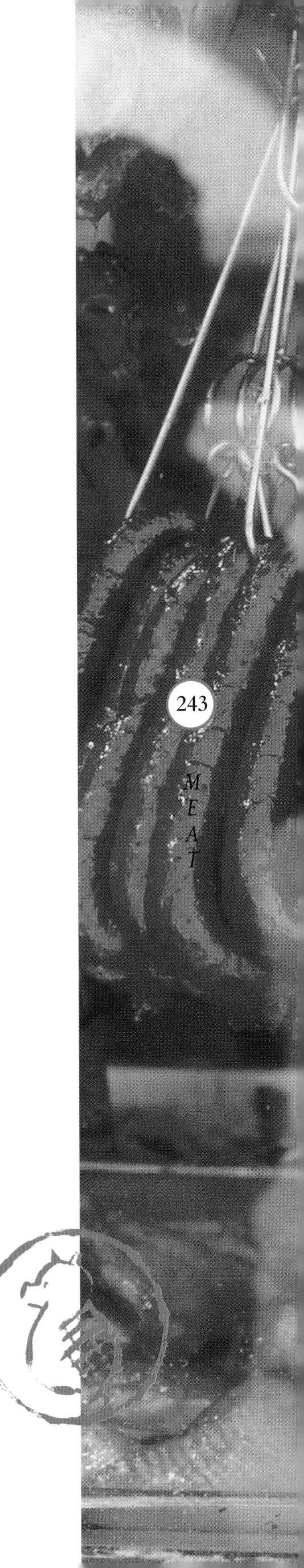

Chinese Barbecued Spareribs

Cantonese restaurants and delicatessens prepare a wonderful roast pork specialty called *char siu*—strips of roast pork with a sweet red glaze—that's served hot or cold and sliced for use in soups, noodle dishes, and dumpling fillings. The same preparation is used for mouthwatering pork spareribs. Here's an easy way to reproduce the effect at home using prepared char siu or hoisin sauce as a base for the marinade.

2 *pounds pork spareribs, cut into 3-inch lengths*

Marinade

⅓ *cup char siu sauce or hoisin sauce*

3 *tablespoons Chinese rice wine or dry sherry*

3 *tablespoons soy sauce*

1 *tablespoon sesame oil*

1 *tablespoon minced ginger*

2 *teaspoons minced garlic*

1 *teaspoon Chinese five-spice*

Char siu sauce or hoisin sauce

Getting Ready

① Cut ribs between every second bone to make serving-size pieces.

② Combine marinade ingredients in a bowl. Add spareribs and stir to coat. Cover and refrigerate for 6 hours or up to overnight.

Cooking

① Preheat oven to 400°F. Place ribs on a rack in a foil-lined baking pan; cover loosely with foil. Bake for 30 minutes. Turn ribs over, baste with char siu sauce, and continue baking, loosely covered, until tender, about 30 minutes.

② Baste again with char siu sauce. Bake, uncovered, for 6 minutes. Turn spareribs over, baste with char siu sauce, and bake until well glazed, about 6 minutes longer.

Makes 4 servings.

Hoisin Sauce

Like soy sauce and oyster-flavored sauce, hoisin sauce is one of those versatile pantry staples I always keep on hand. Made from fermented soybean paste, vinegar, garlic, and sugar, and often seasoned with Chinese five-spice and a touch of chilies, it's served as a condiment for dishes like Peking Roast Duck (page 300) and Mu Shu Pork (page 249). As a marinade and basting sauce for grilled or roasted meats, it adds a sweet, tangy flavor and beautiful reddish brown color. Try mixing it with your favorite bottled barbecue sauce to create your own "secret recipe."

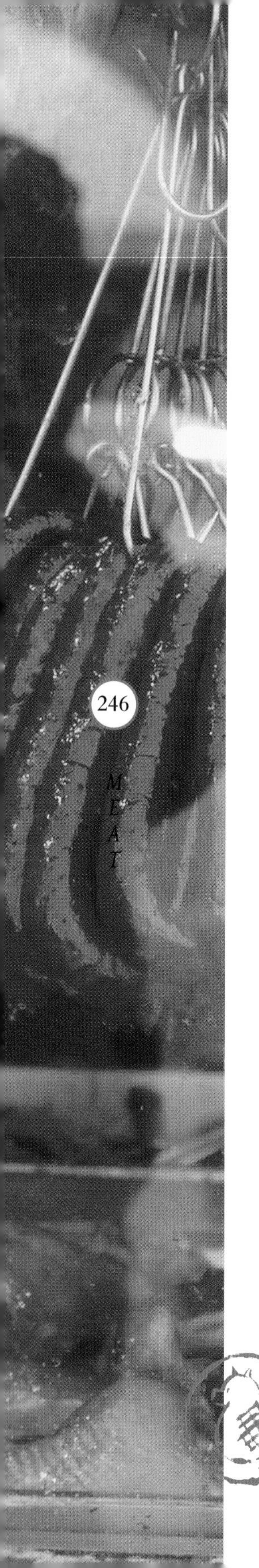

Sweet and Tangy Tangerine Spareribs

Ribs don't have to be barbecued or baked. These succulent pork ribs are cooked in the classic home-style Chinese way my mother taught me: They're simmered in a wok right on the stovetop and finished with a rich tangerine and plum sauce glaze.

1½ *pounds pork spareribs, cut into 3-inch lengths*

Marinade

¼ *cup soy sauce*

2 *tablespoons hoisin sauce*

2 *tablespoons cooking oil*

2 *teaspoons minced ginger*

2 *pieces (each about 1½ in. square) dried tangerine peel, soaked and julienned, or 1 tablespoon julienned orange peel*

2 *whole star anise*

1 *cinnamon stick*

¾ *cup chicken broth*

3 *tablespoons frozen orange or tangerine juice concentrate, thawed*

2 *tablespoons packed brown sugar*

3 *tablespoons orange-flavored liqueur*

1 *tablespoon dark soy sauce*

1 *orange, peeled and cut into segments*

Getting Ready

① Cut ribs between the bones into individual pieces. In a 2-quart pan, parboil ribs in water to cover for 3 minutes; pour into a colander and let drain.

② Combine marinade ingredients in a bowl. Brush onto meat and let stand for 10 minutes.

Cooking

① Place a wok over high heat until hot. Add oil, swirling to coat sides. Add ginger and cook, stirring, until fragrant, about 10 seconds. Add ribs and cook until browned on all sides, 3 to 4 minutes.

② Add tangerine peel, star anise, cinnamon stick, and broth; bring to a boil. Reduce heat to low; cover and simmer until meat is tender, about 45 minutes.

③ Increase heat to high. Add juice concentrate, brown sugar, liqueur, and soy sauce; cook, uncovered, until sauce is reduced and ribs are glazed, 4 to 6 minutes.

④ Place ribs on a serving platter and garnish with orange segments.

Makes 4 servings.

Red-Cooked Country Ribs

Traditional red cooking is slow braising of meat in a highly seasoned reddish brown soy sauce. The method originated in the Shanghai region, where chefs prefer to cook the meat in clay pots. I have updated this technique for modern Western kitchens, but the rich taste of tender braised ribs is absolutely timeless.

- 2 *pounds country-style pork spareribs, cut into 2-inch pieces*

Braising Sauce

- 3 *tablespoons red fermented bean curd*
- 1¼ *cups water*
- ¼ *cup Chinese rice wine or dry sherry*
- 3 *tablespoons regular soy sauce*
- ¼ *cup dark soy sauce*
- 2 *tablespoons hoisin sauce*
- 6 *slices ginger, each the size of a quarter, lightly crushed*
- 4 *cloves garlic, peeled and thinly sliced*
- 2 *green onions, cut in half and lightly crushed*
- 2 *tablespoons packed brown sugar*
- 1 *whole star anise*

Getting Ready

① Trim fat from ribs. In a 4-quart pan, parboil ribs in water to cover for 2 minutes; pour into a colander and let drain. Return ribs to pan.

② In a bowl, evenly blend bean curd with water; add remaining braising sauce ingredients.

Cooking

① Pour braising sauce over ribs. Bring to a boil; reduce heat, cover, and simmer for 1½ hours. Place lid ajar on pan and continue to simmer until meat is very tender and sauce thickens slightly, about 30 minutes.

Makes 4 servings.

Zesty Tips

The zest or peel is the outermost, colored layer of a citrus fruit, and that's where all the fragrant oils are. So when a recipe calls for grated or shredded lemon peel, that's the part you want, not the white layer below it. If you don't have a lemon zester, use a grater. You can also shave off thin pieces of peel with a vegetable peeler, then stack them and slice them into fine shreds with a sharp knife.

福
福

Mu Shu Pork

I've heard that pancakes are not just for breakfast anymore. How true: You can fill Mandarin pancakes with delicious *mu shu* pork stuffings at lunch or dinner. This is a great dish.

- 1/3 *cup dried tiger lily buds*
- 4 *dried black mushrooms*
- 6 *dried cloud ears*
- 2 1/2 *tablespoons cooking oil*
- 2 *eggs, lightly beaten*
- 1 *teaspoon minced garlic*
- 1/2 *teaspoon minced ginger*
- 1/2 *pound boneless pork, julienned*
- 4 *cups finely shredded cabbage*
- 1 *small carrot, cut into 1-inch slivers*
- 2 *green onions, cut into 1-inch slivers*
- 1/2 *cup chicken broth*
- 2 *tablespoons soy sauce*
- 1 *tablespoon Chinese rice wine or dry sherry*
- 1 *teaspoon sesame oil*
- 1 1/2 *teaspoons cornstarch dissolved in 1 tablespoon water*
- *About 16 Mandarin Pancakes* *(see page 189)**, heated*
- *Hoisin sauce*

Getting Ready

① In separate bowls, soak lily buds, mushrooms, and cloud ears in warm water to cover until softened, about 20 minutes; drain. Cut hard knobby ends off lily buds; tie each bud into a knot. Discard mushroom stems. Thinly slice mushroom caps and cloud ears.

② Place a nonstick 8- to 9-inch frying pan over medium heat until hot. Brush with 1/2 teaspoon cooking oil. Add half of eggs and cook until lightly browned on bottom and set on top, about 1 minute. Turn over and cook for 5 seconds; remove from pan. Repeat with 1/2 teaspoon oil and remaining egg. Cut into 1/4-inch-wide strips.

Cooking

① Place a wok over high heat until hot. Add remaining cooking oil, swirling to coat sides. Add garlic and ginger and cook, stirring, until fragrant, about 10 seconds. Add pork; stir-fry until lightly browned, about 2 minutes.

② Add lily buds, mushrooms, cloud ears, cabbage, carrot, green onions, and broth. Stir-fry until vegetables are tender-crisp, about 2 minutes. Stir in soy sauce, wine, and sesame oil. Add cornstarch solution and cook, stirring, until sauce boils and thickens. Toss in egg strips and mix well.

③ Place meat-vegetable mixture on a serving plate. Place Mandarin pancakes and a small bowl of hoisin sauce alongside. To eat, spread a small amount of hoisin sauce and about 3 tablespoons of meat-vegetable mixture on pancake. Wrap like a burrito.

Makes 6 to 8 servings.

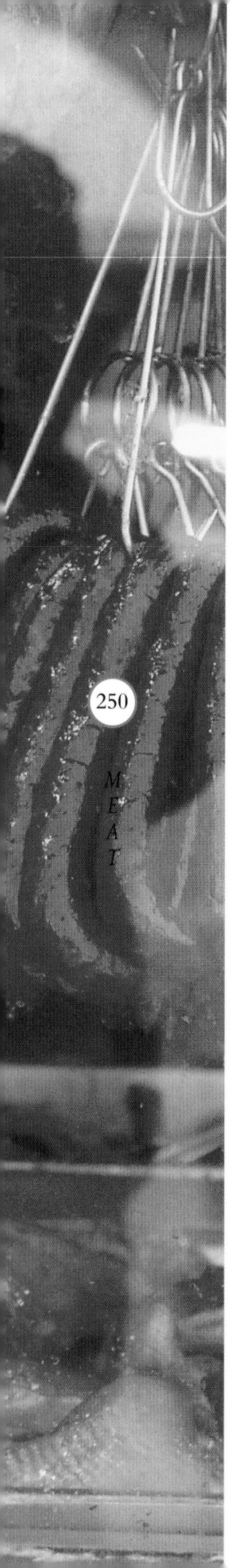

Lion's Head Meatballs

The name of this specialty of eastern China refers to the large size of the meatballs and to their "manes" of sliced cabbage. In this lighter version, I've replaced the traditional pork fat with tofu.

6 *dried black mushrooms*

Meatballs

¼ *pound regular-firm tofu, drained*

¾ *pound ground pork or ground beef*

1 *egg, lightly beaten*

2 *tablespoons oyster-flavored sauce*

2 *tablespoons cornstarch*

2 *teaspoons minced ginger*

2 *teaspoons minced cilantro*

Cooking oil for deep-frying

1½ *cups chicken broth*

2 *tablespoons Chinese rice wine or dry sherry*

1 *tablespoon soy sauce*

¾ *pound napa cabbage, cut into 3-inch sections*

1 *small carrot, thinly sliced diagonally*

16 *snow peas, trimmed and cut in half diagonally*

1 *teaspoon sesame oil*

Getting Ready

① Soak mushrooms in warm water to cover until softened, about 20 minutes; drain. Discard stems and quarter caps.

② Prepare meatballs: Mash tofu in a bowl. Place in a clean towel and squeeze to remove excess liquid. Return to bowl and add remaining meatball ingredients; mix well. Divide mixture into 12 equal portions. Roll each portion into a ball.

Cooking

① In a wok or 2-quart saucepan, heat oil for deep-frying to 350°F. Deep-fry meatballs, half at a time, turning frequently, until browned on all sides, 3 to 4 minutes. Remove with a slotted spoon/spatula; drain on paper towels.

② Place meatballs in a 2-quart pan. Add broth, wine, and soy sauce. Heat to simmering. Cover and simmer for 10 minutes. Add mushrooms, cabbage, and carrot. Cover and cook for 10 minutes. Add snow peas and cook until all vegetables are tender-crisp, about 2 minutes longer. Stir in sesame oil.

Makes 4 to 6 servings.

Pork with Spicy Basil Sauce

This spicy dish is perfect for a hot summer night. The combination of basil, chili, and fish sauce will perk up your appetite. Adjust the hotness by adding or easing off on the chilies.

Sauce

- ¼ *cup chicken broth*
- 1 *tablespoon fish sauce*
- 2 *teaspoons sugar*
- 1 *teaspoon chili garlic sauce*

- 2 *tablespoons cooking oil*
- 1 *teaspoon minced garlic*
- 2 *fresh jalapeño chilies, sliced*
- ¾ *pound boneless pork, thinly sliced*
- ¾ *cup (lightly packed) fresh basil leaves*
- 3 *green onions, cut into 1½-inch pieces*
- 1½ *teaspoons cornstarch dissolved in 1 tablespoon water*

Getting Ready

① Combine sauce ingredients in a bowl.

Cooking

① Place a wok over high heat until hot. Add oil, swirling to coat sides. Add garlic and chilies; cook, stirring, until fragrant, about 10 seconds. Add pork and stir-fry until no longer pink, 2½ to 3 minutes.

② Add basil and green onions; stir-fry for 30 seconds. Add sauce and bring to a boil. Add cornstarch solution and cook, stirring, until sauce boils and thickens.

Makes 4 servings.

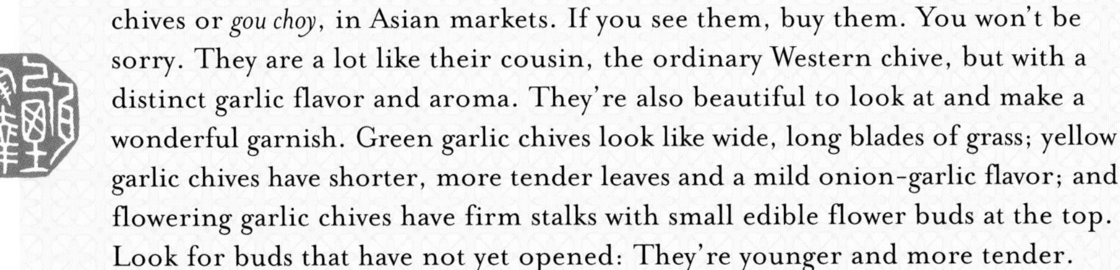

Garlic Chives

In the spring and summer, you can find fresh garlic chives, also known as Chinese chives or *gou choy*, in Asian markets. If you see them, buy them. You won't be sorry. They are a lot like their cousin, the ordinary Western chive, but with a distinct garlic flavor and aroma. They're also beautiful to look at and make a wonderful garnish. Green garlic chives look like wide, long blades of grass; yellow garlic chives have shorter, more tender leaves and a mild onion-garlic flavor; and flowering garlic chives have firm stalks with small edible flower buds at the top. Look for buds that have not yet opened: They're younger and more tender.

Suzhou Braised Pork in a Clay Pot

Suzhou, a city in Jiangsu province, northwest of Shanghai, is well known for its spectacular lakes and canals. But when it comes to beauty, the local cuisine certainly doesn't take a backseat to nature. This classic recipe is a masterpiece in any book.

Marinade

- 2 *tablespoons regular soy sauce*
- 1 *tablespoon dark soy sauce*
- 1 *tablespoon cornstarch*

- 1¼ *pounds boneless pork shoulder*

Seasoned Broth

- 2 *cups chicken broth*
- ⅓ *cup Chinese rice wine or dry sherry*
- 2 *tablespoons oyster-flavored sauce or soy sauce*
- 2 *tablespoons dark soy sauce*
- 4 *green onions, cut in half and lightly crushed*
- 2 *whole star anise*
- 1 *cinnamon stick*
- ¼ *cup crushed rock sugar or packed brown sugar*

- 2 *tablespoons cooking oil*
- 6 *cloves garlic, thinly sliced*
- ½ *pound napa cabbage, cut into 1½-inch squares*
- 1½ *teaspoons cornstarch dissolved in 1 tablespoon water*

Getting Ready

① Combine marinade ingredients in a bowl. Cut meat into 2-inch pieces. Add to marinade and stir to coat. Let stand for 10 minutes.

② Combine seasoned broth ingredients in a 2-quart clay pot or other cooking pot.

Cooking

① Place a wok over high heat until hot. Add oil, swirling to coat sides. Add garlic and cook, stirring, until fragrant, about 10 seconds. Add pork and cook until browned on all sides, 3 to 4 minutes.

② Place meat in pot with seasoned broth. Bring to a boil (over medium heat if using a clay pot); reduce heat, cover, and simmer until meat is tender, 1¼ to 1½ hours.

③ Add cabbage to meat; cover and simmer until cabbage is tender-crisp, about 10 minutes. Add cornstarch solution and cook, stirring, until sauce boils and thickens.

④ Place cabbage on serving plate. Arrange pork over cabbage and pour sauce on top.

Makes 4 to 6 servings.

Pork Cutlets

If you want to order pork cutlet in Japan, ask the waiter for *tonkatsu*. This dish was first made at a Tokyo restaurant in the 1930s, where it became an instant hit. Today, tonkatsu shops all over Japan specialize in the crusty coated pork, each with its own sauce recipe.

Tonkatsu Sauce

- ½ *teaspoon dry mustard powder*
- 2 *tablespoons Japanese rice wine (sake)*
- ¼ *cup ketchup*
- 1 *tablespoon soy sauce*
- 1 *tablespoon hoisin sauce or char siu sauce*
- 2 *teaspoons sugar*
- 2 *teaspoons Worcestershire sauce*

- 1 *pound boneless pork loin chops, cut ½ inch thick*
- *Salt and black pepper*
- ½ *cup flour*
- 1 *egg, lightly beaten*
- 1 *cup Japanese-style bread crumbs (panko)*
- *Cooking oil*
- *Shredded red and green cabbage*
- *Lemon wedges*

Getting Ready

① Combine mustard and sake in a bowl; whisk until smooth. Add remaining sauce ingredients; mix well.

② Lightly pound pork; sprinkle with salt and pepper. Dip pork in flour; shake off excess. Dip into egg, drain briefly, then coat with bread crumbs.

Cooking

① Place a wide frying pan over medium heat. Add oil to a depth of ¼ inch. When oil is hot, add pork and pan-fry, covered, for 2 minutes on each side. Uncover and cook until pork is no longer pink in center, about 2 minutes longer on each side. Lift out and drain on paper towels.

② To serve, cut pork into crosswise slices, then reassemble on a serving plate. Serve with cabbage, lemon wedges, and sauce.

Makes 4 servings.

In Praise of Panko

If you've ever used store-bought bread crumbs to coat fried foods and gotten crummy results, give Japanese-style bread crumbs (*panko*) a try. You'll never look back! You can find panko in the Asian section of most supermarkets. These crumbs, which give Pork Cutlets (recipe above) their wonderfully crisp texture, are lighter, coarser, and flakier than Western-style bread crumbs. When fried, they create a crunchy golden coating that doesn't taste greasy and stays crisp longer than regular bread crumbs do.

Beijing Sweet and Tangy Pork Chops

The sophistication of any cuisine lies in the complex balancing of tastes and textures, and in the presentation. In this dish, sweetness and tanginess complement and contrast each other, making the dish more than the sum of its parts.

1½ *pounds boneless pork chops, cut ½ inch thick*

Marinade

3 *tablespoons Chinese rice wine or dry sherry*

2½ *tablespoons soy sauce*

1 *tablespoon cornstarch*

Sauce

¼ *cup ketchup*

3 *tablespoons Chinese black vinegar or balsamic vinegar*

2 *tablespoons hoisin sauce*

2 *tablespoons Worcestershire sauce*

1 *tablespoon soy sauce*

1 *tablespoon sugar*

1 *teaspoon chili garlic sauce*

1 *egg, lightly beaten*

Cornstarch

Cooking oil for deep-frying

Getting Ready

① Cut pork into 2-inch squares. Place between sheets of waxed paper and pound to ¼ inch thick. Combine marinade ingredients in a bowl. Add meat and stir to coat. Cover and refrigerate for 2 hours.

② Combine sauce ingredients in a small pan and set aside.

Cooking

① Place egg and cornstarch in separate bowls. Dip pork in egg, drain briefly, then dip in cornstarch; shake off excess.

② In a wok or 2-quart saucepan, heat oil for deep-frying to 360°F. Deep-fry pork, a few pieces at a time, turning occasionally, until golden brown, 3 to 4 minutes. Remove with a slotted spoon; drain on paper towels.

③ Cook sauce over medium heat, stirring, until heated through.

④ Place pork on a serving plate. Pour sauce over the top.

Makes 6 servings.

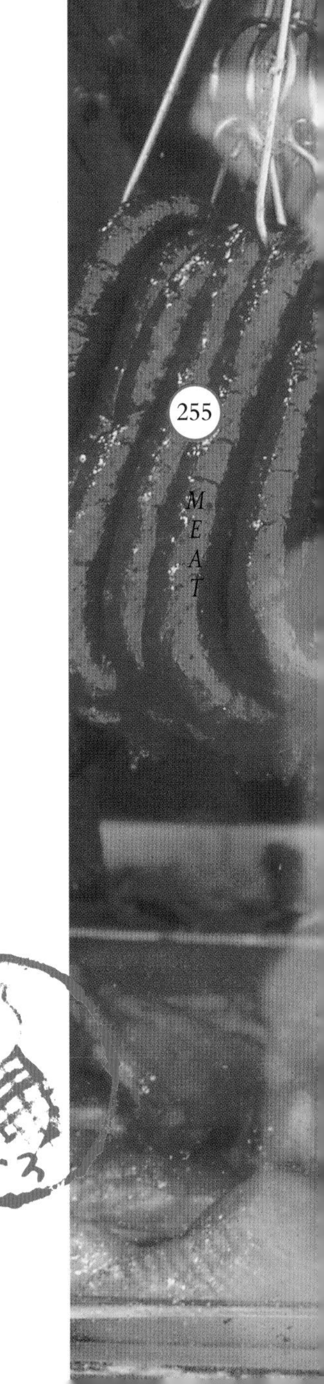

Five-Spice Pork Chops

Chinese five-spice is a blend of star anise, cloves, cinnamon, fennel, and Sichuan peppercorns. When you braise the pork chops slowly, the complex flavors of all these spices really come through.

- ¾ *teaspoon salt*
- ¼ *teaspoon Chinese five-spice*
- 4 *pork chops, cut about ½ inch thick*

Sauce

- ¼ *cup orange juice*
- ¼ *cup chicken broth*
- 1½ *tablespoons soy sauce*
- 1 *tablespoon packed brown sugar*
- 1 *tablespoon grated orange peel*

- 1 *tablespoon cooking oil*
- 1 *small onion, cut into 1-inch cubes*
- 2 *teaspoons minced ginger*
- 2 *teaspoons minced garlic*
- 1 *fresh red jalapeño chili, seeded and sliced*
- 2 *teaspoons cornstarch dissolved in 2 tablespoons water*

Getting Ready

① Combine salt and five-spice in a small bowl. Sprinkle on both sides of pork chops.

② Combine sauce ingredients in a bowl.

Cooking

① Place a heavy frying pan over high heat until hot. Add ½ tablespoon oil, swirling to coat sides. Place pork chops in pan and brown for 2 minutes on each side. Remove meat from pan.

② Heat remaining ½ tablespoon oil in pan, swirling to coat sides. Add onion, ginger, garlic, and chili; cook, stirring, until onion is softened, 1½ to 2 minutes.

③ Return meat to pan; add sauce. Bring to a boil; reduce heat, cover, and simmer until meat is no longer pink, 5 to 7 minutes.

④ Lift meat from sauce and place on a serving plate. Add cornstarch solution and cook, stirring, until sauce boils and thickens. Pour sauce over meat.

Makes 4 servings.

Fabulous Five-Spice

The ancient Chinese believed the number five had curative powers, and the spice blend known as five-spice probably began as an herbal medicine. Like everything else nowadays, inflation has caught up with five-spice, and it usually has a few more than five ingredients, including star anise, cinnamon, fennel, clove, ginger, Sichuan peppercorns, and dried tangerine peel, ground together into fine powder. It's delicious mixed with salt for dipping, and used on grilled or roasted foods.

Hoisin Red-Cooked Lamb

Some say that lamb requires a cultivated taste. I say that no cultivated palate can do without lamb, especially when it is slowly braised in a rich sauce. Many traditional Chinese chefs save their red cooking sauce so that they can use it again and again. They add a little broth, fresh soy sauce, and more seasonings, and the sauce gets richer each time it's used.

1	*piece lamb shoulder (2 to 2½ lb.)*
1	*tablespoon cooking oil*
5	*slices ginger, each the size of a quarter, lightly crushed*
3	*cloves garlic, peeled and lightly crushed*
2	*cups chicken broth*
2	*cups water*
¼	*cup regular soy sauce*
⅓	*cup dark soy sauce*
⅓	*cup Chinese rice wine or dry sherry*
3	*tablespoons sugar*
2	*tablespoons orange peel, julienned*
1	*whole star anise*
¾	*teaspoon cornstarch dissolved in 2 teaspoons water*

Cooking

① In a large pan, parboil lamb in water to cover for 5 minutes; pour into a colander and let drain.

② In the same pan, heat oil over high heat until hot. Add ginger and garlic; cook, stirring, until fragrant, about 10 seconds. Add broth, water, soy sauces, wine, sugar, orange peel, and star anise. Bring to a boil; reduce heat, cover, and simmer for 20 minutes.

③ Return lamb to pan and stir to coat with sauce. Bring to a boil; reduce heat, cover, and simmer until meat is tender, about 2 hours.

④ Remove lamb and place on a cutting board. Cut meat into thin slices and place on a serving plate.

⑤ Strain sauce. Bring ½ cup of the sauce to a boil in a small pan. Add cornstarch solution and cook, stirring, until sauce boils and thickens. Pour thickened sauce over meat to serve. Reserve remaining sauce for other uses.

Makes 6 to 8 servings.

Wok-Seared Lamb with Four Onions

This quick stir-fry of lamb with leeks and red, yellow, and green onions was inspired by more than one restaurant dish I've been served in Beijing. I love the way the sweetness of the onions and the tanginess of the vinegar bring out the flavor of the lamb. This makes a great stuffing for Sesame Seed Pillows (see page 193).

Marinade

- 2 *tablespoons Chinese rice wine or dry sherry*
- 2 *tablespoons dark soy sauce*
- 2 *teaspoons cornstarch*
- ¼ *teaspoon ground toasted Sichuan peppercorns*

- ¾ *pound boneless lamb (leg or loin)*

Sauce

- 3 *tablespoons hoisin sauce*
- 1 *tablespoon dark soy sauce*
- 1 *tablespoon vinegar*
- 2 *teaspoons chili garlic sauce*

- 2½ *tablespoons cooking oil*
- 3 *cloves garlic, thinly sliced*
- 1 *leek (1-in. diameter), white part only, julienned*
- ½ *cup* each *thinly sliced red and yellow onions*
- 6 *green onions, julienned*

Getting Ready

① Combine marinade ingredients in a bowl. Cut lamb into thin slices, then cut slices into thin strips. Add meat to marinade and stir to coat. Let stand for 10 minutes.

② Combine sauce ingredients in a bowl.

Cooking

① Place a wok over high heat until hot. Add 2 tablespoons oil, swirling to coat sides. Add garlic and cook, stirring, until fragrant, about 10 seconds. Add lamb and stir-fry until barely pink, 1½ to 2 minutes. Remove meat from pan.

② Add remaining ½ tablespoon oil to wok, swirling to coat sides. Add leek and onions; stir-fry for 1 minute. Return lamb to wok and add sauce. Cook until heated through.

Makes 4 servings.

On the Lamb

Beijing is known as the lamb capital of China. You can find lamb and mutton (lamb that's over a year old) on most restaurant menus, and in the streets you often smell the distinctive aroma of lamb cooking. To balance the pronounced taste of lamb, northern cooks prepare it with lots of onions, leeks, and garlic, and season it with flavorful condiments like vinegar, chili sauce, rice wine, and hoisin.

Barbecued Mongolian Lamb

Grilling is a not a typical method of cooking in most parts of China, and grilled foods like these small skewers of lamb are most likely to be found at open-air food stands. When preparing them at home, presoak the bamboo skewers in water to keep them from burning on the grill.

Marinade

- 1/3 *cup Chinese rice wine or dry sherry*
- 1/4 *cup soy sauce*
- 2 *teaspoons minced garlic*
- 2 *teaspoons cornstarch*
- 1 *teaspoon ground toasted Sichuan peppercorns*

- 3/4 *pound tender boneless lamb or beef*
- *About 16 bamboo skewers*
- 1/2 *tablespoon cooking oil*
- 1 *medium onion, cut into 1/2-inch pieces*

Getting Ready

① Combine marinade ingredients in a bowl. Cut lamb into thin strips, about 1/2 inch wide and 8 inches long. Place lamb in marinade and stir to coat. Let stand for 10 minutes.

② Soak skewers in water to cover for 15 minutes or until ready to use.

③ Lift lamb from marinade; reserve marinade. Thread one piece of meat on each skewer, stretching meat so it lies flat.

Cooking

① Place a wok over high heat until hot. Add oil, swirling to coat sides. Add onion and stir-fry until onion is tender-crisp, 3 to 4 minutes. Remove wok from heat; cover to keep warm.

② Place skewers on an oiled grill 3 to 4 inches above a solid bed of glowing coals. Cook, basting with marinade and turning frequently, until meat is no longer pink, 2 to 3 minutes.

③ Spread onion on a serving plate. Top with skewers of meat.

Makes 4 servings.

Sichuan Peppercorns

No relation to black peppercorns, Sichuan peppercorns are actually a dried berry that's used as a seasoning throughout western China. Along with star anise, they're one of the main ingredients in Chinese five-spice. When Sichuan peppercorns are toasted, their fragrant oils are released, and they take on a pleasant spiciness that's less sharp than that of chilies or black pepper. Toast them in a heavy frying pan over low heat, stirring occasionally, until they become fragrant.

Mongolian Hot Pot

Mongolian hot pot is the Chinese version of fondue, and it's great for entertaining because it brings people together and once you set it up, the guests do all the work! In northern China, lamb is traditionally the main ingredient, while in the south it might be seafood, chicken, or pork, and lots of fresh vegetables. End the meal by serving the flavorful broth as a soup.

6	*cups chicken broth*
2	*slices ginger, each the size of a quarter, lightly crushed*
2	*green onions, cut in half and lightly crushed*
8	*ounces dried bean thread noodles*
2	*pounds tender boneless lamb or beef*
1	*package (14 oz.) regular-firm tofu, drained*
2	*pounds mixed leafy green vegetables, such as bok choy, spinach, and napa cabbage*

Dipping Sauce

1	*cup soy sauce*
⅓	*cup chicken broth*
2	*tablespoons sesame seed paste or chunky peanut butter*
2	*tablespoons sesame oil*

Getting Started

① Place broth, ginger, and green onions in a large pot; bring to a boil. Reduce heat, cover, and simmer for 30 minutes. Discard ginger and green onions.

② Soak noodles in warm water to cover until softened, about 5 minutes; drain. Cut noodles into 4-inch lengths.

③ Cut lamb into thin slices. Cut tofu into 1-inch cubes. Cut vegetables into bite-sized pieces. Arrange noodles, lamb, tofu, and vegetables attractively on a large platter. Cover and chill until ready to cook.

④ Combine dipping sauce ingredients in a bowl. Pour into individual dipping sauce bowls.

Cooking

① Reheat broth to simmering. Set a Mongolian hot pot or an electric wok in center of table. Pour broth into hot pot and adjust heat so broth simmers gently. Each diner cooks his or her choice of ingredients in the broth and seasons it with dipping sauce.

Makes 6 to 8 servings.

One Hot Pot!

When buying a hot pot, be sure to find one that's suitable for cooking—some are purely ornamental. Always fill the moat with hot broth before adding the coals to avoid damaging the pot. You can start the coals in a barbecue, then use tongs to transfer them to the hot pot, filling the chimney halfway full.

CHAPTER 8

Poultry

Minced Poultry with Walnuts in Lettuce Cups

This is my version of a favorite banquet dish that's often served on festive occasions as a symbol of longevity. The crisp, chilled lettuce makes a wonderful contrast to the warm filling, and the sweetness of the hoisin sauce marries all the flavors.

6	*dried black mushrooms*
¾	*cup walnuts*
½	*pound boneless, skinless chicken, turkey, or duck*
1	*tablespoon oyster-flavored sauce*
2	*tablespoons cooking oil*
1	*teaspoon minced ginger*
1	*small carrot, cut into ¼-inch cubes*
1	*small zucchini, cut into ¼-inch cubes*
1	*cup diced water chestnuts or jicama*
1	*tablespoon Chinese rice wine or dry sherry*
1	*teaspoon sesame oil*
	Hoisin sauce
12	*small iceberg lettuce cups*

Getting Ready

① Soak mushrooms in warm water to cover until softened, about 20 minutes; drain, reserving ¼ cup of the soaking liquid. Discard stems and chop caps.

② Spread walnuts in a pie pan; toast in a 350°F oven, stirring once or twice, until lightly browned, about 10 minutes. Let nuts cool, then coarsely chop.

③ Cut chicken into ¼-inch pieces. Place in a bowl with oyster-flavored sauce; stir to coat. Let stand for 10 minutes.

Cooking

① Place a wok over high heat until hot. Add oil, swirling to coat sides. Add ginger and cook, stirring, until fragrant, about 10 seconds. Add chicken and stir-fry for 1 minute. Add carrot, zucchini, and water chestnuts; stir-fry for 30 seconds.

② Add reserved mushroom soaking liquid; cook until vegetables are tender-crisp, about 2 minutes. Add wine and sesame oil; cook until heated through. Add walnuts and toss to coat.

③ To eat, spread hoisin sauce on a lettuce cup, spoon in some of chicken mixture, wrap in lettuce cup, and eat out of hand.

Makes 4 to 6 servings.

Lychee Chicken

The sweet taste of a fresh lychee is my favorite memory of our next-door neighbors in China. They had a lychee tree in their backyard, and during harvest season, that tree became the delight of the entire neighborhood. The sweetness of lychee will make this chicken dish a delight in your kitchen, too.

Marinade

- 2 *tablespoons oyster-flavored sauce*
- 1 *tablespoon Chinese rice wine or dry sherry*
- 1 *tablespoon cornstarch*
- ¼ *teaspoon white pepper*

- ¾ *pound boneless, skinless chicken, cut into ¾-inch cubes*

Sauce

- 1 *can (15 oz.) lychees*
- 1 *cup cantaloupe balls*
- ¼ *cup sweet chili sauce*
- 3 *tablespoons orange juice*

- 2 *tablespoons cooking oil*

Getting Ready

① Combine marinade ingredients in a bowl. Add chicken and stir to coat. Let stand for 10 minutes.

② For sauce, drain lychees and pour ⅓ cup lychee syrup into a bowl. Add lychees, cantaloupe, sweet chili sauce, and orange juice.

Cooking

① Place a wok over high heat until hot. Add oil, swirling to coat sides. Add chicken and stir-fry until no longer pink when cut, 2½ to 3 minutes.

② Add sauce and bring to a boil; simmer for 1 minute.

Makes 4 servings.

I Love Lychee

Southern China is the land of lychees. But nowadays, so is the American South. Florida growers produce fresh lychees from July through September—which is great news for me, because ever since I was a small boy, I've never been able to get enough of them. If you ever get a chance to taste fresh lychees, you'll understand why. Fortunately too, canned lychees are always available, and I love their sweet flavor and soft texture. In Guangzhou, you'll find lychees used in sweet and sour dishes and sometimes served as a refreshment over a bowl of ice.

Black Bean-Flavored Chicken

Mention black bean sauce, and my mouth starts to water. The strong aroma and pungent flavor of salted black beans do much to enhance the flavor of various dishes, whether steamed, braised, or stir-fried.

Marinade

- 2 *tablespoons oyster-flavored sauce*
- 1 *tablespoon Chinese rice wine or dry sherry*
- 2 *teaspoons cornstarch*

- ¾ *pound boneless, skinless chicken, cut into ½-inch cubes*
- 2 *tablespoons cooking oil*
- 2 *tablespoons salted black beans, rinsed, drained, and coarsely chopped*
- 2 *teaspoons minced garlic*
- 1 *fresh jalapeño chili, seeded and sliced*
- ¾ *pound asparagus, trimmed and cut diagonally into 1½-inch lengths*
- 1 *red bell pepper, seeded and thinly sliced*
- ½ *cup chicken broth*
- 2 *teaspoons sugar*
- 1 *teaspoon cornstarch dissolved in 2 teaspoons water*

Getting Ready

① Combine marinade ingredients in a bowl. Add chicken and stir to coat. Let stand for 10 minutes.

Cooking

① Place a wok over high heat until hot. Add 1½ tablespoons oil, swirling to coat sides. Add chicken and stir-fry until no longer pink when cut, 2½ to 3 minutes. Remove chicken from wok.

② Add remaining ½ tablespoon oil to wok, swirling to coat sides. Add black beans, garlic, and chili; cook, stirring, until fragrant, about 10 seconds. Add asparagus and bell pepper; stir-fry for 30 seconds. Add broth and sugar; cover and cook until vegetables are tender-crisp, 1½ to 2 minutes. Return chicken to wok; cook until heated through. Add cornstarch solution and cook, stirring, until sauce boils and thickens.

Makes 4 servings.

A Chicken Checklist

Here are a few basic safety tips: Defrost in the refrigerator, in the sink under cold running water, or in the microwave, never out on the counter. To avoid cross-contamination, wash your hands, knives, and cutting boards. Cook chicken to an internal temperature of 165°F at the thickest point, or until juices are clear and not pink. If you've used a marinade on raw poultry, either discard it or cook it before serving. If you're using the marinade for basting, be sure the last application has enough time to cook completely.

General Tso's Favorite Chicken

A dish fit for a general is certainly good enough for me. The usual way to make this dish is to deep-fry the chicken. Personally, I prefer stir-frying for a lighter fare. With the rich and flavorful sauce, it's sure to be your favorite chicken dish as well.

Marinade

- 3 *tablespoons Chinese rice wine or dry sherry*
- 1½ *tablespoons oyster-flavored sauce*
- 2 *teaspoons cornstarch*

- 1 *pound boneless, skinless chicken thighs, cut into 1-inch pieces*

Sauce

- ¼ *cup chicken broth*
- 1 *tablespoon rice vinegar*
- 1 *tablespoon regular soy sauce*
- 1 *tablespoon dark soy sauce*
- 1 *tablespoon sugar*
- 2 *teaspoons sesame oil*

- 2 *tablespoons cooking oil*
- 6 *small dried red chilies*
- 1 *tablespoon minced garlic*
- 2 *teaspoons minced ginger*
- 2 *green onions, cut into 1-inch lengths*
- ½ *teaspoon crushed dried red chilies*
- 1½ *teaspoons cornstarch dissolved in 1 tablespoon water*
- ¼ *cup roasted peanuts, coarsely chopped*

Getting Ready

① Combine marinade ingredients in a bowl. Place chicken in marinade and turn to coat. Let stand for 10 minutes.

② Combine sauce ingredients in a bowl.

Cooking

① Place a wok over high heat until hot. Add oil, swirling to coat sides. Add chilies and stir-fry for 10 seconds. Add chicken and stir-fry for 2 minutes. Add garlic, ginger, green onions, and crushed chilies; stir-fry for 1 minute.

② Add sauce and cook, stirring, for 1 minute. Add cornstarch solution and cook, stirring, until sauce boils and thickens.

③ Place chicken on a serving plate and sprinkle with peanuts.

Makes 4 servings.

Glazed Plum-Flavored Chicken with Wolfberries

Chicken thighs quickly braised and glazed with dried fruit make a great autumn or winter dinner. Wolfberries are small, deep red fruits with a sweet, spiced apple flavor. I buy them from an herbalist in San Francisco's Chinatown. If you can't find wolfberries, dried cranberries work well.

Marinade

- 2 *tablespoons dark soy sauce*
- 2 *teaspoons cornstarch*

- ¾ *pound boneless, skinless chicken thighs, cut into 1-inch pieces*
- 6 *small dried figs, halved and stemmed*
- 8 *pitted prunes*
- 2 *tablespoons dried wolfberries or dried cranberries*
- ¼ *cup plum wine*
- 2 *tablespoons cooking oil*
- 2 *tablespoons plum sauce*
- ¼ *cup chicken broth*
- ½ *teaspoon cornstarch dissolved in 1 teaspoon water*
- ½ *cup roasted cashews*

Getting Ready

① Combine marinade ingredients in a bowl. Add chicken and stir to coat. Let stand for 10 minutes.

② Soak figs, prunes, and wolfberries in plum wine until softened, about 10 minutes.

Cooking

① Place a wok over high heat until hot. Add oil, swirling to coat sides. Add chicken and stir-fry for 2 minutes. Add figs, prunes, wolfberries, soaking wine, plum sauce, and broth. Bring to a boil; reduce heat, cover, and simmer until chicken is no longer pink when cut, about 5 minutes longer. Add cornstarch solution and cook, stirring, until sauce boils and thickens. Add cashews and mix well.

Makes 4 servings.

Herb Blurb

The herbal medicine shops of Hong Kong and Chinatowns around the world are renowned for their vast selections of hard-to-find herbal remedies. The most popular shops are the ones that have a full-time doctor on staff to consult with customers and write prescriptions. There's always a not unpleasant, musty odor—something like a cross between wet earth, tea, and lemons. And the walls are lined with cabinets and jars containing an unending array of powders, berries, roots, and more. Chefs and savvy cooks know that these shops are also the best places to find all kinds of premium dried ingredients and seasonings for cooking.

Chicken in a Clay Pot

This is real Chinese home cooking—my mother's home, to be exact. This kind of braised chicken is as popular in China as coq au vin is in France. Note: Unless you are an expert with a heavy cleaver, ask the butcher to cut the chicken thighs in half for you, or simply use boneless chicken thighs.

- 6 *dried black mushrooms*

Sauce

- ½ *cup chicken broth*
- 2 *tablespoons Chinese rice wine or dry sherry*
- 1 *tablespoon soy sauce*
- 1 *tablespoon mashed fermented bean curd (optional)*
- ½ *teaspoon sugar*
- ⅛ *teaspoon white pepper*

- 4 *chicken thighs, cut in half crosswise*
- *Cornstarch*
- 1 *tablespoon cooking oil*
- 1 *teaspoon minced garlic*
- 1 *teaspoon minced ginger*
- 2 *Chinese sausages (2 oz. each), thinly sliced diagonally*
- 3 *green onions, cut into 1½-inch pieces*
- ¼ *cup sliced bamboo shoots*
- 1 *teaspoon cornstarch dissolved in 2 teaspoons water*
- *Green onion slivers*

Getting Ready

① Soak mushrooms in warm water to cover until softened, about 20 minutes; drain. Discard stems and thinly slice caps.

② Combine sauce ingredients in a bowl, mashing bean curd so it is evenly blended in sauce.

Cooking

① Dip chicken in cornstarch; shake off excess. Place a clay pot over low heat; gradually increase heat to medium-high. Add oil, swirling to coat sides. Add garlic and ginger; cook, stirring, until fragrant, about 10 seconds. Add chicken and cook until browned on each side, 4 to 5 minutes.

② Add mushrooms, sausages, green onions, bamboo shoots, and sauce. Bring to a boil; reduce heat, cover, and simmer, stirring occasionally, until meat near bone is no longer pink when cut, 20 to 25 minutes. Add cornstarch solution and cook, stirring, until sauce boils and thickens.

③ Garnish chicken with green onion slivers.

Makes 4 servings.

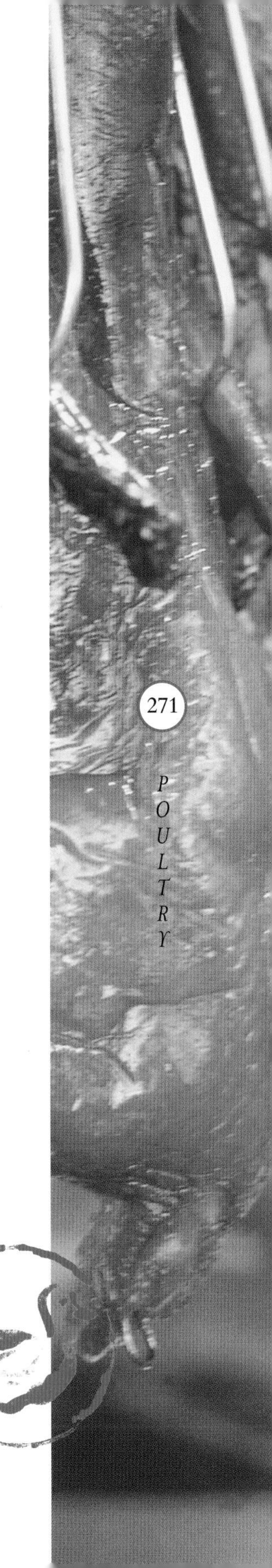

Three-Cup Chicken

The traditional "three-cup" red cooking sauce is so named because it called for 1 cup of soy sauce, 1 cup of cooking wine, and 1 cup of sesame oil. I've reduced the oil and added water for a more contemporary taste. Save the braising sauce. It makes a great addition to future dishes.

Braising Sauce

- 2 *cups water*
- 1 *cup Chinese rice wine or dry sherry*
- ½ *cup regular soy sauce*
- ½ *cup dark soy sauce*
- 2 *tablespoons Worcestershire sauce*
- 2 *tablespoons sesame oil*
- 4 *ounces rock sugar or ⅓ cup granulated sugar*
- 3 *green onions, cut in half*
- 1 *whole star anise*
- ¼ *teaspoon Chinese five-spice*

- 1 *tablespoon cooking oil*
- 8 *chicken thighs or drumsticks*
- 6 *slices ginger, each the size of a quarter, lightly crushed*
- 4 *cloves garlic, thinly sliced*
- 3 *small dried red chilies*

Getting Ready

① Combine braising sauce ingredients in a bowl.

Cooking

① Place a deep frying pan over medium-high heat until hot. Add oil, swirling to coat sides. Place chicken in pan and brown lightly on all sides, 4 to 5 minutes total. Remove chicken from pan.

② Increase heat to high. Add ginger, garlic, and chilies; cook, stirring, until fragrant, about 20 seconds. Return chicken to pan and add braising sauce. Bring to a boil; reduce heat, cover, and simmer until meat near bone is no longer pink when cut, 25 to 30 minutes.

③ Lift chicken from sauce and arrange on a serving platter. Strain sauce. Pass a bowl of sauce at the table; reserve remaining sauce for other uses.

Makes 4 servings.

Fowl Memories

When I was a kid in Guangzhou, a crowing rooster woke me up every morning, and we always had a few chickens scratching around the yard. My mom had a remarkable talent for turning a single chicken into several meals and using every last bit for soup stock, home remedies, and medicinal purposes. The sound of chickens clucking always makes me think of China, where chickens are a universal delicacy; even the poorest families will raise their own for an occasional special meal.

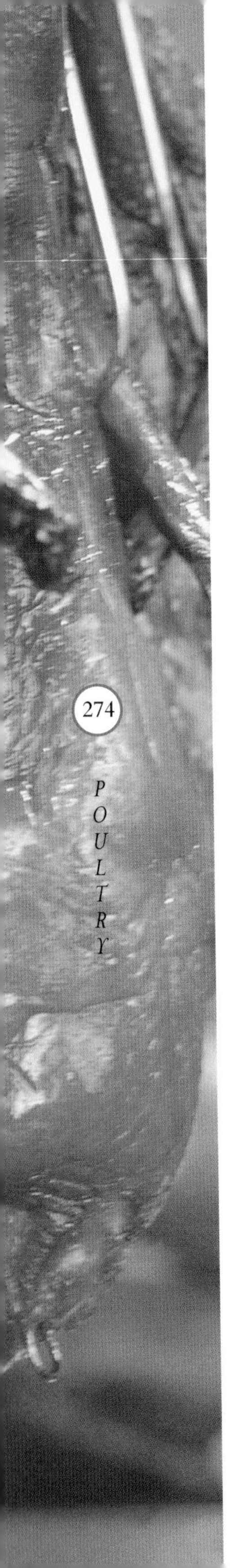

Hainan Curried Chicken

This dish is named after the tropical island of Hainan, southwest of Hong Kong, the only place in China where coconuts are grown commercially. If you use curry paste, be sure to use an Indian or Chinese brand, not the hotter Thai-style curry pastes.

Marinade

3 *tablespoons soy sauce*
1 *tablespoon cornstarch*

6 *chicken thighs*

Curry Sauce

1 *cup unsweetened coconut milk*
¼ *cup chicken broth*
2 *tablespoons Chinese rice wine or dry sherry*
2 *tablespoons oyster-flavored sauce*
1 *tablespoon curry powder or 2 tablespoons curry paste*
½ *teaspoon Chinese five-spice*

1 *tablespoon cooking oil*
2 *teaspoons minced garlic*
1 *fresh red jalapeño chili, seeded and sliced*
1 *small onion, cut into 1-inch squares*
1 *medium potato, cut into 1-inch cubes*
2 *green onions, cut into 1-inch pieces*
1 *tablespoon cornstarch dissolved in 2 tablespoons water*

Getting Ready

① Combine marinade ingredients in a bowl. Add chicken and turn to coat. Let stand for 10 minutes.

② Combine curry sauce ingredients in a bowl.

Cooking

① Place a wok over medium-high heat until hot. Add oil, swirling to coat sides. Add chicken to wok and brown lightly on all sides, 4 to 5 minutes total. Remove chicken from wok.

② Increase heat to high. Add garlic, chili, and onion; cook, stirring, until fragrant, about 20 seconds. Return chicken to wok; add potato and curry sauce. Bring to a boil; reduce heat, cover, and simmer until meat near bone is no longer pink when cut, 25 to 30 minutes.

③ Stir in green onions. Add cornstarch solution and cook, stirring, until sauce boils and thickens.

Makes 6 servings.

Kung Pao Chicken

Here's my recipe for one of the most famous of all Sichuan-Hunan dishes—hot, sour, sweet, and savory Kung Pao Chicken. To make it even hotter, break open one or more of the dried chili pods before adding them to the wok.

Marinade

- 2 *tablespoons oyster-flavored sauce*
- 1 *teaspoon cornstarch*

- ¾ *pound boneless, skinless chicken*

Sauce

- ¼ *cup Chinese black vinegar or balsamic vinegar*
- ¼ *cup chicken broth*
- 3 *tablespoons Chinese rice wine or dry sherry*
- 2 *tablespoons hoisin sauce*
- 1 *tablespoon soy sauce*
- 2 *teaspoons sesame oil*
- 2 *teaspoons chili garlic sauce*
- 2 *teaspoons sugar*

- 2½ *tablespoons cooking oil*
- 8 *small dried red chilies*
- 4 *teaspoons minced garlic*
- 2 *stalks celery, diced*
- ½ *red bell pepper, cut into 1-inch squares*
- 1 *can (8 oz.) sliced bamboo shoots, drained*
- 2 *teaspoons cornstarch dissolved in 1 tablespoon water*
- ⅓ *cup roasted peanuts*

Getting Started

① Combine marinade ingredients in a bowl. Cut chicken into 1-inch pieces. Place chicken in marinade and stir to coat. Let stand for 10 minutes.

② Combine sauce ingredients in a bowl.

Cooking

① Place a wok over high heat until hot. Add 2 tablespoons oil, swirling to coat sides. Add chilies and cook, stirring, until fragrant, about 10 seconds. Add chicken and stir-fry for 2 minutes. Remove chicken and chilies from wok.

② Add remaining ½ tablespoon oil to wok, swirling to coat sides. Add garlic and cook, stirring, until fragrant, about 10 seconds. Add celery, bell pepper, and bamboo shoots; stir-fry for 1½ minutes.

③ Return chicken and chilies to wok; stir-fry for 1 minute. Add sauce and bring to a boil. Add cornstarch solution and cook, stirring, until sauce boils and thickens. Add peanuts and stir to coat.

Makes 4 servings.

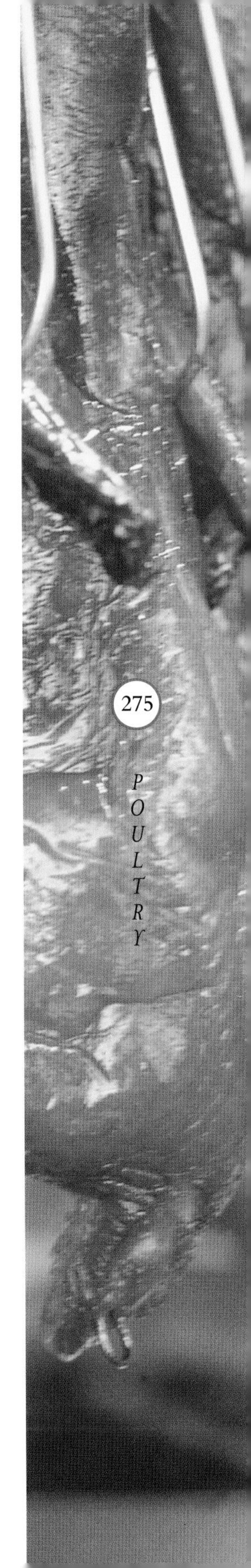

Honey-Glazed Lemon Chicken

In Cantonese restaurants all over the world, lemon chicken is one of the best-known dishes. This version, sweetened with honey and melon, was inspired by a version I was served in Shenzen, southern China.

Marinade

- 2 *tablespoons oyster-flavored sauce*
- 1 *tablespoon cornstarch*

- 4 *boneless, skinless chicken breast halves*

Sauce

- ⅓ *cup lemon juice*
- ¼ *cup honey*
- 2 *tablespoons chicken broth*
- 2 *teaspoons soy sauce*
- 1 *teaspoon grated lemon peel or orange peel*

- *Cooking oil for deep-frying*
- *Cornstarch*
- 1 *egg, lightly beaten*
- ¾ *cup Japanese-style bread crumbs (panko)*
- 2 *teaspoons cornstarch dissolved in 1 tablespoon water*
- ½ *cup diced honeydew melon*
- ½ *cup diced cantaloupe*

Getting Ready

① Combine marinade ingredients in a bowl. Place chicken between waxed paper; pound to an even thickness. Add chicken to marinade and stir to coat. Let stand for 10 minutes.

② Combine sauce ingredients in a small saucepan.

Cooking

① In a wok or 2-quart saucepan, heat oil for deep-frying to 350°F. Dip chicken in cornstarch; shake to remove excess. Dip into egg, drain briefly, then coat with bread crumbs. Deep-fry chicken, turning once, until golden brown, 3 to 4 minutes on each side. Remove with a slotted spoon; drain on paper towels.

② Cook sauce over medium heat, stirring, until it simmers. Add cornstarch solution and cook, stirring, until sauce boils and thickens. Add diced melons; cook until heated through.

③ To serve, cut chicken into bite-sized pieces. Pour sauce on top.

Makes 4 servings.

Sweet Honey in the Rock

For many centuries, honey was the only sweetener available in China. Honey from beehives along cliff faces was called "stone honey." Eventually, sugar was called stone honey (as in "getting water from a stone"), because it was made without bees. Even more confusing, along came "rock sugar," made from sugar *and* honey!

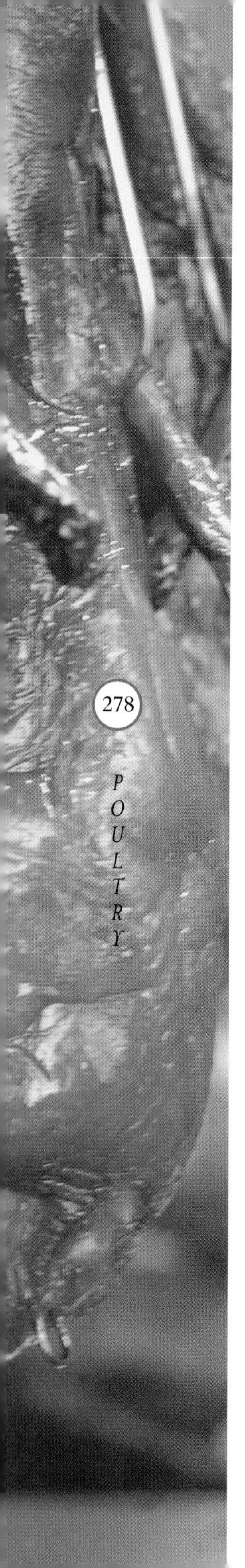

Sweet and Sour Chicken

For many North Americans, sweet and sour chicken was their first introduction to Chinese cooking. Early immigrants from southern China had brought with them their love of sweet and sour dishes. Ironically, this dish is now much better known over here than back in Guangdong.

Marinade

- 2 *tablespoons soy sauce*
- 2 *teaspoons cornstarch*

- 1 *pound boneless, skinless chicken, cut into ¾-inch cubes*

Sauce

- ¼ *cup orange juice*
- ¼ *cup ketchup*
- 3 *tablespoons packed brown sugar*
- 2 *tablespoons plum sauce*
- 2 *tablespoons lemon juice*
- 1 *tablespoon soy sauce*
- 1 *teaspoon grated ginger*
- 1 *teaspoon chili garlic sauce*

Cooking oil for deep-frying

Cornstarch

- 1 *small onion, cut into ½-inch cubes*
- 1 *bell pepper, cut into ½-inch squares*
- 1 *can (11 oz.) lychees, drained*
- 1½ *teaspoons cornstarch dissolved in 1 tablespoon water*

Getting Ready

① Combine marinade ingredients in a bowl. Add chicken and stir to coat. Let stand for 10 minutes.

② Combine sauce ingredients in a bowl.

Cooking

① In a wok or 2-quart saucepan, heat oil for deep-frying to 375°F. Dredge chicken in cornstarch; shake off excess. Deep-fry chicken, a few pieces at a time, turning once or twice, until golden brown, about 3 minutes. Remove with a slotted spoon; drain on paper towels.

② Place a frying pan over high heat until hot. Add 1 tablespoon of the frying oil, swirling to coat sides. Add onion and cook for 1 minute. Add bell pepper and cook for 1 minute. Add lychees and sauce; bring to a boil. Return chicken to pan. Add cornstarch solution and cook, stirring, until sauce boils and thickens.

Makes 4 servings.

Eight-Piece Beijing Chicken

This is fried chicken Beijing-style. Traditionally, chefs cut a whole chicken into eight pieces and deep-fry it. Here's an easy pan-fried adaptation. Cutting slashes in the chicken parallel to the bone shortens the cooking time and allows the marinade to permeate the meat.

Marinade

- 2 *tablespoons Chinese rice wine or dry sherry*
- 2 *tablespoons soy sauce*
- 2 *tablespoons cornstarch*
- 2 *tablespoons finely chopped green onion*
- 1 *tablespoon grated ginger*
- 2 *teaspoons minced garlic*

- 8 *chicken thighs or drumsticks*

Spiced Salt

- 2 *teaspoons salt*
- 1 *teaspoon Chinese five-spice*
- ¼ *teaspoon white pepper*

- 3 *tablespoons cooking oil*

Getting Ready

① Combine marinade ingredients in a bowl. If using chicken thighs, place chicken, skin side down, on a cutting board. With a sharp knife, cut ½-inch-deep slits along both sides of the bone. Place chicken in marinade and stir to coat. Cover and refrigerate for 1 to 2 hours.

② Combine spiced salt ingredients in a frying pan over low heat. Cook, stirring, until toasted and fragrant, about 2 minutes. Let cool.

Cooking

① Place a wide frying pan over medium heat until hot. Add oil, swirling to coat sides. Add chicken and cook until golden brown on all sides, 2 to 3 minutes per side. Reduce heat to medium-low, cover, and cook, until meat near bone is no longer pink when cut, 10 to 12 minutes.

② Serve chicken with spiced salt.

Makes 4 servings.

A Wing and a Prayer

Chickens hold a special place in Chinese ritual and symbology. They were used as sacrificial offerings in ancient China and were thought to possess life-giving powers. The rooster gets a place of honor in the Chinese zodiac, too, and its crowing is credited with driving away the evil spirits of the night. Black chickens (whose skin and bones are naturally dark black) are not only flavorful, they're also believed to restore youthful vigor and good looks. I'm keeping my fingers crossed.

Sesame Chicken with Rice

In Japan, this is one of my favorite one-dish meals. Dusting the chicken lightly with cornstarch before pan-frying seals in the moisture and creates a delicately crispy coating. This makes a well-balanced meal, not to mention a delicious one. For details on sake and *dashi*, see pages 286 and 45.

Sauce

- ½ *cup soy sauce*
- ½ *cup Japanese rice wine (sake)*
- ½ *cup Japanese soup stock (dashi)*
- ⅓ *cup sugar*
- 2 *teaspoons minced garlic*
- ½ *teaspoon minced ginger*
- 2 *teaspoons cornstarch dissolved in 1 tablespoon water*

- 1 *teaspoon sesame seeds*
- ½ *pound spinach*
- ¾ *pound boneless chicken thighs, cut into 2- by 2-inch pieces*
- *Cornstarch*
- *Cooking oil*
- 4 *cups hot cooked rice*

Getting Ready

① In a 2-quart pan, combine soy sauce, sake, dashi, sugar, garlic, and ginger. Cook over medium heat, stirring once or twice, until sugar is dissolved. Reduce heat and simmer, uncovered, for 10 minutes. Add cornstarch solution and cook, stirring, until sauce boils and thickens. Keep sauce warm.

② Place sesame seeds in a small frying pan over medium heat; cook, shaking pan frequently, until seeds are lightly browned, 3 to 4 minutes. Immediately remove from pan to cool.

③ Wash spinach and remove coarse stems. Place spinach in a large pot with 1 inch of water. Parboil for 30 seconds; drain, then rinse with cold water. Drain well and keep warm.

Cooking

① Dip chicken in cornstarch; shake off excess. Place a wide frying pan over medium heat. Add oil to a depth of ¼ inch. When oil is hot, add chicken and pan-fry, uncovered, until no longer pink in center when cut, about 4 minutes on each side. Lift out and drain on paper towels.

② Place rice in 4 individual bowls; top each serving with ¼ of the spinach. Cut chicken into ½-inch-wide strips, dip in sauce, then arrange over spinach. Drizzle 1 to 2 tablespoons additional sauce over each serving, then sprinkle with sesame seeds.

Makes 4 servings.

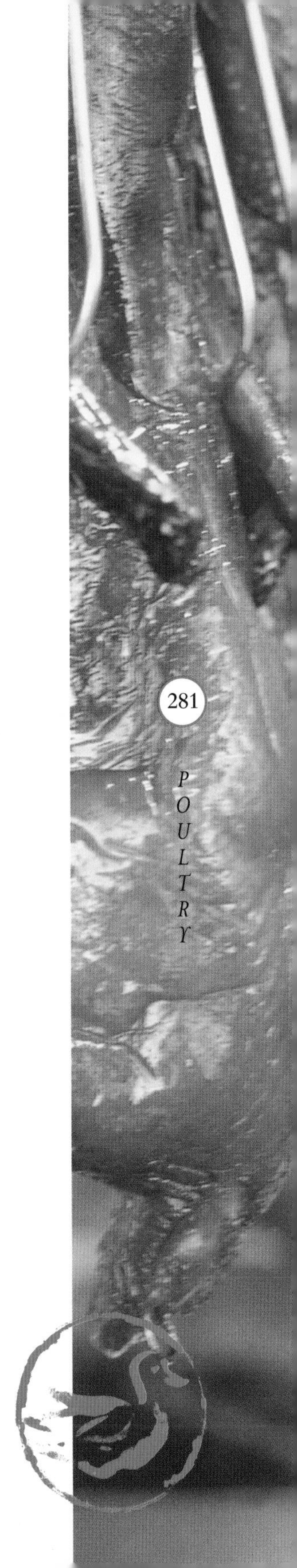

Thai-Style Chicken

So many of the great tastes of Thailand are found in the great outdoors, at roadside food stands. I've discovered that this tasty chicken recipe with all the right seasonings works equally well indoors. With practice, Little Bangkok may be as close to you as your oven.

Marinade

3	*tablespoons fish sauce*
3	*tablespoons finely chopped cilantro*
2	*tablespoons minced garlic*
1	*tablespoon grated ginger*
2	*teaspoons sugar*
2	*teaspoons curry powder*
1	*teaspoon turmeric powder*
½	*teaspoon white pepper*
8	*chicken thighs*
	Sweet chili sauce

Getting Ready

① Combine marinade ingredients in a large bowl. Add chicken and turn to coat. Cover and refrigerate for 4 hours or up to overnight.

Cooking

① Preheat oven to 375°F. Place chicken pieces 1 inch apart in a shallow baking pan. Bake, uncovered, until meat near bone is no longer pink when cut, 40 to 45 minutes.

② Place chicken on a serving plate. Pass a small bowl of sweet chili sauce for dipping.

Makes 4 servings.

Cilantro

Also known as fresh coriander or Chinese parsley, fresh cilantro has a distinctive aromatic flavor that people either love or can't stand. But once cilantro is cooked, it has a less pronounced taste that marries well with fish, poultry, and red meat. I like to use it as a garnish, placing a few leaves at one side of a serving platter or floating individual sprigs on bowls of soup, because its soft, lacy leaves are so attractive. That way, guests can either eat it or set it aside.

Beggar's Favorite Chicken

Who says beggars can't be choosers?

Marinade

- 3 *tablespoons Chinese rice wine*
- 2 *tablespoons regular soy sauce*
- 1 *tablespoon dark soy sauce*
- ½ *teaspoon Chinese five-spice*

- 1 *whole frying chicken (about 3 lb.), cleaned*
- 2 *dried lotus leaves or two 15-inch squares cooking parchment*

Stuffing

- 1 *tablespoon cooking oil*
- 1 *teaspoon minced garlic*
- 1 *Chinese sausage (2 oz.), thinly sliced*
- 1 *stalk celery, chopped*
- 2 *green onions, thinly sliced*
- 2 *tablespoons Sichuan preserved vegetable, chopped*
- 1 *tablespoon hoisin sauce*
- 2 *teaspoons soy sauce*

- 1 *piece foil large enough to enclose wrapped chicken*

Baker's Clay

- 9 *large egg whites*
- 8 *cups regular salt*

Getting Ready

① Combine marinade ingredients. Rub chicken inside and out with marinade. Cover and refrigerate 2 hours.

② Heat a large pot of water, add lotus leaves, and simmer until softened, about 15 minutes; drain.

③ Prepare stuffing: Place a wok over high heat until hot. Add oil, swirling to coat sides. Add garlic and cook, stirring, until fragrant, about 10 seconds. Add sausage and stir-fry until sausage is slightly crisp, 1½ to 2 minutes. Add celery, green onions, and preserved vegetable. Cook for 1 minute. Add hoisin sauce and soy sauce; mix well. Let stuffing cool.

Cooking

① Place stuffing inside chicken; enclose with skewers. Spread 1 lotus leaf on work surface; cover with second leaf. Place chicken in center of leaves; fold leaves over so chicken is completely enclosed. Fold foil around wrapped chicken to enclose.

② Preheat oven to 400°F. Prepare baker's clay: Combine egg whites and salt; mix well. Spread half of clay mixture on a foil-lined baking sheet to make a rectangle 1 inch thick and about 2 inches wider than chicken. Place chicken on clay mixture. Spread remaining clay over top and sides so chicken is enclosed. Bake for 1¼ hours.

Makes 2 to 4 servings.

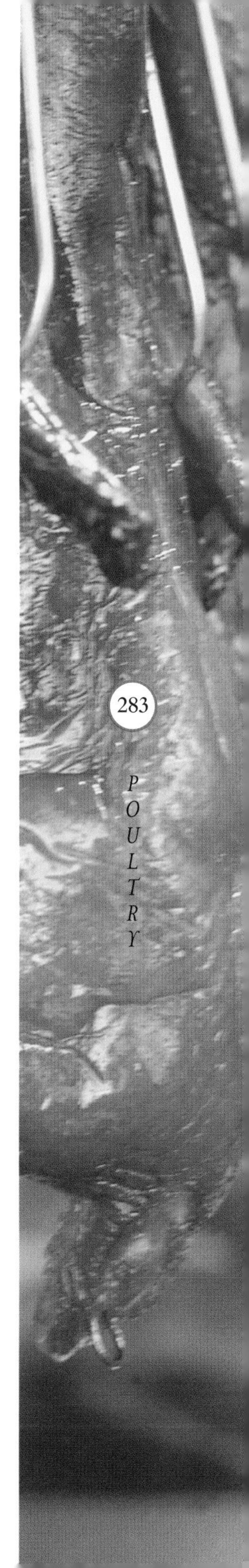

Chicken and Seafood Trio in a Basket

This delicate stir-fry will be a hit if you serve it in a deep-fried edible basket (see recipe below).

- ¾ *pound asparagus, trimmed and cut into 2-inch lengths*
- ½ *pound mixed seafood (choose from firm white fish fillets, scallops, and shrimp)*
- ¼ *pound boneless, skinless chicken breast*
- 1 *tablespoon cornstarch*
- 1 *egg white*
- ½ *teaspoon salt*
- ¼ *teaspoon white pepper*
- 2 *tablespoons cooking oil*
- 2 *teaspoons minced ginger*
- 1 *green onion, finely chopped*
- ¾ *cup chicken broth*
- 2 *tablespoons oyster-flavored sauce*
- 1 *tablespoon fish sauce*
- 1 *teaspoon cornstarch dissolved in 2 teaspoons water*
- *Edible basket (recipe below)*

Getting Ready

① Bring a large pan of water to a boil. Add asparagus. Cook until tender-crisp, about 2 minutes. Drain.

② Cut seafood into ½-inch cubes. Cut chicken into ½-inch cubes. Coat seafood and chicken with cornstarch, egg white, salt, and pepper.

Cooking

① Place a wok over high heat until hot. Add oil, swirling to coat sides. Add ginger and cook, stirring, until fragrant, about 10 seconds. Add seafood, chicken, and green onion; stir-fry for 1 minute.

② Add broth, oyster-flavored sauce, and fish sauce; bring to a boil. Add cornstarch solution and cook, stirring, until sauce boils and thickens. Add asparagus and toss to mix.

③ Spoon seafood mixture into basket.

Makes 4 servings.

Basket-Making 101

To make an edible basket, you need two 6-inch metal strainers. In a wok, heat **cooking oil** for deep-frying to 350°F. Peel and shred or finely julienne 1 medium **potato** (taro root or cooked fresh egg noodles can also be used). Rinse shredded potato under cold running water; squeeze well to remove as much moisture as possible and pat dry with paper towels. Toss potato with 1 teaspoon **cornstarch**. Dip strainers into hot oil to coat them. Line one strainer with potato to a thickness of about ⅜ inch. Nest second strainer on top, and immerse strainers in oil. Deep-fry until golden brown. Remove potato basket and drain on paper towels. Use immediately.

Chicken Teriyaki

Probably the most famous Japanese dish the world over, chicken teriyaki is also one of my favorite backyard barbecue foods. If you don't want to fire up the grill, you can also cook it in the broiler. Just remember to baste and turn it often.

- ⅓ *cup soy sauce*
- ⅓ *cup Japanese rice wine (sake)*
- ⅓ *cup sweet cooking rice wine (mirin)*
- 1 *tablespoon sugar*
- 1 *teaspoon minced garlic*
- 1 *teaspoon minced ginger*
- 1½ *pounds boneless chicken thighs*
- 2 *teaspoons sesame seeds*
- 1 *teaspoon cornstarch dissolved in 2 teaspoons water*
- *Sliced green onion*

Getting Ready

① Place soy sauce, sake, mirin, and sugar in a small pan. Bring slowly to a simmer over low heat; simmer for 5 minutes. Remove from heat; stir in garlic and ginger and let mixture cool.

② Place chicken in a shallow bowl. Pour ½ of sauce over; reserve remainder. Cover and refrigerate chicken for 2 hours, turning occasionally.

③ Place sesame seeds in a small frying pan over medium heat; cook, shaking pan frequently, until lightly browned, 3 to 4 minutes. Immediately remove from pan to cool.

Cooking

① Lift chicken from marinade. Place chicken, skin side down, on a lightly oiled grill 4 to 6 inches above a solid bed of low-glowing coals. Cook, basting with marinade and turning frequently, until meat is no longer pink when cut, 25 to 30 minutes.

② In a small pan, heat reserved sauce to simmering. Add cornstarch solution and cook, stirring, until sauce boils and thickens slightly.

③ Place chicken on a platter and pour sauce over. Sprinkle with sesame seeds and green onion.

Makes 4 to 6 servings.

Sake

Sake, the clear alcoholic beverage made from fermented glutinous rice, is the national brew of Japan—an indispensable part of every special occasion and an important ingredient in cooking. There's no such thing as a vintage sake. In fact, it should be consumed within a year of production, and once a bottle is opened, it should be finished relatively quickly. Sake is served warm in little ceramic cups or chilled in square wooden ones. To warm it, pour a small amount into a porcelain serving bottle (*takkuri*) and place the bottle in a pan of water over low heat. *Kampai!*

Tea-Smoked Chicken

What makes this chicken so special? It is cooked by three methods: quickly browned in oil for color and flavor, cooked with moist heat in a steamer, and finally wok-smoked over tea and rice to give it a distinctive smoky flavor.

Marinade

- 2 *tablespoons dark soy sauce*
- 2 *tablespoons Chinese rice wine or dry sherry*
- 2 *teaspoons cornstarch*

- 4 *chicken thighs or drumsticks*
- 2 *tablespoons cooking oil*

Smoking Mixture

- ½ *cup packed brown sugar*
- ⅓ *cup uncooked rice*
- ¼ *cup black or oolong tea leaves*
- 4 *slices ginger, each the size of a quarter, lightly crushed*
- 2 *whole star anise*
- 2 *teaspoons liquid smoke or ¼ cup hickory chips*

Getting Ready

① Combine marinade ingredients in a bowl. If using chicken thighs, place chicken, skin side down, on a cutting board. With a sharp knife, cut ½-inch-deep slits along both sides of the bone. Add chicken to marinade and stir to coat. Let stand for 10 minutes.

Cooking

① Place a wok over high heat until hot. Add oil, swirling to coat sides. Add chicken and cook until golden brown on all sides, 6 to 8 minutes. Remove chicken and place in a heat-proof dish.

② Prepare a wok for steaming (see page 25). Cover and steam chicken over high heat for 30 minutes.

③ Line wok and inside of wok lid with foil. Combine smoking mixture ingredients; spread evenly in wok. Set a round cake rack over smoking mixture; place chicken on rack.

④ Place wok, uncovered, over high heat. When mixture begins to smoke, cover wok; reduce heat to medium-low and smoke until chicken turns a rich, deep color, 12 to 15 minutes. Turn off heat; let stand for 5 minutes before removing wok lid.

⑤ Serve chicken hot or at room temperature.

Makes 4 servings.

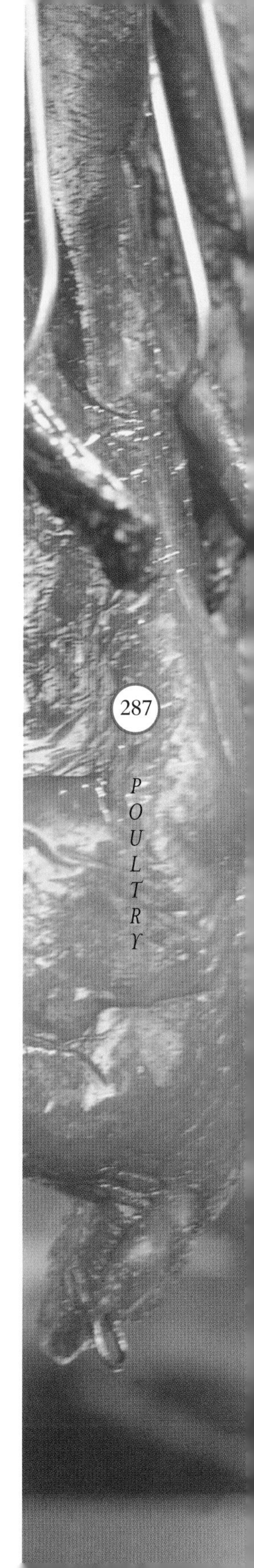

Shrimp-Filled Chicken Breasts

Looking for an elegant entrée to impress your dinner guests? Stop looking and start putting on your chef's apron. This dish pleases all the senses. Make sure you cook enough, because there are bound to be calls for seconds, maybe even thirds.

Filling

5 *dried black mushrooms*

½ *pound medium raw shrimp, shelled, deveined, and coarsely chopped*

¼ *cup chopped water chestnuts*

1 *tablespoon minced ginger*

2 *teaspoons chopped cilantro*

4 *large boneless chicken breast halves with skin on*

Marinade

3 *tablespoons Chinese rice wine or dry sherry*

2 *tablespoons soy sauce*

2 *teaspoons hoisin sauce*

2 *teaspoons cornstarch*

⅛ *teaspoon white pepper*

1 *small carrot, finely julienned*

1 *teaspoon sesame oil*

Getting Ready

① Prepare filling: Soak mushrooms in warm water to cover until softened, about 20 minutes; drain. Discard stems and coarsely chop caps. Place mushrooms in a bowl with shrimp, water chestnuts, ginger, and cilantro; mix well.

② Remove fillet (small muscle) from each chicken breast half; reserve for other uses. Split each breast half horizontally almost all the way through; open it up like a book. Place breast halves between waxed paper; pound to an even thickness.

③ Combine marinade ingredients in a bowl. Add chicken and stir to coat. Let stand for 10 minutes.

④ Lift chicken from marinade. Place chicken, skin side down, on work surface. On each piece, place ¼ of carrot strips and shrimp filling. Roll up breasts; do not fold in sides. Place rolls, seam side down, in a shallow baking pan; brush with sesame oil.

Cooking

① Preheat oven to 350°F. Bake rolls, uncovered, until juices run clear when chicken is pierced, 30 to 35 minutes.

② Serve chicken breasts whole or sliced. Pour pan juices over rolls.

Makes 4 servings.

Spices of Life

Chinese Herbs and Holistic Health

Lately, there's been a lot of interest in the press and in the food world in "nutraceuticals" and "functional foods." These are ingredients that offer specific health benefits when eaten as part of a regular diet.

The Chinese are no strangers to this idea. For almost 3,500 years, Chinese medicine has used herbs and other foods to regulate the system and restore the balance of yin and yang forces in the body (see page 110). Many Chinese believe that illness occurs when these forces are out of balance and that certain foods and herbal ingredients can boost or suppress the body's natural immune functions.

The ancient science of Chinese herbal medicine is based on centuries of experience and observation, and it's amazing how many of its treatments and cures were discovered or accepted by Western medicine only during the 20th century. For example, digitalis, one of the leading heart medications, is extracted from the leaves of the *mao di huang* or foxglove plant, an ancient Chinese medicinal herb. Ephedrin, derived from the *ma huang* or ephedra shrub, is now widely used in the West to treat asthma and allergies; the Chinese have been prescribing *ma huang* for this purpose for centuries.

Chinese herbal remedies are not just a matter of eating certain herbs. They are almost always a carefully balanced combination of herbal ingredients blended together to form a customized prescription. There are more than 200 typical herbal combinations in everyday use, and, though the basic ingredients remain constant, their quantities differ depending on the practitioner and the needs of the patient.

No matter what your medical orientation, a visit to a Chinese herbalist's shop can be a fascinating experience. The walls are lined with drawers and shelves, and the center of the room is filled with all kinds of barrels and bins brimming with pieces of bark, herbs, dried fungus, berries, and roots that create an unmistakable, earthy aroma. You almost feel stronger just from breathing the air!

The practitioner generally makes a diagnosis based on interviewing the patient about symptoms, appetite, mental state, and so on. Other vital signs help give clues about the state of the internal organs—everything from the smell of the breath and the strength of the pulse to the color of the eyes and the skin.

Once the diagnosis has been made, herbs and ingredients are weighed, measured, and combined—often in the form of whole pieces to be taken home by the patient and boiled in water to create a concentrated decoction, which is then strained, cooled, and drunk. Sometimes, ingredients are prescribed in pill or powdered form as well.

Now, you don't have to visit an herbalist to check out the benefits of Chinese medicinal ingredients for yourself. Many Chinese regard all food as part of a holistic approach to health and well-being. The herbal practitioner may be consulted when illness arises, but the everyday maintenance of health and equilibrium is achieved through the simple act of eating. And though some herbs are used only for medicinal purposes, many of the traditional Chinese seasoning ingredients not only add wonderful flavor to foods, but are also believed to have healing powers. Here are a few examples.

Dried black mushrooms and black fungus are used to stimulate the immune system, promote better circulation, and lower cholesterol; wood ears are used to prevent blood clots.

Ginger is known to relieve coughing, nausea, and dizziness, and is also used to aid in digestion. Try adding a little fresh ginger to your favorite tea.

Lychee can help relieve coughs, anemia, and fatigue.

Cinnamon bark stimulates digestion, respiration, and circulation.

Dried tangerine peel can alleviate coughing, hiccups, and nausea, and can also stimulate the appetite and aid in digestion.

Lily buds are used as a sedative and a remedy for coughing and certain disorders of the lung.

Lemongrass, the fragrant herb commonly used in Southeast Asian cooking, is used to induce sweating.

Ginseng is something of a panacea to Chinese herbalists. It's believed to cleanse the blood, provide energy, and act as an aphrodisiac. It is often prescribed as a treatment for anemia, nervous disorders, fevers, excessive sweating, and even memory loss.

Chinese jujubes (also known as Chinese red dates) are reddish brown dried fruits. They are used to treat anxiety, insomnia, and dizziness.

Of course, there's no magic cure or single ingredient that can make everyone live longer and stay healthier. All things don't work for all people. But whatever you believe in, there's one ancient principle of Chinese medicine we can all learn from: Health is part of a larger picture that includes attitude, diet, exercise, sleep, and so on. In other words, the best medicine of all is a life well lived.

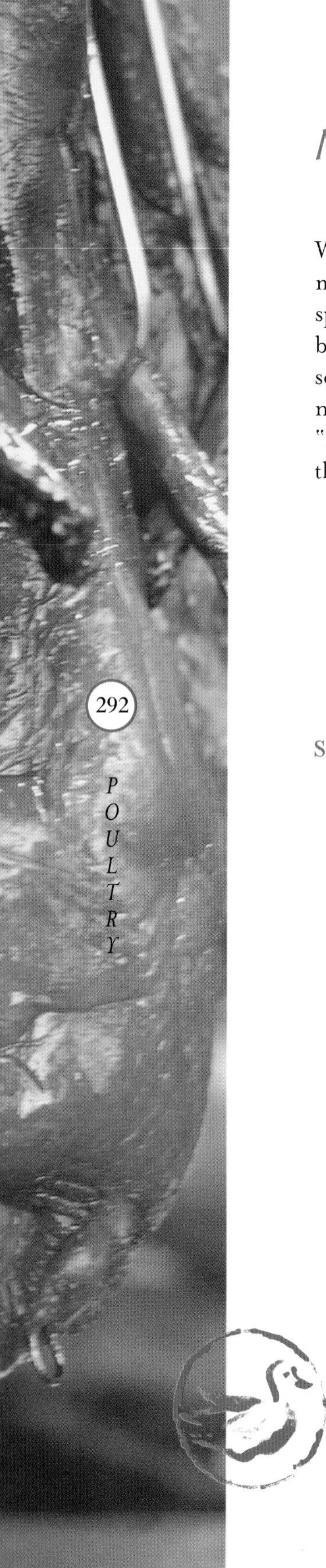

Multiflavored Chicken

When it comes to tastes, the more the merrier. The blending of sweet, sour, spicy, and peanut tastes in this dish is bound to impress even the most sophisticated palates. The Chinese name for this dish literally means "strange-flavor chicken," but only the name is strange.

- ¾ *pound boneless chicken*
- 6 *slices ginger, each the size of a quarter, lightly crushed*
- ½ *teaspoon salt*
- 2 *teaspoons sesame seeds*

Sauce

- ¼ *cup creamy peanut butter*
- ¼ *cup rice vinegar*
- 3 *tablespoons soy sauce*
- 2 *tablespoons Chinese rice wine or dry sherry*
- 1 *tablespoon sugar*
- 2 *teaspoons chili garlic sauce*
- ½ *teaspoon ground toasted Sichuan peppercorns*

- 2 *ounces dried bean thread noodles*
- *Cilantro sprigs*

Getting Ready

① Place chicken, ginger, and salt in a 2-quart pan. Add water to cover chicken. Bring to a boil. Reduce heat, cover, and simmer until chicken is tender, about 20 minutes; drain. Discard ginger and chicken skin. Thinly slice meat and place in a bowl.

② Place sesame seeds in a small frying pan over medium heat; cook, shaking pan frequently, until lightly browned, 3 to 4 minutes. Immediately remove from pan to cool.

③ Combine sauce ingredients in a bowl.

④ Soak bean thread noodles in warm water until softened, about 10 minutes; drain. Cut into 4-inch lengths. Place noodles in the center of a serving plate.

Cooking

① Add half of sauce to chicken; mix well. Place chicken over noodles; sprinkle with sesame seeds. Garnish with cilantro sprigs. Pass remaining sauce at the table.

Makes 4 servings.

Poached Chicken with Pepper Salt

Simple pleasures are best, and that certainly applies to this dish. The traditional preparation of "white-cut" chicken requires several hot- and cold-water baths (for the chicken, not the chef). I have reduced the poaching process to just one step.

Marinade

- ¼ *cup Chinese rice wine*
- 1½ *teaspoons salt*
- ¼ *teaspoon white pepper*

- 1 *whole frying chicken (3 to 3½ lb.), cut in half*

Pepper Salt

- 1 *teaspoon Sichuan peppercorns*
- 2 *teaspoons salt*
- ¼ *teaspoon Chinese five-spice*
- ¼ *teaspoon white pepper*

- 3 *green onions, cut in half and lightly crushed*
- 6 *slices ginger, each the size of a quarter, lightly crushed*
- 1 *whole star anise*

Getting Ready

① Combine marinade ingredients in a bowl. Rub chicken on all sides with marinade. Cover and refrigerate for 2 hours.

② Prepare pepper salt: Place peppercorns in a small frying pan over low heat; cook, shaking pan frequently, until they are aromatic, about 5 minutes. Immediately remove from pan to cool. Coarsely grind in a spice grinder. Combine peppercorns with remaining pepper salt ingredients.

Cooking

① Place chicken, green onions, ginger, and star anise in a pot; add water to cover chicken. Bring to a boil; reduce heat, cover, and simmer for 30 minutes. Turn off heat and let stand, covered, for 30 minutes.

② Drain chicken; reserve poaching liquid for soup stock.

③ Cut chicken into 2-inch pieces with shears, or carve Western-style. Serve with pepper salt.

Makes 4 to 6 servings.

Meet a Star

Star anise, an eight-pointed seed pod that tastes like a stronger version of anise seed, is wonderful used in braising and poaching liquids, soups, stews, and roasted and barbecued foods, and it's particularly tasty when paired with Sichuan peppercorns and soy sauce. The pod is inedible (although some people like to chew on it as a breath freshener), and it's discarded after cooking. In its ground form, star anise plays a starring role in Chinese five-spice.

Cashew Chicken

This popular dish, probably number one for Chinese take-out, is easily mastered at home. My preference is to use unsalted cashews. If your market doesn't stock them, you can reduce the soy sauce to compensate for the salt.

Marinade

- 1 *tablespoon soy sauce*
- 2 *teaspoons Chinese rice wine or dry sherry*
- 2 *teaspoons cornstarch*

- ¾ *pound boneless, skinless chicken*
- 2 *tablespoons cooking oil*
- 2 *teaspoons minced ginger*
- 2 *teaspoons minced garlic*
- 1 *small onion, cut into ½-inch cubes*
- 1 *small red bell pepper, cut into ½-inch cubes*
- 1 *small zucchini, cut into ½-inch cubes*
- ½ *cup chicken broth*
- 2 *tablespoons soy sauce*
- 1 *teaspoon sesame oil*
- ½ *teaspoon sugar*
- 1 *teaspoon cornstarch dissolved in 2 teaspoons water*
- ½ *cup roasted cashews or blanched almonds, toasted*

Getting Ready

① Combine marinade ingredients in a bowl. Cut chicken into ½-inch cubes. Add chicken to marinade and stir to coat. Let stand for 10 minutes.

Cooking

① Place a wok over high heat until hot. Add cooking oil, swirling to coat sides. Add ginger and garlic and cook, stirring, until fragrant, about 10 seconds. Add chicken and stir-fry for 2 minutes.

② Add onion, bell pepper, zucchini, and broth. Cover and cook until vegetables are tender-crisp, about 2 minutes. Add soy sauce, sesame oil, and sugar; mix well. Add cornstarch solution and cook, stirring, until sauce boils and thickens. Add nuts and mix well.

Makes 4 servings.

Drunken Chicken

This popular cold dish is marinated in wine, then steamed and chilled. The wine and chicken juices gelatinize, forming a kind of flavor aspic, which is served over the moist, tender chicken slices. For this dish, I splurge and buy top-of-the-line rice wine that comes from Shaoxing (Shao Hsing), in eastern China.

4 *boneless chicken thighs with skin on*

Marinade

3 *tablespoons Shaoxing wine*

3 *tablespoons soy sauce*

6 *slices ginger, each the size of a quarter, lightly crushed*

2 *green onions, cut in half and lightly crushed*

1 *tablespoon sugar*

2 *cups Shaoxing wine*

Getting Ready

① Place chicken thighs between sheets of waxed paper; pound to an even thickness.

② Combine marinade ingredients in a 1-quart heatproof dish. Add chicken and stir to coat. Place ginger and green onions on top of chicken. Let stand for 10 minutes.

Cooking

① Prepare a wok for steaming (see page 25). Steam chicken over high heat until meat is no longer pink when cut, 10 to 12 minutes. Let cool.

② Stir sugar into wine. Pour wine over chicken and its steaming juices. Cover and refrigerate for 24 hours.

③ To serve, discard ginger and onions. Cut chicken into thin slices; arrange on a plate with the gelatinized juices. Serve chilled.

Makes 4 to 6 servings.

Wine of the Times

The rituals surrounding wine in China are ancient and fascinating. "Scholar's Wine" was buried underground by a father upon the birth of his first son, then unearthed years later and drunk in celebration of the son's graduation from college. "Bride's Wine" was buried at the birth of a daughter and drunk at her wedding. And "Withered Flower" wine was served at the death of a child to ensure peace in the next life.

Chinese Christmas Turkey

Turkey may be as North American as apple pie, but I have the feeling that if the Chinese had landed on Plymouth Rock, the classic American feast would have quite a different look and taste. Next Christmas, try a glutinous rice stuffing instead of a bread stuffing. Your leftovers will definitely be more interesting.

Marinade

- ¼ *cup soy sauce*
- 1 *tablespoon minced ginger*
- 1 *tablespoon minced garlic*
- 1 *teaspoon Chinese five-spice*
- 1 *teaspoon pepper*
- ½ *teaspoon salt*

- 1 *hen turkey (12 to 14 lb.), cleaned*

Stuffing

- 8 *dried black mushrooms*
- ¼ *cup dried shrimp*
- 1 *tablespoon cooking oil*
- 2 *Chinese sausages (2 oz. each), diced*
- 1 *can (8 oz.) sliced water chestnuts*
- 4 *green onions, thinly sliced*
- 3 *tablespoons chopped cilantro*
- 3 *tablespoons oyster-flavored sauce*
- 3–3½ *cups cooked glutinous rice or medium-grain rice*

Getting Ready

① Combine marinade ingredients in a bowl. Rub turkey inside and out with marinade. Cover and refrigerate for 4 hours or up to overnight.

② Prepare stuffing: In separate bowls, soak mushrooms and dried shrimp in warm water to cover until softened, about 20 minutes; drain. Discard mushrooms stems and thinly slice caps. Leave shrimp whole.

③ Place a wok over high heat until hot. Add oil, swirling to coat sides. Add sausage and shrimp; stir-fry until sausage is slightly crisp, 1½ to 2 minutes. Add mushrooms, water chestnuts, green onions, and cilantro. Cook for 1 minute. Stir in oyster-flavored sauce. Remove pan from heat and add rice; mix well. Let stuffing cool.

Cooking

① Preheat oven to 350°F. Just before roasting, place stuffing inside turkey; enclose with skewers. Place turkey, breast side up, on a rack in a roasting pan. Insert a meat thermometer into thickest part of thigh meat, without touching bone. Bake until a thermometer registers 180° to 185°F, about 3 hours. During the last half of roasting time, baste turkey occasionally with pan juices.

Makes 8 to 10 servings.

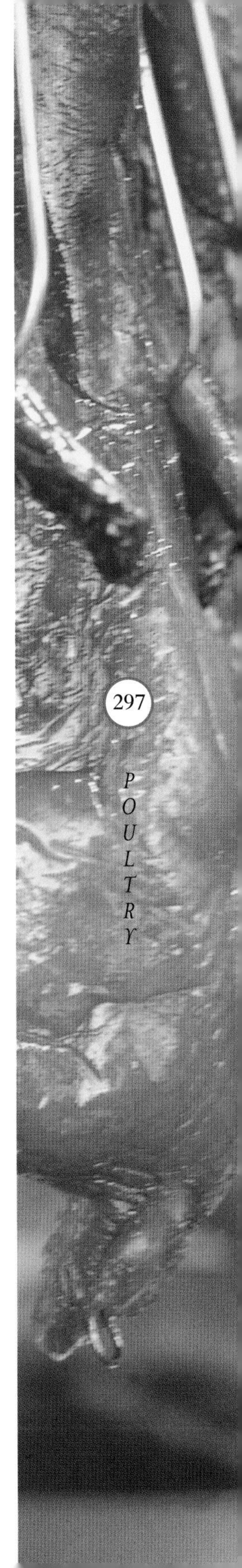

Double-Steamed Chicken

This recipe is based on a method used in the province of Yunnan, to the south of Sichuan. Chicken or game hen is first parboiled to remove some fat, then placed in a pot of aromatic broth, which is, in turn, placed inside a steamer and slowly simmered. This gentle cooking method produces succulent, tender chicken and a rich complex broth.

4	*dried black mushrooms*
2	*dried wood ears (optional)*
1	*small Rock Cornish game hen or 1 pound boneless, skinless chicken*
6	*dried jujubes (optional)*
4	*Medjool dates, pitted*
4	*slices ginger, each the size of a quarter, lightly crushed*
2	*tablespoons chopped ham*
¼	*cup walnut halves or raw skinless peanuts*
3	*cups chicken broth*
¾	*cup Chinese rice wine or dry sherry*
1	*teaspoon salt*

Getting Ready

① In separate bowls, soak mushrooms and wood ears in warm water to cover until softened, about 20 minutes; drain. Discard mushroom stems and halve caps. Cut wood ears into bite-sized pieces.

② In a pan, parboil game hen in water to cover for 2 minutes; pour into a colander and let drain. Place game hen in a 2-quart casserole and add remaining ingredients; cover.

Cooking

① Prepare a wok for steaming (see page 25). Place casserole in steamer. Cover and steam over high heat, replenishing water as necessary, until game hen is tender, 1½ to 2 hours.

② To serve, cut game hen into 2-inch pieces with shears, or carve Western-style. Strain broth and serve in small soup bowls.

Makes 4 servings.

The Yunnan Pot

To prepare this recipe, you can use any casserole that will fit inside your steamer, but if you can find an authentic Yunnan pot, sold in Chinese specialty shops, so much the better. It's a round pot made of red clay with a chimney that comes halfway up its center, stopping just below the lid. Food is placed around the chimney, and the pot is covered and placed inside the steamer. The steam comes up through the chimney into the pot and slowly cooks the food, making it moist and succulent.

Peking Roast Duck

Peking duck is Beijing's most famous specialty—a banquet treat that's seldom prepared at home, since most Chinese kitchens don't have ovens. But since you probably do, here's how you can make your own tasty Peking duck at home.

1 *duckling (4 to 5 lb.), cleaned*

Marinade

2 *tablespoons soy sauce*
2 *tablespoons hoisin sauce*
3 *slices ginger, each the size of a quarter, lightly crushed*

Glaze

1½ *cups water*
¼ *cup rice vinegar*
¼ *cup honey or maltose*
¼ *teaspoon red food coloring (optional)*

16 *Mandarin Pancakes (see page 189) or flour tortillas*
Hoisin sauce
Slivered green onions

Getting Ready

① In a large pan, parboil duck in water to cover for 3 minutes; pour into a colander and let drain. When duck has cooled, pat dry with paper towels.

② Combine marinade ingredients in a bowl; rub inside duck cavity. Cover duck and refrigerate for 4 hours.

③ Combine glaze ingredients in a wide frying pan. Cook, stirring, over medium heat, until heated through. Remove from heat. Tie a string around duck's neck or under its wings. Holding duck over the pan, ladle glaze over duck 6 to 8 times to coat all skin areas. Hang duck in a cool place until skin is taut and dry, 4 to 6 hours (2 hours if you use an electric fan).

Cooking

① Preheat oven to 400°F. Place duck, breast side up, on a rack in a roasting pan. Roast, uncovered, for 40 minutes. Turn duck over; roast for 20 minutes, brushing occasionally with pan drippings. Turn duck breast side up again and brush with pan drippings. Roast until skin is brown and crisp, about 10 minutes.

② Prepare a wok for steaming (see page 25). Wrap Mandarin pancakes in a damp towel and place inside steamer. Cover and steam for about 3 minutes.

③ Carve duck, including the crisp skin, into thin slices; arrange on a serving plate. To eat, spread hoisin sauce on a Mandarin pancake, place 1 or 2 slices of duck on sauce, top with slivered green onions, roll up, and eat out of hand.

Makes 4 to 6 servings.

Braised Orange-Flavored Duck

Orange-flavored duck is a classic in both French and Chinese cuisines. Who inspired whom?

1	*duckling (4 to 5 lb.), cleaned*
¾	*teaspoon salt*
½	*teaspoon black pepper*
2	*tablespoons rice vinegar*
1	*tablespoon dark soy sauce*
1	*tablespoon honey*

Braising Sauce

2½	*cups chicken broth*
3	*tablespoons grated orange zest*
1½	*cups orange juice*
2	*tablespoons regular soy sauce*
2	*tablespoons lemon juice*
2	*tablespoons packed brown sugar*
1	*piece (about 1½ in. square) dried tangerine peel, soaked and julienned*

1½	*tablespoons cooking oil*
4	*walnut-sized shallots, sliced*
2	*tablespoons brandy*
2	*tablespoons orange-flavored liqueur*
½	*teaspoon cornstarch dissolved in 1 teaspoon water*

Getting Ready

① Prick duck all over with a skewer. Parboil duck in water to cover for 3 minutes; drain in a colander. Rinse with cold water. Pat duck dry with paper towels. Rub inside and out with salt and pepper. Combine vinegar, soy sauce, and honey. Brush mixture on duck to coat evenly. Cover and refrigerate for 6 hours.

② Combine braising sauce ingredients.

Cooking

① Preheat oven to 425°F. Place duck, breast side up, on a rack in a roasting pan. Roast, uncovered, until skin is lightly browned, about 30 minutes.

② Place a heavy pot large enough to hold duck over high heat until hot. Add oil, swirling to coat sides. Add shallots; cook, stirring, until limp, 1 to 1½ minutes. Add brandy and braising sauce. Lower duck into pot. Ladle some of the sauce into body cavity and over duck. Bring to a boil. Reduce heat, cover, and simmer, turning occasionally, until duck is tender and skin is a rich brown, about 1¼ hours.

③ Lift out duck. With kitchen shears, split duck lengthwise and remove backbone. Cut duck crosswise into 1-inch pieces, then reassemble in the original shape on a serving platter.

④ Skim fat from cooking liquid. Add liqueur and cornstarch solution; cook, stirring, until sauce boils and thickens slightly. Pour sauce over duck and serve.

Makes 4 to 6 servings.

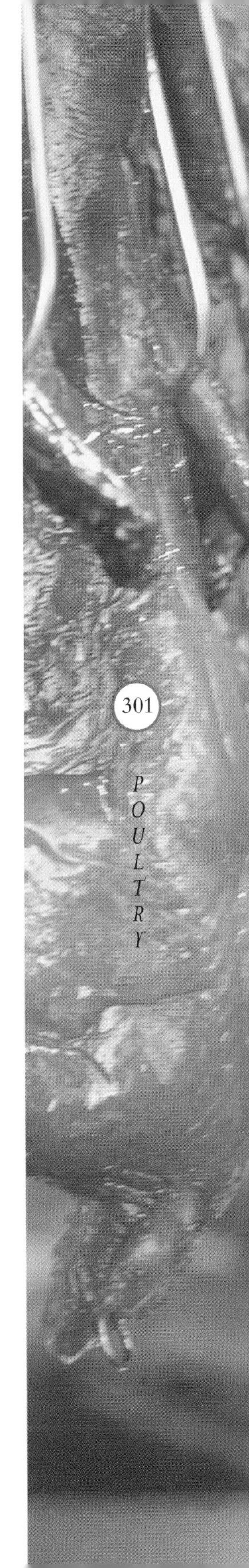

Roast Drunken Duck

Here's my easy home-style version of Cantonese roast duck. It's marinated in wine, filled with an aromatic stuffing, and finished off with a soy and hoisin glaze for a beautifully lacquered look.

Marinade

- 2 *teaspoons regular soy sauce*
- 2 *teaspoons dark soy sauce*
- ½ *cup white wine or dry sherry*
- ½ *teaspoon salt*
- ½ *teaspoon Chinese five-spice*

- 1 *duckling (4 to 5 lb.), cleaned*
- 8 *dried black mushrooms*

Stuffing

- 2 *tablespoons cooking oil*
- 4 *slices ginger, each the size of a quarter, julienned*
- 3 *cloves garlic, minced*
- 2 *medium onions, thinly sliced*
- ¼ *cup shredded bamboo shoots*
- 2 *tablespoons thinly sliced Sichuan preserved vegetable*
- ¼ *cup white wine*
- 1 *teaspoon Chinese five-spice*
- 2 *tablespoons dark soy sauce*
- 1 *tablespoon hoisin sauce*

Glaze

- 2 *tablespoons dark soy sauce*
- 1 *tablespoon hoisin sauce*

Getting Ready

① Combine marinade ingredients in a bowl. Rub duck inside and out with marinade. Cover and refrigerate for 2 hours.

② Soak mushrooms in warm water to cover until softened, about 20 minutes; drain. Discard stems and thinly slice caps.

③ Prepare stuffing: Place a wok over high heat until hot. Add oil, swirling to coat sides. Add ginger and garlic; cook, stirring, until fragrant, about 10 seconds. Add onions and stir-fry for 1 minute. Add mushrooms, bamboo shoots, and preserved vegetable; stir-fry for 2 minutes. Add wine, five-spice, soy sauce, and hoisin sauce; cook for 1 minute. Let cool.

Cooking

① Preheat oven to 400°F. Just before roasting, place stuffing inside duck; enclose with skewers. Place duck, breast side up, on a rack in a roasting pan. Bake until meat is no longer pink when cut near bone, 1 to 1½ hours.

② Increase heat to 475°F. Combine glaze ingredients in a bowl. Brush glaze over duck. Bake until skin is richly glazed, 5 to 7 minutes.

Makes 4 to 6 servings.

Cantonese Pei Pa Roast Duck

Crisp-skinned, succulent, and delicious, *pei pa* duck (named after the Chinese lute the flattened duck resembles) is to southern China what Peking duck is to the north.

1 *duckling (4 to 5 lb.), cleaned*

Marinade

2 *teaspoons cooking oil*
2 *tablespoons minced ginger*
1 *tablespoon minced shallot*
3 *tablespoons hoisin sauce*
2 *tablespoons soy sauce*
½ *teaspoon Chinese five-spice*

2 *cups boiling water*

Glaze

1½ *cups water*
¼ *cup rice vinegar*
¼ *cup honey or maltose*
¼ *teaspoon red food coloring (optional)*

Plum sauce

Getting Ready

① With poultry shears, cut through breastbone of duck; spread duck, skin side up, on a flat surface and press firmly to crack bones. Place duck, skin side down, on a rack in a roasting pan.

② Prepare marinade: Place a saucepan over high heat until hot. Add oil, swirling to coat sides. Add ginger and shallot; cook, stirring, until fragrant, about 10 seconds. Remove pan from heat and stir in remaining marinade ingredients. Brush marinade over duck. Refrigerate duck, uncovered, for 6 hours or up to overnight.

③ Place duck on rack, skin side up. Pour boiling water over skin. Drain water from roasting pan. Let duck dry on rack for 30 minutes. Combine glaze ingredients in a pan; bring to a boil. Pour glaze over duck. Hang duck in a cool place until skin is taut and dry, 4 to 6 hours (2 hours if you use an electric fan).

Cooking

① Preheat oven to 400°F. Place duck, skin side up, on a rack in a roasting pan; roast, uncovered, for 40 minutes. Turn duck over, cover loosely with foil, and roast for 15 minutes. Turn duck skin side up again and brush with pan drippings. Place 5 to 6 inches below a preheated broiler; broil until skin is golden brown and crisp, 3 to 5 minutes.

② Cut duck into serving-sized pieces and arrange on a serving plate. Serve with plum sauce on the side.

Makes 4 to 6 servings.

Pineapple-Lychee Duck Sauté

Fruit and duck are a natural combination in the cuisines of many cultures. They go together splendidly in this quick Cantonese-style stir-fry of tender duck breast with a sweet, fruity sauce and chunks of lychee and pineapple. Boneless duck breast is sold fresh and sometimes frozen in many major supermarkets. A boneless half-breast weighs in at around 8 ounces.

Marinade

- 1 *tablespoon Chinese rice wine or dry sherry*
- 2 *teaspoons dark soy sauce*
- 2 *teaspoons cornstarch*

- ½ *pound boneless, skinless duck breast*

Sauce

- 3 *tablespoons plum sauce*
- 3 *tablespoons pineapple juice*
- 2 *tablespoons chicken broth*
- 1 *tablespoon regular soy sauce*

- 1½ *tablespoons cooking oil*
- 2 *slices ginger, each the size of a quarter, lightly crushed*
- 1 *red bell pepper, seeded and cut into 1-inch squares*
- ½ *cup lychees*
- ½ *cup pineapple chunks*
- ½ *teaspoon cornstarch dissolved in 1 teaspoon water*

Getting Ready

① Combine marinade ingredients in a bowl. Thinly slice duck breast; add to marinade and stir to coat. Let stand for 10 minutes.

② Combine sauce ingredients in a bowl.

Cooking

① Place a wok over high heat until hot. Add oil, swirling to coat sides. Add ginger and cook, stirring, until fragrant, about 10 seconds. Add duck and stir-fry until slices are cooked through but still rosy, 1 to 2 minutes. Remove duck from wok.

② Add bell pepper, lychees, and pineapple to wok; stir-fry for 1 minute. Return duck to wok and add sauce. Cook until sauce boils. Add cornstarch solution and cook, stirring, until sauce boils and thickens.

Makes 4 servings.

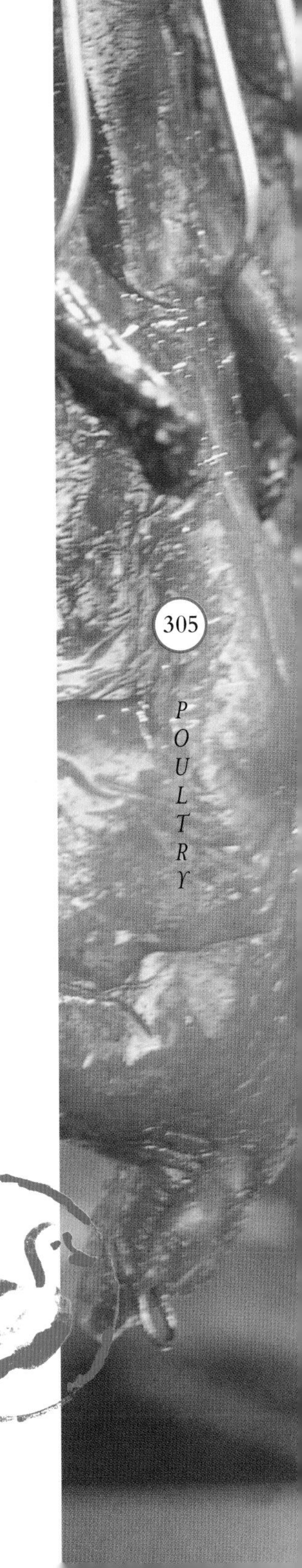

Duck Soup

While in Beijing, I ate at the world-famous Hui Zhen Restaurant, where Peking duck is the specialty of the house, and no duck dinner is complete without a simple soup made from the carcass.

- 5 *cups chicken broth*
- 1 *carcass from a roast duck*
- 2 *slices ginger, each the size of a quarter, lightly crushed*
- 2 *green onions, cut into 2-inch pieces*
- 6 *dried black mushrooms*
- 1 *package (16 oz.) soft tofu, drained*
- 2 *cups sliced napa cabbage*
- ½ *cup sliced bamboo shoots*
- ½ *cup shredded roast duck meat*
- 1 *tablespoon soy sauce*
- 2 *teaspoons Chinese rice wine or dry sherry*

Cooking

① Place broth, duck carcass, ginger, and green onions in a large pot; bring to a boil. Reduce heat, cover, and simmer for 2 hours. Strain broth and discard solids. Return broth to the pot.

② While stock is cooking, soak mushrooms in warm water to cover until softened, about 20 minutes; drain. Discard stems and thinly slice caps. Cut tofu into ½-inch cubes.

③ Heat broth to simmering. Add mushrooms, cabbage, and bamboo shoots. Cook until cabbage is tender, 4 to 5 minutes. Add tofu, duck meat, soy sauce, and wine. Cook until heated through.

Makes 4 to 6 servings.

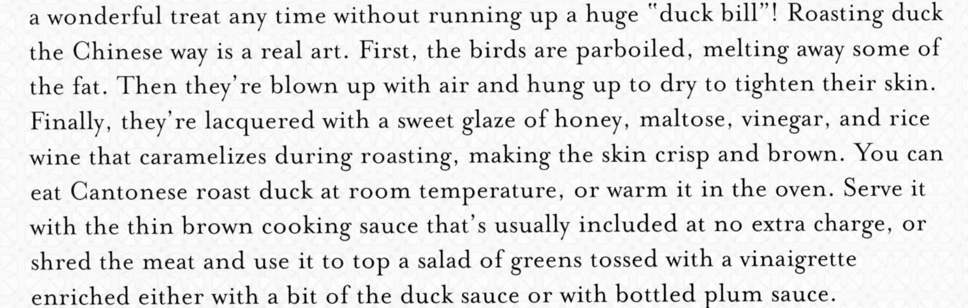

Lucky Duck

If you live near a Chinese deli that sells roast ducks, you're in luck. You can enjoy a wonderful treat any time without running up a huge "duck bill"! Roasting duck the Chinese way is a real art. First, the birds are parboiled, melting away some of the fat. Then they're blown up with air and hung up to dry to tighten their skin. Finally, they're lacquered with a sweet glaze of honey, maltose, vinegar, and rice wine that caramelizes during roasting, making the skin crisp and brown. You can eat Cantonese roast duck at room temperature, or warm it in the oven. Serve it with the thin brown cooking sauce that's usually included at no extra charge, or shred the meat and use it to top a salad of greens tossed with a vinaigrette enriched either with a bit of the duck sauce or with bottled plum sauce.

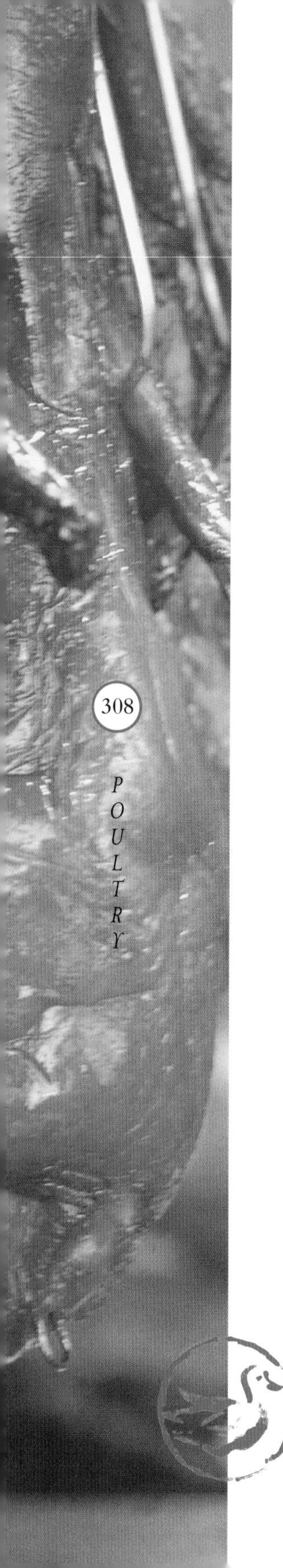

Roasted Duck Salad

This is a great way to make Chinese-style roast duck go further. You can use leftovers from any of the roast duck recipes in this chapter, or buy half a duck at a Chinese deli. The spicy-sweet sauce complements the richness of the duck, and the fried noodles offer a delightful crunchy texture.

1 *ounce dried rice stick noodles*
Cooking oil for deep-frying

Dressing

3 *tablespoons plum sauce*
2 *tablespoons cooking oil*
1 *tablespoon sesame oil*
2 *teaspoons soy sauce*
1 *teaspoon Chinese mustard*
¼ *teaspoon chili oil*

1 *tablespoon sesame seeds*
½ *roast duck*
4 *cups shredded iceberg lettuce*
1 *cup bean sprouts*
4 *green onions, cut into 1½-inch slivers*
½ *cup shredded Chinese sweet mixed pickles or sweet gherkins*
¼ *cup chopped toasted almonds*
1 *small bunch green leaf lettuce*

Getting Ready

① Pull rice stick noodles apart to separate. In a wok or 2-quart saucepan, heat oil for deep-frying to 375°F. Deep-fry noodles, a handful at a time, until they puff and expand, about 5 seconds. Turn over to cook the other side. Remove and drain on paper towels. Let cool, then place in a tightly covered container until ready to use (up to 4 days).

② Combine dressing ingredients in a bowl.

③ Place sesame seeds in a small frying pan over medium heat; cook, shaking pan frequently, until lightly browned, 3 to 4 minutes. Immediately remove from pan to cool.

④ Scrape off and discard fat under duck skin; cut skin into thin strips. Bone duck and shred meat.

Assembly

① Place duck meat and skin, iceberg lettuce, bean sprouts, green onions, pickles, sesame seeds, and half of the almonds in a salad bowl. Add dressing and toss to coat. Add noodles and gently toss again.

② To serve, arrange salad on lettuce leaves. Sprinkle with remaining almonds. Serve at once while noodles are still crisp.

Makes 8 servings.

CHAPTER 9

Seafood

Steamed Fish with Sizzling Lemongrass Oil

There's no better way to enjoy fresh fish than in this classic Chinese method—steaming it whole with aromatic vegetables and dressing it with hot oil and a simple sauce.

3 *dried black mushrooms*

2 *stalks lemongrass (bottom 6 in. only)*

4 *green onions*

Sizzling Lemongrass Oil

3 *tablespoons cooking oil*

2 *teaspoons sesame oil*

1 *stalk lemongrass (bottom 6 in. only), thinly sliced*

Fish Dressing

¼ *cup soy sauce*

3 *tablespoons chicken broth*

1 *tablespoon oyster-flavored sauce*

2 *teaspoons sugar*

1 *whole fish (1½ to 2 lb.), such as sea bass or red snapper, cleaned*

½ *teaspoon salt*

¼ *teaspoon white pepper*

10 *slices ginger, each the size of a quarter, lightly crushed*

Getting Ready

① Soak mushrooms in warm water to cover until softened, about 20 minutes; drain. Discard stems and halve caps. Cut each piece of lemongrass into 3 slanting slices. Julienne 2 green onions; leave 2 green onions whole.

② Combine lemongrass oil ingredients in a saucepan. Combine fish dressing ingredients in another pan.

③ On each side of fish, cut 3 diagonal slices, ¾ inch deep, across body. Sprinkle fish inside and out with salt and pepper. Place a piece of mushroom, lemongrass, and ginger in each slit. Place whole green onions in center of a heatproof dish; lay fish on top.

Cooking

① Prepare a wok for steaming (see page 25). Cover and steam fish over high heat until fish turns opaque, 8 to 10 minutes.

② Sprinkle half the julienned green onions over fish. Heat pans of lemongrass oil and fish dressing until hot. Drizzle oil over fish, then pour dressing over. Garnish with the remaining julienned green onions.

Makes 4 to 6 servings.

Salmon Sandwiches

Can you make a sandwich without bread? Sure! Just follow this recipe closely, and before you can say, "tuna on rye," you will be staring at a light, healthy lunch of pan-fried salmon in a flavorful sauce.

- 6 *dried black mushrooms*
- 1½ *pounds center-cut salmon fillet, skinned*
- ¼ *cup finely julienned carrot*
- ¼ *cup finely julienned celery*
- 8 *snow peas, trimmed and finely julienned*
- 4 *cilantro sprigs*
- ¼ *teaspoon salt*
- ⅛ *teaspoon white pepper*

Sauce

- ⅓ *cup chicken broth*
- ¼ *cup Chinese rice wine or dry sherry*
- 1 *tablespoon oyster-flavored sauce*
- 1 *tablespoon fish sauce*

- 2 *tablespoons cooking oil*
- 1 *tablespoon minced shallots*
- 1 *tablespoon minced ginger*
- 1 *teaspoon minced garlic*
- 1 *teaspoon cornstarch dissolved in 2 teaspoons water*

Getting Ready

① Soak mushrooms in warm water to cover until softened, about 20 minutes; drain. Discard stems and thinly slice caps.

② Cut salmon to make 4 equal-sized pieces, each about 3 inches square. Split each piece horizontally almost all the way through; open it up like a book. To make each sandwich, place ¼ of mushrooms, carrot, celery, snow peas, and cilantro inside of a piece of butterflied salmon; close like a book. Sprinkle fish with salt and pepper.

③ Combine sauce ingredients in a bowl.

Cooking

① Heat a wide frying pan over medium heat until hot. Add 1½ tablespoons oil, swirling to coat sides. Place salmon sandwiches in pan and cook for 2 minutes; turn and cook 2 minutes longer. Remove fish from pan.

② Heat remaining ½ tablespoon oil in pan, swirling to coat sides. Add shallots, ginger, and garlic; cook, stirring, until fragrant, about 30 seconds. Return fish to pan. Add sauce and bring to a boil. Reduce heat, cover, and simmer until fish is opaque, 2 to 3 minutes.

③ With a slotted spatula, transfer fish to a serving platter. Strain sauce into a small pan and bring to a boil. Add cornstarch solution and cook, stirring, until sauce boils and thickens. Pour sauce over the fish.

Makes 4 servings.

Lotus Salmon Patty

When I was a child, my mom used to make a wonderful dish of lotus root slices coated with a flavorful ground pork stuffing. This is the Shanghainese version of that same home-style dish, coated with a purée of salmon, lightly breaded, and pan-fried until golden brown.

- ¾ *pound salmon*

Marinade

- 1½ *tablespoons cornstarch*
- 1 *tablespoon Chinese rice wine or dry sherry*
- 1 *tablespoon oyster-flavored sauce*
- ½ *teaspoon salt*
- ¼ *teaspoon white pepper*
- 1 *egg white*

- ¼ *cup finely chopped water chestnuts*
- 2 *tablespoons minced ham*
- ¾ *pound lotus root*
- *Cornstarch*
- 1 *egg, lightly beaten*
- ¾ *cup Japanese-style bread crumbs (panko)*
- 3 *tablespoons cooking oil*

Getting Ready

① Remove any skin and bones from fish; cut fish into 1-inch pieces. Place in a food processor; process until finely chopped. Add marinade ingredients; process until mixture is smooth. Remove salmon mixture to a bowl; stir in water chestnuts and ham. Let stand for 10 minutes.

② Peel lotus root; cut into ¼-inch-thick rounds.

③ Make each patty: Dust a lotus root round with cornstarch. Use 2 tablespoons fish mixture to cover both sides of lotus root. Dip patty in egg, drain briefly, then coat with bread crumbs.

Cooking

① Place a wide nonstick frying pan over medium heat until hot. Add oil, swirling to coat sides. Add patties and cook until golden brown, 2 to 3 minutes per side.

Makes 4 to 8 servings.

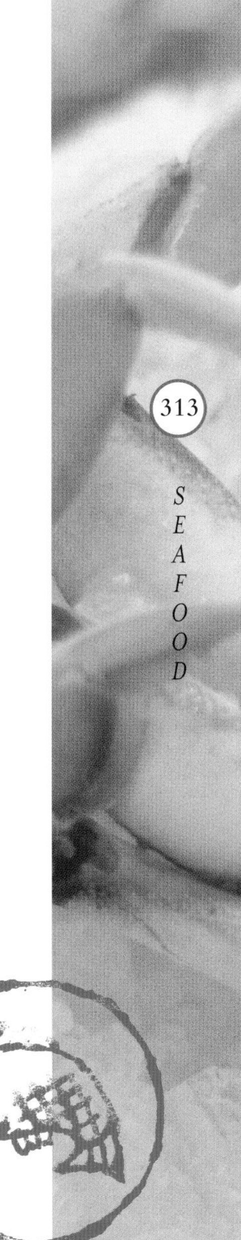

Sweet and Sour Fish Rolls

Tomato-based sweet and sour sauces were introduced to the West by way of southern China. This banquet-style dish is a nice way to add a lot of flavor to mild white fish, and the presentation is elegant and attractive. To save time, you can use a prepared Asian-style sweet and sour sauce.

- 4 *dried black mushrooms*
- 1 *pound firm white fish fillets, such as sea bass or red snapper, each about ½ inch thick*
- ½ *teaspoon salt*
- ¼ *teaspoon white pepper*
- 1 *small carrot, julienned*
- 1 *stalk celery, julienned*
- 2 *green onions, julienned*

Sauce

- ⅓ *cup orange juice*
- ¼ *cup water*
- ¼ *cup catsup*
- 3 *tablespoons sugar*
- 1 *tablespoon lemon juice*
- 1 *teaspoon minced ginger*
- ½ *teaspoon chili sauce*
- ½ *teaspoon salt*

- 1 *tablespoon cornstarch dissolved in 2 tablespoons water*

Getting Ready

① Soak mushrooms in warm water to cover until softened, about 20 minutes; drain. Discard stems and thinly slice caps.

② Cut fish crosswise into four 2- by 3-inch pieces, then butterfly to make 3-inch by 4-inch pieces. Sprinkle with salt and pepper. Make each roll: Place ¼ of the mushrooms, carrot, celery, and green onions across one short side of fish, then roll fish into a cylinder. Place rolls, seam side down, in a heatproof dish.

③ Combine sauce ingredients in a small pan.

Cooking

① Prepare a wok for steaming (see page 25). Cover and steam fish rolls over high heat until fish turns opaque, 5 to 6 minutes.

② With a slotted spatula, transfer rolls to a serving plate. Pour 3 tablespoons steaming juices into pan with sauce ingredients; heat to simmering. Add cornstarch solution and cook, stirring, until sauce boils and thickens. Pour sauce over rolls.

Makes 4 servings.

Poached Fish

There is more than one way to return a fish to water. My favorite is poaching. It is fast and easy, and it seals in all the goodness of fresh seafood. The green onions and ginger in the poaching liquid also give the fish a wonderful flavor even before the sauce goes on.

- 6 *slices ginger, each the size of a quarter, lightly crushed*
- 2 *green onions, cut in half and lightly crushed*
- 1 *teaspoon salt*
- 1 *whole fish (1½ to 2 lb.), such as sea bass or red snapper, cleaned, or 1½ pounds fish fillets*

Sauce

- 1 *tablespoon cooking oil*
- 2 *teaspoons minced ginger*
- ¼ *cup rice vinegar*
- 3 *tablespoons sweet chili sauce*
- 2 *tablespoons sugar*
- 2 *tablespoons soy sauce*
- 1 *teaspoon chili garlic sauce*

- 1½ *teaspoons cornstarch dissolved in 1 tablespoon water*

Cooking

① Pour 2 inches of water into a pan large enough to hold fish. Add ginger, green onions, and salt; bring to a boil. Reduce heat to low. Add fish, cover, and simmer until fish turns opaque, 10 to 12 minutes for a whole fish, about 8 minutes for fillets. Remove fish with a slotted spatula and place on a serving plate; cover to keep warm.

② Prepare sauce: Heat a small pan over medium heat until hot. Add oil, swirling to coat sides. Add ginger and cook, stirring, until fragrant, about 10 seconds. Add remaining sauce ingredients; mix well. Bring to a boil. Add cornstarch solution and cook, stirring, until sauce boils and thickens.

③ Pour sauce over fish and serve.

Makes 4 servings.

The Whole Fish

What makes whole fish so popular in China? First, the bones, the head, the gills, and the fins all add a lot of flavor to the fish as it cooks. Then there's the symbolic value. A whole fish is a regular fixture at special meals because it symbolizes abundance and fullness. It's such an important symbol that in landlocked regions where fish is unavailable, a stand-in wooden fish is sometimes presented! When serving a whole fish, it's customary in China to point the head toward the guest of honor.

Fish Tail with Brown Sauce

In China, eating a fish is like flipping a coin: Heads or tails, you're always a winner. Chinese chefs know that the head and tail of a fish contain some of the juiciest and most flavorful bits of meat, and this Shanghai-style recipe is delicious proof. Ask your fish market to save you a 5- to 6-inch tail piece from any medium-sized fish. You can also make this recipe using fish fillets.

1 *fish tail (about 1½ lb.), cleaned*

Marinade

3 *tablespoons soy sauce*

¼ *teaspoon white pepper*

Sauce

¾ *cup chicken broth*

3 *tablespoons Chinese rice wine or dry sherry*

2 *tablespoons dark soy sauce*

1½ *tablespoons sugar*

1 *teaspoon sesame oil*

¼ *teaspoon white pepper*

4 *slices ginger, each the size of a quarter, julienned*

Cornstarch

3 *tablespoons cooking oil*

1 *green onion, cut into 2-inch pieces*

1 *stalk lemongrass (bottom 6 in. only), minced*

1 *teaspoon cornstarch dissolved in 2 teaspoons water (optional)*

Getting Ready

① Cut fish lengthwise in 1-inch-wide strips, leaving strips attached at the tail. Combine marinade ingredients in a bowl. Add fish and turn to coat. Let stand for 10 minutes.

② Combine sauce ingredients in a bowl.

Cooking

① Dust fish with cornstarch; shake to remove excess.

② Place a wide frying pan over high heat until hot. Add oil, swirling to coat sides. Add fish and cook, turning once, until golden brown, about 2 minutes on each side. Add sauce, green onion, and lemongrass. Bring to a boil. Reduce heat, cover, and simmer until fish turns opaque. If desired, add cornstarch solution and cook, stirring, until sauce boils and thickens.

Makes 4 servings.

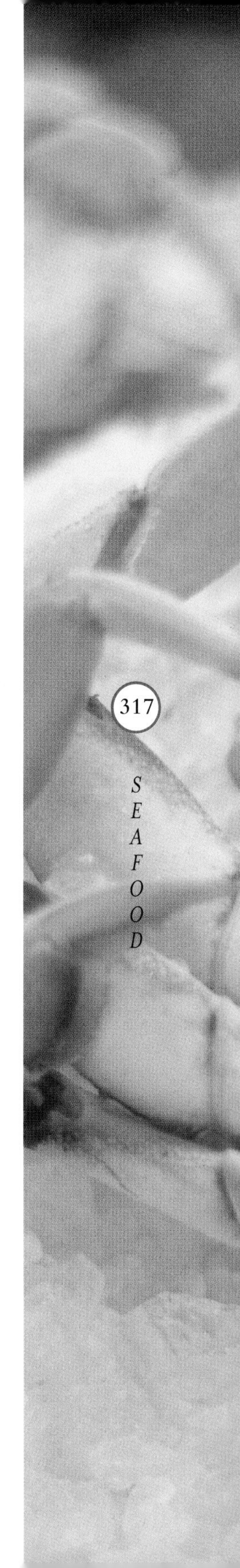

Steamed Fish in a Bamboo Leaf

Perhaps you've tried fish baked in a parchment wrapper. Why not serve it the Asian way, wrapped and steamed in a leafy packet? The leaves impart a subtle flavor and perfume to the dish. Dried bamboo leaves can be found in many Asian markets; fresh ti leaves are sold in florists' shops.

2 *dried bamboo leaves or fresh ti leaves*

Sauce

2 *tablespoons black bean garlic sauce*

2 *tablespoons chicken broth*

2 *tablespoons dark soy sauce*

1 *tablespoon sugar*

2 *teaspoons minced ginger*

2 *teaspoons chili garlic sauce*

2 *teaspoons sesame oil*

2 *teaspoons cornstarch*

1½ *pounds firm white fish fillets, such as sea bass or red snapper, each about ¾ inch thick*

3 *green onions, julienned*

2 *ounces thinly sliced ham, julienned*

Getting Ready

① If using dried leaves, soak in warm water to cover until softened, about 30 minutes; drain. Cut leaves in half crosswise.

② Combine sauce ingredients in a bowl.

③ Cut fish crosswise to make 2- by 3-inch pieces. Make each packet: Place 1 leaf half, ribbed side up, on work surface. Center a piece of fish on leaf. Top with a heaping tablespoon of sauce and a few pieces of green onion and ham. Fold sides of leaf around fish to enclose; secure with a wooden pick. Ends of packet will be open. Place packets in a heatproof dish.

Cooking

① Prepare a wok for steaming (see page 25). Cover and steam fish packets over high heat until fish turns opaque, 6 to 8 minutes.

Makes 4 servings.

A New Leaf

Leave it to the Chinese to come up with all kinds of wonderful ways to cook fish in leaves! Lotus leaves, which are sold dried and must be soaked before using, are large and round (almost 2 feet in diameter), with a pointed peak at the center that's perfect for stuffing. They give food an exotic, sweet, tealike flavor. I love the classic dish *nor mai gai*: sticky rice cooked with chicken, ham, or Chinese sausage, then wrapped in a lotus leaf and steamed. Bamboo leaves, also used for wrapping and steaming food, are, like the lotus leaves, inedible (unless you're a panda bear).

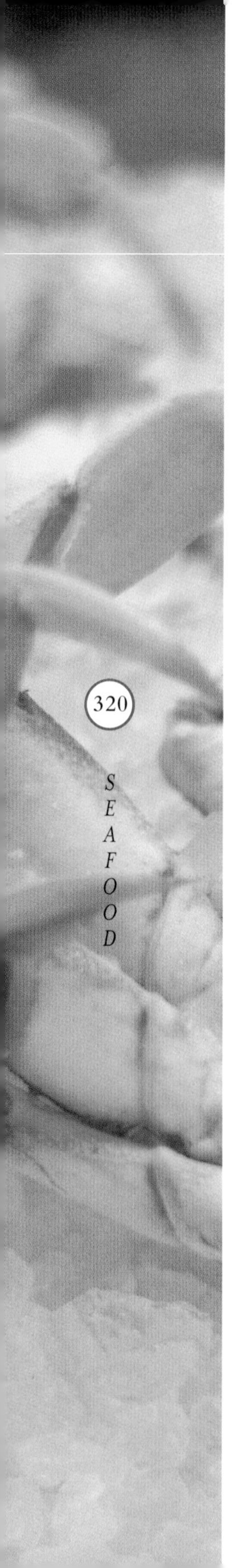

Pan-Fried Fish with Fruited Chili Sauce

Golden sautéed fish fillets topped with chili sauce are classic Hong Kong fare. For an extra kick of sweetness, I like to add fresh mango and apple—my tribute to the spirit of international culinary exchange that makes today's Hong Kong cuisine so vibrant and dynamic.

Marinade

- 2 *tablespoons Chinese rice wine or dry sherry*
- 2 *teaspoons cornstarch*
- ¼ *teaspoon white pepper*

- 1¼ *pounds firm white fish fillets, such as sea bass, trout, or red snapper; or 1 whole fish*

Fruited Chili Sauce

- ½ *cup orange juice*
- 3 *tablespoons packed brown sugar*
- 2 *tablespoons rice vinegar*
- ¼ *cup diced apple*
- ¼ *cup diced mango*
- 1 *teaspoon minced garlic*
- ½ *teaspoon chili garlic sauce*
- ¼ *teaspoon salt*
- ⅛ *teaspoon white pepper*

- 2 *teaspoons cornstarch dissolved in 1 tablespoon water*
- 2 *tablespoons cooking oil*
- 3 *green onions, julienned*

Getting Ready

① Combine marinade ingredients in a bowl. Add fish and turn to coat. Let stand for 10 minutes.

② Combine fruited chili sauce ingredients in a small pan and bring to a boil. Add cornstarch solution and cook, stirring, until sauce boils and thickens.

Cooking

① Place a wide frying pan over medium heat until hot. Add oil, swirling to coat sides. Fry fish until golden, 4 to 5 minutes on each side. Reheat sauce.

② Arrange fish on a serving plate. Pour sauce over fish. Garnish with green onions.

Makes 4 servings.

Wok-Smoked Fish

Wok-smoking over rice and tea is a common food preservation technique in hot, humid Sichuan. It's also a wonderful way to flavor foods, no matter where in the world you live.

- 1½ *pounds firm white fish fillets, such as sea bass or red snapper, ½ to ¾ inch thick*

Marinade

- ¼ *cup Chinese rice wine or dry sherry*
- 3 *tablespoons regular soy sauce*
- 3 *tablespoons dark soy sauce*
- 2 *teaspoons minced ginger*
- 2 *teaspoons sugar*
- ½ *teaspoon Chinese five-spice*
- ½ *teaspoon ground toasted Sichuan peppercorns*
- ½ *teaspoon liquid smoke (optional)*

Smoking Mixture

- ½ *cup packed brown sugar*
- ⅓ *cup uncooked rice*
- ⅓ *cup black or oolong tea leaves*

Sliced honeydew melon or cantaloupe

Getting Ready

① Cut fish crosswise to make pieces about 3 inches square. Combine marinade ingredients in a bowl. Add fish and turn to coat. Let stand for 10 minutes.

Cooking

① Line wok and inside of wok lid with foil. Combine smoking mixture; spread evenly in wok. Set a round cake rack over smoking mixture; place fish on rack.

② Place wok, uncovered, over high heat. When mixture begins to smoke, cover wok; reduce heat to medium-low and smoke for 7 minutes. For ¾-inch-thick fish, smoke for 1 to 2 minutes longer. Turn off heat; let stand for 5 minutes before removing wok lid.

③ Serve fish hot or at room temperature. Garnish with melon slices.

Makes 4 servings.

Fresh Fish Facts

Living in coastal California, I'm spoiled by all the wonderful fresh seafood. When buying a whole fish, judge it first by your eyes and the fish's, which should be clear, not cloudy. Check the gills, which should be bright red. Then use your nose to detect any off or fishy odors. Finally, use your ears: Get the salesperson to tell you what's fresh that day. For fillets and steaks, avoid those that are sitting in a pool of liquid. Chances are, they've gone the way of all fish.

Salmon in Parchment with Black Bean Sauce

Cooking fish in parchment seals in its juices and flavor. The black bean topping for the salmon may sound like an unlikely combination, but its flavors add delightful highlights.

Black Bean Topping

- 6 *dried black mushrooms*
- 3 *tablespoons salted black beans, rinsed, drained, and coarsely chopped*
- 3 *tablespoons finely julienned ginger*
- 2 *green onions, julienned*
- 2 *teaspoons minced garlic*
- 2 *teaspoons sugar*

- 1½ *pounds salmon fillet*

Marinade

- 3 *tablespoons Chinese rice wine or dry sherry*
- 2 *tablespoons soy sauce*
- 2 *teaspoons cornstarch*
- 2 *teaspoons sesame oil*
- ⅛ *teaspoon white pepper*

- 4 *pieces cooking parchment, each 12 inches square*
- 2 *teaspoons sesame oil*

Getting Ready

① Prepare black bean topping: Soak mushrooms in warm water to cover until softened, about 20 minutes; drain. Discard stems and thinly slice caps. Combine mushrooms in a bowl with remaining topping ingredients; mix well.

② Remove salmon skin. Cut fillet into 4 equal portions. Combine marinade ingredients in a bowl. Add fish and turn to coat. Let stand for 10 minutes.

③ To make each packet: Place a square of parchment on work surface. Brush ½ teaspoon sesame oil on parchment 2 inches from one edge. Place fish on oiled area; top with ¼ of black bean topping. Fold parchment over fish, then roll over twice more to enclose fish completely. Double-fold ends of parchment; tuck ends under packet to hold in place.

Cooking

① Preheat oven to 400°F. Place packets, folded ends down, slightly apart in a shallow baking pan. Bake until fish turns opaque, about 15 minutes. To test, cut a tiny slit through parchment into fish.

Makes 4 servings.

Grilled Fish in a Wrap

To keep something under wraps is to keep it a secret. But it is no secret that banana leaves make great wrappers on the grill. They help to keep the fish moist, and they also minimize the smoky taste. Grilled fish should be flaky, not sticky.

Marinade

2 *tablespoons chopped cilantro*

1 *tablespoon minced garlic*

1 *tablespoon minced ginger*

1 *walnut-sized shallot, minced*

2 *tablespoons oyster-flavored sauce*

2 *tablespoons fish sauce*

1 *tablespoon lemon juice*

1 *teaspoon cooking oil*

1½ *pounds firm white fish fillets, such as sea bass or red snapper, each about ¾ inch thick*

4 *pieces banana leaf or foil, each about 8 by 12 inches*

8 *fresh basil leaves*

Getting Ready

① Combine marinade ingredients in a bowl. Cut fish into 4 equal portions; place in marinade and turn to coat. Let stand for 10 minutes.

② Dip banana leaves into a pot of boiling water for 3 to 4 seconds to soften; wipe dry. Make each packet: Center leaf, shiny side down, on work surface. Lift a portion of fish from marinade and center on leaf. Bring 2 long sides of leaf together and double-fold to seal; fasten ends with wooden picks.

Cooking

① Place packets on an oiled grill 4 to 6 inches above a solid bed of medium-glowing coals. Grill until fish turns opaque, about 8 minutes on each side. If leaves begin to burn, move to a cooler spot on the grill.

② Place packets on a serving platter. Cut packets open with scissors and scatter basil over the fish.

Makes 4 servings.

Love It or Leave It

In Malaysia, Singapore, and the Philippines, banana leaves are used as plates, place mats, and wrappers for cooking food over steam or charcoal. I've also seem them sold frozen by the pound in many Asian, Filipino, and Central American markets. Frozen leaves do not need to be dipped in boiling water for 3 to 4 seconds, they can be used as soon as they are thawed. If you can't find banana leaves, you can bake food in fresh ti leaves from a florist. And if you can't find ti leaves, don't let that foil your plans. Just use foil!

Clear-Simmered West Lake Fish

West Lake Fish is a popular Chinese restaurant dish that's served all over the world. This healthful version is poached whole and served with a Shanghai-style sweet and sour sauce. Fish fillets can be substituted for the whole fish.

Sauce

- 6 *tablespoons Chinese black vinegar or balsamic vinegar*
- 3 *tablespoons packed brown sugar*
- 2 *tablespoons Chinese rice wine or dry sherry*
- 1 *tablespoon regular soy sauce*
- 1 *tablespoon dark soy sauce*
- 2 *teaspoons sesame oil*
- 1 *teaspoon chili sauce*

- 1 *whole fish (1½ to 2 lb.), such as sea bass or red snapper, cleaned*
- 6 *slices ginger, each the size of a quarter, lightly crushed*
- 3 *green onions, lightly crushed*
- 1 *teaspoon salt*

Getting Started

① Combine sauce ingredients in a small pan.

② On fish, cut a ¾-inch-deep slit along each side of dorsal fin.

Cooking

① Pour 2 inches of water into a pan large enough to hold fish. Add ginger, green onions, and salt; bring to a boil.

② Slide fish into water. Reduce heat, cover, and simmer until fish turns opaque, 8 to 12 minutes, depending on thickness of fish. Remove fish with a slotted spatula and place on a serving plate.

③ Place sauce over low heat. Cook, stirring, until sauce is heated through. Pour sauce over fish.

Makes 4 to 6 servings.

Black Vinegar

I love to use a splash of vinegar in cooking to add sparkle and intensity to a dish. For lighter color and flavor, I'll often use distilled white vinegar, but for darker, deeper taste, Chinese black vinegar is the way to go. It's sold in Asian markets (sometimes as "Chinkiang vinegar"), and it's really worth tracking down. Black vinegar is made by fermenting a mixture of rice, wheat, and millet or sorghum. It's flavor is smokier, sweeter, and less tart than that of Western white or red vinegars. If you can't find it, don't be sour: Balsamic vinegar is a perfect substitute, though you may want to reduce the amount of sugar in your recipe.

Baked Fish in Banana Leaf

Your family and friends may think you've gone bananas when you bring a whole fish baked in a banana leaf to the table. But when they discover the fish's delicate, succulent texture and marvelous spicy flavor, they'll realize you haven't taken "leave" of your senses after all! You can also cook this fish on the grill, as people often do in Malaysia.

- 1 *whole fish (1½ to 2 lb.), such as sea bass or red snapper, cleaned*
- ½ *teaspoon salt*
- ¼ *teaspoon white pepper*

Spice Paste

- 1 *stalk lemongrass*
- 6 *walnut-sized shallots*
- 3 *cloves garlic*
- 6 *fresh red jalapeño chilies, seeded*
- ½ *teaspoon dried shrimp paste (optional)*
- ½ *tablespoon lime juice*
- ¼ *cup water*

- 1–2 *pieces banana leaf large enough to wrap around fish*
- 1 *piece foil large enough to enclose wrapped fish*
- *Lime slices*

Getting Ready

① Cut 3 diagonal slits, each ½ inch deep, across each side of fish. Sprinkle fish inside and out with salt and pepper.

② Very thinly slice bottom 6 inches of lemongrass; discard remainder. Place in a blender with remaining spice paste ingredients and process until smooth.

③ Dip banana leaf into a pot of boiling water for 3 to 4 seconds to soften; wipe dry. Center leaf, shiny side down, on foil. Fill the cavity and slits of fish with about ⅓ of the spice paste. Spread another ⅓ of spice paste on banana leaf. Lay fish on paste and top with remaining paste. Fold leaf over fish, then fold foil around fish to enclose. Place wrapped fish on a baking sheet.

Cooking

① Preheat oven to 425°F. Bake until fish turns opaque, about 30 minutes.

② Place fish on a serving platter. Open foil and banana leaf, and turn foil back and under fish. Garnish with lime slices.

Makes 4 servings.

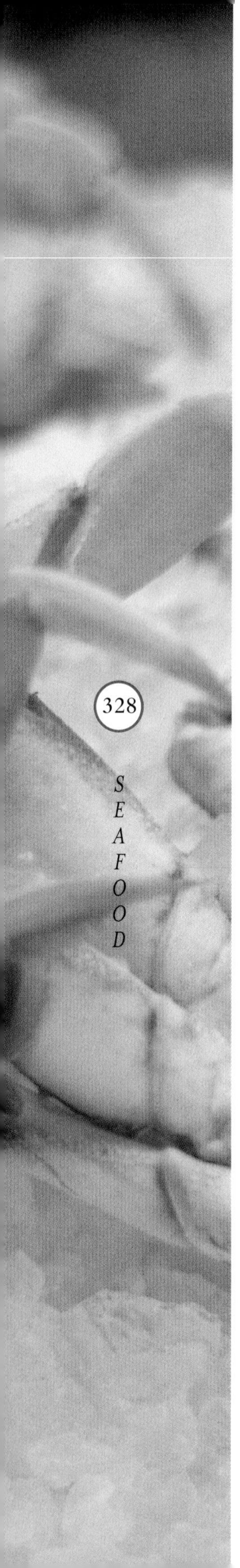

Fish Fillet in Wine Sauce

Fish steamed in rice wine and rice wine lees (a byproduct of making rice wine) is a classic regional specialty of eastern and northern China. You can find fermented rice at Asian groceries, sold as a semiliquid paste in jars. It imparts a wonderful yeasty flavor and a delicate rice wine aroma.

- 6 *dried cloud ears*
- 1½ *pounds firm white fish fillets, such as sea bass or red snapper*
- 1 *tablespoon cornstarch*
- ¾ *teaspoon salt*
- ¼ *teaspoon white pepper*

Wine Sauce

- ⅓ *cup Chinese rice wine or dry sherry*
- ¼ *cup chicken broth*
- 1 *tablespoon oyster-flavored sauce*
- 1 *tablespoon regular soy sauce*
- 1 *teaspoon dark soy sauce*
- 2 *tablespoons fermented rice (optional)*
- 1 *teaspoon sugar*

- 2 *tablespoons cooking oil*
- ½ *cup sliced bamboo shoots*
- 2 *teaspoons cornstarch dissolved in 1 tablespoon water (optional)*

Getting Ready

① Soak cloud ears in warm water to cover until softened, about 20 minutes; drain. Thinly slice.

② Cut fish to make pieces roughly 2 inches by 4 inches. Combine cornstarch, salt, and pepper in a bowl. Add fish and turn to coat. Let stand for 10 minutes.

③ Combine wine sauce ingredients in a bowl.

Cooking

① Place a wide frying pan over high heat until hot. Add oil, swirling to coat sides. Add fish and cook for 1½ minutes on each side. Remove fish from pan.

② Add cloud ears and bamboo shoots to pan; stir-fry for 1 minute. Return fish to pan and add sauce; bring to a boil. Reduce heat and simmer, uncovered, for 5 minutes. If desired, add cornstarch solution and cook, stirring, until sauce boils and thickens.

Makes 4 servings.

Savory Fish Cakes

Who says you can't have your cake and eat it, too? Not Martin Yan! When I make these savory fish cakes, I always make enough for another meal. They are wonderful appetizers, and, of course, everybody who tastes them asks me for the recipe. Don't be tempted to use anything but fresh fish.

Fish Cakes

- 1 *pound firm white fish fillets, such as cod or red snapper*
- 2 *tablespoons finely chopped water chestnuts*
- 2 *tablespoons finely chopped carrot*
- 2 *teaspoons chopped cilantro*
- 2 *tablespoons oyster-flavored sauce*
- 2 *teaspoons cornstarch*
- ½ *teaspoon salt*
- ⅛ *teaspoon white pepper*
- 1 *egg white*

- ¾ *cup Japanese-style bread crumbs (panko)*
- 2½ *tablespoons sesame seeds*
- *Cooking oil for deep-frying*

Getting Ready

① Remove all bones from fish; cut fish into 1-inch cubes. Finely chop fish in a food processor. Remove to a bowl and add remaining fish cakes ingredients; mix well.

② Combine bread crumbs and sesame seeds in a wide bowl.

③ Shape fish mixture into eight 2-inch patties. Coat on all sides with crumb mixture.

Cooking

① In a wok or 2-quart saucepan, heat oil for deep-frying to 360°F. One half at a time, deep-fry fish cakes, turning once, until golden brown, about 1½ minutes on each side. Remove with a slotted spoon; drain on paper towels.

Makes 8.

Porcupine Fish with Sweet Chili Sauce

My favorite way to eat deep-fried fish is with a spicy sweet and sour sauce. The traditional method of scoring the fillets before deep-frying exposes more surface area, allowing the light, seasoned egg coating to cover more of the fish.

Sauce

- ¼ *cup chicken broth*
- ¼ *cup rice vinegar*
- 3 *tablespoons ketchup*
- 2 *tablespoons sugar*
- 1 *tablespoon soy sauce*
- 1 *teaspoon chili sauce*

- 1 *large firm white fish fillet (about 1 lb., 1 in. thick) with skin intact, such as sea bass or red snapper*
- ½ *cup flour*
- ¼ *cup cornstarch*
- ¾ *teaspoon salt*
- ¼ *teaspoon white pepper*
- *Cooking oil for deep-frying*
- 2 *eggs, lightly beaten*
- 2 *teaspoons cornstarch dissolved in 1 tablespoon water*

Getting Ready

① Combine sauce ingredients in a small pan.

② Score skinless side of fish with shallow diagonal cuts; score again at a 90° angle to the first cuts. Combine flour, cornstarch, salt, and pepper on a plate.

Cooking

① In a wok or 2-quart saucepan, heat oil for deep-frying to 375°F. Dip fish in egg, drain briefly, then dust with flour mixture. Shake to remove excess. Deep-fry fish, turning once, until golden brown, 2 to 3 minutes. Remove with a slotted spoon; drain on paper towels.

② Place sauce over medium heat and cook, stirring, until it simmers. Add cornstarch solution and cook, stirring, until sauce boils and thickens.

③ To serve, place fish on a plate and pour sauce over the top.

Makes 4 servings.

Cornstarch Comments

Starches of all kinds are an essential part of Chinese cooking, but in the Western world, the kind most widely used in Chinese food is cornstarch. The recipe above is a good illustration of what it can do. Cornstarch dissolved in water is used to thicken sauces, giving them an attractive transparent glaze. As a coating, it seals in the juices of deep-fried foods and gives them a crispy exterior. In marinades, it helps coat foods evenly and gives them a velvety texture.

Seafood Hot Pot

Running low on ideas on how to entertain your guests while dinner is cooking? Hand each of them an apron, and make each one a Hot Pot Chef. This is a dish they will enjoy making as much as eating. Use this recipe as a guide when preparing a hot pot, but your imagination and creativity are the most important ingredients.

- 4 *ounces dried bean thread noodles*
- ½ *pound fish fillet, thinly sliced*
- ¼ *pound medium raw shrimp, shelled and deveined*
- ¼ *pound sea scallops*
- 1 *package (14 oz.) medium-firm tofu, drained and cut into ½-inch cubes*
- 1 *bunch spinach (coarse stems discarded)*
- ¼ *pound snow peas, trimmed*
- ¼ *pound mushrooms, thickly sliced*
- 8 *green onions, cut into 1½-inch pieces*
- 1 *can (8 oz.) sliced bamboo shoots, drained*

Dipping Sauce

- ¼ *cup soy sauce*
- ¼ *cup rice vinegar*
- 3 *tablespoons chicken broth*
- 1 *tablespoon chili garlic sauce*
- 2 *teaspoons sesame oil*

- 8 *cups chicken broth*

Getting Ready

① Soak bean thread noodles in warm water to cover until softened, about 5 minutes. Drain and cut into 4-inch lengths. Arrange noodles, fish, shrimp, scallops, tofu, spinach, snow peas, mushrooms, onions, and bamboo shoots attractively on a platter; cover and chill until ready to cook.

② Combine dipping sauce ingredients; pour into 4 individual dipping bowls.

Cooking

① In a pot, heat broth to simmering. Set a Mongolian hot pot or an electric wok in center of table. Place platter of food on the table. Arrange individual plates and dipping bowls around hot pot. Pour broth into hot pot and adjust heat so broth simmers gently. Each diner cooks his or her choice of ingredients in the broth and seasons it with dipping sauce.

② When all the seafood, tofu, and vegetables are cooked, add noodles to broth and cook until heated through. Ladle noodles and broth into 4 soup bowls and serve.

Makes 4 servings.

Coconut Curried Fish

Singapore chefs cook fish many ways, and one of the best is done in a style introduced from South India: seasoning fish with a fragrant spice paste and simmering it in coconut milk. Serve this in deep bowls. Spoon some of the sauce over rice.

Spice Paste

- 2 *stalks lemongrass*
- 2 *walnut-sized shallots*
- 4 *slices ginger, each the size of a quarter, lightly crushed*
- 3 *cloves garlic*
- 8 *almonds*
- 2 *fresh red jalapeño chilies, seeded*
- ¼ *cup water*

- 1½ *pounds halibut*
- *About ½ teaspoon salt*
- 1 *tablespoon cooking oil*
- ½ *medium red onion, thinly sliced*
- ¼ *teaspoon turmeric powder*
- 1 *can (13½ oz.) unsweetened coconut milk*
- ⅓ *cup water*
- 1 *fresh red jalapeño chili, seeded and cut into thin strips*

Getting Ready

① Thinly slice bottom 6 inches of lemongrass; discard remainder. Place in blender with remaining spice paste ingredients and process until smooth.

② Remove skin and bones from fish, then cut fish into 1-inch cubes. Sprinkle with ½ teaspoon salt.

Cooking

① Place a wok over medium-low heat until hot. Add oil, swirling to coat sides. Add spice paste and cook, stirring, until fragrant, 6 to 8 minutes.

② Add onion, turmeric, coconut milk, and water; mix well. Simmer, uncovered, for 5 minutes.

③ Add fish; simmer, uncovered, until fish turns opaque, 8 to 10 minutes. Season to taste with salt. Sprinkle with chili.

Makes 6 servings.

"Milking" a Coconut

Did you know that the liquid that sloshes around inside a coconut isn't coconut milk? It's called coconut water. The milk and cream of a coconut are actually extracted from its meat. To make your own, chop the meat of a coconut (remove brown outer layer first) in a food processor, then add 1 cup of hot water, then purée. Press the coconut mixture through a fine sieve to extract the rich cream. Return the meat to the food processor and blend with another cup of hot water, then strain again to extract the thinner milk.

Fish with Spicy Salsa

Fried fish topped with a cold fresh tomato sauce—this is my interpretation of a simple dish that my cousin threw together for dinner one warm night during one of my trips to Asia. I like the contrast of the crisp, golden fish and the cool, sweet, and slightly spicy salsa.

- 2 *teaspoons cornstarch*
- ½ *teaspoon salt*
- ¼ *teaspoon white pepper*
- 1 *pound fish steaks, such as striped bass, cod, or salmon, each about ¾ inch thick*

Salsa

- ¼ *cup diced tomatoes*
- ¼ *cup* each *diced red and green bell peppers*
- ¼ *cup chopped red onions*
- 1 *tablespoon chopped cilantro*
- 3 *tablespoons plum sauce*
- 1 *tablespoon seasoned rice vinegar*
- 2 *teaspoons soy sauce*
- 1 *teaspoon chili sauce*

- 2 *tablespoons cooking oil*
- *Cornstarch*

Getting Ready

① Combine the 2 teaspoons cornstarch, salt, and pepper in a small bowl. Sprinkle on both sides of fish. Let stand for 10 minutes.

② Combine salsa ingredients in a bowl. Let stand for 10 minutes for flavors to blend.

Cooking

① Place a wok or wide frying pan over medium-high heat until hot. Add oil, swirling to coat sides. Dust fish with cornstarch; shake to remove excess.

② Place fish in pan and cook, turning once, until golden brown, 3 to 4 minutes on each side. Remove and drain on paper towels.

③ Serve fish with salsa.

Makes 4 servings.

Go Fish

Fresh fish holds a special place in the hearts of the Chinese. And when they say fresh, they mean it! The more recently a fish was alive before cooking the better, and that can be a matter of just a few minutes. Restaurants often pluck live fish from tanks and cook them to order, and in many villages fish ponds are used to cultivate a variety of freshwater fish and edible aquatic plants.

Seafood Purses

A purse is where you keep your valuables, and that's certainly the case with this dish. Picture the pleasure of opening up this purse and discovering a steamy treasure of seafood inside. Another great thing about this purse: No need to run out to buy matching shoes!

- 5 *dried black mushrooms*
- 6 *garlic chives, green onion tops, or leek leaves*
- ¼ *pound medium raw shrimp*
- ¼ *pound firm white fish fillet*

Marinade

- 2 *tablespoons Chinese rice wine or dry sherry*
- 2 *teaspoons cornstarch*
- ½ *teaspoon salt*
- ¼ *teaspoon white pepper*

Sauce

- ¼ *cup chicken broth*
- 2 *tablespoons oyster-flavored sauce*
- 1 *tablespoon hoisin sauce*

- 2 *tablespoons cooking oil*
- ⅓ *cup finely diced carrots*
- ¼ *cup finely diced water chestnuts*
- 1 *teaspoon cornstarch dissolved in 2 teaspoons water*
- 6 *Mandarin Pancakes (see page 189), heated, or 6 spring roll wrappers*

Getting Ready

① Soak mushrooms in warm water to cover until softened, about 20 minutes; drain. Discard stems and finely chop caps.

② Split chives lengthwise, then blanch in boiling water for 20 seconds. Use as ties for purses.

③ Cut shrimp and fish into ½-inch cubes. Combine marinade ingredients in a bowl; add seafood and stir to coat. Let stand for 10 minutes.

④ Combine sauce ingredients in a bowl.

Cooking

① Place a wok over high heat until hot. Add oil, swirling to coat sides. Add shrimp and fish and stir-fry for 1 minute. Add mushrooms, carrots, and water chestnuts; stir-fry for 1 minute. Add sauce and bring to a boil. Add cornstarch solution and cook, stirring, until sauce boils and thickens.

② Make each purse: Place about 3 tablespoons seafood mixture in center of a Mandarin pancake; gather up edges to form a pouch, and secure with a chive tie.

Makes 6 servings.

Wok-Seared Scallops with Chili-Wine Sauce

I discovered this dish on board the Eastern and Oriental Express bound up the Malay Peninsula toward Thailand. The talented chefs have a monumental task wok-searing scallops while the train is going 60 miles per hour! Now that's fast food with panache!

- ¾ *pound sea scallops*
- 2 *teaspoons cornstarch*
- ½ *teaspoon salt*

Chili-Wine Sauce

- ¼ *cup tomato sauce*
- ¼ *cup Chinese rice wine or dry sherry*
- 2 *teaspoons chili garlic sauce*
- 2 *teaspoons oyster-flavored sauce*
- 1½ *teaspoons sugar*

- 1 *tomato*
- 2 *tablespoons cooking oil*
- 1 *teaspoon minced garlic*
- 1 *teaspoon minced ginger*
- *Cilantro sprigs*

Getting Ready

① Pat scallops dry with paper towels. Place in a bowl with cornstarch and salt; let stand for 5 minutes.

② Combine sauce ingredients in a small bowl.

③ Slice tomato and reserve for garnish.

Cooking

① Heat 1 tablespoon oil in a small pan over high heat. Add garlic and ginger; cook, stirring, until fragrant, about 10 seconds. Add sauce; simmer over medium heat, 2 to 3 minutes. Remove sauce from heat and keep warm.

② Place a wok over medium heat until hot. Add remaining 1 tablespoon oil, swirling to coat sides. Add scallops; cook until they turn opaque, about 2 minutes on each side.

③ Pour sauce onto a rimmed serving plate; arrange scallops over sauce. Garnish with tomato and cilantro.

Makes 4 servings.

Scallops

The two types of scallops most commonly sold in the U.S. are sea scallops and bay scallops. Larger sea scallops have a nice chewy texture that's great for stir-fries. You can cut them in half horizontally so that they cook more evenly. Bay scallops are smaller and sweeter, and have a more delicate texture. In fine restaurants in China, scallops are more likely to be used dried than fresh. A prized delicacy along the lines of shark's fin, dried scallops are used as a flavoring in soups and sauces.

A Menu for Success

Making the Most of a Chinese Restaurant Meal

When I'm traveling around the country and around the world, I do a lot of entertaining in Chinese restaurants. Over the years, I have literally ordered thousands of Chinese meals. (It was a tough job, but somebody had to do it.) So now, let me share with you my ten commandments for enhancing your Chinese restaurant dining experience.

1. **Look before you leap.** You can tell a lot about a Chinese restaurant before you sit down to order. Never mind about the decor. Check out the menu. Does it look interesting? Does it offer options beyond the old standards? Does the restaurant specialize in a particular region of China? Are there lots of people inside? Are many of them Asians? (I know this sounds politically incorrect, but I usually find it to be a good indicator of quality and value.) Does the food on the tables look colorful, fresh, clean, and nongloppy? Are you getting hungry from all the wonderful aromas in the air? If you can answer "yes" to most of these questions, proceed. If not, time for the next stop.

2. **Go as a group.** The more people in your party, the more dishes you can try. A party of four to six is usually just right for ordering a well-balanced menu.

3. **Be adventurous.** The risks are low, and the potential for dining pleasure is high. Make the most of the moment, and try new dishes you've never had before—at least one on each outing.

4. **Go beyond the ABCs.** A lot of Chinese restaurants offer a series of set menus. Menu A for two or three people, Menu B for four to six, etc. Sure, these set menus are easy to use, but people who order from them often seem to have the attitude: "The sooner we get this over with, the sooner we can all go home." You're here to explore and discover new things. Avoid the set menus. Relax, slow down, and savor the moment.

5. **Ask what's special.** Most Chinese restaurants feature seasonal specials based on what's fresh—from crab to fresh asparagus. And there's a reason they're called "specials." They're often the best-tasting dishes in the house. Always start by asking for a list of the specials. It's more than just a way to get information. It's a way of signaling to the staff that you're interested in

trying new things. Also, ask about regional specialties. (And please, be friendly, polite, and respectful. You might even try learning a few Chinese words and expressions. It can't hurt, and chances are, you will get better service and better food in return!)

6. **Ask to see the Chinese menu.** Yes, it will be in Chinese. And yes, it will have some things on it that you may not want to try—innards, "variety meats," and the like. But again, it's a way of showing interest and starting a dialogue. Even if you don't order from the Chinese menu, you'll avoid being directed to old stand-bys like Lemon Chicken or the neon-red Sweet and Sour Pork.

7. **Look around the room.** The best menu in any restaurant is the food itself. If you see wonderful looking things on other tables, find out what they are and give them a try.

8. **Go for the "see food."** In Chinese cooking, "fresh" often means food that was live until it was cooked. Many Chinese restaurants feature display tanks teeming with live fish, crab, lobster, prawns, eels, frogs, geoduck clams, and more. Even if you can't find these items on the menu, ask how they're prepared and give them a try. Stick with a simple cooking method and sauce, so the fresh flavor of the food comes through. (And by the way, to avoid going "tankrupt," always ask how these live items are priced. They're generally seasonal and a bit more expensive than the standard menu items.)

9. **Keep it balanced.** Order an array of dishes that contrast and complement each other: a soup, dumplings, plus one dish per person (to be shared communally, needless to say), including poultry, meat, fish, seafood, and vegetables, served with plain cooked rice throughout. I find it helpful to write the whole order down on a napkin rather than trying to balance everything in my head. This also makes things easier when it's time to order.

10. **More is more.** I always tell people to replace the phrase "We can always order more" with "We can always take it home." After all, prices are usually low, and this is your chance to try new things. Chinese restaurants expect you to take home the leftovers. They make a wonderful midnight snack, or you can reheat them for lunch or dinner the next day.

A good Chinese restaurant offers wonderful flavor, fresh, healthful eating, speedy service, and reasonable prices. What more could a person want? So remember, when you're dying for Chinese food, but you're too busy to cook, there's one thing you always have time to make: reservations!

Velveted Scallops with Sugar Snap Peas

Scallops are sweet and tender, sugar snap peas are sweet and crunchy—a match made in heaven! I stir-fry the peas, then the scallops, and top them both with a light wine sauce.

Marinade

- 2 *teaspoons cornstarch*
- 1 *egg white*
- ½ *teaspoon salt*
- ¼ *teaspoon white pepper*

- ¾ *pound sea scallops, butterflied*

Sauce

- ⅓ *cup Chinese rice wine or dry sherry*
- 2 *teaspoons black bean sauce*
- 2 *teaspoons oyster-flavored sauce*
- ½ *teaspoon sugar*

- 4 *teaspoons cooking oil*
- ½ *pound sugar snap peas or snow peas*
- 1 *fresh red jalapeño chili, seeded and thinly sliced*
- 1 *teaspoon cornstarch dissolved in 2 teaspoons water*

Getting Ready

① Combine marinade ingredients in a bowl. Add scallops and stir to coat. Let stand for 10 minutes.

② Combine sauce ingredients.

Cooking

① Bring a pan of water to a boil. Add scallops and parboil for 1 minute; drain and pat dry with paper towels.

② Place a wok over high heat until hot. Add 2 teaspoons oil, swirling to coat sides. Add peas and stir-fry for 2 minutes; add a few drops of water if wok appears dry. Remove peas to center of a serving plate.

③ Add remaining 2 teaspoons oil, swirling to coat sides. Add scallops and stir-fry for 1 minute. Add chili and cook for 30 seconds. Add sauce and bring to a boil. Add cornstarch solution and cook, stirring, until sauce boils and thickens.

④ Arrange scallops around peas. Pour sauce over peas and serve.

Makes 4 servings.

Edible Velvet

Have you ever wondered how Chinese restaurants make scallops so plump and tender? Allow me to reveal the chef's secret: First, the scallops are marinated in cornstarch, egg white, and salt to seal in their juices and make them plumper. Then they're quickly blanched in water or oil, drained, and patted dry. Now, half-cooked, they are ready to be quickly stir-fried. This technique, often used on seafood and poultry, is called "velveting" because it gives foods such a soft, smooth texture.

Seafood over Singing Rice

Talk about singing for your supper! In this dramatic banquet-style dish, a flavorful stir-fry of seafood and vegetables is poured over sizzling rice crusts (see page 113) for a showstopping tableside presentation.

- 2 *teaspoons cornstarch*
- ½ *teaspoon salt*
- ¼ *pound sea scallops, cut in half horizontally*
- ¼ *pound medium raw shrimp, shelled and deveined*

Sauce

- ⅓ *cup chicken broth*
- ⅓ *cup sweet chili sauce*
- 2 *teaspoons soy sauce*
- 1 *teaspoon sesame oil*

- 2 *tablespoons cooking oil*
- 1 *can (8 oz.) sliced bamboo shoots, drained*
- ½ *cup canned straw mushrooms*
- ½ *cup sliced carrots*
- ¼ *pound snow peas, trimmed and cut in half*
- 2 *teaspoons cornstarch dissolved in 1 tablespoon water*
- *Cooking oil for deep-frying*
- 12 *pieces rice crusts (see page 113), each about 2 inches square*

Getting Started

① Combine cornstarch and salt in a bowl. Add scallops and shrimp; stir to coat. Let stand for 10 minutes.

② Combine sauce ingredients in a bowl.

Cooking

① Place a wok over high heat until hot. Add oil, swirling to coat sides. Add scallops and shrimp; stir-fry for 1 minute. Add bamboo shoots, straw mushrooms, carrots, and snow peas. Stir-fry until carrots and snow peas are tender-crisp, about 2 minutes. Add sauce and bring to a boil. Add cornstarch solution and cook, stirring, until sauce boils and thickens. Remove from heat, cover, and keep warm while you deep-fry rice crusts.

② In a wok or 2-quart saucepan, heat oil for deep-frying to 375°F. Add rice crusts, ½ at a time, and deep-fry, turning continuously, until puffed and golden, 15 to 20 seconds. Remove with a slotted spoon; drain on paper towels.

③ Place hot rice crusts on a serving plate and immediately pour hot seafood mixture over the top.

Makes 4 servings.

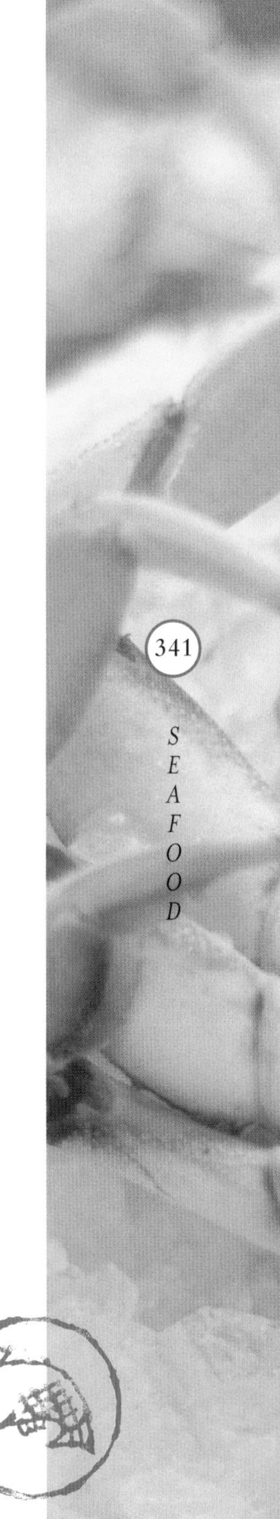

Mussels in Black Bean Sauce

Salted black beans lend a distinctly pungent, smoky flavor to foods. You'll find recipes in this book that call for whole beans, which must be rinsed and coarsely chopped before using. But when I'm in a hurry, I use black bean sauce, one of the sauces I keep in the refrigerator for quick cooking, such as in this dish of mussels in broth.

- 2 *pounds mussels*
- 1½ *tablespoons cooking oil*
- 2 *teaspoons minced garlic*
- 2 *teaspoons minced ginger*
- 1 *fresh jalapeño chili, seeded and thinly sliced*
- ½ *cup chopped onion*
- ¼ *cup seafood bouillon (from bouillon cube and water)*
- 1 *tablespoon black bean sauce*
- 2 *tablespoons Chinese rice vinegar*
- 1½ *teaspoons sugar*
- 1 *teaspoon cornstarch dissolved in 2 teaspoons water*

Getting Ready

① Scrub mussels; remove beards and discard any with open shells that don't close when tapped.

Cooking

① Place a wok over high heat until hot. Add oil, swirling to coat sides. Add garlic, ginger, and chili; cook, stirring, until fragrant, about 10 seconds. Add onion and stir-fry for 1 minute. Add mussels, bouillon, black bean sauce, vinegar, and sugar. Cover and cook over medium heat until mussel shells open, 6 to 8 minutes. Add cornstarch solution and cook, stirring, until pan juices thicken slightly, 1 to 2 minutes longer.

② Place mussels in a serving dish. (Discard any mussels whose shells have not opened.)

Makes 4 servings.

Make a Mussel

Fresh mussels may look a little intimidating, but don't be put off: Their flavor is sweet and delicate, and they're easy to clean and cook—especially the farmed mussels that are now sold in most fish markets. Mussels must be alive when you buy them, which means that they should be tightly closed, or they should close quickly when you tap them. Avoid chipped shells or shells that slide back and forth easily. Scrape off the "beard" with a small knife, and rinse each mussel well under cool running water. Keep mussels iced until you cook them, because they're quite perishable. Once cooked, mussels lose their muscle and open up. If they don't open, don't eat them.

Shaoxing Savory Prawns

Leaving the shells on these quickly stir-fried prawns steeped in a tangy wine sauce gives them extra flavor; but if you don't want the bother of having to remove the shells at the table, you can prepare this dish with shelled prawns, too.

½ *pound medium raw prawns*
1 *tablespoon cornstarch*
½ *teaspoon salt*

Sauce

⅓ *cup Shaoxing wine*
3 *tablespoons ketchup*
2 *tablespoons soy sauce*
2 *tablespoons rice vinegar*
2 *teaspoons sugar*
1 *teaspoon chili sauce*
1 *teaspoon sesame oil*

2 *tablespoons cooking oil*
1 *green onion, thinly sliced*

Getting Ready

① Remove legs from prawns. If desired, cut through back of shells with scissors and rinse out sand veins; pat dry with paper towels. Combine cornstarch and salt in a bowl. Add prawns and stir to coat. Let stand for 10 minutes.

② Combine sauce ingredients in a bowl.

Cooking

① Place a wok over high heat until hot. Add oil, swirling to coat sides. Add prawns and stir-fry until they turn pink, 1 to 2 minutes. Add sauce and bring to a boil. Reduce heat and simmer for 5 minutes.

② Place prawns on a serving plate and sprinkle with green onion.

Makes 2 or 3 servings.

Shaoxing Wine

The rice wine of Shaoxing in Zhejiang province is renowned throughout the world, not only as an accompaniment to Chinese food, but also as a flavoring ingredient in cooking. It's made by a process that has remained unchanged for more than 2,000 years. In outdoor urns covered with seaweed mats, rice is fermented with local lake water and an ancient strain of yeast that has been cultivated for centuries. The process can't be rushed; the wine ages at least 18 months, and sometimes up to 100 years.

Eight-Flavored Shrimp

These shrimp are fried in the shell for extra flavor and texture, then tossed in a wok with garlic, chilies, and green onion, and seasoned at the last minute with one of my favorite spice mixtures, Sichuan pepper salt. This magical mix makes a terrific seasoning for roasted chicken and grilled steaks and chops, too.

1 *pound medium to large raw shrimp*

Pepper Salt

¾ *teaspoon salt*

¼ *teaspoon black pepper*

¼ *teaspoon sugar*

⅛ *teaspoon Chinese five-spice*

⅛ *teaspoon ground toasted Sichuan peppercorns*

½ *cup cooking oil*

1 *teaspoon minced garlic*

1 *teaspoon crushed dried red chilies*

1 *green onion, chopped*

Shredded lettuce

1 *fresh red jalapeño chili, sliced*

Getting Ready

① Remove heads from shrimp, keeping shells and legs intact. Rinse shrimp and pat very dry with paper towels.

Cooking

① Prepare pepper salt: Place a small frying pan over medium-high heat until hot. Add salt and cook, stirring continuously, until slightly gray in color, 2 to 3 minutes. Place in a bowl and add remaining pepper salt ingredients.

② Heat oil in a wok over high heat until hot. Add shrimp and stir-fry until they turn pink, about 2 minutes. Lift out with a slotted spoon; drain on paper towels.

③ Remove all but 2 teaspoons oil from wok. Add garlic, crushed chilies, and green onion; cook, stirring, until fragrant, about 30 seconds. Return shrimp to wok and stir-fry for 1 to 1½ minutes. Add pepper salt and toss to coat.

④ Line a serving plate with lettuce. Place shrimp on top and garnish with chili rings.

Makes 4 servings.

East-West Eats

Mayonnaise in Chinese food? Why not? Creamy Shrimp with Candied Walnuts (recipe on opposite page) is a perfect example of a new kind of cross-cultural Chinese cooking that's particularly popular in restaurants in Shanghai, Guangdong, and Hong Kong. You'll find ingredients like mayonnaise, Worcestershire sauce, and ketchup (which, by the way, originated in Malaysia) being used to create new dishes that blend the best of East and West.

Creamy Shrimp with Candied Walnuts

You may find candied walnuts in the store, but I always prefer to make my own (recipe below). They are great to keep on hand. Toss them on a chicken salad or in stir-fries, and you will have an instant winner. In this dish, they provide great texture contrast to the velvety shrimp. Mayonnaise makes them that way.

Marinade

- 1 *tablespoon Chinese rice wine or dry sherry*
- 1 *tablespoon cornstarch*
- ½ *teaspoon salt*
- ⅛ *teaspoon white pepper*

- 1 *pound medium raw shrimp, shelled and deveined*

Sauce

- ⅓ *cup mayonnaise*
- 2 *teaspoons sugar*
- 2 *teaspoons oyster-flavored sauce*
- 2 *teaspoons sesame oil*
- 1 *teaspoon grated lemon zest*
- 1 *teaspoon chili garlic sauce*

- 2 *tablespoons cooking oil*
- 2 *tablespoons chicken broth*
- 1 *cup Candied Walnuts (recipe below)*

Getting Ready

① Combine marinade ingredients in a bowl. Add shrimp and stir to coat. Let stand for 10 minutes.

② Combine sauce ingredients in a bowl.

Cooking

① Place a wok over high heat until hot. Add oil, swirling to coat sides. Add shrimp and stir-fry until they turn pink, about 2 minutes. Add broth and cook for 30 seconds. Add sauce and cook for 30 seconds.

② Place shrimp on a serving plate and sprinkle with candied walnuts.

Makes 4 servings.

Candied Walnuts

In a pan of boiling **water**, blanch 1 pound **walnut halves** for 2 minutes; drain. Combine 1 cup **sugar** and ½ cup **water** in a 3-quart pan; cook over medium heat until sugar is dissolved. Add nuts and cook, stirring continuously, until sugar caramelizes, about 5 minutes. Pour into a colander to drain excess syrup. In a wok, heat **cooking oil** for deep-frying to 300°F. Add nuts and deep-fry, stirring often, for 5 minutes. Gradually increase heat to 350°F and cook nuts until they turn deep brown and glossy, and float to the surface. Remove nuts, drain well, and place in a shallow pan to cool. Shake pan often to prevent nuts from sticking. When they are cool, package airtight; refrigerate or freeze.

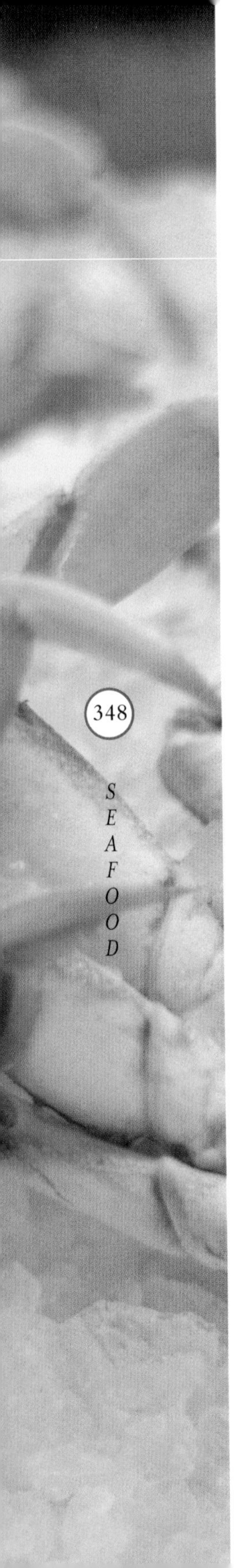

Asparagus Shrimp

For years my appreciation for asparagus was restricted to the West, so imagine my delight when I finally discovered fresh asparagus in Asia! It now appears regularly on Hong Kong dining tables.

Marinade

2 *tablespoons Chinese rice wine or dry sherry*

2 *teaspoons cornstarch*

¼ *teaspoon salt*

⅛ *teaspoon white pepper*

¾ *pound medium raw shrimp, shelled and deveined*

½ *pound asparagus*

2 *tablespoons cooking oil*

2 *teaspoons minced garlic*

2 *teaspoons minced ginger*

1 *can (8 oz.) sliced water chestnuts, drained*

⅓ *cup chicken broth*

2 *tablespoons Chinese rice wine or dry sherry*

2 *tablespoons oyster-flavored sauce*

1 *teaspoon sugar*

1 *teaspoon sesame oil*

2 *teaspoons cornstarch dissolved in 1 tablespoon water*

Getting Ready

① Combine marinade ingredients in a bowl. Add shrimp and turn to coat. Let stand for 10 minutes.

② Snap off and discard tough ends of asparagus; cut spears into 1½-inch diagonal slices.

Cooking

① Place a wok over high heat until hot. Add 1½ tablespoons oil, swirling to coat sides. Add garlic and ginger; cook, stirring, until fragrant, about 10 seconds. Add shrimp and stir-fry until they turn pink, about 2 minutes. Remove shrimp from wok.

② Heat remaining ½ tablespoon oil in wok, swirling to coat sides. Add asparagus and water chestnuts; stir-fry for 30 seconds. Add broth; cover and cook until asparagus is tender-crisp, about 1½ minutes. Return shrimp to wok and add wine, oyster-flavored sauce, sugar, and sesame oil. Add cornstarch solution and cook, stirring, until sauce boils and thickens.

Makes 4 servings.

Crispy Shrimp with Sauces

Crisp on the outside, succulent inside, these shrimp are perfect as an appetizer or as a main course. Make extras. The biggest challenge is getting them to the dining table. There will be plenty of tasting and dipping beforehand in the kitchen.

¾ *pound medium raw shrimp*

Marinade

1 *teaspoon Chinese rice wine or dry sherry*

½ *teaspoon salt*

⅛ *teaspoon white pepper*

Ketchup Dip

¼ *cup ketchup*

1 *teaspoon Worcestershire sauce*

½ *teaspoon chili oil*

Soy-Mustard Dip

¼ *cup soy sauce*

2 *teaspoons mustard powder*

2 *teaspoons water*

Batter

¾ *cup flour*

¼ *cup cornstarch*

1¼ *teaspoons baking powder*

½ *teaspoon sugar (optional)*

¾ *cup cold water or flat beer*

1 *teaspoon cooking oil*

Cooking oil for deep-frying

Getting Ready

① Shell and devein shrimp, leaving tails intact. Make several cuts across backs of shrimp, then butterfly. Combine marinade ingredients in a bowl. Add shrimp and stir to coat. Let stand for 10 minutes.

② In separate bowls, combine ingredients for ketchup dip and soy-mustard dip.

③ Prepare batter: In a bowl, mix flour, cornstarch, baking powder, and sugar. Gradually add cold water and oil, beating with a wire whisk until smooth.

Cooking

① In a wok or 2-quart saucepan, heat oil for deep-frying to 375°F. Dip shrimp, a few at a time, into batter, shaking off excess, then put immediately into hot oil. Deep-fry until batter is crispy and golden brown, 3 to 4 minutes. Remove with a slotted spoon/spatula; drain on paper towels.

② Serve with dipping sauces.

Makes 4 servings.

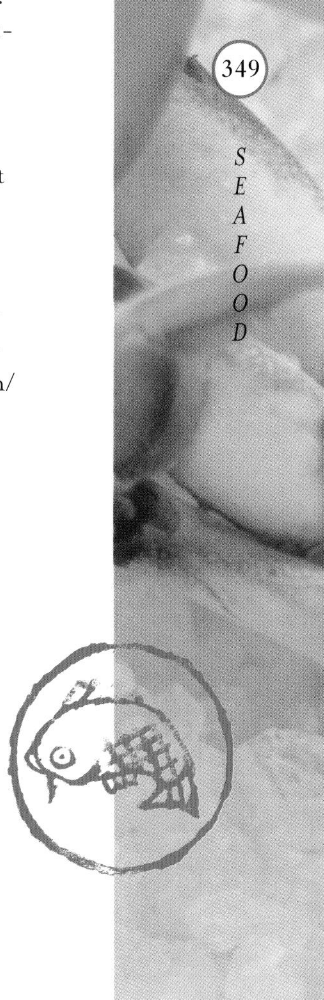

Seafood Stew

When French bouillabaisse made its way to Vietnam, chilies and lemongrass joined the medley of seafood.

Stock

- 1 *tablespoon cooking oil*
- 1 *small onion, chopped*
- 1 *walnut-sized shallot, minced*
- 1 *tablespoon minced garlic*
- 1 *tablespoon minced ginger*
- 1 *fresh jalapeño chili, seeded and thinly sliced*
- 3 *cups seafood bouillon (from bouillon cube and water) or chicken broth*
- 1½ *cups water*
- 1 *bottle (8 oz.) clam juice*
- 1 *cup dry white wine*
- 3 *tablespoons soy sauce*
- 2 *tablespoons fish sauce*
- 2 *stalks lemongrass (bottom 6 in. only), lightly crushed*

- 1 *dozen hard-shell clams*
- ½ *pound firm white fish fillet, cut into bite-sized pieces*
- ½ *pound medium raw shrimp, shelled and deveined*
- 1 *large tomato, peeled, seeded, and chopped*
- 3 *green onions, thinly sliced*
- 4 *fresh basil leaves*
- 2 *teaspoons sesame oil*

Cooking

① Prepare stock: Place a 5-quart pan over medium-high heat until hot. Add cooking oil, swirling to coat sides. Add onion, shallot, garlic, ginger, and chili; cook, stirring, for 1 minute. Add remaining stock ingredients and bring to a boil. Reduce heat, cover, and simmer for 30 minutes. Discard lemongrass.

② Scrub clams and discard any with open shells that don't close when tapped. Add clams, fish, and shrimp to the stock. Cover and simmer until clam shells open, 6 to 8 minutes. Add tomato, green onions, and basil; cook for 1 minute. Stir in sesame oil.

③ Ladle soup into deep bowl. (Discard any clams whose shells have not opened.)

Makes 4 servings.

Stalking the Wild Lemongrass

That mysteriously floral, delicately lemony aroma and flavor in Southeast Asian dishes is lemongrass. After peeling away dry, fibrous outside layers, gently crush the stalk and use it to flavor soups; or mince, pound, or grind it for use in sauces. You can find it in Asian markets, and even in supermarkets, too. In a pinch, substitute 1 teaspoon fresh lemon peel for one stalk lemongrass.

Tempura

Did you know tempura was brought to Japan in the 1500s by Spanish and Portuguese missionaries?

Dipping Sauce

- 1 *cup Japanese soup stock (dashi)*
- ¼ *cup sweet cooking rice wine (mirin)*
- ¼ *cup soy sauce*
- 2 *tablespoons sugar*

Batter

- 1 *cup flour*
- ¼ *cup cornstarch*
- ⅛ *teaspoon baking soda*
- 1 *egg yolk*
- 1⅓ *cups ice water*

- 8 *large raw shrimp*
- 1 *zucchini*
- 1 *medium onion*
- 1 *green bell pepper*
- 1 *carrot*
- 2 *Asian eggplants*
- 1 *sweet potato*
- 8 *white button mushroom caps*
- ¼ *pound green beans, trimmed*
- ¼ *pound broccoli florets, trimmed*
- *Cornstarch*
- *Cooking oil for deep-frying*
- 2 *sheets Japanese seaweed (nori), cut into 2-inch squares*
- *Grated daikon, grated ginger, and lemon slices*

Getting Ready

① Combine dipping sauce ingredients in a saucepan. Cook until sugar dissolves; cool. In a bowl, mix flour, cornstarch, and baking soda for batter. Refrigerate.

② Shell and devein shrimp, leaving tails intact. Make several cuts across backs of shrimp, then butterfly; set aside.

③ Cut zucchini into 2½-inch pieces, then lengthwise into ¼-inch-thick slices. Cut onion in half lengthwise, then crosswise ¼ inch thick; run a wooden pick through all layers to hold rings together. Cut bell pepper lengthwise into ¼-inch-wide strips, 2 inches long. Cut carrot, eggplants, and sweet potato diagonally into ⅛-inch-thick slices. Halve mushroom caps if large. Dry all vegetables. Dust with cornstarch.

Cooking

① Finish batter: Mix egg yolk and ice water; stir quickly into dry ingredients (batter will be lumpy). Do not overmix.

② In a wok or 2-quart saucepan, heat oil for deep-frying to 350°F. Dip shrimp, vegetables, and nori, a few pieces at a time, into batter, shaking off excess, then deep-fry immediately until batter is golden brown and shrimp and vegetables are cooked, about 1½ minutes. Remove with a slotted spoon; drain on paper towels.

③ Serve with dipping sauce and daikon, ginger, and lemon.

Makes 4 servings.

Cashew Shrimp

The great taste and texture of shrimp really come through in this stir-fry dish. I prefer to use unsalted cashews. Buy them already roasted or, if you have time, roast them in the oven.

Marinade

1 *egg white*

2 *teaspoons cornstarch*

2 *teaspoons Chinese rice wine or dry sherry*

¼ *teaspoon salt*

⅛ *teaspoon white pepper*

1 *pound medium raw shrimp, shelled and deveined*

Sauce

¼ *cup chicken broth*

1 *tablespoon Chinese rice wine or dry sherry*

1 *teaspoon sesame oil*

½ *teaspoon sugar*

¼ *teaspoon salt*

2½ *tablespoons cooking oil*

1 *teaspoon minced garlic*

1 *teaspoon minced ginger*

¼ *teaspoon crushed dried red chilies*

½ *cup frozen peas, thawed*

1½ *teaspoons cornstarch dissolved in 1 tablespoon water*

½ *cup roasted cashews*

Getting Ready

① Combine marinade ingredients in a bowl. Add shrimp and stir to coat. Let stand for 10 minutes. Combine sauce ingredients in a bowl.

Cooking

① Place a wok over high heat until hot. Add 2 tablespoons oil, swirling to coat sides. Add shrimp and stir-fry for 2 minutes. Remove shrimp from pan.

② Heat remaining ½ tablespoon oil in wok, swirling to coat sides. Add garlic, ginger, and chilies; cook, stirring, until fragrant, about 10 seconds. Add peas and sauce; cook for 30 seconds. Return shrimp to wok. Add cornstarch solution and cook, stirring, until sauce boils and thickens.

③ Place shrimp on a serving plate. Sprinkle cashews on top.

Makes 4 servings.

Tempura Tips

For light, crispy tempura (recipe at left): Keep the oil at 350°F (an electric wok or fryer is helpful). Ice water in the batter makes lacier tempura. Make batter just before frying so it's light and cold. Don't overbeat. Dry ingredients, then dip them in flour or cornstarch to help the batter adhere. Cook only a few pieces at a time.

Shrimp on Lemongrass Skewers

My mom comes from the "whole hog" school of cooking—in other words, "use every part, from the feet to the ears." She'd love this recipe, because it makes thrifty use of the otherwise unusable lemongrass stalks as skewers. For me, it's the unusual appearance of the skewers and the subtle flavor they impart to the shrimp that make this cooking method so special.

Spice Paste

- 6 *small dried red chilies*
- 1 *stalk lemongrass*
- 4 *walnut-sized shallots*
- 5 *cloves garlic*
- 4 *almonds*
- 1 *teaspoon turmeric powder*
- ½ *teaspoon dried shrimp paste (optional)*
- ¼ *cup water*

- 4 *stalks lemongrass*
- ¾ *pound large raw shrimp*
- 2 *tablespoons cooking oil*
- ½ *cup unsweetened coconut milk*
- 1 *tablespoon packed brown sugar*
- 1 *tablespoon lime juice*
- 1 *tablespoon soy sauce*
- *Cooking oil*

Getting Ready

① Soak chilies in warm water to cover for 20 minutes; drain. Thinly slice bottom 6 inches of lemongrass stalk. Place chilies and lemongrass in a blender with remaining spice paste ingredients and process until smooth.

② Cut off bottom 6 inches of 4 lemongrass stalks and save for another use. Cut the remaining woody stalks in half to make 8 skewers.

③ Shell and devein shrimp, leaving tails intact.

④ Place a wok over medium-low heat until hot. Add 2 tablespoons oil, swirling to coat sides. Add spice paste and cook, stirring, until fragrant, 6 to 8 minutes. Add coconut milk, brown sugar, lime juice, and soy sauce. Cook for 1 minute. Let mixture cool; divide in half.

⑤ Place shrimp in half of the coconut milk mixture; cover and refrigerate for 30 minutes.

Cooking

① Remove shrimp from marinade and drain briefly. Thread onto lemongrass skewers and place on an oiled grill 4 to 6 inches above a solid bed of low-glowing coals. Grill, turning and basting with oil, until shrimp turn pink, 3 to 4 minutes on each side.

② Reheat remaining coconut milk mixture and serve with shrimp.

Makes 8 skewers, 4 servings.

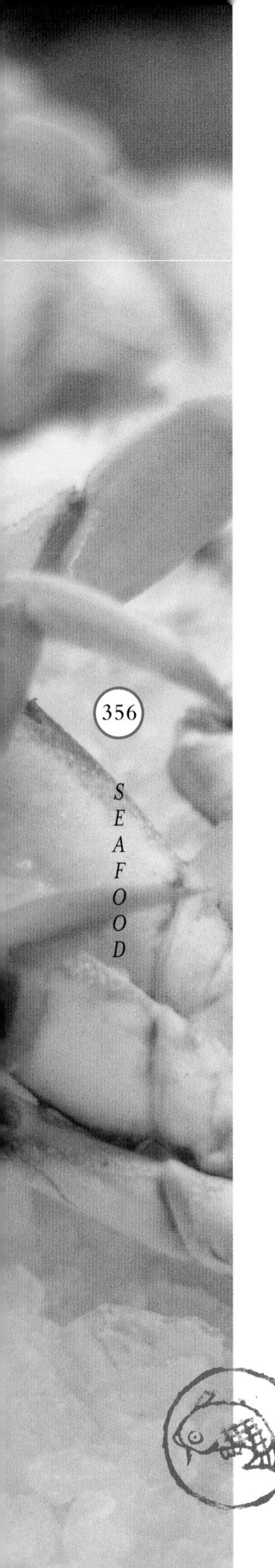

True Lovers' Prawns

Are we but mere pawns in the sea of love? Well, better pawns than prawns, I'd say, unless you don't mind ending up as someone's idea of a romantic dinner. All kidding aside, this is a perfect dish for that special someone. Shrimp are presented in two different ways sharing the same plate. True love means never having to say you are hungry.

- 2 *teaspoons cornstarch*
- ½ *teaspoon salt*
- ¾ *pound medium raw shrimp, shelled and deveined*

Tangy Tomato Sauce

- 3 *tablespoons ketchup*
- 1 *tablespoon plum sauce*
- 1 *teaspoon sugar*
- ½ *teaspoon chili paste*

Curry Sauce

- 2 *tablespoons prepared curry sauce*
- 2 *tablespoons Chinese rice wine or dry sherry*

- 2 *small tomatoes, cut in half and thinly sliced*
- 1½ *tablespoons cooking oil*
- 1 *teaspoon minced garlic*
- 1 *teaspoon minced lemon peel*

Getting Started

① Combine cornstarch and salt in a bowl. Add shrimp and stir to coat. Let stand for 10 minutes.

② Combine tomato sauce ingredients in one bowl. Combine curry sauce ingredients in another bowl.

③ Arrange tomato slices in center of a serving plate to form a tomato "wall."

Cooking

① Place a wok over high heat until hot. Add oil, swirling to coat sides. Add garlic and lemon peel; cook, stirring, until fragrant, about 10 seconds. Add shrimp and stir-fry until they turn pink, about 2 minutes. Remove half of shrimp from pan.

② Add tomato sauce to shrimp in wok; stir-fry for 30 seconds. Arrange shrimp on one side of serving plate. Wipe wok clean. Return remaining shrimp to wok. Add curry sauce and stir-fry for 30 seconds. Arrange on other side of serving plate.

Makes 4 servings.

Shrimp with Spicy Tomato Sauce

Some call this the best thing that ever came out of Hong Kong (for what it's worth, some say I am the second best). In Hong Kong, these shrimp are cooked and served with their shells on. If you feel adventurous, try them this old-fashioned way.

Marinade

- 1 *tablespoon Chinese rice wine or dry sherry*
- 1 *tablespoon cornstarch*
- ¼ *teaspoon salt*

- 1 *pound large raw shrimp, shelled and deveined*

Sauce

- ¼ *cup ketchup*
- 2 *tablespoons hoisin sauce*
- 2 *teaspoons chili garlic sauce*
- 2 *teaspoons Worcestershire sauce*
- 1 *teaspoon sesame oil*

- 2 *tablespoons cooking oil*
- 1 *tablespoon minced ginger*
- 2 *teaspoons minced garlic*
- ½ *small onion, diced*
- 1 *fresh red jalapeño chili, seeded and thinly sliced*

Getting Started

① Combine marinade ingredients in a bowl. Add shrimp and stir to coat. Let stand for 10 minutes.

② Combine sauce ingredients in a bowl.

Cooking

① Place a wok over high heat until hot. Add oil, swirling to coat sides. Add ginger, garlic, onion, and chili; cook, stirring, for 30 seconds. Add shrimp and stir-fry until they turn pink, 2 to 3 minutes.

② Add sauce and cook until shrimp are well glazed, about 1 minute.

Makes 4 servings.

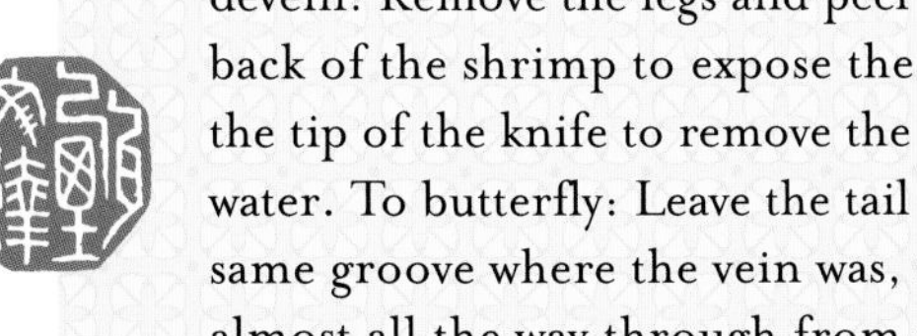

Shrimp Made Simple

Deveining and butterflying a fresh shrimp is easier than you might think. To devein: Remove the legs and peel off the shell; run a sharp paring knife along the back of the shrimp to expose the black vein (which is actually the intestine); use the tip of the knife to remove the vein, then rinse the shrimp quickly under cold water. To butterfly: Leave the tail on during peeling. Make a deeper cut along the same groove where the vein was, slicing along the entire length of the shrimp, almost all the way through from the back to the other side. Open the shrimp along the cut and flatten it.

Sizzling Oysters and Mussels

Even if you don't have a sizzle platter to serve this on, it's got plenty of sizzle of its own from fresh chili, garlic, ginger, and green onion.

- ¾ *pound mussels*
- 2 *teaspoons cornstarch*
- ½ *teaspoon salt*
- 1 *jar (10 to 12 oz.) shucked oysters, drained*

Sauce

- ¼ *cup chicken broth*
- 3 *tablespoons Chinese rice wine or dry sherry*
- 1 *tablespoon black bean garlic sauce*
- 1 *tablespoon dark soy sauce*
- 1 *teaspoon cornstarch*
- ½ *teaspoon sugar*

- 2 *tablespoons cooking oil*
- 1 *fresh jalapeño chili, seeded and minced*
- 3 *cloves garlic, thinly sliced*
- 4 *slices ginger, each the size of a quarter, lightly crushed*
- 1 *green onion, thinly sliced*
- 2 *teaspoons cornstarch dissolved in 1 tablespoon water*
- ½ *teaspoon sesame oil*

Getting Ready

① Scrub mussels; remove beards and discard any with open shells that don't close when tapped. Place mussels in a heatproof dish. Prepare a wok for steaming (see page 25). Cover and steam mussels over high heat until shells open, 3 to 4 minutes. Let cool. Strain and reserve ½ cup of mussel steaming liquid; discard sandy residue.

② Combine cornstarch and salt in a bowl. Add oysters and stir to coat. Let stand for 10 minutes. Parboil oysters in a pot of boiling water for 1 minute; drain.

③ Combine sauce ingredients in a bowl.

Cooking

① Place a wok over high heat until hot. Add cooking oil, swirling to coat sides. Add chili, garlic, ginger, and green onion; cook, stirring, until fragrant, about 10 seconds. Add sauce, steamed mussels, reserved mussel steaming liquid, and oysters; bring to a boil. Add cornstarch solution and cook, stirring, until sauce boils and thickens. Stir in sesame oil.

② Place on a serving plate. If you wish to make dish sizzle, serve in a preheated cast-iron serving plate.

Makes 4 servings.

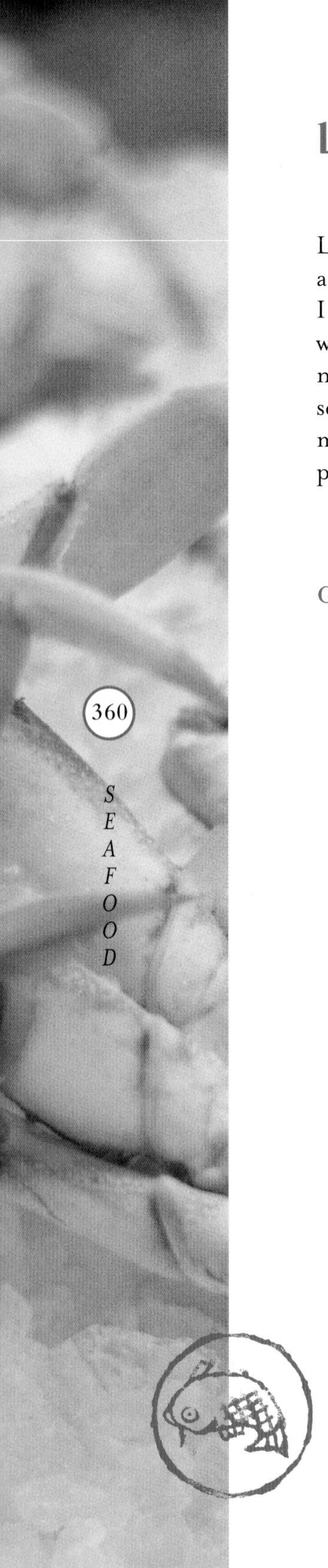

Lobster with Ginger-Scallion Oil

Lobster is a special dish, and it calls for a steam bath (for the lobster, not me). I add green onion and garlic to the water so my lobster will steam up with a nice flavor. When pouring the ginger-scallion oil over the exposed lobster meat, take time to enjoy the sizzle—it's part of the dish.

2 *lobster tails (each about 8 oz.)*

Ginger-Scallion Oil

¼ *cup cooking oil*

3 *green onions, cut into 1½-inch slivers*

2 *tablespoons slivered ginger*

1 *teaspoon minced garlic*

1 *fresh jalapeño chili, seeded and thinly sliced*

2 *teaspoons sesame oil*

¼ *teaspoon salt*

2 *tablespoons oyster-flavored sauce*

4 *slices ginger, each the size of a quarter, lightly crushed*

3 *green onions, cut in half and lightly crushed*

6 *sprigs cilantro*

Getting Ready

① Prepare each lobster tail: With scissors, cut along edges of undershell, clipping off fins along outer edges as you cut. Peel back and discard soft undershell. Bend tail backward, cracking some of the joints in overshell (this reduces curling when cooking) Place lobster, meat side up, in a heatproof dish.

② Assemble ginger-scallion oil ingredients: Place cooking oil in a small pan. In a bowl, combine green onions, ginger, garlic, chili, sesame oil, and salt. Have oyster-flavored sauce near stove.

Cooking

① Prepare a wok for steaming (see page 25). Drop ginger, green onions, and cilantro sprigs into steaming water. Place lobster in steamer; cover and steam over high heat until meat turns opaque, 6 to 7 minutes.

② Complete ginger-scallion oil: Heat oil in pan until hot. Add green onion mixture and stir once. Remove from heat and stir in oyster-flavored sauce (oil will sizzle).

③ Place lobster on a serving plate. Immediately drizzle ginger-scallion oil over each serving.

Makes 2 servings.

Drunken Crab with Ginger-Wine Sauce

Here's my interpretation of a famous dish from Shaoxing, China's rice wine capital. If the idea of cooking a live crab doesn't appeal to you, you can make this dish with cooked crab in the shell, omitting the first step of the recipe.

4 *live blue shell crabs or 1 live Dungeness crab*

Sauce

½ *cup chicken broth*

⅓ *cup Shaoxing wine*

2 *tablespoons soy sauce*

2 *tablespoons oyster-flavored sauce*

1 *teaspoon chili garlic sauce*

Flour

3 *tablespoons cooking oil*

8 *slices ginger, each the size of a quarter, lightly crushed*

6 *green onions, thinly sliced*

¼ *cup fresh basil leaves*

1 *teaspoon cornstarch dissolved in 2 teaspoons water (optional)*

Getting Ready

① In a pot of boiling water, parboil crab for 2 minutes. Drain, rinse with cold water, and drain again. Pull off the top shell. Remove and discard the gills and spongy parts under the shell. Twist off the claws and legs; crack them with a cleaver or mallet. Cut blue shell crab bodies in half; if using Dungeness crab, cut body into 4 pieces.

② Combine sauce ingredients in a bowl.

③ Dust crab pieces with flour.

Cooking

① Place a wok over high heat until hot. Add oil, swirling to coat sides. Add crab and stir-fry for 1 minute. Add ginger and green onions; cook for 2 minutes. Add sauce and basil; bring to a boil. Reduce heat, cover, and simmer, stirring once or twice, until crab is cooked, 8 to 10 minutes.

② Uncover and cook 1 to 2 minutes to reduce sauce; or add cornstarch solution and cook, stirring, until sauce boils and thickens.

Makes 4 servings.

Drunken Dishes

At one of Shaoxing's most famous wine bars, we sat in the garden drinking bowls of Shaoxing (Shao Hsing) wine and feasting on an amazing variety of "drunken" dishes, from chicken and duck to fish and even octopus. My favorite is the legendary Drunken Freshwater Crab, kept alive in wine for three days before it's cooked. At least you know the crab died happy! You have to watch your step eating in Shaoxing, or you may experience another local specialty: Drunken Guests!

Steamed Crab over Rice

While this marinated whole crab steams over a bed of seasoned rice, the rice and crab engage in a wonderful exchange of flavors. Glutinous rice is traditional in this recipe, but long-grain rice will also work. If you like, you can substitute walnuts for the peanuts.

- 2 *tablespoons dried shrimp*
- 2 *dried black mushrooms*
- 3 *water chestnuts*
- 3 *tablespoons raw peanuts*
- 2 *tablespoons cooking oil*
- 1 *teaspoon salt*
- 4 *cups cooked rice*
- 1 *live Dungeness crab*

Marinade

- 2 *tablespoons oyster-flavored sauce*
- 1 *tablespoon Chinese rice wine or dry sherry*
- 1 *tablespoon cornstarch*
- 1 *teaspoon minced ginger*
- ½ *teaspoon salt*

- 1 *green onion, thinly sliced*

Getting Ready

① In separate bowls, soak dried shrimp and mushrooms in warm water to cover until softened, about 20 minutes. Drain shrimp and coarsely chop. Reserve about ¼ cup of mushroom-soaking liquid. Discard mushroom stems; dice caps. Dice water chestnuts. Remove skins from peanuts.

Cooking

① Place a wok over high heat until hot. Add oil, swirling to coat sides. Add dried shrimp, mushrooms, water chestnuts, and peanuts; stir-fry for 1 minute. Add reserved mushroom-soaking liquid and salt; stir-fry for 1 minute. Turn off heat; add rice and mix thoroughly.

② In a pot of boiling water, parboil crab for 2 minutes. Drain, rinse with cold water, and drain again. Pull off the top shell in one piece and reserve. Remove and discard the gills and spongy parts under the shell. Twist off the claws and legs; crack them with a cleaver or mallet. Cut the body into 6 pieces.

③ Combine marinade ingredients in a large bowl; add crab and stir to coat. Marinate in the refrigerator for 30 minutes.

④ Spread rice mixture in a shallow heatproof dish. Reassemble crab in its original shape over rice; place top shell over body pieces. Sprinkle green onion around crab. Prepare a wok for steaming (see page 25). Cover and steam over high heat for 15 minutes. Serve hot.

Makes 4 to 6 servings.

Chili Crab

When I ask my Singaporean friends to name their national dish, those who don't say "fish head curry" say "chili crab." When you taste this crab in chili sauce, you'll understand why.

Sauce

- ¾ *cup chicken broth*
- ½ *cup ketchup*
- 2 *tablespoons soy sauce*
- 1 *tablespoon chili garlic sauce*
- 1 *tablespoon rice vinegar*
- 1 *tablespoon sugar*

- 1 *live Dungeness crab*
- 2 *tablespoons cooking oil*
- 2 *tablespoons minced garlic*
- 1 *tablespoon minced ginger*
- 1 *fresh red jalapeño chili, seeded and minced*
- 1 *egg, lightly beaten*
- *Sliced green onion*

Getting Ready

① Mix sauce ingredients in a small bowl and set aside.

② In a pot of boiling water, parboil crab for 2 minutes. Drain, rinse with cold water, and drain again. Pull off the top shell in one piece and reserve for garnish. Remove and discard the gills and spongy parts under the shell. Twist off the claws and legs; crack them with a cleaver or mallet. Cut the body into 4 pieces.

Cooking

① Place a wok over high heat until hot. Add oil, swirling to coat sides. Add garlic, ginger, and chili; cook, stirring, for 1 minute. Add crab and stir-fry for 2 minutes.

② Add sauce and reduce heat to low; cover and simmer, stirring once or twice, until crab is cooked, 6 to 7 minutes.

③ Stir in egg and cook just until it begins to set, about 1 minute.

④ Arrange crab and top shell on a serving plate. Pour sauce over all and garnish with green onion.

Makes 4 servings.

Grab a Crab

There's no substitute for the sweet, delicate flavor of fresh, live crab. In the western U.S., fall and winter are Dungeness crab season. Summer and fall are peak for the East Coast's blue crab. When you buy live crabs, refrigerate quickly, and cook and eat them within 24 hours. If you're not comfortable with "crab-icide," have your fish seller kill and clean the crabs for you just before use and skip the boiling step. For a dramatic touch, retain the whole top shell.

CHAPTER 10

Desserts and Drinks

Tofu Custard with Tropical Fruits

Few desserts are this easy, this healthy, and this beautiful. The "custard" is simply cubes of chilled soft tofu. But when topped with a lemon syrup and a colorful array of berries and tropical fruits, the tofu tastes creamy, silky, and refreshingly light. You can use any fresh or canned fruit, from orange, grapefruit, and mandarin orange sections to pineapple, papaya, and mango chunks.

- 1½ *cups water*
- ⅔ *cup crushed rock sugar or honey*
- 2 *tablespoons lemon juice*
- ½ *cup jackfruit chunks*
- ½ *cup longans*
- ½ *cup loquats*
- ½ *cup raspberries or blueberries*
- ½ *cup diced cantaloupe*
- 2 *packages (16 oz. each) soft tofu, drained*

Cooking

① Combine water, sugar, and lemon juice in a nonreactive pan. Cook over low heat, stirring occasionally, until sugar dissolves, 6 to 8 minutes. Remove from heat and add all the fruit. Let cool; cover and refrigerate until chilled.

② Cut tofu into ½-inch cubes and place in a serving bowl. Spoon fruit and syrup over tofu. Serve chilled.

Makes 8 servings.

The Topic Is Tropical

The longan, also known as "dragon's eye," looks like a lychee, small and round with a smooth brown shell. In the West, I've seen fresh ones in Asian markets during the summer, and they're sold in cans year-round. The loquat originated in China, and looks and tastes like a cross between an apricot and a plum. Canned loquats are easier to find than fresh ones. The gigantic jackfruit is a sweet tropical fruit that reaches weights of up to 100 pounds! In the U.S. jackfruit is sold only in cans.

Pears Poached In Plum Wine

During warmer months, poached pears make a nice light dessert. If you can find Asian pears—also called "apple pears" because they look like a cross between a pear and an apple—give them a try. They have a pleasantly sweet flavor and a crunchy texture that stand up well to poaching. When the conversation lags, you can impress your guests with this piece of pear trivia: Asian pears are the oldest known cultivated pears in the world!

- 3 *cups water*
- ⅔ *cup sugar*
- ¼ *cup plum wine*
- 3 *tablespoons lemon juice*
- 4 *slices ginger, each the size of a quarter, lightly crushed*
- 4 *Asian pears or medium-firm Bartlett or Bosc pears*
- 2 *tablespoons plum sauce*
- *Chopped crystallized ginger*

Cooking

① In a large pan, combine water, sugar, wine, lemon juice, and ginger. Bring to a boil over medium heat.

② Peel pears with a vegetable peeler, keeping stems intact. If you wish, remove cores from bottom of pears with a melon baller.

③ As you peel each pear, place it in the liquid. Simmer, uncovered, until pears are barely tender, 20 to 30 minutes, depending on ripeness of fruit. Turn pears occasionally during cooking.

④ Lift out pears with a slotted spoon and place in a wide bowl. Simmer syrup until it is reduced to 1 cup. Add plum sauce to syrup; cook until heated through. Pour syrup over pears. Let stand until cool.

⑤ Serve at room temperature, or cover and refrigerate to serve cold. Sprinkle crystallized ginger over each serving.

Makes 4 servings.

Sweet Talk

If you ever have the good fortune to be invited to a banquet in China and you're served a sweet dessert, don't get up and leave—the meal's not over! The northern and western Chinese sometimes serve sweets throughout the meal in the form of soups and fruit concoctions, and they don't build in a grand finale dessert as Western cooks do. A meal is likely to end with slices of fresh fruit and a bowl of rice to aid digestion. Fortune cookies, by the way, are a Chinese restaurant invention, originally from San Francisco, not China.

Fresh Ginger Ice Cream

Ginger ice cream is one of those things that I wish I had discovered much, much earlier in life. As a child, I would have gone nuts over this yummy treat. But perhaps the long delay explains my current enthusiasm: I have plenty of catching up to do.

- 1/3 *cup water*
- 1/4 *cup sugar*
- 1/4 *cup minced peeled ginger*
- 1 *cup milk*

Custard

- 4 *egg yolks*
- 1/3 *cup sugar*
- 1 *cup hot milk*

- 1 *cup whipping cream*
- 2 *tablespoons minced crystallized ginger*

Cooking

① Combine water and sugar in a small pan; cook over medium heat until sugar is dissolved. Add ginger; simmer, covered, for 5 minutes. Strain syrup and discard ginger. Whisk milk into syrup. Chill until ready to use.

② Make custard: In a heavy 2-quart pan, beat egg yolks with a wire whisk. Whisk in sugar. Gradually stir in hot milk. Cook over medium-low heat, stirring, until custard has thickened enough to lightly coat a metal spoon in a smooth layer. (Don't boil custard or it will curdle.) At once, set pan into a bowl of ice water; stir often until custard is cool. Lift pan from water, cover, and chill until cold.

③ In a large bowl, whip cream until it holds soft peaks; fold in chilled custard and syrup, and crystallized ginger. Freeze according to manufacturer's directions in an electric or manual ice cream maker. Serve, or freeze in an airtight container.

Makes 1 1/2 quarts, 6 to 8 servings.

Mango Pudding

In southern China, mangoes turn up in sweet soups and puddings like this one made with creamy coconut milk. This molded pudding is easy to prepare ahead of time. For an elegant dinner party, I make it in individual ramekins, unmold them onto small plates, and garnish with fresh tropical fruit.

- 2 *mangoes, each about 12 ounces*
- 1¼ *cups cold water*
- 2 *envelopes unflavored gelatin*
- ⅔ *cup sugar*
- ½ *cup milk*
- ½ *cup unsweetened coconut milk*
- *Sliced starfruit*

Cooking

① Peel mangoes and cut flesh from pits. Cut enough flesh into ¼-inch cubes to make ½ cup. Chop remaining flesh to make about 1½ cups. Place chopped fruit in a blender with 1 cup cold water; purée until smooth.

② Sprinkle gelatin over the remaining ¼ cup cold water in a bowl; let soften for several minutes.

③ Combine sugar and milk in a 2-quart pan. Cook, stirring, over medium-low heat, until sugar dissolves; remove from heat. Add softened gelatin; stir until dissolved.

④ Add coconut milk (shake can before opening to mix the heavy coconut cream with the thin coconut milk) and mango purée; whisk until blended. Fold in diced mango. Pour into a 1-quart mold, or divide among 5 individual 1-cup ramekins or custard cups. Cover and refrigerate until firm, 3 to 4 hours, or overnight.

⑤ To serve, dip base of mold in a bowl of warm water to loosen pudding. Place a serving plate over mold, then invert to unmold. Arrange sliced starfruit around pudding.

Makes 5 servings.

Let Them Eat Fruit

So many people are thrown into a tailspin when they're planning dinner for friends and it comes time to think about dessert. Why not follow the lead of home cooks all over Southeast Asia and make dessert a simple array of tropical fruit? Cut up chunks of mango, papaya, pineapple, fresh coconut, banana, and—if you're feeling wild—some passion fruit. Sprinkle a little lime juice and shredded coconut over everything and garnish with a few pineapple leaves. It's a light, refreshing way to finish off a meal, and your friends will think you're exotic. What could be sweeter than that?

Mandarin Orange Tofu Mousse

Whipped cream, custard, and gelatin are the building blocks of a mousse, but I prefer a nondairy version made with silken tofu. It's light and luscious. For a party presentation, chill the mousse in wineglasses and garnish each serving with a sprig of mint.

- 1 *envelope unflavored gelatin*
- ¼ *cup cold water*
- ¾ *cup sugar*
- ½ *cup boiling water*
- 1 *can (6 oz.) frozen orange juice concentrate*
- ½ *of a 16-ounce package soft tofu, drained*
- 1½ *cups (4 oz.) frozen whipped topping, thawed*
- 1 *can (11 oz.) mandarin oranges, drained*
- *Mint sprigs*

Cooking

① In a small bowl, sprinkle gelatin over cold water; let stand 1 minute to soften.

② In a blender, process sugar, boiling water, and softened gelatin until gelatin is dissolved. Add juice concentrate and tofu; process until smooth.

③ Pour into a large bowl. Refrigerate until mixture mounds slightly when dropped from a spoon. Fold in whipped topping. Pour into 6 dessert dishes; chill until firm, 3 to 4 hours.

④ Before serving, top with oranges and a mint sprig.

Makes 6 servings.

Ginger Date Wontons

Wontons aren't just for appetizers and soups. Versatile wonton wrappers have a neutral flavor that goes perfectly with sweet ingredients, too. These crispy treats, with a chewy filling of dates, nuts, and candied ginger, make a delicious dessert. I sometimes serve them warm with a scoop of vanilla ice cream, but they're equally tasty at room temperature.

Filling

- ⅓ *cup chopped walnuts*
- 6 *Medjool dates, pitted and coarsely chopped*
- 3 *tablespoons chopped crystallized ginger*
- 1 *tablespoon grated lemon peel*
- 2 *teaspoons butter, softened*

- 24 *wonton wrappers*
- *Cooking oil for deep-frying*

Getting Ready

① Combine filling ingredients in a bowl; mix well.

② Make each wonton: Place 1 teaspoon filling in center of a wonton wrapper; keep remaining wrappers covered to prevent drying. Brush edges of wrapper with water and fold wrapper in half to form a triangle. Pinch edges to seal. Pull two opposite corners together, moisten one corner with water, and overlap with the other corner; press to seal. To prevent drying, cover filled wontons with a dry towel.

Cooking

① In a wok or 2-quart saucepan, heat oil for deep-frying to 360°F. Deep-fry wontons, a few at a time, turning occasionally, until golden brown, 2 to 3 minutes. Remove with a slotted spoon; drain on paper towels. Serve hot or cold.

Makes 24 wontons.

Up-To-Date

In China, dates date back centuries. The jujube, or Chinese red date, is small and wrinkled, with a sweet-tart flavor. In the U.S., it's sold only in dried form. The jujube bears no relation to the palm date—the kind familiar to Western cooks—or to the chewy jujube candy! Palm dates came to China from Persia more than a thousand years ago. If you're looking for a great palm date, I recommend the large, moist, and sweet Medjool, grown in California.

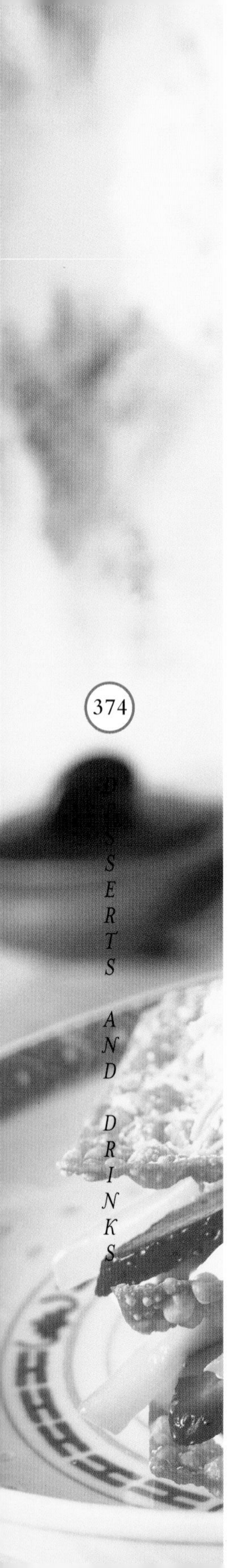

Mandarin Glazed Apples

Why bring your favorite teacher a plain apple when you can offer this elegant dessert? It's most often found in restaurants, but with an extra pair of hands to help deep-fry and caramelize the apples, your kitchen can become a five-star establishment.

1 *tablespoon sesame seeds*

Syrup

¾ *cup sugar*

⅓ *cup water*

1 *teaspoon cooking oil*

Batter

⅔ *cup flour*

¼ *cup cornstarch*

½ *teaspoon baking powder*

¾ *cup water*

3 *teaspoons sesame oil*

2 *tart-sweet crisp apples*

Cooking oil for deep-frying

Getting Ready

① Place sesame seeds in a small frying pan over medium heat; cook, shaking pan frequently, until lightly browned, 3 to 4 minutes. Immediately remove from pan to cool.

② Place syrup ingredients in a heavy pan; set aside.

③ Prepare batter: Sift flour, cornstarch, and baking powder into a medium bowl. Gradually pour in water, whisking until smooth. Add 1½ teaspoons sesame oil; mix well. Rub remaining 1½ teaspoons sesame oil onto a serving platter.

④ Peel and core apples; cut each apple into 8 wedges. Place apples in batter and turn to coat evenly.

Cooking

① In a wok, heat oil for deep-frying to 365°F. Using chopsticks or a spoon, lift 1 piece of apple at a time from batter, let excess batter drip off, then lower fruit into hot oil. Deep-fry several pieces at a time, turning frequently, until coating is golden brown, about 3 minutes. Remove with a slotted spoon; drain on paper towels.

② Fill a large bowl with ice cubes and enough water to cover the ice.

③ Stir syrup to blend. Cook over medium heat, stirring constantly, until mixture caramelizes and turns a pale straw color, about 9 minutes. Immediately remove from heat. (Syrup will continue to cook after you remove it from heat, and color will turn golden in a few seconds.)

④ Drop fruit into syrup and swirl to coat evenly. Sprinkle with sesame seeds. Using two spoons, remove each piece of fruit and dip into ice water so coating hardens, then place on oiled serving plate. Serve immediately.

Makes 6 servings.

Lemon Tofu Custard

What makes this steamed custard so creamy and silky, yet so light? Surprise! It's soft tofu, puréed in the food processor. The versatile soybean strikes again! I developed this recipe for a program on cooking with kids, and my pint-sized guest chefs gave it high marks.

- 2 *slices white sandwich bread*
- 1 *package (16 oz.) soft tofu, drained*
- ½ *cup milk*
- 3 *eggs*
- ⅔ *cup sugar*
- 2 *teaspoons grated lemon peel*

Getting Ready

① Trim bread crusts. Cut bread into ½-inch cubes to make 1 cup.

② Mash tofu. Place in a clean towel and squeeze to remove excess liquid. In a food processor, whirl tofu until smooth. Add bread, milk, eggs, and sugar; process until smooth.

③ Stir in lemon peel.

④ Pour tofu mixture into 5 individual 1-cup ramekins or custard cups.

Cooking

① Prepare a wok for steaming (see page 25). Place ramekins in steamer; set a piece of waxed paper loosely over ramekins. Cover and steam over medium heat until a knife inserted in center comes out clean, about 15 minutes.

② Remove ramekins from steamer and let cool for 1 hour.

Makes 5 servings.

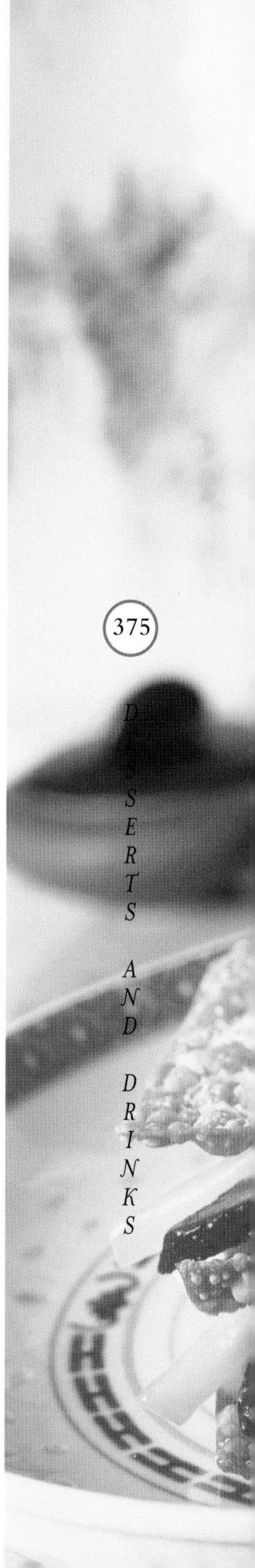

All the Tea, Beer, and Wine in China

A Look at Chinese Beverages

If you've ever been to a Chinese restaurant, you've had the chance to enjoy tea with a meal. But did you know that in most of China, tea is not usually a mealtime beverage? You're more likely to be served one or more soups throughout the meal.

Tea is drunk between meals as a refreshment, a quick pick-me-up, or a digestive. It's a Chinese tradition that dates back close to 2,000 years and one that still holds sway in our house. I love to drink tea, by itself, in a quiet moment of communion and meditation, preferably while staring out my kitchen window at the vegetable garden. Just the act of making a pot of tea and sitting down to drink it relaxes and reenergizes me.

Chinese teas fall into four general categories: green, black, oolong, and flavored. Categories are determined not by the plant variety but by how the tea leaves are treated after picking.

Green or unfermented tea is the most common throughout China. It is sun-dried and roasted right after picking, and its flavor is clean and delicate. Look for Dragon Well (*Lung Ching*), Gunpowder, or *Lu An*.

Black or fermented tea is allowed to ferment in the hot, humid air before roasting, giving it a deep, full-bodied flavor. The most famous black teas are Keemun from northern China (the precursor to English Breakfast tea) and Yunnan from southern China.

Oolong teas, my favorite, are allowed to ferment partially before roasting, creating a nice combination of black and green tea flavors. This is the tea served most often in Chinese restaurants in Europe and North America.

Finally, flavored teas are made from green or oolong teas scented with aromatic ingredients, like jasmine or chrysanthemum. Lapsang Souchong is cured with smoldering logs to give it its distinctive smoky flavor.

Here are eight secrets for brewing tea:

1. Start with a good pot—one made of porcelain, earthenware, glass, or cast iron. Avoid aluminum or other metals that can give tea an off flavor.

2. Use filtered water (not distilled water, which is flat and flavorless).

3. Bring the water to a full boil for black or oolong tea. For green tea, heat it to just below boiling.

4. Rinse the pot with boiling water to warm it, then pour the water out.

5. Add 1 teaspoon of tea leaves to the pot for every cup of water.

6. Bring the pot to the kettle (to keep the water from cooling) and pour the boiling water over the leaves (never add the leaves to the water).

7. Let the tea steep for 3 to 5 minutes (1 to 2 minutes for a lighter flavor), then remove the leaves or strain the tea.

8. You can reuse these leaves for a second pot by simply adding more boiling water and steeping 2 to 3 minutes before serving. Try not to let the tea leaves steep too long; if you don't drink all the tea, pour it out and refrigerate the pot until you're ready to reuse the leaves. After three or four refills of boiling water, you might want to start again with new leaves.

Of course, tea isn't the only thing that goes with Chinese food. *Chiew* is the Chinese term for alcoholic beverages, which range from mao tai, a strong, distilled, vodkalike liquor (up to 120 proof) to Shaoxing rice wine (about 30 proof), which can be served warm or chilled like Japanese sake and also used extensively in cooking.

In China, *chiew* is regarded less as a complement to food and more as a "recreational" beverage and palate cleanser to be consumed with friends as toasts between courses.

But what about pairing Western grape wines with Chinese foods? The simple answer is Yes! Although grapes are not native to China, and drinking grape wines, especially during meals, is generally unheard of there, I find that the complexity and depth of these wines make them an ideal counterpoint to the flavors of many Chinese dishes.

With lighter, more delicate dishes (much of Cantonese food, for example) I might serve a fruity white wine, like a Riesling, Colombard, or Chenin Blanc. A sweet, spicy Gewürztraminer makes a tasty counterpoint to the flavors of ginger and garlic as well as curry and some pickled foods. The robust and spicy flavors of Sichuan and Hunanese food go well with medium-bodied red wines, such as Burgundy or Chianti. And lighter reds—Beaujolais and some Zinfandels—can be a good choice with the rich and savory flavors of many northern-style dishes. The important thing is to pair the wine with the flavor of the dish rather than with the protein.

If you're eating courses in sequence—as is the case in many Chinese dinners, especially banquets—it's best to start with lighter wines and build up to heavier ones. But if you're eating a lot of dishes all at once, you may find it hard to find a single wine that works well with all of them. In that case, I suggest either a dry Champagne or beer.

A relative newcomer to the Chinese beverage scene, beer first showed up in China around the turn of the century. It's been gaining popularity ever since. A glass of ice cold beer can balance the heat of chilies and garlic, and beer (especially a light, crisp Pilsner) almost magically enhances the flavor of just about any Chinese dish.

So many beverage options! So many flavors to pair them with! Don't be discouraged. In the end, there are really no hard-and-fast rules. When in doubt, offer a few options and let your guests choose for themselves. And when all else fails, evoke this magic toast: "*ho yum, ho sick*", "good eating and good drinking." It always seems to put people in a good mood.

Chinese Napoleons

The classic French napoleon is made with rectangles of puff pastry put together with a filling of whipped cream or custard. As a time-saver, I deep-fry wonton wrappers and stack them with layers of fruit and whipped cream. The dessert looks beautiful, and it's fun to eat. Cut a bite: the wrapper goes crunch, the filling goes squish.

Cooking oil for deep-frying

12 *wonton, potsticker, or gyoza wrappers*

¼ *cup sweetened shredded coconut*

Sauce

⅓ *cup packed brown sugar*

2 *tablespoons honey*

2 *tablespoons lemon juice*

¼ *cup orange-flavored liqueur*

1 *cup strawberries, hulled and sliced*

1 *mango, peeled and diced*

1 *can (11 oz.) mandarin oranges, drained*

1 *cup whipping cream*

¼ *cup powdered sugar*

½ *teaspoon coconut extract*

Cooking

① In a wok or 2-quart saucepan, heat oil for deep-frying to 350°F. Deep-fry wonton wrappers, a few at a time, until lightly browned, 15 to 20 seconds on each side. Remove with a slotted spoon; drain on paper towels. Let cool, then place in a tightly covered container until ready to use (up to 4 days).

② Spread coconut in a pie pan; toast in a 350°F oven, stirring frequently, until lightly browned, 4 to 5 minutes.

③ Combine sauce ingredients in a small pan; cook over medium heat, stirring frequently, until sugar dissolves and sauce becomes syrupy, 3 to 4 minutes. Let cool.

Assembly

① In a bowl, combine strawberries, mango, mandarin oranges, and cooled sauce. In another bowl, whip cream with 1 tablespoon powdered sugar and coconut extract until it holds soft peaks.

② Place remaining powdered sugar in a sieve; shake a light dusting over wonton wrappers.

③ For each serving, place a wrapper on a dessert plate, top with a spoonful of cream and a spoonful of fruit. Repeat for second and third layers. Sprinkle with coconut.

Makes 4 servings.

Mangoes and Sticky Rice

This Southeast Asian recipe features sweet mango and sticky, or glutinous, rice. With toasted coconut, coconut milk, and cashews, this is not exactly your Aunt Sadie's rice pudding.

- 2 *cups glutinous rice*
- 3 *tablespoons sweetened shredded coconut*
- 1 *can (13½ oz.) unsweetened coconut milk*
- ½ *cup packed brown sugar*
- ¼ *teaspoon salt*
- 2 *mangoes*
- 2 *tablespoons chopped cashews or peanuts*

Getting Ready

① Soak rice in warm water to cover for 1 hour.

② Spread coconut in a pie pan; toast in a 350°F oven, stirring frequently, until lightly browned, 4 to 5 minutes.

Cooking

① Drain rice. Place in a medium pan with the 2¼ cups water. Bring to a boil; cover, reduce heat, and simmer until small craterlike holes appear on the surface and rice is tender, 20 to 25 minutes.

② While rice is cooking, simmer coconut milk in a pan over low heat, stirring constantly, until it is reduced to about ¾ cup. Add brown sugar and salt; simmer, stirring, until sugar is dissolved.

③ Scrape warm rice into a wide, shallow bowl. Pour coconut milk mixture over rice and stir gently to mix. Let stand until coconut milk is absorbed, about 30 minutes.

④ Just before serving, peel and slice mangoes. Divide rice among 6 dessert plates and arrange 2 or 3 slices of mango alongside each serving. Sprinkle with coconut and nuts.

Makes 6 servings.

Managing a Mango

Preparing a mango can be tricky. Try this "chef's secret." Stand an unpeeled mango (not too ripe) on its end, with a narrow side facing you. Using a sharp knife, cut straight downward about ½ inch from the center of the mango so you clear the pit. Turn the mango around and make the same cut on the other side. Lay the cut slices face up and, with the tip of the knife, make diagonal cuts about ½ inch apart in a crosshatch pattern; be careful not to cut through the peel. Turn the slice inside out and your crosshatch pattern will open up into a beautiful "flower." You can use this flower as a garnish, or you can trim away the peel and the flesh will fall way into perfect chunks. Repeat this with the other slice, then use your knife to cut away the flesh that's left around the pit.

Banana Rolls

Jackfruits grow in abundance in the fertile soil of Southeast Asia. I wanted to combine the unique texture and taste of this noble fruit with the familiar banana. The result: goodness of fruit fiber and a heavenly treat for the sweet tooth. How much closer to perfection can one get?

4	*medium firm, ripe bananas*
½	*cup packed brown sugar*
1	*tablespoon sesame seeds*
1	*teaspoon ground cinnamon*
½	*cup canned jackfruit*
8	*lumpia wrappers or egg roll wrappers*
	Cooking oil for deep-frying

Getting Ready

① Peel bananas; halve each lengthwise and crosswise. With a teaspoon, scoop out a channel on the cut side of each banana piece.

② In a small bowl, combine brown sugar, sesame seeds, and cinnamon. Drain jackfruit and cut into 8 strips to fit along channels in banana pieces.

③ Make each roll: Spoon 1 tablespoon brown sugar mixture in channel of 1 banana piece, top with a thin strip of jackfruit, then cover with a second piece of banana placed cut side down.

④ Place a wrapper on work surface with one corner facing you. Place filled banana across wrapper, slightly above the corner. Fold corner over banana, then roll over once. Fold in left and right sides. Brush edges with water and roll up completely to enclose filling.

Cooking

① In a wok or 2-quart saucepan, heat oil for deep-frying to 350°F. Deep-fry banana rolls a few at a time, turning occasionally, until golden brown, about 3 minutes. Remove with a slotted spoon; drain on paper towels.

② Let cool for 10 minutes before serving.

Makes 8 rolls.

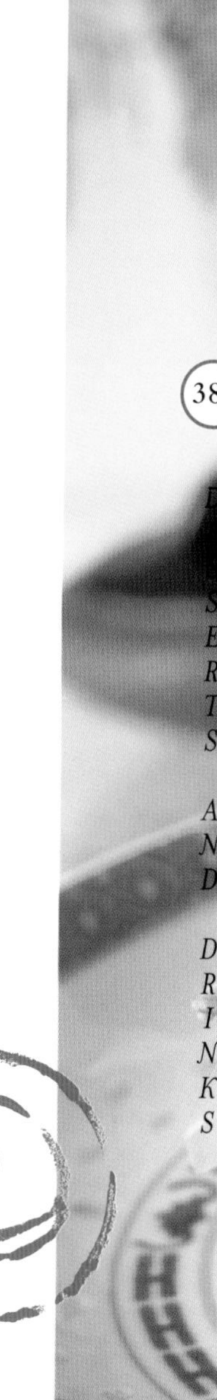

Fortune Cookies

There's a Chinese proverb: A big fortune comes by the grace of the heavens and a small one by the grace of one's hard work and savings. Based on that, these heavenly giant cookies must truly be a godsend.

- 4 *strips of paper, each 1 by 3 inches*
- ½ *cup flour*
- 1 *tablespoon cornstarch*
- ¼ *cup sugar*
- ¼ *teaspoon salt*
- ¼ *cup cooking oil*
- ¼ *cup egg whites*
- 1½ *teaspoons water*
- 1 *teaspoon vanilla extract*

Getting Ready

① Write individual fortunes on strips of paper.

② Sift flour, cornstarch, sugar, and salt into a medium bowl. Add oil, egg whites, water, and vanilla extract; stir until smooth.

Cooking

① Preheat oven to 300°F. Bake 1 cookie at a time. Drop ¼ cup batter onto an oiled baking sheet; spread evenly to make an 8-inch circle. Bake until cookie turns light golden brown, 12 to 14 minutes. (Don't allow edges to become overly brown or cookie will crack when folded.)

② Using pot holders to protect your hands, immediately remove hot, pliable cookie from baking sheet and place a fortune in center. Fold cookie in half to form a half-moon, then grasp ends of cookie and gently pull together to crease. Hold folded cookie for a minute to maintain its shape as it cools and becomes crisp. Repeat with remaining batter.

Makes 4 cookies.

Tea for Two

To the Chinese, tea is a symbol of friendship and fidelity, and there's a courtship ritual based on tea that dates back 1,500 years. First, a suitor would send a gift of tea to the family of his intended. If he was invited to her house, and met with the family's approval, he would be served three teas—one bitter, one sweet and gingery, and the third mellow and lingering. If the engagement were later broken, it was said in polite conversation that "the tea has been spilled."

Pineapple Ginger Soda

Everybody knows that ginger is a popular spice in many Chinese dishes, but do you know that it is also a great thirst quencher? Try this pineapple ginger drink over ice and see if it reminds you a bit of old-time ginger beer.

- ½ *fresh pineapple*
- 1 *piece ginger (3 oz.), about 1½ inches across and 3½ to 4 inches long*
- 1 *cup water*
- 1½ *cups sugar*
- 2 *tablespoons lime juice*
- 1½ *cups lemon-lime soda*
- *Ice cubes*

Getting Ready

① Peel and core pineapple; dice flesh to make 2 cups fruit. Peel and thinly slice ginger.

Cooking

① Combine ginger, water, and sugar in a 2-quart pan; cook over medium heat until syrup simmers and sugar is dissolved. Simmer for 4 minutes longer. Let syrup cool.

② In a blender, process syrup until ginger is finely chopped. Strain syrup and discard ginger. Return syrup to blender; add pineapple and lime juice. Process until pineapple is puréed.

③ Pour into a large pitcher and chill until ready to serve.

④ Just before serving, stir in lemon-lime soda. Serve over ice.

Makes 6 servings.

Limeade

Here's a refreshing change from iced tea on a hot day. Or serve this lime-ginger drink to temper the spiciness of Sichuan- or Hunan-style dishes. In a nonreactive pan, heat 6 cups **water** to boiling. Off heat, add 6 **English Breakfast tea bags**, and let steep for 10 minutes. Remove tea bags. Add ½ cup **honey** and ¼ cup **sugar**; stir to dissolve sugar. Stir in the juice of 9 **limes**. Let mixture cool, then refrigerate until ready to use. To serve, pour into glass pitcher filled with **ice cubes**, or fill glasses with equal parts of limeade and **ginger ale**. Garnish with a slice of **lime** and a sprig of **mint**. Makes 10 to 12 servings.

Egg Custard Tarts

Ask any 7-year-old in Hong Kong what his or her favorite treat is, and you will get an earful: Egg Custard Tarts! These sweet tarts are great for a dim sum brunch, and they are perfect for a proper afternoon tea. And in the very unlikely event that you have any left over, they make a great after-dinner dessert, too.

Pastry Dough

- 1¾ *cups flour*
- ½ *up solid vegetable shortening, chilled*
- ¼ *cup butter, chilled*
- 1 *egg*
- 2 *tablespoons ice water*
- 1 *teaspoon vanilla extract*

Filling

- ⅔ *cup water*
- ⅔ *cup sugar*
- 4 *eggs*
- ⅓ *cup evaporated milk*
- ½ *teaspoon vanilla extract*

Getting Ready

① Prepare dough: Place flour in a food processor. Cut shortening and butter into ½-inch chunks and distribute over flour. Process with on-off bursts until fat particles are the size of peas. Add egg, ice water, and vanilla. Process until mixture just begins to form a ball. (Do not process completely to the ball stage, and don't worry if dough has shortening streaks in it.) Remove dough, shape into a patty 1 inch thick, and cover with plastic wrap. Chill for at least 1 hour or up to 2 days.

Cooking

① Prepare filling: In a small pan, heat water and sugar until sugar dissolves; let cool. In a bowl, beat eggs slightly. Whisk in sugar-water syrup, evaporated milk, and vanilla extract, blending until smooth.

② Preheat oven to 300°F. On a lightly floured board, roll out pastry to about ¼ inch thick. Cut into fourteen 4-inch circles (reroll scraps and cut again if necessary). Fit circles into 2½-inch tart pans. Lightly press dough into bottoms and sides of pans; trim edges.

③ Pour filling into pastry-lined pans to within ¼ inch of top. Place filled pans on a baking sheet; bake in preheated oven until a knife inserted in center comes out clean, about 35 minutes. Place pans on rack; let cool for 10 minutes. Remove tarts from pans. Serve warm or at room temperature.

Makes 14 tarts.

Walnut Cookies

These are the flaky short-dough cookies you find in Chinese bakeries all over the world. My version replaces the traditional lard with a combination of butter and shortening, producing a crisper, more tender cookie.

- 1¾ *cups flour*
- ¾ *teaspoon baking powder*
- ½ *teaspoon baking soda*
- ½ *cup butter, softened*
- ½ *cup solid vegetable shortening*
- ⅔ *cup granulated sugar*
- ½ *cup packed brown sugar*
- 1 *egg, lightly beaten*
- 1 *teaspoon vanilla extract*
- ¼ *cup finely chopped walnuts*
- *About 40 walnut halves*

Getting Ready

① Sift flour, baking powder, and baking soda into a bowl.

② With an electric mixer, beat butter, shortening, and sugars in a large bowl until fluffy. Add egg and vanilla; beat until blended. Add flour mixture; mix well. Stir in chopped walnuts. Shape dough into a ball, cover with plastic wrap, and refrigerate for at least 1 hour or up to 2 days.

Cooking

① Preheat oven to 350°F. Divide dough into four pieces and each piece into 10 portions. Roll each portion into a ball, then place 2 to 3 inches apart on a baking sheet. Press a walnut half into center of each ball.

② Bake until golden brown, 14 to 16 minutes. Let cool on baking sheet for 5 minutes, then transfer to a rack to cool completely. Store in an airtight container.

Makes about 40 cookies.

Almond Cookies

Follow recipe for Walnut Cookies (above), but increase **flour** to 2 cups and leave out the finely chopped walnuts. Reduce **vanilla extract** to ½ teaspoon, and add ¾ teaspoon **almond extract**. After placing balls of dough on the baking sheet, press a whole **blanched almond** in the center of each ball. Bake cookies until very lightly browned, 10 to 12 minutes.

INDEX

Also from Martin Yan

If you've enjoyed this book and the public television series *Yan Can Cook*, wait till you see what else we have in store! For more information about these and other culinary inquiries, please contact us at: Yan Can Cook, P.O. Box 4755, Foster City, CA 94404. Fax: 650-525-0522. E-mail: yccook@aol.com

Books

Martin Yan's Culinary Journey Through China

Take a delicious trip through the techniques and best-loved specialties of China's many regional cuisines! Over 120 authentic, delicious—and surprisingly easy—recipes make Chinese food come alive for American cooks. From Canton to Beijing, Shanghai to Sichuan, this is a culinary journey you will want to take again and again.

Martin Yan's Asia

Discover the culinary secrets of Asia with Yan Can Cook! The rich and varied cuisines of Asia are America's fastest growing culinary phenomenon, and here we explore the cuisines of Hong Kong, Singapore, Malaysia, the Philippines, and Japan. The book contains over 150 easy-to follow recipes, step-by-step instructions on the techniques of Asian cooking, and insights into the customs and cultures of Asia, plus Yan Can Cook's favorite secret ingredient—fun!

Martin Yan's Simple Guide to Chinese Ingredients and Other Asian Specialties

This handy guidebook takes the mystery out of shopping for Asian ingredients. It's packed with color photos, cooking tips, and storage information. And best of all, it's small enough to carry with you every time you shop.

Basic tools and networking

Martin Yan's Ultimate Chinese Chef's Knife

I spend so much time slicing, dicing, and chopping that I finally decided to create my very own Chinese chef's knife to make cooking easier...and a lot more fun! It was designed with durability and ease of handling in mind and features a high-carbon stainless steel blade, so you can look forward to years of reliable, precision performance.

Yan Can Cook Online

Now you can visit us on the worldwide web at **http://www.yancancook.com**. It's a place to share our recipes, send us e-mail, and learn about our exciting culinary tours. You'll also find information about the latest trends and specialty items from Asia from my friends and partners on the internet at **www.asianconnections.com**.